W9-CMP-664

SPIRITED AMERICANS

SPIRITED AMERICANS

A COMMENTARY ON AMERICA'S OPTIMISTS—
FROM THE PURITANS TO THE CYBER-CENTURY

A.E. Jeffcoat

Top news medium, 1903.

Winslow House Books

With thanks to the Poe Fratt Writers Room of the Seattle Public Library
for providing the solitude and research materials that so enhance a writer's
productivity. Thanks also to James MacGregor Burns—scholar, political
scientist, Pulitzer Prize author and presidential biographer—who encouraged the author and gave prompt, sage advice to a student many years
gone from his class. And to LTCP, J and J for their forbearance, and to RCJ
for his technical prowess.

Front cover illustration: John F. Clymer's painting of trappers cavorting
with a group of frontiersmen, titled *Alouette*. This is one of the many
strikingly lifelike representations of pioneer activities by this great painter
of Western frontier life.

Book design by Stephen Herold.
This book is set in Monotype Columbus, a clear, classical font based on
late 18th century Spanish typefaces.

ISBN:
0-9672022-0-5
LCC No. 99-93842
SAN 299-8890

10 9 8 7 6 5 4 3 2

Winslow House Books
321 Lovell Avenue SW
Bainbridge Island, WA 98110

National Distributor:
Midpoint Trade Books, New York
Fax: (212) 727-0195
E-mail: midpointny@aol.com
Small Sales:
Books AtoZ, Seattle
Fax: (206) 547-2026
E-mail: steve@booksatoz.com

"These—the expanse of space, the mixture of race, the pluralism of region and religion, the fresh start, the release of energies, the access to opportunity, the optimism and pragmatism of a society in motion, the passion for equality—were the crucial shaping forces of the American heritage."

Max Lerner
America as a Civilization

CONTENTS

PROLOGUE

A chorus of complaint in recent times, particularly in contemporary books, has been telling us that America has lost its spirit, its traditional optimism, its sense of purpose and direction. These morose commentaries are troubling as we enter the new millennium. Among the many headlined wails in books and newspapers have been: "The Withering of the American Dream", "America: Who Stole the Dream?", "Silent Depression—the Fate of the American Dream," "Is Government Dead?", "A Nation of Finger-Pointers", "Slouching Towards Gomorrah" and "The End of Everything." A new word, "declinists", has emerged to describe these pessimists. The trend sinks all the way down to the song of the militia movement, "America is going down the drain."

Many of today's commentators seem to lose all historical perspective, engrossed as they are with the new social and global problems of a high-velocity world. America's traditional optimism is being deflated further by the media's technology-driven ability to give us scary news from anywhere just as fast as it happens.

Many Americans are asking: *Have we lost the sense of optimism and self-confidence that played such a great part in our past? Is America in decline? Have we become an endangered species?* This book attempts to answer the basic question: *Where has the remarkable spirit of Americans come from, and will it survive in the new world of the 21ˢᵗ century?*

One reason why Americans today are confused about the direction of the nation and of their own lives is that they are virtually drowning in information like no other race before them. In their mailboxes, on their TVs, over the Internet and in telemarketing phone calls, fax messages, E-mail messages and palm pilot beepers, the torrent of information and advice from every quarter breeds anxiety and confusion. The art of living has become to some extent the art of sifting through this colossal mess for meaningful insights.

I believe the first step in understanding and recapturing the enthusiasm of earlier Americans is to look back at the historical sources of their optimistic outlook—the obvious ones and the not-so-obvious ones—from the very beginning of European emigration to America to the beginning of the unraveling of national confidence in the present age of cynicism and prosperity. Americans for the most part have lost touch with this history. They give scant thought to the meaning of their lives in historical perspective. They have missed "that transmission of the value of the past as a force still miraculously fertile and moving—mostly absent from American education at all levels," as Anthony Burgess once wrote.

No one can glean more meaning from American history than the millions of American descendants of the immigrants who fled from religious persecution in many lands and the branded and manacled Africans who entered the country in servitude, all working their way eventually from terror and bondage to freedom and a share of the American dream—not to mention the one in ten Americans today who were born abroad.

At many if not most educational institutions the subject of American history has been demoted, competing with social studies or other electives that aim to build students' self-esteem or address contemporary issues. It is not just possible but more likely probable today that an American student will go all the way through high school and graduate from college with only the most rudimentary familiarity with the American past, wholly ignorant of such prime accomplishments as the Constitution and the Bill of Rights. As historian Sean Wilentz has noted, "students may learn nothing about the presidency of Abraham Lincoln except as it pertains to the persistence of American racism."

Studs Terkel, the indefatigable oral historian, found young people in America lacking a sense of history about the American past. A national survey in 1994 found that more than half of high school seniors do not know the basic facts of American history. A mid-1996 report of the Department of Education found that six in 10 high school seniors lack even the most basic knowledge of U.S. history. "Students now arrive at the university ignorant and cynical about our political heritage, lacking the wherewithal to be either inspired by it or seriously critical of it," wrote Allan Bloom in his "meditation on the state of our souls", *The Closing of the American Mind.* Washington's home in Virginia draws fewer visitors each year and now holds a weak second place ahead of Elvis Presley's home as a visitor attraction. The birthday of Lincoln is lumped with other presidents in a bland celebration of "Presidents' Day", known primarily for highly touted automobile sales. Young vandals have desecrated Lincoln's tomb in Springfield, Illinois three years running. A survey in 1995 indicated that nearly a fifth of the American public cannot even explain what we celebrate on the Fourth of July.

It was not always so. For example, that most perceptive foreign chronicler of early American society, Alexis de Tocqueville, noted on his visit to America in 1831 that in New England every citizen was taught "the doctrines and the evidences of his religion, the history of his country, and the leading features of its Constitution. In the states of Connecticut and Massachusetts, it is extremely rare to find a man imperfectly acquainted with all these things, and a person wholly ignorant of them is a sort of phenomenon."

Stark evidence of the gap between then and now was provided by none other than the President of the United States who, on the stump in California in October 1996, during the presidential election campaign, quoted Lincoln's famous phrase from the Gettysburg Address ("Of the people, by the people and for the people") and told his audience those words were from the U.S. Constitution and the Declaration of Independence.

Surely our failure to teach American history to so many citizens is one reason why many young people today do not vote in elections. They are absorbed by the immediacies of a whirlwind world. The consuming habit of television, which is fast merging with multi-media technologies and the digitalized Information Highway, has caused people to focus on the here and now—on whatever crime or criminal trial, whatever terrorist attack, whatever scandal or earthquake or tornado or plane crash happened in the last hour or the last few minutes. "The din of the contemporary drowns out the quiet voices of the past," said former Librarian of Congress Daniel J. Boorstin in a London radio broadcast in 1975. "Despite our facilities for all other forms of travel," he said, "we find ourselves peculiarly ill-equipped and ill-disposed to travel back through time."

In the film and television media there are more examples of gross distortions of history than of faithful portrayals. Oliver Stone's attempts to remake history, in "J.F.K", for example, implied a conspiracy to assassinate President Kennedy by the CIA, the FBI and an imagined military-industrial complex, and, in "Nixon", which insinuated that President Johnson also was involved in this plot and falsely accused Nixon of complicity in plots against Castro.

Scarcely worth mention are the synthetic presidents played in major Hollywood films by actors like Bill Pullman and Michael Douglas. Among screen versions of political figures the ne plus ultra surely was the comedy, "My Fellow Americans", depicting two former presidents as vulgar bozos and an incumbent president as not above murder—all of them "as lost on the American highway as everybody else," as one critic put it.

A few exceptional television productions—most notably the ground-breaking PBS series, "The Civil War" and "The American Experience"—have shown how the powerful media of film and television could enlighten their huge audiences if only Hollywood used the left side of its brain as well as the right. In its 50 years, TV has in general been a poor educator, despite the admirable efforts of the National Endowment for the Humanities and the "Biography" and "History" cable channels.

Our educational system, the natural habitat for a contemplative study of history, has too often mimicked the trend of the media, giving increasing emphasis to contemporary issues, especially race, ethnicity, gender and media techniques—subjects that in many colleges and universities today characterize the "majors". Courses with names like "Murder" (at Amherst), "Gangster Films" and "Prison Literature" (at Georgetown), "The Year My Voice Broke" (at Sarah Lawrence), "The Uses of Deviance" (at Oberlin), "Girl Talk" (at Wesleyan)", "Creation/Procreation" (at Stanford), "Sex Work: the Labor of Pornography" (at the University of California, Santa Cruz), "Queer Histories" (at Yale), "Queer Lives" (at Hampshire College), "Fetishism, Gender, Sexuality and Capitalism" (at the University of Chicago) and "Thinking Queer" and "The Souls of Animals" (at Bowdoin) are some examples of the smorgasbord of options for college students in recent times. One sign of the times: a college was established not long ago in Redmond, Washington offering a four-year diploma in video games (no humanities courses here, where nose and eye rings are chic.)

The focus in all these cases, devolved from the 1960s when activists derided the classic curriculum, is on problems and issues of the here and now. A report of the National Association of Scholars in March 1996 decried the purging from the curriculum of many formerly required courses including those in history that familiarize students with the cultural and political foundations of our society. Nationwide, the number of college students majoring in history took a precipitous slide from the 1970s to mid-1980s.

The project to draw up national history standards for schools, initiated by the federal government and supported by educational groups, has been discouraging. These standards skew American history, casting white Americans very often as racist, sexist oppressors of minorities, while giving attention to subjects like the 14th century Muslim ruler of the West African empire of Mali and omitting subjects like the Federalist Papers. We pander to special interests, attempting to right past wrongs with new distortions, even in some cases imputing corruptness in our Constitutional foundings. We are in danger of becoming a nation of groups and minorities, "each following its own beliefs and inclinations", in Allan Bloom's phrase, in contrast to our Founders' pursuit of common good.

This trend is a tragedy, the more so because, our contemporary troubles notwithstanding, no other country for centuries has had such a dramatically upbeat past—filled with men and women who were truly remarkable for their courage, their wisdom and intelligence, their fortitude and their faith in the future. As one of my professors at Williams College, Max Lerner, used to say, with typical hyperbole: "America is the only fabulous country."

There is a wealth of literature about American history, particularly the biographies of early leaders such as James Flexner's Washington, Dumas Malone's Jefferson, Carl Sandburg's Lincoln and Edmund Morris's Theodore Roosevelt, to mention just a few. Any young adult who grows up ignorant of such works is missing the real joys of being an American. As Daniel Boorstin has put it, "There are few things more important to the survival of our country than the discovery of our history."

The fact that about one-third of our population will be of Hispanic or Asian origins by the middle of the next century underlines the wisdom of that remark. At a United States vs. Mexico soccer match in Los Angeles, in February 1998, thousands of mostly Mexican-American or Mexican fans threw bottles at the U.S. players and attacked a spectator who tried to unfurl an American flag, according to a *National Review* reporter. Describing the "assimilation crisis" that such events demonstrate, this writer quoted an Hispanic-American law professor in Florida as suggesting that "Americanization must either be completely reworked or abandoned as a premise of American identity." The U.S. immigration service, the reporter wrote, was even flirting with the idea of abolishing the required test on American history for new citizens.

Surely the study of American history is an important way to foster assimilation of new Americans, as well as to reinforce the patriotism of *all* Americans. Our forbears, starting with Washington and Jefferson, saw an enlightened electorate and an intellectual and moral climate that would nourish and preserve the Republic in future years as the best "kettle" in which to brew wise leaders.

This book is a focused look at historical highlights, attempting to suggest a frame in which to relate past, present and future—the kind of thing so many people seem to be calling for these days ("What is the meaning, the direction of this country?") Its purpose is to broaden readership beyond the relatively small audience that exists for the many big, grand scholarly books that have inspired me but for which, sadly, most people today simply don't have time in their busy lives.

I have chosen the theme of our historical optimism and individual self-confidence as the admittedly narrow line on which to hang this particular interpretation of American history. As suggested by the opening quote from that polymath, Max Lerner, the single quality of Americans that has been most remarked upon in the past by observers, foreign and domestic, is the quality of optimism and faith in the future that ran so forcefully through Americans for two centuries, helping us to create the greatest nation on earth.

To some extent this is an unabashed paean to a unique nation and its better angels. The American presidents, poets or philosophers who walk these pages are the apostles of optimism, the thinkers who articulated their optimism so well that it actually was the most important formative influence on the spirits and the welfare of the nation.

As I wrote this book I became more aware than ever before that, especially during the most crucial crises of American history, it was our chief executive, the President himself, who had the greatest influence on the state of public spirits. In general, as the revered *New York Times* reporter James Reston put it in his memoir, the most successful presidents have been the "cheerful optimists." This is why some half dozen presidents occupy such space here. And this is why we should regard our presidential elections, today and ever, as key to the health and vitality of the nation.

American history has not been one long parade of heroes and victories, not by a long shot. It would take another book to cover all the downers left out here, such as the sufferings of immigrants in New York tenements and sweatshops, even up to the present day, the bloody battles of labor and management, the scandals of administrations like Harding's and Nixon's and the heartbreaking abuse of native Americans and black Americans before their rights, which Jefferson wrote into our Declaration of Independence, were finally but still not completely recognized. But optimism is a trait so entwined with our two centuries of history that it provides a focus for parsing American society. I believe it is also the trait most needed in our leaders as we move along, so full of doubts, into our new millennium.

There are good reasons to believe that our traditional optimism has simply been obscured in the modern world's chaos, not lost. I feel about America much the way the British scholar D.W. Brogan did when he visited a corner drugstore in a small Illinois farm town in late summer 1936. He described the "boys and girls" in their bright summer clothes, the endless cars, the general friendliness and "that indefinable American air of happiness and ease, at least for the young." What was remarkable about this was that the region was in the throes of very bad times, a serious draught, crop failures and bank failures, and yet displayed "an air of confident adaptation."

In the preface to his book *The American Character* that described this scene, Brogan observed that whatever its problems, America still had to be recognized as the greatest experiment of free government on a grand scale in history. He acknowledged that there is "apparent justification at some periods and in some departments of American life for pessimism about the present or the future of America."

But he concluded: "In the past, the pessimists have always been wrong. I think they are still wrong."

A.E. Jeffcoat
Bainbridge Island, Washington

PART ONE

FROM A NEW EDEN TO
A NEW NATION

The First Three Centuries

LANDFALL

Don Cristóbal Colón, *Almirante del Mar Océano*, was the first great optimist as well as the first discoverer to reach what is now the United States from the Old World. The 41-year-old mariner believed, and for a time persuaded Queen Isabella and King Ferdinand, that God had intended him to discover a new sea route to the Indies, where gold and other riches awaited him to take back to his Catholic monarchs. Even after four voyages he clung to the illusion that this discovered paradise was in the Far East.

What makes the benighted admiral a fair starting point for America's story is not just that his voyage became the world's metaphor of discovery but that he himself became a totemic presence in the cultural imagination. He became a point of reference, a star for future explorers, whether public leaders, entrepreneurs, scientists or whatever. He personifies the optimist-in-action who built the new nation. It is this almost mystical Columbus, the explorer with his vision of a paradise in the new land that would glorify God who deserves a place at the beginning of our story.

He fits the picture of the self-made man, the kind of quintessential self-reliant, courageous and tenacious character who was exalted in the writings and lectures of America's two great early philosophers, Ralph Waldo Emerson and William James. Emerson read the ancient mariner's shipboard notes and found him a gifted letter-writer. His notes and letters left a sharp portrait of this inspired optimist. He speaks even today to the very core of Americans' adventurous spirit, to all the Americans who came after him, emboldened to take leaps of faith—from Puritans to pioneers, from the soldiers who stormed Normandy and Iwo Jima to the astronauts and the heroes of sport.

Born lowly, the son of a Genoa weaver, Columbus went to sea at 14, and as a young seaman was cast overboard from a vessel sunk by a French pirate corsair off Portugal's southern coast. Grasping a floating long oar, he paddled with one arm six miles to the shore and made his way to Lisbon, where he studied the Portugese language and the exploits of Portugal's mariners. In the Genoese quarter he learned the art of maritime chart-making and studied books such as Marco Polo's *Description of the World* and the Egyptian scientist Ptolemy's *Geography*. He learned enough Latin to read ancient and medieval cosmographers, and found that Seneca had written that an ocean crossing from Spain to the Indies could be done in a few days.

By 1483 he had the nerve to submit to the Portugese king and the royal court his own bold plan "to sail West to reach the East", based on his own original conception of world geography and his self-confidence based on mastery of dead-reckoning navigation and other skills. Turned down by the king and his advisors, he traveled to Spain, continued his studies at a Franciscan monastery and, with the help of a priest versed in astronomy and nautical studies, managed to obtain audiences with two of Spain's wealthiest grandees. With their help he was received at the court of Spain's King Ferdinand and Queen Isabella.

Displaying before these royals his own original map of the world, and appealing to the devout Queen for a chance to carry the Christian gospel to yet-undiscovered lands, he appealed for support of an exploratory voyage. He was promptly rejected by a royal commission of experts. But with an assist from the sympathetic rector of the monastery where he'd been living, he was given a second chance to present his novel proposal to the Queen and her advisory committee.

This time he shrewdly described the riches he might bring back to Spain from a voyage to the Indies, which he mistakenly thought he could reach by the shortcut of crossing the Atlantic. He asked for nothing less than the title of Admiral of the Ocean Sea, the governorship of any lands he discovered, and ten percent of all gold and silver and other discovered riches. Turned down again, he headed for Cordoba on a mule given him by the Queen. A court messenger overtook him on the Cordoba road with the news that the monarchs, on reflection, and with some persuasion by their finance chief, had changed their minds.

The zealous adventurer's persistence had paid off. With money from the crown, and even larger venture capital funds borrowed from wealthy backers, the nervy explorer had the wherewithal to ready within two weeks two square-rigged caravels and a cargo ship, for a venture that many of Spain's best minds considered risky, foolhardy, dangerous and contrary to the beliefs of the best scientists and mariners of the time. Columbus believed, and persuaded the Spanish monarchs, who gave him introductory letters to the "Grand Khan" (the Chinese emperor) and royal princes, that by sailing westward, the opposite direction from Marco Polo, he would discover a shorter route to Asia and its gold and other riches. His courage, and his feat of sailing thousands of miles into an unknown ocean relying simply on dead reckoning, caused Samuel Eliot Morison to call him "the greatest navigator of his age."

Besides Columbus's ambition to discover new riches for his king and queen and for himself (which also made him the first American materialist), he was profoundly inspired by visions based on Biblical lore. Like many who would follow him, the able and fearless mariner was a pious visionary, buoyantly hopeful of finding an earthly paradise. He was driven by his faith that God "gives all those who walk in His way victory over things which appear impossible."

On the October dawn more than five hundred years ago when Columbus first set foot on a Caribbean island, he and his officers dropped to their knees to thank God and ask his blessing, just as the Puritans did more than a century later. Almost immediately he noted in his journal that the natives on the island would be better converted to the Holy Faith by love than by force, so he presented them with red caps, glass beads and other trinkets. Foreshadowing from the start an evil that was to plague America right up to the present day, Columbus and his crew and the conquistadors who followed them immediately regarded the American Indians as slaves to their superior European masters.

Convinced that he had reached Asia, he surmised that he was within reach of the Garden of Eden described in the Book of Genesis, "the spot of the Earthly Paradise," he wrote, "whither no one can go but by God's permission." Imagining himself to be on a planet half the size of earth, he dreamed of pointing the way for a new crusade to retake Constantinople and Jerusalem from the Ottoman Turks. Growing up in Genoa he had heard soldiers returning from war with the Turks exhorting citizens to avenge the loss of Christendom's birthplace in the East.

Writing home about "the great victory which our Lord hath given me", Columbus described the harbors, plants and fruits and the natives of Guanhani, as they called the island where he landed. The people there, whom he called "Indians" because he thought he had reached India, "all go naked, men and women, just as their mothers bring them forth. Of anything they have, if it be asked for, they never say no, but do rather invite the person to accept it, and show as much loving kindness as though they would give their hearts." He wrote that "they all believe that power and goodness are in the sky, and they believe very firmly that I, with these ships and crew, came from the sky... Christendom should give solemn thanks for the great exaltation they shall have by the conversion of so many peoples to our Holy faith..."

Columbus imagined that God had chosen him to be "the messenger of the new heaven and the new earth" and that his discovery would lead to fulfillment of the Biblical prophesies. Morison wrote that Columbus "had a deep conviction of the immanence, the sovereignty, and the infinite wisdom of God, which transcended all his suffering and enhanced all his triumphs."

Columbus compared the innocent Caribbean Indians to Adam and Eve. Although his vision made little progress among the skeptics of Spain and Italy he dreamed that Spaniards were destined to become the chosen people, recreating the story of the children of ancient Israel. The huge Spanish-speaking populations of Los Angeles and New York today are not exactly what he had in mind, though like Columbus they too harmonize Catholic religion with ambitions for earthly riches. In the mind of Columbus there was no contradiction between these spiritual aspirations and his eagerness to find gold, jewels, spices and other material Edenic riches.

By chance, in a marvelous quirk of circumstances, Columbus had opened up the hidden half of the globe and the opportunity to create a whole new civilization from scratch. "A mere sea captain's ambition to trace a new trade route gave way to a moral adventure for humanity," wrote Woodrow Wilson more than four centuries later. In his rhapsodic, campaign-speech prose, Wilson added:

Never can that moment of unique opportunity fail to excite the emotion of all who consider its strangeness and richness... The race was to found a new order here on this delectable land, which no man approached without receiving, as the old voyagers relate, sweet airs out of woods

aflame with flowers and murmurous with the sound of pellucid waters...
The whole thing springs into the imagination like a wonderful vision, an
exquisite marvel which once only in all history would be vouchsafed. One
other thing only compares with it, only one other thing touches the springs
of emotion as does the picture of the ships of Columbus... and that is
the choke in the throat of the immigrant of today as he gazes from the
steerage deck at the land where he has been taught to believe he in his turn
shall find an earthly paradise..."

The world's most famous sailor-explorer became an icon, a reminder to future generations that America was built by immigrants—for the most part independent, self-asserting, entrepreneurial people willing to take great risks for the hope of a better life. Risk-takers made the nation what it is today and if there is a single phrase that has set America apart among nations it is "risk-taking."

Whatever his faults, and however shortsighted his image of the planet, it must be admitted that the admiral was a bold adventurer with great imagination and a genuine sense of divine mission. In that sense he set something of a tone for the millions who followed him in settling the American continent. "Every ship that comes to America got its chart from Columbus," wrote Emerson.

His persuasive salesmanship with his royal patrons, his penchant for hyperbole, his stubborn determination to overcome natural and human obstacles to reach his goal—all these characteristics foreshadowed the characteristics of the race that followed Columbus.

The *persistence* of Columbus in his quest was a quality recognized by his family and his supporters: after all, he had promoted his ideas for at least 12 years at the courts of Spain and Portugal and even, through his brother Bartholomew, at the courts of England and France. But perhaps the most lasting impact Columbus made on the American spirit was through the national fuss that was made of him time after time, long after his exploits. With Columbus-like exaggeration, Americans virtually crowned him and made him a permanent national hero.

Columbus and Columbia became common names of places and events across the country, including the 1893 World's Columbian Exhibition in Chicago, Columbus Circle in New York and more than 30 American cities and towns named after him. One of those cities, Columbus, Ohio, was chosen by Franklin Delano Roosevelt for the start of his momentous 1932 Presidential campaign (and his trust-buster speech, blaming laissez-faire Hoover economics and self-serving financial leaders for the collapsed state of the country and offering his own program for federal regulation of security exchanges, holding companies and banks.)

In the present age characterized by collective enterprises, reliance on technology and frustrating attempts to understand the world, it is impossible not to admire Columbus, the lone genius who so confidently believed he could change the world. His private vision, his defiance of authorities and his faith in his God and his mission transformed the admiral's creative ideas into history-making action and led the way for the creation of the world's most powerful nation.

Nearly 500 years later two other explorers, Neil A.Armstrong and Edwin E. ("Buzz") Aldrin, Jr., bundled in oxygen cocoons, left their command module called Columbia and dropped in the Apollo landing craft to the surface of the moon, the first human steps onto another planet. No nation had ever conceived such an optimistic undertaking—an eight-year, $25 billion mobilization of technology and talent, spurred by the Russian launching of the first artificial satellite, Sputnik 1, twelve years before. Speaking over a scratchy radio link to an awestruck, worldwide audience, Armstrong said: "That's one small step for man, one giant leap for mankind." On a rocky plain called the Sea of Tranquility the space voyagers left a plaque declaring: "Here Men From the Planet Earth First Set Foot Upon the Moon… We Came in Peace for All Mankind." They had traveled 240,000 miles in three days.

That first moon landing was part of the largest scientific and technological undertaking in history, the response of American scientists and technicians to President John F. Kennedy's 1961 commitment to land men on the moon by the end of the decade. For some Americans this achievement raised the hope that if the nation could carry out a commitment to make a lunar landing, perhaps it could solve remaining earthbound problems, such as poverty among its citizens.

Twelve years later, the United States launched the first manned space shuttle. Of course it too was named Columbia, one more derivation from Columbus.

8

SPIRITUAL SHAPERS

One hundred and twenty-two years after Columbus's discovery, the English adventurer John Smith, sailing beside the coast of New England, compared the new land of America to Eden, just as Columbus did. The comparison took on special meaning for him when he settled in the warm and hospitable climate of Virginia, where he found an Eve in the new world paradise. Pocahontas, the daughter of Indian chief Powhattan, reportedly saved Smith's life when he was attacked by Indians, and continued to befriend the settlers and eventually marry one of them. But the early settlements in Virginia, sponsored by business interests for commercial purposes, were plagued with disasters of weather, disease, Indian attacks, internal conflicts and bad management.

Smith later sailed north to explore New England, which he named, and dreamed of establishing a colony in Massachusetts Bay, which he never managed to do. That historic task was accomplished by other English settlers of a different stripe altogether with very unique, high goals. The great Puritan migration of the 1630s, essentially a religious movement, had an enduring effect on the American mind and character. These settlers were united by a faith in God's purpose for them so strong that it is nearly impossible for present-day Americans to understand. They were convinced, like the Israelites of ancient times with whom they compared themselves, that it was their destiny to begin nothing less than a new millennial chapter in the history of mankind.

The Puritans who settled on the shores of New England had only spiritual motivations for their enterprise. Many of them had given up comfortable lives and careers in England, pulling up their stakes because they felt the Church of England had moved too far away from the purity of the first church of Christ by interposing Episcopal practices inherited from the Pope of Rome between Christians and the one solid anchor of their faith—the supreme and absolute law proclaimed by the Bible.

They were to a large extent highly intelligent, very well educated middle-class people who had found it impossible to square their religious beliefs with the Anglican Church of England. Tocqueville observed that the Puritans "possessed, in proportion to their number, a greater mass of intelligence than is to be found in any European nation of our own time. All, perhaps without a single exception, had received a good education."

The early settlers came to America with intellectual ambitions, and one of their first priorities in 1636 was to set up a college of higher education with high standards in religious and classical studies. Harvard's 17th-century purpose has more or less applied, give or take some, to the present time ("the advancement and education of youth in all manner of good literature, arts and sciences... and all other necessary provisions that may conduce to the education of the English and Indian youth of this Country in knowledge and godliness.")

The Bible above all

In the words of historians Perry Miller and Thomas Johnson, the Puritans thought the Bible was "the word of God from one end to the other, a complete body of laws, an absolute code in everything it touched upon". The Puritans believed that with proper religious training Christians could establish rules not only for worship but also for public policy and for every facet of private life from dress and sexual behavior to the conduct of business.

While the Puritans' absolute faith in scripture put obvious restraints on their adherents, these early settlers believed equally in the principle of personal freedom that was to become, besides religion, the other defining strand of early American character. After all they had sacrificed their wealth, their inheritances, their careers and their considerable creature comforts in order to declare their independence from the dictates and practices of Anglican England.

The first-generation Puritans believed they had a historic mission to set the example for all nations, and indeed theirs were the binding threads of morality and freedom that ran prominently through American life for more than 300 years. One of their lay leaders, John Winthrop, the first governor of the colony, delivered a sermon aboard the Arabella as it headed for Massachusetts Bay, emphasizing the spiritual opportunities that lay ahead. In its most-quoted passage he spoke of New England as "a city upon a hill", a model for future generations, a moral community where justice and mercy would rule.

Another Puritan leader, John Cotton, told the emigrants departing from England that they had a patent from heaven, because of "the grand charter given to Adam and his posterity in Paradise." Massachusetts was the place, said another settler, Edward Johnson, "where the Lord will create a new Heaven and a new Earth." As the Bible taught them, chosen people had to overcome harsh trials and burdens before they reached their promised land, just as the Israelites had to do in passing from Egyptian bondage through the wilderness. As Cotton Mather put it, "The wilderness through which we are passing to the Promised Land is all over fill'd with Fiery flying serpents." And indeed the American virtues of rugged individualism were bred in the wilderness of forests, wild animals and flying Indian arrows that these first pioneers had to face.

Puritan "spirits"

To the Puritans, the words "spirit" and "spirits" had special meaning, and no better models of spiritual believers can be found than Increase Mather and his son Cotton, second and third-generation Puritans and the last true exponents of the Puritan culture that peaked in the 1660s. Increase was so named by his father because of the "never-to-be-forgotten increase of every sort wherewith God favoured the country." All of the men in this family were ministers; in fact, nearly half of the graduates of Harvard in the 17th century became ministers of the gospel. While acting in succession as ministers of the North Church in Boston, both Mathers, through their sermons and writings, inspired their flocks with their own spiritual experiences and theories.

A prodigious scholar, Increase, among other things, studied and preached about angels and published a book on angels not long after the most famous Salem witchcraft trials that helped to end the trials and reaffirm more traditional teachings about the world of the spirit. That world preoccupied both Mathers. Increase himself had experienced conversion to Christ when he was only 15. He was the first to take full advantage of the new printing presses in America in the 1670s decade, according to Michael Hall, in *The Last American Puritan*. He gave hope to the faithful that "salvation is certain" if they reconciled themselves with God.

His son Cotton, after one period of fasting and meditation, claimed to have personally witnessed a shining, winged angel in his study. Cotton had entered Harvard College, where his father had been president, at the age of 12, receiving his degree at 15. He learned to read and write Greek and Latin as well as English; at the age of 17 he preached his first sermon and starting in his early twenties he succeeded his father as pastor of the Second Church of Boston.

Believing that he was marked by God through an angel to awaken his people, he turned out massive studies of the Bible and of the history of New England. He initiated the first important medical advance in America, innoculation for smallpox. He strove to make himself worthy of having been chosen by God to set the example of Christian purity for his fellow men. He was so intense and flamboyant that he has been ridiculed for what seemed to many Americans from his late years on as a narrow-minded, long-winded priggish zealot, a sort of Puritan Ichabod Crane, and in fact he became the model for the negative image of Puritanism that has suffered derision right up to modern times.

Among the early Puritans, prospective church members were screened on the basis of their testimony about their spiritual life before a "gathering of visible saints", lay people who, like Increase and Cotton, believed themselves recipients of God's holy spirit. To be eligible to vote or hold office in Massachusetts a man had to be thus admitted to church membership. Nevertheless, the civil authority had no rule over spiritual life and church ways, so church and state were kept separate.

The punishment for those who challenged Old Testament strictures, however, was harsh, as Mistress Anne Hutchinson found out. A clever woman on the radical fringe of the Puritan movement, she debunked the authority of ministers and preached (in her home) that God communicated directly to people rather than through church officials. She was prosecuted as a heretic, banished from Masschusetts Bay Colony to Rhode Island and eventually killed by Native Americans in New York.

Puritanism respected all worthwhile forms of work, not just the ministry. A merchant or a farmer could earn God's redeeming grace by conducting his business by the lights of Christian ethics, surrendering himself to God and fulfilling his social responsibilities. All human life was a divine enterprise, and each person who made the necessary effort could find salvation.

The roots of optimism

Such optimism as there was about their lot among the Puritans was based in part on whole-hearted faith in God and an absolute, literal belief in heaven and hell. "Man belonged to God alone," wrote Samuel Eliot Morison. "His only purpose in life was to enhance God's glory and to do God's will, and every variety of human activity, every sort of human conduct presumably unpleasing to God must be discouraged if not suppressed."

Disasters in the "visible" world—such as Indian attacks and house burnings, smallpox epidemics and premature deaths—were taken to be signals from above, acts of punishment by God for evils done below. After one minister's wife was captured and held by Indians, for example, she said she had witnessed "the wonderful power of God" when she was returned safely for ransom by Indians who had torched her home. When Increase's own house burned down in the huge Boston fire of 1676 he said he had been corrected by God "with gentleness" because most of his possessions were saved. When he witnessed a comet one cold winter night this too was seen as an awakening sign from God, and Increase produced a book on comets after some typically thorough research.

Of course another source of optimism was the Puritans' conviction that New England was "a blessed land" and that the very emptiness of the new world afforded them a unique opportunity to create their New Jerusalem, new institutions and a wholly new, holy life. What later was called the "outrageous optimism" of Americans sprang in no small part from the conviction that America really was a New Jerusalem. American writers—from Hawthorne to Thoreau, Melville and Mark Twain to Saul Bellow and Philip Roth—were to use Jerusalem as a totem of American identity.

The Puritan influence extended also to the philosophy of democratic political organization. Their creation of churches whose leadership came from the group of self-governing lay "saints", rather then from a church hierarchy or a minister, and their democratic town meeting form of civil government, were examples of the innovation and the democratizing tendencies that characterized their short but influential period.

For more than three centuries the Puritans have been pictured in the public mind more or less like the flinty prudes in Hawthorn's story, *The Scarlet Letter*. The real truth about their lives belies the images that have come down to us through the years of dour, repressed killjoys in black clothes, scornful of merrymaking and any kind of fun. "There was much opportunity for love and laughter in colonial New England," wrote Morison, "though not as much as there should have been."

The joys of churchgoing

It's true that Puritan laws concerning the Sabbath forbade sexual intercourse as well as any unnecessary work or traveling and frivolous behavior on the holy day. (One Harvard tutor and poet agonized over whether closing his neighbor's barn door when it blew in the wind constituted an act of work that profaned the Sabbath, according to Bruce C. Daniels in his book, *Puritans at Play*.) A hard-working lot, these people had little time for leisure. Their time aside from work was filled largely with religious duties. Theirs was a virtuous community if ever there was one.

So great was the zeal of the early Puritans to manifest their faith by attending church that a weekly limit had to be set on the number of sermons they could enjoy. Throughout the century "the New England people never seemed to have enough sermons," Morison wrote. It has been estimated that the Puritan, on average, listened to no less than 7,000 sermons in a lifetime. Their code of behavior was Old Testament-strict. In Connecticut, in the middle of the 17th century, death was the prescribed punishment for worshipping a false god, for blasphemy, sorcery, adultery or rape. In New Haven a young woman was fined and reprimanded for using bad language and allowing herself to be kissed.

There was another, more human side of these people, however. The fact is that the communal spirit of this covenanted group gave them considerable joy. "A society swithout seams", as Daniels called it, the Puritan community bound its people together cohesively—all of the people, of all classes, trades and professions—not just in church but also in civic enterprises, work and recreation.

The colonies recognized their ties to mother England but the nucleus of their lives was the independent township, which named its own magistrates, established schools, levied its own taxes and provided for the poor, the maintenance of roads and records. The people were close to their government; their town meetings, a form of direct democracy, enhanced local public spirit and the vitality of their public life, and they were close to the land, since most of them did their own farming. This strong sense of community guaranteed civic order and tranquility.

Just as the township was the guarantor of democracy, the church was the guarantor of good morals, and the ultimate sovereign was God. Tocqueville wrote that "there is no country in the world where the Christian religion retains a greater influence over the souls of men than in America; and there can be no greater proof of its utility and its conformity to human nature than that its influence is powerfully felt over the most enlightened and free nation on earth."

The Puritans called their churches "meetinghouses" because these simple, unheated and undecorated places, used for town meetings as well as worship, linked the religious world to the workaday world. This close-knit community believed that all aspects of their lives—work, family, religion, government, entertainment—were bound together in the moral life of the community. Sunday was the highlight of the 17th-century Puritan's week. At nine o'clock a bell, drum or conch shell summoned the locals, a volley of gunfire called out to those farther out of town. Each church had two sermons, each one often two hours long, and attendance was compulsory. Many worshippers brought pads and paper to take notes for later discussions and arguments. Hopefully, a sermon might produce "conversion" of a listener on the spot.

Villagers greeted parishioners coming in from surrounding areas, and refreshments and spirited conversations in homes and outdoors filled up the day between morning services and afternoon meetings. Thursday afternoon lecture meetings were also commonplace at the meetinghouses, and taverns were open in the evening following these meetings, with music and sometimes dancing.

Also binding everyone together were community harvests, wood-cuttings and cornhuskings, as well as quilting, spinning and sewing bees and house-raisings, when people helped each other build and hoist frames of new houses, barns, mills and shops. When a youngster shimmied out on a ridgepole to nail home the last beam, the crowd celebrated. Everyone, including children, women and ministers, drank alcohol, usually beer or fermented cider at home or on special occasions. It wasn't unusual for a parish to brew its own ordination beer to honor a new cleric. They never tried to ban all alcoholic beverages.

Simple pleasures, under God

As the Puritans saw it, simple pleasures were the key to good living under their God. Fishing (New England's most popular sport in the 17th and 18th centuries), hunting and martial competitions all met their standard that leisure activities should be engaged in moderation and should have a useful purpose. Fowling, hawking, leaping, "vaulting", wrestling and running were recognized as "laudable, cheap and harmless exercises." Fishing stories stand out in the first-generation Pilgrim diaries and letters. Something as simple as a fish jumping in Cape Cod Bay was regarded as "marvelous merry sport". The New World was a sportsman's paradise, and Puritans appreciated the environment, celebrating "the promised land" more than they bewailed "the howling wilderness."

One of the most moving examples of Puritan joy in "the wondrous world of nature" found in the untamed New England countryside and the religious faith it inspired is the poetry of Anne Bradstreet, mother of eight children and the only early New England writer whose poems survived the later years. She also expressed the simple purity that was the ideal of these people in some verses about her love for her husband, a local magistrate, that began:

"If ever two were one, then surely we.
If ever man were lov'd by wife, then thee;
If ever wife was happy in a man,
Compare with me ye women if you can."

At home, whist was the recreation best embodying the virtues of companionship and moderation, as well as sharpening the skills of logic and arithmetic. Dancing was practiced, in moderation. John Cotton felt that "dancing or leaping is a natural expression of joy" if done "men with men" or "women with women". Mixed-sex dancing nonetheless was common within homes and after celebrations such as ordinations. The Puritans were a "people with sex drives, appetites, a sense of humanity and an appreciation of the need for pleasure and joy in everyday life," wrote Daniels, who noted that sometimes even their sermons extolled the pleasures of sex within the marriage bed.

One of the quiet joys most popular with Puritans was simply reading. They read a lot, with great intensity, and reading played a more important part in their lives, it has been said, than it did in Elizabethan England or Enlightenment Europe. In the early years they read the Bible, sermons and moral tracts for entertainment as well as for instruction on how to prepare for the next life. *The Bay Psalm Book* was the first book published in colonial America. The Puritans' absorption in books is what caused New England, by Revolutionary times, to be one of the world's most literate places.

The Puritans liked humor in their reading, especially when it was tied somehow to salvation. A popular work was the witty, satirical The *Simple Cobbler of Aggawam*, written by the minister Nathaniel Ward, about a cobbler who gave advice from his workbench on family, religion, love and other matters, interspersed with (what was considered risqué) sexual puns. His humor was a contrast to the jeremiads preached by so many ministers warning that the world was going to hell in a handbasket. Ben Franklin's elder brother James published New England's first witty, satirical newspaper, the *New England Courant,* beginning in 1720. It's been described as a cross between the *Harvard Lampoon* and the *National Enquirer*, and when it finally overstepped Puritan bounds it was shut down by the Massachusetts General Court.

Free beer, free cider

The Puritans kept taverns or inns (which they called "ordinaries") in almost every town. Showing themselves to be anything but strict Calvinists, the Puritans provided beer, cider and even hard liquor at town expense, according to Morison. In 1697, 26 ordinaries dotted the Boston Post Road from Boston to the Connecticut shoreline. Boston had over 30 taverns, alehouses and grog shops about that time, which grew to more than 80 in the decade that followed.

Simple church music—the psalms sung without accompaniment—was part of regular religious services in early Puritan days. Music grew more important in the 1720s and became a central part of recreational activities. Concerts became part of Boston life in the 1730s, and church choirs and itinerant singing teachers and singing schools helped raise the musical pulse. By the 1760s most parishes had hired a singing teacher, and the '60s and '70s were a time of singing-school mania among young people. Dancing became the most popular recreation of the young, and of some not so young, by the second half of the 18th century. Diaries of the time sparkled with accounts of dancing pleasures. In the 1760s and 1770s dances were held every fortnight by Boston's upper classes. Music, especially in the form of ballads and ditties, played a role in inspiring camaraderie and esprit among the Revolutionary soldiers.

One of the things that contributed to the reformation and ultimate erosion of strict Puritanism was the inherent conflict between the belief that every man and woman is born a sinner and doomed at birth—underlined in the scarifying early jeremiads of Increase Mather—and the preachers' exhortations to declare for Christ, build an earthly kingdom based on the Bible and lead lives of extreme asceticism, so as to gain a place in heaven.

Increase and Cotton Mather anticipated the decline of Puritan piety, warning that the excesses of the Puritans in their time were leading them down the road to sin—and indeed, the excesses of tavern life in particular marked the real passing of the Puritan era and its commitment to "sober mirth". Increase warned that "wine is from God but the drunkard is from the Devil." As ordinaries proliferated, became known as taverns and assumed meetinghouse functions, serious problems of drunkenness and violence arose, just as the Mathers had feared. Forgotten were the days when a drunkard was fined five shillings for a first offense, 10 for a second and a public whipping for the third, and when, under Governor John Winthrop's rule, one famous drunk was sentenced to wear a red "D" around his neck for a year.

After not much more than a half-century of pietistical Puritanism, with its faith in a second coming and a thousand-year rule of the saints, there was an inevitable loosening of this stern culture. Increase himself came to be criticized for belaboring the sinfulness of his parishioners. The politicians and tradesmen didn't appreciate his tirades about drinking. When Increase went to England to become a virtual lobbyist for a new Massachusetts Charter in 1690, even he was most likely softened up by his contact with the wealth and sophisticated life of London. Over time the tenor of his sermons softened, and his recipe for salvation became a simple belief in Christ, an appeal to his listeners simply to shun the sinful world. There was a new mood of confidence and hope.

The fraying of the spiritual

A special church Synod in 1679 took note of a decline in peoples' commitment to God and, in its place, "an insatiable desire after Land and worldly Accommodations." Increase responded by calling on his people to renew their covenant with God. But the spiritual underpinning of the society was fraying. Boston was becoming more cosmopolitan—its port was booming, construction was underway everywhere, people were building grander residences and, though they went to church, they were losing interest in joining churches. In the fall of 1685 a Boston dancing master for a short time got away with scheduling his classes in competition with the traditional Thursday church lectures and was quoted as claiming he could teach more divinity in one dance floor lesson than could be learned from the Old Testament.

By 1679 Congregational churches were welcoming people at large, and the church of the select visible saints lost its primacy. The New Massachusetts Charter of 1691 based the voting franchise on property, not church membership, and provided a bill of rights unrelated to church and religion. As Michael Hall wrote, "Life, liberty and property were now the concerns of the Massachusetts government, not religion."

So the pietistical, providential world of the Puritans was being succeeded by a new, more materialistic world by the time Increase Mather died in 1723, although "he himself, its greatest exemplar, remained true to the very end," wrote Hall. By the 1760s the citizens of Massachusetts were more interested in private property and speculation than in Christian fellowship. Commercial trade among the colonies and with England became the great force in economic life.

Revolutionary New England brought many more changes that further diminished the old restraints, creating a new society that was a far cry from the old "community of saints". Troops whooped it up in the taverns and played ball on the village greens; people began thinking of life more as a contest or sport than as a pilgrimage; novels became favorite reading; couples could dance the night away and end their dates with a kiss; premarital sex raised eyebrows but wasn't punished, and the Sabbath was shortened, beginning Sunday morning instead of Saturday sundown.

Yet brief as was their reign, the imprint of the early, pious Puritans was writ large on the American character. It was to emerge in Ben Franklin's and George Washington's efforts to achieve moral perfection; in Thomas Jefferson's studies and writings on the Bible, even while he was President; in Woodrow Wilson's heraldic invocation of God's blessing in the Allied war against Kaiser Wilhelm, and in Lincoln's rock-ribbed character and consistent principles based on religious faith, which he placed above all personal considerations. Tocqueville saw America's destiny "embodied in the first Puritan who landed on those shores, just as the whole human race was represented by the first man."

Kenneth Clark once wrote: "Civilized man must feel that he belongs somewhere in space and time; that he consciously looks forward and looks back." Certainly this was true of the early Puritans, perhaps more so than any generation of Americans that was to follow them. Their legacy included a commitment to education and literacy, a devotion to simple fellowship and shared concerns with fellow men and women, a belief in hard work and enterprise, a deeply-planted social conscience, a plain style in language and art and a sense of a new mission on earth under God. All of these Puritan characteristics became very much part of the American identity.

"A veneration for learning, a respect for the humanities and a habit of considering values other than the material," Morison said in a lecture, "had been so firmly established among the ruling class of the New England people by 1701 that they were as well prepared as any people in the world to be quickened by new ideas, and to play their part in the coming drama of the Rights of Man."

POLITICAL SHAPERS

Life in colonial, pre-revolutionary America was rural, and to understand the political and social philosophy developed later by Jefferson and others, as well as the themes of early American literature, it is worthwhile looking back to see just what this life was like. No one described it more charmingly than a Frenchman who farmed in Orange County, New York in the last quarter of the 18th century. His name was Michel-Guillaume Jean de Crevecoeur and he wrote a book called *Letters from an American Farmer* containing essays by a third generation farmer to an imaginary friend in London. D.H. Lawrence called it a classic of American literature. It explained the high and open spirits of Americans in his time.

Crevecoeur penned his letters to give Europeans an idea of the life of a happy, freedom-loving farmer-citizen of his day, the embodiment of Jefferson's later idyl of the man of the soil as the totem of the new society, "the most perfect society now existing in the world." Crevecoeur maintained that Americans were literally, biologically, a new race, in contrast to the decadent Europeans of the Old World. He marveled at the congealing of nationalities and religions that he found around him, "that strange mixture of blood, which you will find in no other country."

At a time when America was about to break from the embrace of mother England he asked the question, "What is an American?" His answer was that the American was a "new man", essentially a new kind of human being, in part because he was free of the contesting nationalities, social ills and inequalities of Europe. Besides being tied to his land, and very much a family person, Crevecoeur's American was resolutely middle class, of a single class, compared with the Europeans, who were divided into the very rich and the very poor, the powerful and the powerless. Like other philosophers of natural rights and natural law, from John Locke to Jefferson, Crevecoeur emphasized the connections between property, political rights and personal freedom.

"The instant I enter on my own land, the bright idea of property, of exclusive right, of independence exalt my mind," he wrote. The process of working his own land gave him almost magical pleasure and he wrote that as a farmer tilled his land, with his child seated on the plow, "the odoriferous furrow exhilarates his spirits and seems to do the child a great deal of good." He said that the American ought to love his country above all others in the old world because "Here the rewards of his industry follow with equal steps the progress of his labour."

He called the middle colonies of Pennsylvania and New York "these shores of Eden" and gloried in the fertility and emptiness of the continent, the "general decency of manners" that prevailed and the hospitality shown to one another by peoples of English, Dutch, Scots, Irish and other ancestries. And he marveled that in this new land it was not unusual to find a new type of man "whose grandfather was an Englishman, whose wife was Dutch, whose son married a Frenchwoman and whose other four sons have now four wives of different nations."

Traveling to Nantucket in Massachusetts, the farmer was inspired by the 5,000 hardy souls then inhabiting the island to a lyrical celebration of free enterprise. He rhapsodized at how these islanders, having made their barren island support what little agriculture it could, turned to the ocean for their livelihood and became the most expert whalers in the world. Except for their habit of taking a dose of opium in the morning, the tastes of the people were simple, drunkenness was unknown, as were the temptations of music, singing and dancing. The chief social amusements were described as storytelling and the sharing of "puddings, pies and custards".

"We are the most perfect society now existing in the world," wrote this farmer. "Here man is free as he ought to be..." Jefferson painted a similar picture of America's place in history in his first Inaugural Address, when he said:

"Kindly separated by nature and a wide ocean from the exterminating havoc of one quarter of the globe; too high minded to endure the degredations of the others; possessing a chosen country, with room enough

for our descendants to the hundredth and thousandth generation; enter-taining a due sense of our equal right to the use of our own faculties, to the acquisition our own industry, to honor and confidence from our fel-low citizens, resulting not from birth but from our actions and their sense of them; enlightened by a benign religion, professed, indeed, and prac-ticed in various forms, yet all of them inculcating honesty, truth, temper-ance, gratitude, and the love of man; acknowledging and adoring an overruling Providence, which by all its dispensations proves that it de-lights in the happiness of man here and his greater happiness hereafter. With all these blessings, what more is necessary to make us a happy and prosperous people?"

The founding gentlemen

If the Puritans laid a rock-solid moral foundation under the future America, and gave it spiritual substance, the Founders established the political, social and legal framework to assure long life for the emerg-ing nation. They elevated spirits well beyond their time by giving Ameri-cans leadership worthy of respect. The leaders of the revolutionary era that followed early colonialism were similar to the Puritans in their firm belief in God. But they were very different in their motivations, their social condition and their views of society. They were Anglican "gentlemen", very much products of British culture and loyal subjects of the British Royal Crown until that Crown squeezed too hard.

They were the nation's finest. Jefferson and especially Franklin be-came recognized even in Europe as among the world's first citizens in intelligence, character and talents. "Over the past two centuries," histo-rian Paul Johnson wrote recently, "few of the key offices in the world have been so consistently occupied by such good men", referring to Washington, "the magisterial head of state" and all his early successors as "men of gravity, distinction and even nobility."

The revolutionary leaders—including Washington, Madison, Edmund Pendleton and Patrick Henry—were all good Anglicans, "se-curely within the fold of the Church," as Daniel J. Boorstin put it. Civic duties and church duties were all the same. Washington was a vestryman of Truro Parish, as were a number of his fellow prominent citizens of Virginia.

They were also affluent landowners. They can fairly be described as entrepreneur-capitalists. Jefferson, Washington, Franklin and scores of other leaders of the time were shareholders of big land companies, making claims to western lands. Between the revolution and his ascent to the presidency Washington was president of a company formed to build canals and push the frontier beyond the Allegheny (eventually he gave all his shares in inland waterway companies to charity schools for poor children.) But perhaps most important, these early leaders were for the most part, like the Puritans, highly educated individuals who cherished the freedom to act on their consciences in a way that was possible in this new society separated by an ocean from mother England.

The greatest of the nation's early leaders contrast with many more recent political leaders. Washington, Franklin and Jefferson each entered politics reluctantly and only after being persuaded that it was their duty to society to do so. Each of them had roots in private enterprise. Each of them tried to return to private life either in managing estates or practicing a profession, but again, with great reluctance, were persuaded by their countrymen that their character, talents, and intelligence were indispensable to the new nation (by comparison with modern-day politicians who have chosen to make lifetime careers of government, with little if any first-hand experiences in private enterprise.)

Perhaps most important, Jefferson and Franklin in particular established the vision of America as a land of virtue in the public mind, though each of them had wavered from the straight and narrow in their personal lives—lapses that would be judged differently in different ages to come. Both of them associated virtue chiefly with nature and agricultural pursuits and with the conversion of wilderness into a paradise of plenty for all who were willing to make the effort. Throughout the 19th century the United States was virtually dominated by what David Riesman called such "inner-directed moralists." *

---

* In his autobiography Franklin actually stated that in 1733 he had "conceived the bold and arduous project of arriving at moral perfection". He tracked his progress with daily charts of 13 virtues (including humility as exemplified by Christ and Socrates.) He wrote: "I wished to live without committing any fault at any time; I would conquer all that either natural inclination, custom, or company might lead me into. As I knew, or thought I knew, what was right and wrong, I did not see why I might no always do the one and avoid the other. But I soon found I had undertaken a task of more difficulty than I had imagined." Yet he later attributed his cheerfulness and evenness of temper to his faithful pursuit of these virtues.

The King who spurned the crown

Just as the name of Columbus became the iconic image inspiriting the high risk-taking entrepreneurs of America, Washington, on a grander scale, became the image of righteous political leadership, an image that grew larger with the years and became an article of faith for generations. Washington was a true original. A legend even in his own time, he was often compared to Cincinnatus, the Roman who left the plow to serve his republic and then surrendered power to return to farming. Writing to his wife Martha in June 1775 to tell her the Congress had put him in charge of the army, Washington said: "You may believe me, my dear Patsy, when I assure you, in the most solemn manner, that, so far from seeking this appointment, I have used every endeavor in my power to avoid it, not only from my unwillingness to part with you and the family but from a consciousness of its being a trust too great for my capacity, and that I should enjoy more real happiness in one month with you at home than I have the most distant prospect of finding abroad..."

After his election, the new president and his wife, under constant public attention, drew some criticism from the anti-federalists for their fortnightly "levees" and drawing room parties and for the way the general drove about New York in a coach and six. A few of the critics found the president dull and stiff. But mostly, the public adored him, and the adulation ran to excesses, especially in *The Gazette of the United States*. Along with his storied probity there were very human sides to the first president. He charmed women and danced with gusto. He speculated in land on a large scale. He made a passable molasses brew as well as one of the country's first commercial rye whiskies.

This immortal American is pictured clearly in the words of those who were closest to him. Jefferson wrote in a letter to a friend in January 1814 that Washington was "incapable of fear" and that his strongest quality was prudence, "never acting until every circumstance, every consideration was maturely weighted; refraining if he saw a doubt but, when once decided, going through with his purpose whatever obstacles opposed." Although he was often at odds with his chief, Jefferson acknowledged that "his integrity was most pure, his justice the most inflexible I have ever known, no motives of interest or consanguinity, of friendship or hatred, being able to bias his decision. He was, indeed, in every sense of the words, a wise, a good and a great man."

Jefferson also called the general "the best horseman of his age, and the most graceful figure that could be seen on horseback." In this same letter he wrote that Washington often had said that he considered the new Constitution an experiment in the practicability of republican government "and with what dose of liberty man could be trusted for his own good"; Washington vowed that he "would lose the last drop of his blood in support of it."

Washington had a moral stature among his contemporaries that has never been surpassed by any of his successors, though his image was reflected in later presidents with high moral standards such as Jefferson, Lincoln, Wilson and the two Roosevelts. Washington's personal rectitude and impeccable manners can be traced all the way back to the notebooks he kept mostly in his pre-teen years, which included 110 rules for good behavior written by French Jesuits. These rules for morals and manners, among other things, stuck with Washington throughout his life. One of them ("Associate yourself with men of good quality, if you esteem your own reputation, for 'tis better to be alone than in bad company") presaged the preoccupation with his own reputation that marked him for life.

The secretary of the French Legation in America during the revolution, the Marquis de Barbe-Marbois, witnessed Washington with his army, wearing his large blue sash of the republic and "preserving in battle the character of humanity which makes him so dear to his soldiers…" The Marquis also observed that Washington "sometimes throws and catches a ball for whole hours with his aides-de-camp. He is reverent without bigotry, and abhors swearing, which he punishes with the greatest severity. As to his public conduct—ask his compatriots, and the universe."

Washington's famous biographer, James Thomas Flexner, sought to disentangle the real-life Washington from the myth he had become. "In all history," he concluded, few men who possessed unassailable power have used that power so gently and self-effacingly for what their best instincts told them was the welfare of their neighbors and all mankind."

In an essay on Washington as constitutional leader, author Garry Wills described him as "forceful though somewhat tongue-tied, gigantic even by Virginia's standards, a Natty Bumppo, a John Wayne, a natural leader of men." During the early stages of the nation's development he remained throughout the "unifying icon, the symbol of the whole process," Wills wrote. Even as a young colonial militiaman, Washington had shown that he meant to stand out, that he had a theatrical flair for impressing others, even to designing his own special uniform.

Washington was a model for his successors in his readiness to yield military and political power when he felt the time had come to pass the baton. He first retired from the military at age 27, after participating in a series of blundering efforts by British troops fighting the French and Indians, an experience that taught him how not to lead troops and after which he sought, as he did many times afterwards, to return to his favorite vocation, which was farming (he exchanged tips on seeds and fertilizers with Jefferson, among others).

In the summer of 1782 an army colonel, one of the legion of his admirers, wrote Washington urging him to set himself up as king of the 13 former colonies, since all major countries then were monarchies. Washington told the colonel to forget it, declaring that nothing in the course of the war had given him more pain than thinking that such ideas existed in the army and among the public. "You could not have found a person to whom your schemes are more disagreeable," he wrote. Washington's determination to yield power when he felt his work was done was truly remarkable in comparison with other revolutionary heroes who had risen to power in other nations.

By what miracle did this modest Virginia planter and surveyor, a self-made man with practically no formal education, become a symbol in his country and throughout the world of the ideal chief executive of a democratic republic? He had less formal education than probably any other president, "not beyond what we would consider the eighth grade", wrote Flexner. As a teen-ager, Flexner said, he couldn't get to a dance because he could not afford the oats to feed his horse.

He had started at 16 as a land surveyor, entering the military at 20 as a volunteer soldier for the British Crown, becoming at 23 the commander-in-chief of all Virginia's forces fighting the Indians and, at 43, the commander in chief of the ill-equipped, rag-tag Continental Army. At 55 he became president of the Constitutional Convention and first president of the new nation. From experience leading his farm-boy troops, he developed a strategy appropriate for those irregulars that enabled him to outlast four British commanders.

Washington was a miracle of nature, thought Jefferson, who wrote of his chief that "never did nature and fortune combine more perfectly to make a man great." Washington stood out among the revolutionary leaders for his dignity and composure, and for the towering presence he lent to every gathering; his contemporaries thought him "the most exciting man in the room"—no small compliment considering the stature of the other leaders at those key formative meetings of the new republic. Madison thought that the sole reason the Constitution was ratified was the trust held by Washington. Surely one reason why Washington was so revered was the fact that he always cherished above all things his reputation and his loyalty to the Constitution and the general public interest. As Jefferson put it, "he had the purest motives."

A spirited inaugural

Washington's inauguration was a blazing highlight in the creation of the new nation. At every town and ferry crossing in that warm April of 1789, cheering crowds thronged around the president-elect and his entourage. "Militia marched, dragoons pranced, cannon fired," wrote Willard Sterne Randall in his biography of Washington. In New Jersey "young girls with women in long white gowns strewed flower petals at the feet of his horse." On his way to Manhattan Washington boarded a large ceremonial barge full of dignitaries.

Washington wrote in his diary, with a trace of anxiety, that "the display of boats which attended and joined us on this occasion, some with vocal and some with instrumental music on board—the decorations of the ships, the roar of cannon and the loud acclamations of the people which rent the skies... filled my mind with sensations as painful (considering the reverse of this scene which may be the case after all my labors to do good) as they are pleasing."

In the inaugural parade the new president rode to Federal Hall, where the Congress was waiting, in a white presidential coach of state. There, he stepped out on the balcony to receive the cheers of ten thousand jubilant citizens. The nation had its first president—church bells rang, cannon fired, and the crowd shouted: "God bless our Washington!" and "Long live our beloved president!" Randall wrote that "virtually every window in the city was illuminated by candlelight for the occasion" and taverns "sported larger-than-life paintings" of the president.

Washington's fears that his thin political experience for the job might bring disaster were, of course, all for naught. In his last annual message to Congress, on December 7, 1796—his eighth and last State of the Union message—he concluded in words typical of his combination of regal tone and personal humility. He left no doubt about how he felt about his presidency as he concluded: "I cannot omit the occasion to congratulate you and my country on the success of the experiment, nor to repeat my fervent supplications to the Supreme Ruler of the Universe and Sovereign Arbiter of Nations that his Providential care may still be extended to the United States; that the virtue and happiness of the people may be preserved and that the government which they have instituted for the protection of their liberties may be perpetual."

Washington has "a centrality in the American national consciousness for which there is no close analogue in other great modern nations", as Boorstin put it. Flexner, whose multi-volume biography of Washington, along with that of Douglas Southall Freeman, has been so important in fixing Washington's place in history, said that his own long writing labors "have persuaded me that he became one of the noblest and greatest men who ever lived." Flexner observed that this great American "was not born that way.... He perfected himself gradually through the exercise of his own will and skill." He was a self-made man within the Virginia colonial planter aristocracy.

The model chief executive

The first President's most important legacy was in setting a model for the nation's chief executive, with little to guide him but with a personal conviction that the citizen's personal character was the foundation of the nation's character. One of his many English admirers, Samuel T. Coleridge, wrote of Washington: "Tranquil and firm he moved with one pace in one path, and neither vaulted nor tottered... among a people eminently querulous and already impregnated with the germs of discordant parties, he directed the executive power firmly and unostentatiously. He had no vain conceit of being himself all..."

Washington had a large vision of the new nation's future. He respected the Congress and considered himself the servant of the Congress and the people. He had a marvelous talent for keeping political adversaries "in double harness". Nowhere was his philosophy better expressed than in his final address to the nation, after 45 years of public service, which, along with the Declaration of Independence, the Constitution and *The Federalist Papers* is one of the great documents of American history (as a timely book by Matthew Spalding and Patrick J. Garrity reminded a forgetful nation during the 1996 presidential election campaign.)

Washington was concerned over what he viewed as the tide of corruption in public and private morals that had risen by the mid-1780s. He was extremely proud of his "beloved" country and of the new course it had struck among nations, but because of the threat that declining morals posed to national life, he wanted the new democracy to revitalize its early principles and commitments.

He believed public virtue depended on individual virtue. He believed that religion was essential to the formation of good citizens and that it should be an essential part of public education. Offering final advice to his fellow citizens, which he said was "the result of much reflection" on these and other matters, he warned against the "baneful effects" of excessive political party discriminations, the accumulation of public debt and foreign entanglements.

Two of his themes were union at home and independence abroad. But his other great theme was character—the inseparability of the character of individual citizens, their leaders and their nation, founded in religion, which was "the necessary spring of popular government." With the other Founders he believed in separation of religion and politics—and believed that this separation actually strengthened both private morality and public virtue—but he also was certain the private virtue had to be the cornerstone of successful democracy. In his final address, one of America's greatest state papers, he said:

"Of all the dispositions and habits which lead to political prosperity, religion and morality are indispensable supports. In vain would that man claim the tribute of patriotism who should labor to subvert these great pillars of human happiness, these firmest props of the duties of men and citizens... And let us with caution indulge the supposition that morality can be maintained without religion. Whatever may be conceded to the influence of refined education... reason and experience both forbid us to expect that National Morality can prevail in exclusion of religious principle."

John Quincy Adams, who followed Washington as president, said he hoped not only that the American people would take this address to heart but also that it would become the foundation upon which the whole system of American policy would rise, "the admiration and example of future time."

Of course in his time Washington had enemies at least as vicious as those of other presidents who followed. Malicious rumors, lies and partisan disputes, and charges of usurping power, fouled the air throughout his presidency. He was demonized in early 1795 for the treaty his emissary, John Jay, negotiated with Britain, which included provisions for payoff to England of old debts (mostly by Virginians) and restrictions on U.S. shipping to the West Indies. "If ever a nation was debauched by a man," growled one Philadelphia newspaper, "the American nation has been by Washington." Nor was that newspaper, owned by Ben Franklin's grandson, the only one to rejoice when Washington left office in March 1797.

The transfiguration of Washington into a virtual demigod, which took place mostly after his death in December 1799, was at first largely the creation of several best-selling biographies celebrating the man as national hero. But it was also a consequence, in the view of Boorstin, of "the desperate need Americans felt for a dignified and worshipful national hero" as well as "the special potency of the will to believe in this New World." Ever afterwards the legendary Washington stirred the souls of Americans. The noble, stately leader's reverence for God and love of fellow men were in great part true but in some part were the concoction of the legions of Washington worshippers who never knew him first-hand.

The optimist who lit the candle

Another one of history's greatest casting jobs was the choice of that six-foot-two-and-a-half-inch freckled redhead, 33-year-old Thomas Jefferson, to write the Declaration of Independence, with a nudge from John Adams, who turned over the task to his young colleague. Jefferson was one of the most broadly gifted, best-read leaders of any age, so much so that from the perspective of later generations he seems a man who might very well have been created to inspire the building of a society more likely to succeed and survive than any before it.

Jefferson was "the eternal optimist", according to Willard Sterne Randall, in his bountiful biography *Thomas Jefferson*— not only because of Jefferson's long vision of the nation's future, far ahead of his countrymen, but also because he had a profound, well-thought-through faith in democracy and in the good sense of free people, based upon his own extraordinary studies of history. As a historical figure he could fairly be compared to Plato and Aristotle in his deep concerns for truth, freedom and learning. Among the Founders, no one had more profound convictions about the rights of man and the ability of free people to govern themselves. And, in part because of his taste of Europe when he was minister in revolutionary France, no one appreciated his country more. Writing to urge James Monroe to visit him in Paris, Jefferson said the trip "will make you adore your own country...My God! How little do my countrymen know what precious blessings they are in possession of, and which no other people on earth enjoy."

The thing about Jefferson that gives you the greatest lift is "his belief in the human mind and his belief in human beings," Jefferson biographer Dumas Malone once said. "You always have the feeling of springtime with Jefferson's mind—a new era, getting rid of superstition and prejudice and tyranny, with the human race launched on an endless conquest of freedom and knowledge." He was obsessed, Stanley Elkins and Eric McKittrick wrote more recently, "with the virtuous uses of time."

Jefferson's scholarly admirers were taken aback in late 1998 when it was reported that DNA research among his descendants suggested that he might have fathered a child by one of his slaves, which, if true, would tarnish his reputation as an advocate of freedom for slaves, not to mention his reputation for the highest character. The truth about this story will probably never be known because, as the pathologist who reported the DNA test pointed out, the genetic study did not prove anything conclusively and the scientists who did the study never made the claim that Jefferson fathered one of the slave's children.

Some scholars and some Jefferson descendants dispute the DNA-link story, and they have circumstantial evidence to back them up. The young slave girl, Sally Hemings, was only eight years old when Jefferson last resided at his Monticello home in Virginia before taking up his duties as minister to France. Sally was only 13 when she went to Europe as an au pair with Jefferson's daughter Polly. Jefferson, Polly and his other daughter Patsy were a close and loving family during his diplomatic tour in Paris and neither daughter ever mentioned anything about their father having an affair with the young sister of his chef. Prior to the DNA test, the main evidence for the "Dusky Sally" story was the rumor spread by a political enemy of Jefferson, an alcoholic journalist whom Jefferson had refused to employ in government service. The integrity of this blackguard was questioned particularly when he died drunk and disgraced in the James River on a Sunday morning in July 1803.

Furthermore, the story seems somewhat incompatible with the two well-documented romances of Jefferson's life. The first was his ardent love affair with the beautiful young Virginia widow "Patty" who became his wife and died after her third childbirth, leaving Jefferson devastated and in stupor for months afterward. The other, four years later, was his hot pursuit in Paris of a 27-year-old Boticelli-like blond English portraitist named Maria Conway, which was a case of love at first sight.

If there is truth in the Jefferson-Hemings story, one explanation may be that Sally Hemings was the daughter of Jefferson's wife's father, thus the half-sister of his widow (and said by some to resemble his widow), to whom he had given a promise never to marry again. The other, less palatable, explanation could be that in the colonial culture of Virginia it was not at all unusual for a plantation owner (including Jefferson's father-in-law) to have a clandestine affair with a slave; a number of people living in Jefferson's time had assumed that it was one of Jefferson's nephews who had sired one or more children with the slave girl. The fact that such stories were not considered unusual in those times throws considerable light on the status of women—in particular black women—in that "man's world" of plantation society.

Jefferson's true legacy

Despite this recent cloud shrouding the history of a great American, especially among African-Americans, there can be no doubting the optimism, learning and devotion to democracy that Jefferson brought to his time. His optimism was remarkable partly because his views departed from those of most people in an age of monarchies. Most Americans before the Declaration of Independence accepted their roles as loyal subjects of King George III. Jefferson's superb mind and writing skills helped him set the path to freedom for people in this and many other nations for ages to come. His studies of the historical relationships between kings and their subjects went back to King Alfred the Great, who unified England in the ninth century, and King William who established Norman rule in England in the eleventh century. His comparative studies of law and governance ranged from Plato to Blackstone.

His heroes were the Enlightenment philosophers Bacon, Newton and Locke and his French favorite, Montesquieu, and his own writings reflected the optimistic faith of the Enlightenment. Jefferson credited Tacitus, "the first writer of the world", for his own understanding of history and the place of morality in public life and his guide to avoiding the errors and the moral decay that undermined the Greco-Roman civilization. As with the other principal founders, Jefferson's serious study of Greek and Roman classics deeply informed his notions of liberty, justice and the good life, his convictions about what government should and should not do. His studies bred in him a deep conviction that a free people could make progress, generation after generation, through the use of their God-given reason.

That conviction, as Randall made clear, was the basis of Jefferson's optimism. He really believed in limitless progress, if not perfection, for the human race—through education, so long as there was free discourse and a free press. This belief in the perfectability of man and society, and the essential wisdom of the common people, is one of Jefferson's legacies that was well planted in the American character. His Enlightenment view of man explains much of the history of hope in America and provided inspiration for freedom-seeking people throughout the world.

In the midst of World War II, two hundred years after Jefferson's birth, Franklin D. Roosevelt, dedicating the Jefferson Memorial, reiterated Jefferson's belief in man. "He believed, as we believe", the 32nd president said of the third president, "that men are capable of their own government, and that no king, no tyrant, no dictator can govern for them as well as they can govern for themselves."

The transcendental Declaration

Jefferson wrote the Declaration of Independence in two weeks on the second floor of a Philadelphia lodging house at a desk which he himself designed. He cobbled it together mostly from two sources: the preamble for the Virginia Constitution that he had written and the draft of Virginia's Declaration of Rights written by George Mason. The Declaration then was edited by virtually the entire Congress of remarkable, sophisticated citizens to the point where it truly could be called "an expression of the American mind."

Jefferson's purpose and his vision transcended colonial America, and the text spoke to an international audience. In lucid style, "life, liberty and the pursuit of happiness" were described as the most important rights of every human being. The cheerfulness of the phrase, "the pursuit of happiness" was in sharp contrast to the Puritan's emphasis on the pursuit of godliness, and reflected the more optimistic view about earthly life that characterized Jefferson, who was more hopeful about the future than many of his contemporaries.

The Declaration left no doubt about the religious faith that undergirded this most transforming of America's revolutionary pronouncements, basing its entitlement on the "Laws of Nature and of Nature's God." The people's rights, it asserted, were "endowed by their Creator." It appealed "to the Supreme Judge of the world" to grant the rectitude of their intentions, and concluded by affirming reliance "on the protection of divine Providence." The authors believed they had inaugurated a new order, a new age ("by Heaven decreed", as stated in the "Ode to the Fourth of July" poem composed at the time with a classical nod to Virgil's Aeneid, which had claimed that the founding of Rome was part of a divine plan, that its leaders, Aeneas and Augustus, were divinely appointed and its people were a Heaven-born generation.)

The Declaration capped a period of rising revolutionary fervor. Colonial leaders had been holding emergency meetings all up and down the eastern seaboard. In the tiny St. John's Church in Richmond, Virginia Patrick Henry, declaring that war had already begun, stirred great excitement at that meeting (at least one person present declared himself "sick with excitement.") When the Declaration was announced at the Boston State House the crowd pulled down a statue of George 3rd, which was then made into bullets. Washington had the Declaration read to his unready but inspired troops.

The Declaration gave birth to the new democracy, but as Jefferson biographer Merrill D. Peterson has written, it also gave the world a philosophy of human rights. Late in his life Jefferson wrote that "all eyes are opened or opening to the rights of man...These are the grounds of hope for others." In another letter he wrote that his purpose had been no less than "to place before mankind the common sense of the subject in terms so plain and firm as to command their assent..." He wanted the Declaration "to be to the world, what I believe it will be, to some parts sooner, to others later but finally to all, the signal to assume the blessings and security of self-government." Based on his ever-growing convictions about peoples' ability to govern themselves without "saddles on their backs", Jefferson's trust in people and his belief in democracy probably ran deeper in his veins than in any other person of his time. "The good sense of the people will always be found to be the best army," he wrote in one of his 28,000 letters to friends and associates.

The depth of Jefferson's belief in democracy translated into one act after another leading up to the birth of the American nation. He had no fears of public protests, even asking pardon for those revolutionaries who instigated Shay's Rebellion in Massachusetts. He showed courage when he suggested in another letter that "the tree of liberty must be refreshed from time to time with the blood of patriots and tyrants". Two years before shots were fired at Concord and Lexington, he wrote a resolution in the Virginia House of Burgesses to protest tyrannical British acts, calling for the first revolutionary committee to represent all the colonies. At a time when most Americans accepted their roles as royal subjects, he wrote a Declaration of Rights for Virginia, defending the "natural and legal rights" of the American people, putting his own life in danger of a hangman's noose.

Jefferson was a radical by comparison with the general population when he spoke out to support Patrick Henry in urging armed preparedness for the colonies. At 32 he was already one of Virginia's foremost leaders in standing up to the royal governor. He drank patriotic toasts with other colonial leaders at the Raleigh Tavern in Williamsburg, while volunteers were arming themselves and General Washington was already leading impromptu parades of riders and carriages, prompting John Adams to remark even then on "the pride and pomp of war."

The nascent revolution did not inspire the whole American population to enthusiastic fervor because it represented such a radical change, and because communications were so slow by today's standards. But the major developments of 1775 and 1776 certainly stirred up the people who were leading the key events, their followers and other citizens close to those events. And Jefferson's eloquent rhetoric as a young representative in the Constitutional Congress helped to stiffen the backs of the colonials when the British made conciliatory gestures, trying to keep their grip on their colonies.

As Governor of Virginia, the largest colonial state, Jefferson was a prime target of British forces when Cornwallis invaded that state in May 1781, a low point for the colonial cause and a frustrating time for Jefferson, whose military resources were no match for the British. Loyalist light infantry swarmed into the streets of Charlottesville. Jefferson, at Monticello, spied a troop of horsemen charging up the hill to capture him. Five minutes before the British dragoons arrived to pillage his house and destroy his crops of corn and tobacco, Jefferson sprang on his fastest horse, Caractacus, and galloped north through the forest to join his family. He was a superb, fearless rider with a lifelong passion for breeding and riding some of Virginia's finest horses. Although he had to face some criticism from his political rivals for his flight from the British, his narrow escape in this case was a blessing to his country, whose history would have been very different if he'd been taken prisoner that day by the British cavalry.

To cite Jefferson's accomplishments is to confound most minds, because the expanse of his knowledge and curiosity, and the richness of his public and private life eclipse the lives of our public figures today. Like Washington, he was a reluctant politician, drawn into politics by the urgings of others who believed his abilities were indispensable to the new republic. Time after time he tried to retire to his beloved Monticello, each time being called back to public service.

The Declaration of Independence was a radical pronouncement at a time when "all men" did not even have the right to vote. It set forth eloquently high aspirations for a free and just society. The Constitution, a more conservative document, spelled out comprehensively the government bodies and rules that became the means for realizing the promises of the Declaration of Independence. It put an economic foundation under the new republic, making clear that private rights of property were out of bounds to government.

What excited hope in these formative days was the novelty of the experience—never before in modern history had there been an opportunity for a people to create a nation on *tabula rasa*—from scratch, on lands without precedent of government, moated by two great oceans that protected it from the direct influence of other cultures. In his first year as president, Jefferson expressed the headiness of it in a note to Joseph Priestley: "For this whole chapter in the history of man is new," he wrote. "The great extent of our republic is new. Its sparse habitation is new." A new generation had freedom for the first time to create an original constitution and laws, unbeholden to history and preceding generations. Even in government, Americans from the start were innovators.

The framers were keenly aware that every republic before them had decayed and cracked under the influence of power abuses and corruption in high places. Their great concern was to make tyranny impossible; that is why they decided to require more than a majority vote to amend the Constitution, and that is why they created a tricameral system with three branches, dispersing power among the three, one to make laws, one to enforce the laws and one to interpret the laws.

The fact that this blueprint for a free society enabled the new democracy to survive longer than any other system of governing is, as much as anything, a tribute to the extraordinary character of the leaders of the time. Those ever astonishing people seem to grow in stature as each succeeding generation looks back on them. In character, intellect and talents the Founders stand high among leaders of any nation in world history, not least for their knowledge of world history and the strengths and weaknesses of past societies.

The assembly of representatives of the thirteen colonies that produced the U.S. Constitution in Philadelphia in 1789 included Washington, its president, Madison, Hamilton and fifty others. This relatively small group, bound together not only by their common enemy but also by the same religion, the same language and customs and devotion to democracy, represented the finest minds and noblest characters of the new nation. The major issue dividing them was the question of independence for the separate states versus the conflicting desire for a union representing the whole nation. This conflict they resolved by a division of the Congress into two bodies, responding to both sides of the argument, as well as the separation of powers among three distinct branches of government.

While the Declaration of Independence alone would have clinched Jefferson's place as an emblematic figure in history, his life and his years of public service were to have wide influence on the future development of the nation and in fact the world.

The cultivation of an intellect

Born in a farmhouse beside Virginia's western frontier, Jefferson by age 14 was reading Greek, Latin and French, and throughout his life kept notebooks that included passages from these works. The son of a surveyor and map-maker who turned these skills to very profitable use in land speculation, Jefferson too became a surveyor at age 16, and at the same age entered the College of William and Mary. He left the college after two years for self-study supervised by some of the finest minds in the country. By age 32 he was the leading colonial property lawyer.

His early studies of law and philosophy were unusually rigorous and wide-ranging by the standards of any age. "A hard student", as he described himself, he spent nearly 20 years studying the laws of biblical, Greek and Roman eras as well as English common law and Continental law, according to Randall, preparing him to become America's most learned president as well as a political philosopher and scientist and acutely observant traveler abroad.

His work in helping frontier people take title to western lands helped him see how the open frontier and cheap land enriched freedom, democracy and prosperity. It led to his expanding vision of his country's future and eventually to his greatest presidential coup. Thanks to Napoleon's needs for money at the time, Jefferson secretly bought the huge Louisiana Territory from France for $15 million, in one stroke doubling the size of the United States. While some eyebrows were raised at the private way in which Jefferson handled this deal, the news of his coup made his countrymen proud. The purchase was trumpeted on the Fourth of July by Philadelphia's National Intelligencer newspaper. According to the paper "It was a proud day for the President, a day of widespread joy of millions at an event which history will record among the most splendid in our annals."

That sudden expansion cleared the way for Jefferson to ask Congress, again secretly, for $2,500 to finance the first scientific expedition of the United States, led by Meriwether Lewis. Instructed down to the fine details by Jefferson, Lewis and Clark spent two years in their journey to the Pacific, amassing the scientific records the President wanted, including the records of animals and plants never described before.

Jefferson had an extraordinary intellectual curiosity and thirst for knowledge throughout his life, which prepared him for his historic role. Science was one of his passionate interests. For three decades he kept notes on plant, animal and bird life, weather and other manifestations of nature. He invented farm equpment to streamline the process of harvesting. When he arrived in Philadelpia in 1789 for the Constitutional Convention he carried in his bags the bones of a prehistoric animal for the collection of the American Philosophical Society, the nation's principal scientific organization founded by Benjamin Franklin, of which he was to become president that year.

He gathered books in such quantities ("I could not live without my books," he said) that his own 6,000-volume library became the core of the Library of Congress. Honored for his botanical experiments, over his lifetime Jefferson also introduced into American life many culinary delights enjoyed today, principally from his European experience. He was a wine connoisseur, called by some "the father of American wines." From his European experience he introduced America to olives, macaroni and ice cream. One of his contemporaries described him as a man who could "calculate an eclipse, survey an estate, tie an artery, plan an edifice, try a cause, break a horse, dance the minuet and play the violin."

Most important down the years were the practical benefits of Jefferson's philosophical studies and the convictions that grew out of them. Foremost among these, after the Declaration, was Jefferson's bill, the Statute of Virginia for Religious Freedom, passed in 1786, which established religious freedom and the separation of church and state and whose principles found their way into the U.S. Constitution by way of the First Amendment in the Bill of Rights. He was exceedingly proud of this document, and he translated it into French and Italian and had it distributed throughout Europe. He also drafted 126 laws for the government of Virginia, largest of the Colonial states, which were later to provide a model for the Federal Government. Almost immediately after he entered the Virginia House of Burgesses he proposed legislation to allow the freeing of slaves, arguing that the slave trade was a war against human nature, for which he was denounced as an enemy of his country.

Putting into action his belief that education could bring progress to society, Jefferson became the founder and moving force behind the

University of Virginia, which he sought to make "the most eminent in the United States". Besides organizing the university's curricula and recruiting its faculty, he supervised construction and drew up architectural plans for the domed building that presides over its campus and the Rotunda modeled after drawings for the Pantheon in Rome by the 16th Century architect Palladio. He also designed the state capital in Richmond and designed and supervised construction of his own mountaintop home, Monticello, based on his studies of Palladio's Villa Rotonda near Vicenza, Italy.

"He not only did it all," the curator at Jefferson's home in Monticello once said, "he was damn near expert in everything, maybe because he didn't have to answer a phone or have television to look at—he wouldn't have looked at it anyway."

Jefferson greatly influenced the ideas that shaped the federal government. He was one of the first to urge strengthening the powers of Congress. Three years before the Constitutional Convention he proposed a constitution that would include the doctrine of the balance of powers. He worried and wrote about the dangers of centralized power in America, especially the tendency of the Judiciary to make decisions that led to further extension of federal power. He sent some 300 books to James Madison, helping his protege play the major role in formulating the central government.

All his life Jefferson believed unshakably that mankind was advancing steadily, that education and scientific progress would eliminate social evils such as slavery. But he also believed that the process was gradual. At age 73 he wrote that "laws and institutions must go hand in hand with the progress of the human mind."

Daniel Boorstin put Jefferson's role in historical perspective in his book, *The Lost World of Thomas Jefferson*. He wrote: "While the folk figure of Benjamin Franklin has tended to become quaint and sententious, and George Washington towers over us, marbleized, monumental and superhuman, Jefferson somehow has remained relevant to our nation's crises and great concerns."

OPTIMISTIC POETS

"You're from New England. That's wonderful. That's the place to be from. It all began there—Emerson, Thoreau, Melville, Hawthorne, Longfellow. They started it. If it weren't for them there would be nothing." The renowned South American writer Jorge Luis Borges paid this tribute to early American writers in a talk with Paul Theroux in Buenos Aires. In a poem about the New England writers, Borges wrote: "They have changed the shapes of my dreams."

The poets and philosophers of the new nation changed the shapes of many dreams. They gave a sturdy literary foundation to the optimism of the new breed. Indeed the most striking aspect of the years 1830 to 1870 was the rise of literary New England, a new romantic movement that came to its climax after the decline of romanticism in Victorian England and was a match for Victorian literature in quality and range. Men of letters were held in highest regard in Boston and Cambridge of those days ("universal humanists" Santayana called them) and one resident of Cambridge, which was still just a village, commented that poets and other writers, literary statesmen and scientists were "as thick as blackberries in our little world."

Tocqueville wrote: "The foundation of New England was a novel spectacle, and all the circumstances attending it were singular and original." When the French traveler came to America in 1831, Emerson was 28, Thoreau 14 and Whitman 12. Emerson entered Harvard at the age of 14 and worked his way through college by waiting on tables and instructing delinquent students. He was class poet at graduation. The single greatest influence in his education was his tiny aunt, Mary Moody Emerson, a very poor but self-educated, naturally brilliant woman who wrote highly original commentaries all her life. And just as Jefferson's political philosophy grew out of intense studies of Enlightenment thinkers, Emerson's philosophy of life and religion emerged from a lifetime ferment of helter-skelter reading—everything from Plato and Plutarch to the idealistic German philosopher Hegel and poet Goethe, to Ruskin, Coleridge, Montaigne and Quetelet to India's Bhagavad Gita and to Sufi poetry such as the 14th-century Persian poet Hafez, as well as Islamic books like the 15th-century Akhlak-I-Jalaly.

From his wide reading and independent thinking, Emerson cast his own original philosophy and became, as Brooks Atkinson once put it, "the first philosopher of the American spirit." The distinguished poet Edwin Arlington Robinson called Emerson "the greatest American poet." Emerson struck a purely American chord, dismissing class distinctions or titles and regarding true aristocracy as "any natural excellence or unusual daring or striking effort", as one of his biographers, Robert Richardson, wrote. Emerson was fascinated by the West, where "everyone has mud up to his knees". He observed that out on the prairies "the people are kings."

He spread his gospel of optimism first in his sermons, as a minister for three years at Boston's old Second Church, the church of Increase and Cotton Mather and their Puritan tradition, where he gave his first sermon before he was twenty. He left the ministry after becoming convinced that church orthodoxy and ritual meant less to him than the direct revelation of God in his own mind and in the natural world about him. He was increasingly active as lecturer and writer from 1834 on, preferring the role of teacher to that of preacher.

One visitor at Emerson's home in Concord in 1838 saw a sight not unlike a characteristic gathering of free thinkers of the 1960s, "men with long beards, men with bare feet" Emerson's wife said. And indeed the 1840s, like the 1790s and the 1960s, was to some extent a decade of rebels and reformers, like the Brook Farm community and other communes, who believed whole-heartedly that society could be remade to their wishes. "Not a reading man but has a draft of a new Community in his waistcoat pocket," said one of these reformers.

Emerson's influence spread mostly from his long career as essayist and speaker on lecture circuits. He gave some 1,500 lectures (40 pages to a typical lecture) over four decades, traveling daily from town to town and becoming a familiar figure throughout the country. He averaged 47 lectures a year in his last 14 years, 80 in 1867 alone at the age of 64. For the rest of the century, his wide public exposure gave an intellectual boost to the cities, villages and frontiers of America and the spirits of its citizens.

Optimist and teacher

Returning from Europe with Emerson in 1873, the scholar and teacher Charles Eliot Norton wrote in his journal that Emerson was the greatest talker on the ship. "His optimistic philosophy had hardened into a creed...", wrote Norton. "To him this is the best of all possible worlds.... Order is the absolute law; disorder but a phenomenon; good is absolute, evil is but good in the making.... He breathed in the confident, sweet morning spirit of a time when America believed that the Fourth of July, the Declaration of Independence, the common school and the four-year presidential term were finalities in political science and social happiness; of a time when society was simple, and comparatively innocent..."

Emerson was the wise man, the Brahmin Buddha , the philosopher whose aphorisms gave freshness and depth to the original character of the American. His wise, succinct sayings fell in the tradition of history's other wise men from Moses and Jesus to Confucius, Buddha and Mohammed, and from Greek and Roman writer-philosophers to Montaigne and Bacon. He had the philosopher's habits, as William James was to define them, "of not taking the usual for granted, of making conventionalities fluid again, of imagining foreign states of mind." He pointed the way for the American philosophers of pragmatism that were to follow him.

Emerson was a "champion of cheerfulness", in Santayana's phrase, but he was also a philosopher who believed more in the ageless unity of the human spirit than in progress as it is measured by most people. Like Socrates, he drew a linkage between the minds and souls of men, in the unity and truth that comes from God. His most unique influence on American character came from his preaching that the genius of men arose from each person's following his own star—what was true in the private heart—relying on inner selves more than on any outside influences.

For him, intuition was infallible. His theme was the infinite capacities of the private individual—that is the prime thought that resonates all through Emerson, pure and valid, he thought, for all people every-where in all times. "Man is his own star," he wrote in his essay "Self Reliance", and again, "Whoso would be a man, must be a nonconform-ist." He wrote: "To believe your own thought, to believe that what is true for you in your private heart is true for all men-that is genius." In the introduction to his first book he asked: "Why should not we also enjoy an original relation to the universe?" He believed that the great-ness of Moses, Plato and Milton was that they over-rode books and traditions and spoke to what was in the minds of individuals.. "In all my lectures," he wrote in his journal, "I have taught one doctrine, namely, the infinitude of the private man."

One reason for Emerson's optimism was his separation of the mind's world—the beautiful, joyful world of intellect and truth—from the experience "on the ground" in the actual world of time and place. He accepted that "there is a crack in everything that God has made." He wrote: "If we did not die, there would be no room for grandchildren; if we were never sick, the amiable profession of medicine would be unknown…" Without war, he wrote, "no soldiers; without enemies, no hero…what would poet do or what would painter paint but for the crucifixions and hells?" Everything is beautiful "seen from the point of view of intellect, or as truth," he wrote. "But all is sour if seen from experience… In the actual world… dwell care, and cancer and fear. With thought, with the ideal, is immortal hilarity… But grief clings to names, and persons, and the partial interests of today and yesterday."

According to Emerson's view of the world, wrote Harold Clark Goddard, "the one reality is the vast spiritual background of existence, the 'Over-Soul', God, within which all other being is unified" and from which the world derives its life. Giving coherence to the world, as Emerson saw it, was the power of the individual soul to draw en-ergy from the "over-soul" that embraces all life.

This transcendental view held that every part of the world "is a microcosm, comprehending within itself, like Tennyson's flower in the crannied wall, all the laws and meaning of the whole." From these conceptions, wrote Goddard, were derived the "doctrines of self-reli-ance and individualism, the identity of moral and physical laws, the essential unity of all religions… and the spirit of complete tolerance and absolute optimism, their defiance of tradition and disregard for all external authority."

46

Transcendentalism, the philosophical movement Emerson led with his essays and lectures around the country, embodied an essentially optimistic view of man and nature.

His hopeful prescriptions for life, such as "Trust Thyself: every heart vibrates to that iron string", were the more remarkable because his own personal life was fretful and tragic. He lost his wife at age 19 to tuberculosis a few months after their first anniversary; their first son, Waldo, died at age five; Emerson himself suffered from symptoms of tuberculosis and eye trouble; three of his younger siblings died in childhood and two in early adulthood, one of them after a spell in a lunatic asylum. None of these things seemed to keep *his* heart from vibrating to that iron string: for him, the life of the mind transcended the tragedies of daily life, of which he had more than his share.

One of his essays, "Circles", sounded a theme that seems pertinent in the modern world of accelerating changes wrought by technology and global development. It scoffs at fixed or finite things or pauses, celebrating instead the energizing spirit of change, "that every end is a beginning, that there is always another dawn... and under every deep a lower deep opens." He affirms that "Nothing great was ever achieved without enthusiasm. The way of life is wonderful. It is by abandonment." He admired energy, whether it be the energy of a locomotive, the rage for road-building or the energy of a "blast furnace" like Daniel Webster. In some of his lectures Emerson reflected on the subject of American identity. He saw the linkage between New England character and the Puritans and said once that 17th-century religious aspirations were "the most creative energy in our experience."

He described America as "another word for Opportunity... There never was such a combination as this of ours, and the rules to meet it are not set down in any history. We want men of original perception and original action, who can open their eyes wider than to a nationality, namely to considerations of benefit to the human race, can act in the interest of civilization."

Emerson's views of enterprise

Emerson's philosophy accommodated an acceptance of the need for productive labor and gainful wealth-creation. "How does man get his living?", he asked in one essay. "He fails to make his place good in the world, unless he not only pays his debt, but also adds something to the common wealth." He said man must apply his mind to nature to create wealth, "from the rudest strokes of spade and axe, up to the last secrets of art", the greatest extension of man's powers. "He is the richest man," he wrote," who knows how to draw a benefit from the labors of the greatest number of men, of men in distant countries, and in past times." His imagination conjured up hopes for the new developments of his day like the electric telegraph and the railroads.

He regarded property as "an intellectual production; commerce a game of skill; money, the delicate measure of civil, social and moral changes." He traced a pattern from wealth to money to spending, recognizing that investment is the seed for higher goods, greater welfare and greater freedom ("A dollar in a university is worth more than a dollar in a jail..."). Even adversity seemed to give him a sort of elation. He cautioned against setting store too much by material things. "What is the end of human life?" he asked in one talk. "It is not, believe me, the chief end of man that he should make a fortune and beget children whose end is likewise to make a fortune, but it is, in few words, that he should explore himself." For society as a whole he believed the goal should be "a voluntary association of fulfilled individuals".

Emerson feared that the vibrant American national spirit would simmer down. "I think we Yankees have marched on since the revolution to strength, to honor and at last to ennui," he worried. He fretted about a settling down of the national spirit. And indeed, by the middle of the 18th century, the Puritan ardor of New England had abated and a new secularism was taking its place, bringing its own form of energy, led by backwoodsmen, traders and later families heading out to the western wilderness and producing a new breed of heroes.

Like Columbus, Whitman and other sky-high idealists, Emerson, as he grew older, became more accepting of the limitations of freedom, the idea of failure, defeat and the imperfections of man and country. Though he was more respectful of worldly wealth than most philosophers and authors (after all, wealth was one outcome of the aggressive self-reliance he preached) he was also troubled by the growing materialistic spirit of Americans, the vulgarity that came with it and the absence of "worthy purpose" in so many lives. "It is the vulgarity of this country," he told the students in a talk at Williams College in the Berkshires in 1854, "...to believe that naked wealth, unrelieved by any use or design, is merit."

He declared: "I too am an American and value practical ability. I delight in people who can do things, I prize talent—perhaps no man more. But I think of the wind, and not of the weathercocks." Urging the students to put intellectual values above materialism, faith above works, he said "it is thoughts that make men great and strong; the material results are bubbles..." In an essay he wrote: "In our large cities, the population is godless, materialized—no bond, no fellow feeling, no enthusiasm. These are not men, but hungers, thirsts, fevers and appetites walking."

Emerson became a virtual institution in his time. In his 79 years, through his essays, poems and lectures, he influenced American thought more profoundly than any writer of his time, perhaps of any time. He set the philosophical base for the unique optimism of the American spirit. His lectures were covered widely in the newspapers. When his house in Concord was destroyed by fire his devotees raised money for him to rebuild it and to take a recuperative trip to Europe, where he was greeted as a celebrity. When he returned, on a train with its whistle blowing in celebration, the entire town of Concord welcomed him, even closing school for the day. His funeral in 1882 drew admirers from far and near, with special trains arranged to bring them to Concord.

Critic of the times

One truly unique mind influenced by Emerson was that of Henry David Thoreau, 14 years his junior, who lived for a time with the Emersons. "They were both modern stoics, interested in self-rule and autonomy", wrote Richardson. Emerson said that "no truer American existed than Thoreau," recognizing the uniqueness of the man who became the most penetrating critic of his generation.

Thoreau found that by working as a handyman or surveyor for six weeks a year he could make all the money he needed for his simple life of study. Like Jefferson and Emerson, he believed that "the less government we have the better." Emerson helped him to see a divinity in man and nature that spoke in the glow of a sunrise, the scampering of squirrels and woodchucks, the sound of frogs and the flowers in a meadow. All these Thoreau had plenty of time to observe during his two years and two months in the little cabin he built beside Walden Pond. Emerson said that "Thoreau dedicated his genius with such entire love to the fields, hills and waters of his native town that he made them known and interesting to all reading Americans, and to people over the sea."

By simplifying life, Thoreau separated the essential from the trivial. He turned his back on material things, in contrast to the Americans of the Gilded Age that was to follow him. An Emersonian man if there ever was one, Thoreau found everything he wanted in life in the woods, fields and waters in the meridian of Concord. Emerson dubbed him "the wood god". He respected the truth that he personally found, or sensed, in nature and in his own imagination, rather than in the opinions of others. Reading Thoreau today is to recognize acutely an independence of mind that has been lost in today's synchronized urban shuffles.

Musing about his solitary time at Walden Pond, Thoreau wrote: "I learned this at least by my experiment: that if one advances confidently in the direction of his dreams, and endeavors to live the life which he has imagined, he will meet with a success unexpected in common hours." Many years later *New Yorker* editor E.B. White recalled how reading that passage resuscitated and exhilarated him when he was a "youth drowning in his sea of doubt."

A poet who dazzled

Walt Whitman was another story, but equally unique and uniquely American. Leaving school to start work in Brooklyn, New York before his teens, he became a newspaper reporter, editor, compositor (setting the type himself for his *Leaves of Grass* in 1855) as well as carpenter and builder. The city was his university: its artists and writers, its politicians and preachers, its carpenters, stage drivers, sailors, street vendors, cabdrivers, ferrymen and other ordinary folk, as well as its libraries and museums, were all his familiars. William Dean Howells once recalled seeing him regaling the bohemian crowd at Pfaffs beer cellar in Brooklyn. The poet reached out his hand, said Howells, "as if he were going to give it to me for good and all."

Whitman read Emerson's "Poet" again and again, and clearly imagined himself rising to the role of that ideal artist. Emerson had written that "America is a poem in our eyes; its ample geography dazzles the imagination and it will not wait long for metres." In 1891 Whitman wrote, "I hear America singing, the varied carols I hear..." and no writer before or since has ever embraced the whole land so robustly, so warmly as he did in his poems.

He was a good match for the rough, open-hearted Americans who were throwing back the nation's frontiers and enjoying democracy "with considerable swagger and gusto," as one writer of the time put it. The giddy transport of the poetry Whitman wrote in his prime took American exuberance and optimism to new heights. Inspired and inspiring, this poet exulted in the sheer joy of freedom in the new land. Boldly speaking for all people, presuming himself to represent the spirit of all the people, he put in soaring verse the ultimate expression of humanity in all the forms that freedom allowed it to take.

Whitman was and is a polestar for Americans, his own expansiveness of spirit speaking for a race of open people, glad in their freedom and their good fortune to live in a land of opportunities. For most of his life he was such a positive personality that, William James wrote, he was actually unable to feel evil. One of Whitman's contemporaries, a writer and disciple of the poet, wrote that "his favorite occupation seemed to be strolling or sauntering about outdoors by himself, looking at the grass, the trees, the flowers, the vistas of light, the varying aspects of the sky, and listening to the birds, the crickets, the tree frogs and all the hundreds of natural sounds… Perhaps, indeed, no man who ever lived liked so many things and disliked so few as Walt Whitman." He had a naturally omnivorous mind, partly derived from his work as a newspaperman.

Whitman never deprecated persons of any class or nationality, according to this friend. He never spoke badly of any occupations or trades, "not even against any animals, insects or inanimate things, nor any of the laws of nature, nor any of the results of these laws, such as illness, deformity and death. He never complained or grumbled either at the weather, pain, illness or anything else. He never swore. He could not very well, since he never spoke in anger and apparently never was angry. He never exhibited fear, and I do not believe he ever felt it."

In his freedom-celebrating, chanting poetry Whitman struck new highs of enthusiasm for life, and he penned raptures that lifted American spirits. A loafer and gadabout as well as a carpenter, editor and schoolteacher, Whitman wrote intuitively, like Emerson. But having none of the rather Puritanical constraints of New Englanders like Emerson and Thoreau he plunged into the midst of life and action with gusto. "My ideas were simmering and Emerson brought them to a boil," he declared.

Like Emerson, Whitman believed American literature should express the American spirit, with a fresh and open style. The free verse style that he adopted after abandoning conventional forms was to transform future American poetry. With quick foresight, Emerson wrote him a letter immediately after reading *Leaves of Grass* to say that he found it "the most extraordinary piece of wit and wisdom that America has yet contributed" and praised it for "fortifying and encouraging" readers. He said he felt like dropping his own work then and there to go pay his respects to this new, courageous poet.

"I greet you at the beginning of a great career," he wrote Whitman, adding later that Whitman's writings were "more deeply American, democratic and in the interest of personal liberty than those of any other poet." Many other people were shocked by Whitman's rough language and references to sex and even Emerson warned that the reader had to hold his nose through certain passages. In a note to Carlyle he called Whitman's book "a nondescript monster which yet had terrible eyes and buffalo strength, and was indisputably American."

America's poet of self-fulfillment

Whitman became America's greatest poet, singing songs of healthy Americans in a healthy land, using their freedom to be themselves, each man and each woman finding fulfillment in himself or herself. America's westward movement and the pioneers found resonance in his lines. His poetry echoes with his ideal of comradely love among the people as the basis of a new democratic society. For him the American experiment was not only working—it was an epochal event that called for celebration, and he fancied himself as leading the celebration. For him, at least until his high spirits were severely tempered by the bloody Civil War, all else in history was just "sleepwalking" compared with the settling of the American continent.

In his exuberance, and his virtual worship of democracy, Whitman embraced all people, in all walks of life, holding all sorts of opinions. He celebrated material progress and technology at the same time he celebrated the human spirit and man's love for his fellow people. His joyful yawps celebrated just about everything. In "Song of Myself", which has been called the first truly modern poem in American literature, he even celebrated the paradox created by his stance of wide-open arms:

"Do I contradict myself?
Very well then I contradict myself,
(I am large, I contain multitudes.")

One paradox of Whitman's verses is what has been called "the paradox of democracy"—the double allegiance, so often conflicted, of the democratic citizen. While proclaiming the primacy of "the self", the citizen of a workable democracy must also give heed to the needs and interests of all citizens together. But this contradiction didn't much restrain this full-throated warbler of American chansons, who said boastfully that his aim was "to cheer up slaves and horrify despots." He saw himself as a spiritual leader too, and the Bible had a big influence on his style. Passages like the first lines of "Song of Myself" ring with the kind of music found in the Psalms:

"I celebrate myself, and sing myself,
And what I assume you shall assume,
For every atom belonging to me as good
belongs to you.
I loafe and invite my soul,
I lean and loafe at my ease observing a spear
of summer grass."

The poet's all-embracing verses are sometimes close in tone to the Biblical effusion found, for example, in Psalm 148:

"Praise the Lord from the earth ye
Dragons and all deeps;
Fire and hail; snow, and vapor;
Stormy wind fulfilling his word:
Mountains, and all hills; Fruitful
Trees and all cedars:
Beasts, and all cattle; creeping
Things, and flying fowl;
Kings of the earth, and all people;
Princes and all judges of the earth:
Both young men, and maidens; old
Men and children:
Let them praise the name of the
Lord: for his name alone is excellent;
His glory is above the earth and heaven."

In "Song of Myself" the "self" is identified in broad terms—with the nation, with all people everywhere, and with the divine. It celebrates human creativity and democratic life. There is also great wit and wisdom in Whitman, along with the boisterous humor that makes him appealing in any age. His esprit knows no limits: "Hurrah for positive science!" he explodes:

"Long live exact demonstration,
Unscrew the locks from the doors!
Unscrew the doors themselves from their jambs!"

In his poetic soliloquy he compares himself to the spotted hawk that flies by:

"I too am not a bit tamed, I too am untranslatable,
I sound my barbaric yawp over the roofs of the world."

In his "Song of the Open Road" Whitman prefigures later American writers like Kerouac, Dos Passos, Saul Bellow and Robert Penn Warren who portrayed Americans on the road:

"Afoot and light-hearted I take to the open road,
Healthy, free, the world before me,
The long brown path before me leading wherever I choose.
"Henceforth I ask not good-fortune, I myself am good fortune,
Henceforth I whimper no more, postpone no more, need nothing,
Done with indoor complaints, libraries, querulous criticisms,
Strong and content I travel the open road.
"The earth, that is sufficient,
I do not want the constellations any nearer,
I know they are very well where they are
I know they suffice for those who belong to them."

Whitman's poetry was not, however, all one-note optimism. His subjects included ghosts, impossible loves, graveyard imagery and death, which fascinated him. *Leaves of Grass* was written while his father lay ill in another room of their Brooklyn house, where he died only days after the book was published. Death haunted many of Whitman's poems—in the metaphor of the ocean, the voice of an old woman, the amorphous shapes that troubled a night.

War, greed and crime dampen the spirit

Whitman wanted to enlighten Americans and regenerate the ideals of the American republic. But after witnessing the suffering of the Civil War, in which he nursed wounded soldiers, both Union and Confederate, in Washington hospitals, he returned to New York exhausted, and somewhat disillusioned that America had not fulfilled its earlier promise. His belief in progress—including material progress—was muted by these later concerns. He felt the country had become driven by greed and was indifferent to the oppression of industrial labor. And indeed his era had many downsides besides the Civil War. Graft, vote-buying, patronage tainted all levels of government; pollution (especially from swine, hogs, dogs and cows roaming the muddy streets) and gang violence and crime—all of these things haunted Whitman's New York. He considered the three presidents before Lincoln—Fillmore, Pierce and Buchanan—a shame to the nation, but his growing disgust with politicians deepened his faith in the common people.

Although "Democratic Vistas", his most important prose work, bears an unquestioning belief in progress, he was by no means blind to society's weaknesses at the outset of the Gilded Age. Recognizing the failures of his celebrated democracy, and the disappointments of the Grant administration, he satirized the "dry, flat Sahara of American life," and assailed "the depravity of the business classes" and the decadence of "fashionable life." He longed for a moral and spiritual regeneration of a nation that he felt had delivered its promises only to the rich, "a nation which had failed all but the rich." Post-Civil War America, as he saw it—and as other writers like Mark Twain, Howells and Henry Adams later saw it—had lost some of its heroic, purposeful, plain and honest character.

As Whitman's superb confidence faltered, he wondered whether Americans could summon the "grandeur of vision" needed for successful self-government. What the country needed, he felt, was a new faith, a new social myth in the liberal tradition of Jefferson, "permeating the whole mass of American mentality, taste, belief, breathing into it a new breath of life, giving it decision... radiating, begetting appropriate teachers, schools, manners, and, as its grandest result, accomplishing... a religious and moral character beneath the political and productive and intellectual bases of the states."

The contrast between Whitman's hopes for progress and his frustration with America's failures mirrors the mentality of most Americans today, celebrating their success while at the same time being made uncomfortable by the shadow of fellow citizens who have definitely not had success and do not share in the bounties of the greatest wealth-producing society that ever existed. This, America's own greatest paradox, is one of the ironic truths at the heart of Whitman's genius and his all-embracing, passionate concern for everything and everyone around him.

Whitman's radicalism of style and expression was certainly ahead of his time. His effect on the American public in general, and the public's recognition of him as a major writer, grew mostly after his death in 1892. But in the century that followed him he came to epitomize the core of optimism underlying the American spirit.

Writing about the "youthfulness" of this whole period of American culture, James Truslow Adams said that the Romantic literary period was not "America's maturity or even its coming of age, but its adolescence—the sudden discovery of romance, of culture, of altruism, of opportunism, of self–reliance, and the sense of one's own individuality. In a time of pessimism and self–criticism like that of today it is sometimes difficult to relate to the complacent optimism of the latter–half 19th century. Apart from slavery there was little serious dissatisfaction with American institutions, whether those institutions were economic, social, political or religious. Victorian England was becoming disillusioned, but America still cherished the Romantic belief in the perfectibility of man."

On Walt Whitman's 70th birthday he received a congratulatory letter from the great humorist Mark Twain. In an uncharacteristically serious, upbeat mood, Twain gave the poet reasons for clinging to his original optimistic spirit:

> You have lived the 70 years which are greatest in the world's history and richest in benefit and advancement to its peoples. These 70 years have done more to widen the interval between man and the other animals than was accomplished by any of the five centuries which preceded them. What great births you have witnessed! The steam press, the steamship, the railroad, the perfect cotton gin, the telegraph, the phonograph, photogravure, the electrotype, the gaslight, the electric light, the sewing machine…the application of anesthesia to surgery practice, whereby the ancient dominion of pain, which began with the first created life, came to an end on this earth forever; you have seen the slave set free…But tarry for a while, for the greatest is yet to come. Wait 30 years and then look out over the earth! You shall see marvels upon marvels…"

A philosopher of action

The philosophical foundation of American optimism created especially by Emerson's fulsome outpouring of writings and speeches and Whitman's poems was fortified by the next great American philosopher, William James, the most influential American thinker of the late 19th into the early 20th centuries, as well as the greatest American psychologist. James reached an audience far beyond his Harvard students and the academic community because thousands attended his popular public lectures and he was the most widely read philosopher at a time when the public, at least in places like New England, actually took the time to read philosophy.

In a biography of James, Gerald E. Myers wrote that "the theme of optimism versus pessimism occupied James throughout his life." James explored the arguments for an ethics of optimism and concluded from his analysis that the makings of an optimist were a mixture of ideals and values, energy, pluck and will, courage and endurance. Nothing is more certain, he wrote, than that no one need assent to pessimism "unless he freely prefers to do so..."

If James's conclusions, and those of Emerson, seem unduly idealistic to some people today, an echo of a different time, they are important nonetheless in expressing the core of early-American character. If we believe in the possibility of something happening, James reasoned in *The Will to Believe*, our belief helps power us to make it happen when the time comes for action.

Together with John Dewey and C.S. Pierce, James led the movement called pragmatism, the most important philosophical movement in America in the early 1900s, which developed the theory of empirical truth that is based on practical results of ideas, not just on ideas alone. James articulated the message—the very American conceit—that by acting on our ideas we can change the nature of truth, and actually change the world around us.

WESTWARD TREKKERS

If liberty and republicanism were the sparks of public enthusiasm in the time of Jefferson and the philosophers and poets who sang optimistic songs, the next source of national uplift was the vast, beckoning unsettled West. A virtually vacant continent lured pioneers over the Alleghenies, across the Mississippi Valley and over the plains and mountains to the western coast, in search of ever-wider horizons and opportunities for new lives and fortunes. The West was a siren luring brave hearts. The westward trek was the corollary of the political movement that had established liberty—equally important in creating the independent, optimistic American character.

Life was good in America when this new phase of development was taking place, at least in the major seaboard cities. Harriet Martineau, the enormously popular English journalist, wrote in "Society in America" in 1837 that "by a happy coincidence of outward plenty with liberal institutions, there is in America a smaller amount of crime, poverty and mutual injury of every kind than has ever been known in any society..." While she was by no means always flattering to the American way of life, she observed in this piece about Americans that "no peculiarity in them is more remarkable than their national contentment..."

In the same year that Martineau's book was published, Peck's *New Guide to the West* came out, tracing the stages of the epochal westward movement of peoples, rolling one after another "like the waves of the ocean". First were the "over-mountain men", the hunters and traders, the farmers who struck out into the wilds, took claim to virgin lands and eventually became founders of new counties and states. The next emigrant class purchased lands, laid road, threw up bridges and built hewn log houses, planted crops and orchards, built mills and schools and courthouses. The settler who reached the Middle West cleared the woods with his ax, but the vastness of the wilderness kept alive his dreams of exploration. After these settlers came the enterprising capitalists who bought out those who were ready to move on and developed commerce, turned villages and towns into cities and organized the institutions that became the foundation of urban America.

In one of his lectures Frederick Jackson Turner said that as the pioneers "wrested their clearing from the woods and from the savages who surrounded them, as they expanded that clearing and saw the beginnings of commonwealths where only little communities had been, and as they saw these commonwealths touch hands with each other along the great course of the Mississippi river, they became enthusiastically optimistic and confident of the continued expansion of this democracy. They had faith in themselves and in their destiny. And that optimistic faith was responsible both for their confidence in their own ability to rule and for the passion for expansion. They looked to the future."

They embodied Jefferson's belief in progress based on a world improved by reason. Self-reliance bloomed into self-confidence. In the three decades before the Civil War the territory of the United States doubled, the population more than doubled, industrial and agricultural production soared, science and technology advanced and the standard of living reached new heights, at least among the dominant whites.

The movement of people that started off this prodigious period of growth was constant, enhancing the qualities of boldness and adventurousness that characterized the new western breed, the classless democracy of the prairies. Peck's guide noted that "hundreds of men can be found, not over 50 years of age, who have settled for the fourth, fifth or sixth time on a new spot. To sell out and remove only a few hundred miles makes up a portion of the variety of backwoods life and manners." The movement of population was the final guarantee that American society would develop on its own independent lines, looking westward rather than eastward (as it once did, to Europe) and developing its own customs, its own character, its own rude code of justice.

In the spring of 1843 the muddy streets of the riverport towns of

Independence and Westport (now Kansas City) were feverish with activity as nearly a thousand men, women and children readied their gear and prepared for the five or six-month trip that would take them to the Pacific coast and a new life. Paddlewheel and stern-wheel steamers, brightly painted and tall-chimneyed, blew their whistles and clanged bells, carrying their motley emigrant cargoes into the waterfront slips. The migrants disembarked into street scenes jammed with other emigrants and with cattle, traders, hunters in buckskin, Mexicans in sombreros, Indians in blankets, mountain men, Negroes, gamblers, roustabouts and settlers in tall beaver hats.

The migrants' dreams had started as far back as 1806 when Lewis and Clark returned from their trek to the Pacific commissioned by Jefferson. President Jefferson suggested such an expedition to Clark's older brother, to search for a land route to the Pacific, as early as 1783. The fire was fanned when John C. Freemont published his revelation that ordinary families in wagons could cross the Rockies via the South Pass in Wyoming.

Freemont's reports were like adventure books, and his father-in-law, Senator Thomas Hart Benton, became the greatest promoter in Congress of "Manifest Destiny" (the belief that the nation was destined to expand across the continent) and "western wayfaring".

The annexation of Texas in 1845, the acquisition of southern Oregon from the British in 1846 and the 1848 peace treaty with Mexico that gave the U.S. a vast stretch of land from Texas west to the Pacific and north to Oregon were huge steps in fulfilling this dream.

The migrants of the 1840s were led on by one of the most effective promotional campaigns in history. Expectations east of the Mississippi were heightened by "emigration societies" where those considering a trip West could exchange information about their prospects. One of these groups produced a whole series of books and pamphlets and poured out letters to newspapers urging western settlement. Young men particularly fell for the bright lure of adventure and hired on as stock tenders and wagon drivers. The first magic word that stirred emigrant heartbeats was "Missouri".

"Jump-offs" and the Great Migration

The "jump-offs", as they were called, of westward-bound emigrants in the spring of 1843 were the start of what became known as the

Great Migration, beginning with some 120 wagons that year and growing year by year into a tide of 23,000 trekkers in 1849. The pioneers of 1843 were the first large-scale migration of families, known as the "movers", in ordinary farm wagons topped with flimsy white canvass roofs. They traveled with all their earthly possessions chiefly by paddlewheelers and sternwheelers along the Ohio, Mississipi and Missouri rivers to the towns that had been starting points for the fur traders, adventurers and roustabouts who had ridden the Santa Fe trail to the Southwest for about 20 years. The gathering place for most of those arriving from the East was the bustling river port town of St. Louis, "The Gateway to the West".

Many of the travelers were farmers fleeing from the hard lives, glutted markets and malaria and other troubles back home. They had built their own wagons; they slept in tents; and day after day, teamsters walked beside their big, plodding, heavy-gaited oxen or mules, coaxing them to pull the wagons on the back-breaking journey across a wild continent. Most of the emigrants relied on oxen, because they were the cheapest and easiest-to-handle beasts of burden. In the 1850s penniless immigrants from Europe, organized by the Mormons, actually pushed or pulled two-wheeled handcarts loaded with their belongings; as many as 5,000 members of these "handcart brigades" made their way to Utah over four years, at a cost of less than $25 a person.

Crossing the Kansas River by rafts, the travelers headed northwest over rolling hills and through wildflowers that inspired one of them to note "a wild and scarcely controllable ecstacy of admiration." Indiana historian Frederick Ogg, writing in 1904, described the wonder of the western lands to immigrants from countries abroad where there was almost no free land. The pioneer settler, he wrote, after crossing the Alleghenies "stood on the threshold of the most magnificent heritage that has ever been vouchsafed to an enterprising people." No other region of the world could match the economic possibilities of the open lands from the Gulf of Mexico to the Rockies and the Great Lakes, and no part of the Old World matched the Mississipi Valley for richness of soil and variety of climate.

Contrasting with occasional joys over wildflowers and inspiring vistas were the thunderstorms and the ordeals of hauling wagons up canyons, through icy waters, over boulders and ravines, with the men having to chop their way through forests, guarding against wolves that drove off their cattle, not to mention facing Indian raids and other dangers. The North Platte Valley was the main course of travel. Wide and shallow, the Platte was hard to ford, too muddy for washing and too sandy for drinking.

The emigrants started overland through treeless prairies, something new to them ("those barren wastes," wrote Francis Parkman, "the haunts of the buffalo and the Indian, where the very shadow of civilization lies a hundred leagues behind...") In his book, *The Oregon Trail*, Parkman, a Boston Brahmin who bravely traveled the famous trail in 1846 at the age of 23, noted that the trekkers' initial enthusiasm for prairie scenery was quickly dampened by what followed. "His wagons will stick in the mud; his horses will break loose; harness will give way; and axle-trees prove unsound. His bed will be a soft one, consisting often of black mud of the richest consistency". That was typical of the notes this young tenderfoot scribbled in his notebook.

As they progressed westward the trekkers had to dig ramps down the banks of rivers and creeks, double up their teams to pull wagons up the opposite banks, sometimes chopping down trees to build huge rafts nearly 50 feet long to carry wagons, while prodding their livestock and horses to swim from one side to the other. One pioneer of the early 1800s wrote to his friends back east: "If you can bear grief with a smile, can put up with accommodations like the soft side of a plank before the fire (and perhaps three in a bed at that), if you are never at a loss for ways to do the most unpracticable things without tools; if you can do all this and some more, come on....It is a universal rule here to help one another, each one keeping an eye single to his own business."

Two points on the trail in particular raised these weary travelers' spirits and made them at least momentarily forget their struggles. One was Fort Laramie, whose adobe walls were a welcome sight, and where they could rest, treat their oxen's bleeding feet, pasture cattle, repair wagons, lay in supplies if they had any cash and celebrate with dancing. They were almost to the Rocky Mountains. They had covered 640 miles on the trail, with 1,400 still to go. The other blissful sight, which they came upon at the end of the Oregon Trail just short of the Pacific, was another fort, Fort Vancouver, the economic center of the Oregon Country, where they found welcome and easy credit at the end of their overland trip. Just south of this fort was the Willamette Valley, a fertile, green Eden with a gentle climate, where the British and the Indians were welcoming, at least to the first waves of trekkers.

When the migrants reached the sloping sagebrush plain crossing the Rockies known as South Pass, in present–day Wyoming, the half-way point and the start of the continent's Pacific Slope, some of the weary travelers whooped and fired their guns in the air. Still ahead, though, was the mighty Columbia River that had to be forged by rafts and—for those heading to Mexican California—the high peaks of the towering Sierra Nevada, through which no rivers offered passage. The Columbia River or the Cascades Mountains—that was the wrench-ing choice they faced. Either choice often meant disaster for those who tried either route up to 1846. The emigration of 1843 had gone to pieces at the Cascades—some trying to make the river passage on rafts, which accounted for most of the fatalities, others trying to build a wagon road over the mountains.

The much larger emigration of 1844 was delayed by muddy prai-ries and swollen streams. The emigration of 1845, about 3,000 per-sons, had to undergo suffering far greater than anything before. At Fort Boise a large party was induced to try a new road to avoid the Blue Mountains and the Columbia descent; plagued with panic, mass frenzy and starvation, they lost about 75 lives. Beside the graves that marked the trail, including those of many children, family possessions such as old carved–oak bureaus, claw–footed tables and carpets and books were abandoned along the way as the travelers stripped their wagons down after losing the oxen that had pulled them. Against this background of struggles one can imagine the jubilation of the pio-neers when they eventually reached such places as the Sacramento Valley or the paradise of the Willamette Valley with its fertile land, long growing seasons and abundant timber.

Bernard DeVoto, who chose the year 1846 as the subject of his classic book on the emigration, *The Year of Decision,* said the phrase "Manifest Destiny" expressed "the very core of American faith… the peculiar will, optimism, disregard and even blindness that character-ized the 1840s in America", the belief in a continental destiny. He described how "a national emotion welled" in the American, how "the lodestone of the West tugged deep in his blood, as deep as desire." The talk in farm kitchens all over the midwest that year was about the westering travelers. Back in New York, editor Horace Greeley (who later urged young men to "Go West") at this time said the migration "wears an aspect of insanity."

The promoters of westward expansion, led by President James Polk, had an ally at the Brooklyn Eagle in New York, which was calling for the takeover of both Mexico and California. There, Walt Whitman's fervor for expansion inflated further the expanding chests of his readers. Whitman's purple prose and poetry, which DeVoto described as "adolescent but perfectly expressive of Whitman's countrymen in 1846" spoke in high tones of "democracy, with its manly heart and its lion strength, spurning the ligatures wherewith drivelers would bind it" and leading to "the great FUTURE of this Western World, a scope involving such unparalled human happiness and rational freedom, to such unnumbered myriads, that the heart of a true man leaps with a mighty joy only to think of it!"

Mormons make a wilderness bloom

Like the Puritans, many pioneers thought of themselves as people of destiny, but none more so than the Mormons, the Church of Jesus Christ of Latter-Day Saints, many of whom believed that making a wilderness bloom was an exercise of morality. Some of the other emigrants passed them off as wierd fanatics. But the obstacles these people had to overcome before reaching their Eden were fierce tests of human fortitude and endurance.

In one of the worst excesses of prejudice and mob terrorism in American history, the Mormons were driven from their Illinois homeland on the Mississippi by zealots who had murdered their prophet Joseph Smith after jailing him in Carthage in June of 1844. Mobs and armed gangs burned Mormon houses, chased off and killed their stock and their chickens and broke into their Temple, defecating its floors by turning them into latrines. Fleeing from their homes in 1846 to begin their long trek west, the "Saints" were ravaged by dysentery and pneumonia as well as fear, but they pressed on through snow and sleet and rains, sometimes only able to travel a mile a day. Some of them who had no wagons carried all their possessions in wheelbarrows. Along the trail they had to cope with sick women and children, mountain fever, frostbitten feet, prairie mosquitoes and rattlesnakes, as well as Indian raids, mostly to steal cattle and horses. More migrants died of accidental gun discharges than were killed by Indians, who seldom attacked wagon trains drawn up in a circle, as was the custom.

Ironically, one of the qualities that drew the most scorn from their oppressors—the Mormons' remarkable cohesion—was a key factor in making this particular trek one of the historic pageants of American history, "the children of Israel moving into the land of Canaan", as DeVoto put it. Their new leader Brigham Young, president of the quorum of the Twelve Apostles, performed an incredible feat of managing this enormous emigration. He and his staff ruled tightly over a huge procession stretching from the Missouri River across the country.

They managed supplies, handled the bookkeeping and kept up the spirits of 15–20,000 uprooted people, and kept moving the thousands of wagons and tens of thousands of livestock, horses, goats, chickens, geese and even canaries, through sleet and drought and hot prairie summer. Observers marveled, when they came upon the white wagons of the Mormons, to find them sometimes in serious discussion of the fine points of theology after a day's work in the wilderness. Sometimes they heard rolling drums and a blast of trumpets from the Mormon caravans. After camp-down, their bands played hymns and quadrilles and hoedowns to keep hopes alive, and the Saints danced to fiddles under the stars.

Brigham Young had decided on Great Salt Lake Valley as the place for Mormon settlement, the new Zion—a place that other emigrants would pass up, and a place that he said he had seen in a vision. In July 1847 the Mormons in the lead drew within sight of the valley where the Great Salt Lake glistened ahead. One of the apostles fell on his knees, dedicating the land to the Lord. Another said, "We could not refrain from a shout of joy which almost involuntarily escaped from our lips". One man wrote in his diary, "I could not help shouting hurrah! hurrah! hurrah! …here is my new home at last." They prayed, organized committees and almost immediately began to plow, to build an irrigation dam and begin the cultivating and planting that would bring a dead land to life, all under instructions from their prophet who, they believed, spoke with the authority of God.

Of all their non-conformities, the practice of multiple wives did more than anything to offend other Americans and continue to produce hostility whenever the Mormons settled outside their own community. Brigham Young more than once called back to the Salt Lake base community those Mormons who had gone elsewhere, as it became clear that things would go best for them if they settled amongst their own.*

The rush west turned into a human stampede when news of the discovery of gold in California electrified the nation and altered the history of the state and the nation. In the year after a New Jersey carpenter found a small pea-size piece of gold in the mill race at Sutter's ranch near Sacramento on the Oregon Trail in 1848, some 90,000 people from every part of the country pulled up stakes to head west, their heads full of dreams of finding fortunes. In this stampede, which continued to the end of the 19th century, a million wishful thinkers were caught up in this usually unsuccessful rush for quick riches.

Gold and the "'Forty-Niners"

They came by overland trail, around the Horn, across the Isthmus of Panama. These were mostly young adventurers, who remained lighthearted in the face of appalling problems, including cholera epidemics. They were the "Forty–Niners", or "Argonauts" as Bret Harte called them in his mining–town stories that established the tradition for "westerns" in print and film. Some of the greenhorns from the East dressed up to "look the part" for the Wild West by decking themselves out with fancy uniforms or buckskins decorated with porcupine quills, sombreros, red-flannel shirts, flashing spurs and 20-inch bowie knives. These lighthearted vagabonds painted colorful names on their wagons, like "Rough and Ready" and "Wild Yankee", and "swapped endless misinformation about routes and procedures, boomed out songs around campfires and drank more than they should have while waiting for the prairies to green", according to historian David Lavender.

Bret Harte noted that the "faith, courage, vigor, youth and capacity for adventure necessary to this migration produced a body of men as strongly distinctive as were the companions of Jason." Many from towns and cities of the East had to learn how to build dugout rafts and cook meals over Buffalo "chips" and circle wagons round to make a corral and keep off the Indians when they stopped for the night or for

---

* Propelled by the optimism of their young, especially the influence of a growing force of 60,000 missionaries in over 160 nations, the Mormons claimed over ten million adherents by the end of the '90s.

a rest on the trail. Harte, whose short story, "The Luck of Roaring Camp" launched him on a prolific literary career, not only described the colorful mix of characters and races in the mining camps but also stood up, in his writing and in his own life, for the victims of prejudice and brutality in these wild times, mostly Indians who were brutalized and Chinese who were treated as "cheap labor." His vigorous opposition to racial injustice helped awaken the country to "the immigrant problem" that was to linger long afterward.

Yet Harte was optimistic about basic human nature. As G.K. Chesterton wrote, Harte "tells the truth about the wildest, the grossest, the most rapacious of all the districts of the earth—the truth that, while it is very rare indeed in the world to find a thoroughly good man, it is rarer still… to find a man who does not either desire to be one, or imagine that he is one already."

Harte scholar Wilton Eckley noted that social distinctions gave way easily enough to a pragmatic frontier democracy that judged a man on his conduct and not on his ancestry or background. Loyalty, generosity and practical sagacity were some of the most notable traits of the Argonauts. From this life Harte selected the material he would make into stories that captured the popular imagination and established a tradition for the Western story that continues undiminished today.

Of course only a lucky few found the vast riches they had come for (either in California or in the Klondike, where another gold frenzy erupted in 1897 with the arrival in Seattle of Yukon prospectors and their bags of gold from that rugged terrain). But gold fever virtually created the cities of San Francisco and Seattle. Most failed and many died in the search for gold but as Lavender wrote, "all who finished were able to look back in pride on what they had achieved. And for the foresighted ones who started well prepared and traveled light, who fished and hunted and relished the natural wonders along the way, it was, many said afterwards, the most exhilarating experience of their lives."

California, which had been a foreign state populated mostly by Mexican ranchers and some scattered Americans, by mid-19th century had a population of about a hundred thousand and was bursting with life. Other lures besides gold kept hopes rising among those left behind in the East and Midwest—including the 1850 land act, which made generous awards of land in Oregon to settlers, and the Homestead Act of 1862, which gave 160 acres of public land to each homesteader for a small fee after five years of residence, or for $1.25 an acre after six months' residence. (All these frontier opportunities notwithstanding, it's interesting to note that the richest 10% of the population owned 70% or more of the country's wealth during the 1850–1870 period.)

After documenting the westward movement of 1846, DeVoto wrote that "one theme that recurs is the basic courage and honor in the face of adversity that we call gallantry. It is always good to remember human gallantry, and it is especially good in times like the present." The frontier, through its encouragement of democracy and self–reliance, became more important than the European heritage in shaping American society. It was a time of torments, but it was also a grand triumph of human spirits over nature.

A gallant lady

No story illustrated better this triumph of spirit over adversity than that of an extraordinary woman by the name of Sarah Eleanor Bayliss Royce, who joined the movement west in 1849, the first gold-rush year. Born in Stratford-on-Avon, she was only six weeks old when she was carried aboard ship to emigrate to America at the very moment when British guns were celebrating the birth of Queen Victoria.

At the age of 30 Sarah Royce left behind a comfortable life in New York to head for El Dorado with her husband and two-year-old daughter, Mary, in a covered wagon drawn by three yoke of oxen and one yoke of cows, the latter valued more for their milk than their part-time help pulling the load.

The Royce party followed the Mormon trail on the north side of the Platte River from Council Bluffs, Iowa to Fort Laramie, in the land where the Plains Indians followed the bison herds, past Independence Rock to the South Pass, then down to Fort Bridger and Salt Lake City and on to the Carson desert and, eventually, Hangtown, California (so named because thieves were hung to deter crime in the small settlement.) They had nothing to guide them but Fremont's *Travels* and tips from other westering travelers. Sarah's diary was a story of crises and sufferings punctuated repeatedly by her bursts of joy and thanks to God for safely crossing a desert, reaching the rim of a valley, sighting a landmark, finding deliverance from perils—all set down in her *Pilgrimage Diary* written on the overland trail.

The diary describes an odyssey of perils that would have sorely tested anyone's endurance. In her first entry, as the little party was crossing Iowa, she showed her initial anxiety. The family had awakened to find that the oxen and cows had "gone off". Sarah had the task of "staying by the stuff" with Mary while the men chased down the animals. "It soon became plain," she wrote, "that the hard facts of this pilgrimage would require patience, energy and courage fully equal to what I had anticipated when I had tried to stretch my imagination to the utmost."

The daunting challenges ahead included passing through bottomlands where water stood two feet deep from rains; building bridges to cross creeks "so swollen by rains as to be impassable"; dealing with cholera that was "raging among the emigrants" they encountered at crossing points on the Missouri River (and disinfecting the wagon and all its contents); fending off "begging and pilfering Indians" who swarmed about them on the western side of the Missouri (as well as roving bands of armed Indian hunters "seeking food and plunder"); coping with stampedes of their own cattle in lightning storms, when the wagon was overturned, breaking the chains that had held the cattle to the wagon; pulling hay out of their bed mattresses to feed starving oxen as they crossed the Great Salt Desert, bare of grass or water; and digging out wagon wheels "in very miry places, in the rain" when they slipped into sloughs (called "sloos") which required unloading the whole wagon so it could be pushed free.

One week in June, after burying several fellow travelers felled by cholera, and waiting through "one of the most terrible storms I ever recollect witnessing", which drove rain into the wagon, Sarah admitted that "heavy gloom hung around us" as they wondered which one of them would be next struck by disease. "But I poured out my heart to God in prayer," she wrote, "and He gave me comfort and rest. I felt a full assurance that He would not afflict us beyond our strength to bear. I committed my precious child into His hands entirely, claiming for her His promises and His guardianship. I said from my heart, 'Thy will be done'. Then peace took possession of my soul, and in spite of threatening ills, I felt strong for duty and endurance."

Occasionally there was respite in "social meetings" with other travelers on the trail, who gathered together "for prayer, reading and singing," Sarah wrote. Along the jolting passage as they crossed the country,

Sarah recounted moments of joy with childish wonder and enthusiasm—like her thrill at coming in sight of famous Chimney Rock in the valley of the Platte on the Fourth of July, "an immense natural tower visible for many miles," where they halted to celebrate, enjoy a bit of dancing and "a cheerful sing".

Another such lift was on July 26 when they reached Independence Rock and Sarah yanked her little Mary behind her in a determined climb up "the lone mass of granite" that rose above the plain, which she knew to be the most famous landmark of the overland trail. Still another high for Sarah was reaching the point where they passed from the Atlantic to the Pacific Slope. "I had looked forward for weeks to the step that would take me past that point," she wrote. She took a last look back at the waters flowing east "to mingle with the streams and wash the shores where childhood and early youth had been spent." Crossing this line, she knew, "would separate me from all these, perhaps forever. Through what toils and dangers we had come to reach that point!"

Having endured "the blank dreariness of prairies", the rains and swollen rivers, the muds and quicksands and countless other obstacles, this remarkable woman still had the spirit from time to time to rush ahead of her party, as she often liked to do, climbing hills or rock formations with childish wonder in order to be the first to enjoy a great view.

At the entrance of Great Salt Lake Valley "we paused to take breath and faced each other with mutual looks of wonder", so covered with plains dust that they could barely recognize each other. Later, at the journey's climax, she recalled being the first person in her party to venture out on a rocky height overlooking Sacramento Valley where the rosy glow over the valley seemed "a smile of welcome" to the new land. "California, land of sunny skies," she wrote, "that was my first look into your sunny face." On this occasion she was riding a borrowed mule, having abandoned wagon and oxen because they couldn't make it through the passes. As her companions, including husband and daughter, caught up with her on the trail that day, she recalled how "boisterous shouts and snatches of song made rocks and welkin ring."

Years later, Sarah's son Josiah, a Harvard professor, said he felt sure that his mother's "devout and unfailing religious belief stood by her through all difficulties and dangers and enabled her to keep her courage and to help others keep up theirs, whatever happened." She shared in "the optimism of the age in America," her son wrote. "Wherever Sarah was, *she* made civilization, even when it seemed that she had little indeed with which to make it."

Often, when she was passing through the deserts, Sarah thought of the sacred stories of the Bible. Sometimes the loneliness of the desert inspired mystical feelings, especially when she witnessed a burning sage bush or the discovery of precious springs and streams or when she looked at the stars or a sunset, "signs from heaven." At those times "God's presence was no longer a matter of faith but of divine direct sight," Josiah wrote. "Who else was there but God in the desert to be seen? One was on a pilgrimage whose every suggestion was of the familiar sacred stories."

As Yale history professor Ralph Henry Gabriel wrote many years later, Sarah Royce's fortitude was squarely based on two things: her religious faith and her devotion to family. She was a 19th-century Puritan, free of the 17th-century Puritan's devils and fears of Hell but possessed of an abiding faith in a loving God who, as she put it, "through all the devious paths of life ever guides safely those who trust and obey Him." Over and over again Sarah and her diary taught the lesson to her children that high spirits and courage in dangerous times commonly spring from strong religious faith and loyalty to family.

Her daughter thought it was very characteristic of Sarah that, having been forced in times of danger to abandon virtually all her worldly possessions, "she rescued and brought through to California her Bible, her Milton and a tiny lap writing desk."

Near the end of her diary Sarah recorded a patriotic high when she was settled at last in her own home on the edge of San Francisco Bay overlooking North Beach within sight of Telegraph Hill. On that day in October 1850, she and her neighbors "were all excitement to hear the result of California's knock on the door of the Union", waiting for the steamer *Oregon* to arrive with news from the nation's capital.

Sarah watched through field glasses from a high veranda as the steamer entered the harbor with flying colors, "gay with streamers and flags of all nations—the Stars and Stripes most prominent, and above them, straightened out by the generous wind that seemed to blow a long breath on purpose, floated the longest streamer of all, displaying the words 'California Admitted'. The roar of cannon rolled over the waters, and met answering roars from fort and ships. Everyone was laughing."

One of the watching crowd shouted out that at last the pioneers could feel they had a real homeplace to replace the ones they had left behind. "Yes," another person replied, as noted in Sarah's journal, "and remember, all, we must no more talk of going 'to the States'. We are *in* the States!"

The ending of the frontier

The most massive emigrant movements took place in the 1850s, with 45,000 people in 1850 alone crowding the trail to California, twice as many as the previous year. Travel peaked in 1852 with 52,000 people spread out over more than a thousand miles on what by then had become a wide and well-beaten highway. By that time the duration of the trip from the Missouri River to the coast had been reduced from about six months to little more than three months.

The days of the open frontier were numbered, however. In 1893, when the stupendous celebrations began at the Chicago World's Fair marking the 400th anniversary of the arrival of Columbus in the New World, Frederick Jackson Turner delivered his historic address titled "The Significance of the American Frontier in American History", warning that the fair coincided with the end of both America's frontier and the lure of free land. Turner described the classic American frontiersman, whose era was ending, as unique in having learned to live "between savagery and civilization" and to adapt to both dangers and opportunities as he moved west. Later Turner noted also that the frontier that produced Andrew Jackson was "free from influence of European ideas and institutions. The men of the Western World turned their backs upon the Atlantic Ocean, and with a grim energy and self-confidence began to build up a society free from the dominance of ancient forms."

At the same historic Chicago fair where Turner spoke, Governor Theodore Roosevelt of New York was moved by the grandeur of the scene, including the flying banners of Old Glory, the great statue of the Republic with arms reaching west, and the first massive demonstration of electricity, hinting of new wonders to come in the next chapter of American history. By contrast with Roosevelt's bully confidence about the nation's future, Henry Adams was moved to anxiety by this fair. He recognized the epochal change that "the dynamo" symbolized for society but wondered whether Americans had any idea where they were going.

Turner, more than anyone, articulated the legacy of frontier life and its importance in explaining American character and in acting as "a tonic for the times", as historian Ray Allen Billington expressed it. Never before had the individual been so exalted, never before given such free play. Turner believed that the American intellect owed its core characteristics to frontier influences, including "a dominant individualism" with its belief in grass–roots democracy and antipathy to control; a coarseness and strength combined with acuteness and inquisitiveness; that practical, inventive turn of mind, quick to find expedients; that masterful grasp of material things, lacking in the artistic but powerful to effect great ends; that restless, nervous energy; that dominant individualism working for good and evil, and with that buoyancy which comes from freedom—these are the traits of the frontier."

Turner was an inveterate optimist. "I prefer to believe that man is greater than the dangers that menace him," he wrote in 1924; "that education and science are powerful forces to change these tendencies and to produce a rational solution of the problems of life on the shrinking planet. I place my trust in the mind of man seeking solutions by intellectual toil rather than by drift and by habit, bold to find new ways of adjustment…"

Turner felt that the "fluidity" of frontier life, the opportunities afforded by the open frontier and the contact with simple, primitive society were key forces that dominated American character. In the essay he read at the Chicago exposition he pointed out that the American citizen was "a new product" in the world, a new race that had steadily grown away from its European roots. He believed that while free land offered an escape from poverty, the frontier also fostered economic equality. Both of these factors enhanced democracy, which, Turner said, "came stark and strong and full of life out of the American forest, and gained new strength each time it touched a new frontier." Free land constantly rejuvenated man and society when civilization came into contact with the wilderness.

"Western democracy has been from the time of its birth idealistic," Turner wrote. "The very fact of the wilderness appealed to men as a fair, blank page on which to write a new chapter in the story of man's struggle for a higher type of society. The Western wilds, from the Alleghanies to the Pacific, constituted the richest free gift that was ever spread out before civilized man."

American democracy, Turner believed, was fundamentally the outcome of the experiences of Americans in dealing with the West. Early Western democracy's most distinctive characteristic was "the freedom of the individual to rise under conditions of social mobility, and whose ambition was the liberty and well-being of the masses. This conception has vitalized all American democracy, and has brought it into sharp contrasts with the democracies of history, and with those modern efforts of Europe to create an artificial democratic order by legislation."

The wilderness had served as a safety valve for American society, according to Turner. So long as the wilderness offered escape, Americans could solve social problems by moving. (Gertrude Stein put it this way: "In the United States there is more space where nobody is than where anybody is. That is what makes America what it is.") The wilderness "opened wide its portals to all who were oppressed," wrote Turner, " to all who with strong arms and stout heart desired to hew out a home and a career for themselves." First the trappers and traders, then the teamsters and the axmen who hacked a way for the wagons through the forests and the pioneer families in their caravans—all these were the making of a hardy new breed.

Of course there were also those in the westward movement who could not meet the challenge-who turned back, depressed and shorn of their dreams. The pioneers who kept going were fully taken up in activity, shared with others, as they hacked their way across the vast expanse, uncowed by its perils. But there were perils not only for those in the vanguard but also for those who did not try to go all the way West, those who settled in the vast area between the frontier and eastern settlement. Ironically, another element was to be mixed into the American spirit by these people who followed the pioneers and actually settled down to live and farm in places like the midlands and the plains memorialized by writers like Hamlin Garland and Willa Cather. The trials of homesteading women in the high, dry prairie country of Nebraska were memorably painted by Cather, who was only nine when she herself was brought to Nebraska in 1883. It was still frontier territory, settlers lived in sod houses or caves and roads were faint wagon trails in seas of red grass. Forlornness, loneliness, deprivation of body and spirit were often the mix of life in those days. But the new American became increasingly gregarious and "good natured, generous, hospitable and sociable, and he reversed the whole history of language to make the term 'stranger' a term of welcome," wrote Henry Steele Commager in *The American Mind.* "The front porch was an American invention."

"Free land" was the lure that brought thousands of homesteaders streaming into Nebraska and other states after the Civil War to stake their claims on the wild prairie, after the Homestead Act was passed in 1862. The act gave any American citizen (or anyone declaring an intent to become one) 160 acres of government land. A popular song of the time had the cheery message: "Uncle Sam is rich enough to give us all a farm!" But the reality of the homesteaders' lives, as documented by Cather in *My Antonia,* was filled with hardships and uncertainties, draughts, frosts, grasshopper plagues and prairie fires that threatened wheat and corn fields and sorghum fields for winter fodder. The neighborliness that came to characterize Midwesterners was born of their dependence on each other to meet these common foes.

The frontier as proving ground

The wilderness represented the final proving ground of man, a metaphor for the obstacles against which all men and women struggle in life. The joy of those who "made it" was comparable to the elation felt by all human beings who overcome life's most daunting problems. This was the point of view of Francis Parkman, whose amazing chronicle based on notebooks written on the trail during the same year chronicled by DeVoto was a first-hand account as well as a literary window on the frontier era.

The vivid impressions that frontier life made on the young, alert mind and quick eye of this daring tenderfoot, a 23-year-old Boston Brahmin, compliment DeVoto's description of the momentous events of 1846. Parkman not only wandered and camped among emigrant caravans, sleeping on his buffalo robe with a rifle by his side, but also showed amazing grit by joining a pack of Sioux Indians as they hunted across prairies black with buffalo, breakfasting on antelope head, dining on raw buffalo liver and dogmeat while traveling along the Laramie and Medicine Bow mountains.

Fortunately setting forth on his adventure at a time when the Sioux were not making war on whites, Parkman accompanied a moving "village" of Ogillallah, staying in the lodge of its chief, Kongra Tonga or Big Crow, and "passing the pipe" with Indian braves. Though he was disillusioned by the unromantic nature of the Indians as he found them (thorough savages "of the stone age", he called them), Parkman valued highly his sojourn with them, and regretted parting from what he rightly guessed was a disappearing race of peoples.

Looking back in retrospect today, frontier life appears as a paradox. On one hand it was characterized by obstacles and dangers that would turn off all but the strongest and most resilient men and women. On the other hand, the very existence of the vast unoccupied domain stretching from the eastern shores to the Pacific offered exciting opportunities to all with strong bodies and stout hearts to hew out homes and make new lives for themselves and their families. Because these opportunities existed, the society would keep renewing itself and freeing itself—so long as the frontier existed—from social problems like class conflict and urban poverty. As Turner put it, "Here was an opportunity for social development continually to begin over again, wherever society gave signs of breaking into classes. Here was a magic fountain of youth in which America continually bathed and was rejuvenated."

The wilderness was indeed the proving ground for a new breed of man and woman. "What the Mediterranean Sea was to the Greeks," Turner wrote, "breaking the bonds of custom, offering new experiences, calling out new institutions and activities—that and more the ever– retreating frontier has been to the United States… In America, the presence of practically free land into which pioneers might move from the older settlements prevented, so long as this movement continued, the emergence of class divisions or of a dominant or privileged class based on property or custom".

The significance of Turner's prescient, landmark essay in 1893 was that it drew the curtain down on this never–to–be–repeated era of American expansion. It could not go on indefinitely once the continent had been spanned. For nearly four centuries after Captain John Smith had made a forest clearing in Virginia, pioneers, from one generation to the next, had been crossing one frontier only to move on to the next one. "Their experiences," said Turner, "left abiding influences upon the ideas and purposes of the nation." And now, Turner concluded, "the frontier has gone, and with its going has closed the first period of American history."

Turner recognized the problems confronting 20th-century America, wrote Commager—"urbanization, industrialism, class conflicts, the rise of the giant corporation—but his deep-rooted optimism did not permit discouragement" and in fact Turner wrote, rather lyrically: "We shall continue to present to our sister continent of Europe the underlying ideas of America as a better way of solving difficulties."

Naturally the ending of such an important, defining era of American life—with its implications not only for the frontier spirit but also for the relatively new problems of preserving natural resources and unifying the new, expanded nation—was regarded with foreboding by some perceptive people. One indication of this came in 1907, when President Theodore Roosevelt gathered the governors of the 46 states to consider the consequences of exhausting the nation's natural resources.

While the pioneers may have contributed little to the nation's culture in the most refined sense of that word, and while their lives often had aspects that are unpleasant to recollect—from coarse habits and discourse to brutality as they faced the extremes of fighting for survival, most chillingly in the horrors of the Donner party—the trekkers, the mountain men and their hardy leaders cannot be denied a central place in the shaping of the American spirit.

An enterprising generation risked everything for its dreams. The slowly lurching, canvass–topped prairie schooners of the emigrants became, in David Lavender's words, "one of the most enduring symbols of accomplishment that the nation possesses as a part of its heritage." The story of their adventures in taming a wild continent, like the story of Columbus, rests permanently in American memory. The spirit of adventure, the independent and innovative mind, and the neighborliness, especially in the Midwest and West today, that characterize Americans, have been passed down from the those pioneer dreamers. The story of the West also gave a vision of hope to oppressed people everywhere, an assurance to them that there was a nation that had great faith in man and had the will to give men and women the opportunity to grow to the full measure of their capabilities.

Just as the Puritans, and after them the Founders, had left their stamps on American character, so too did these hardies who pushed back the frontier of the new nation, and in the process created a new person— highly individualistic, self-sufficient and philosophically optimistic.

Young Francis Parkman, whose fortuitous timing put him right into the heart of the greatest westward migration, had an inherently optimistic view of history, believing in progress and perceiving a transition from the absolutism of the medieval mind to "a liberty crude, incoherent, and chaotic, yet full of prolific vitality." But while recognizing that America was taming a vast continent, he worried whether the new democracy could produce a civilization that would be truly superior to those before it.

As for Turner, he faced a more specific dilemma in contemplating America's future. He believed that democracy, the greatest value of American life, had been based on free land, and that nature as the emigrants found it was the source of spiritual values. Free land was not only the guarantor of democracy but it also led to the rise of the common man, relieved poverty back east and led to development all across the country. The frontier and the free land that beckoned people to it had fostered economic freedom and opportunity. But the westward movement had caused free land to disappear. So the sobering question then arose: Would democracy survive?

PART TWO

COMING OF AGE

Three Presidents, in Three Great Wars

THE "LORD PROTECTOR"

In the relatively placid times before the Civil War, most Americans had no inkling of the epochal changes that lay ahead. Booming cities, fueled by new immigrants, were challenging the simplicity and moral absolutes of frontier days. Fortune hunters were buying farms, drilling wells and striking oil.

A transition was underway from small businesses to big corporations controlled by a few tycoons. A Cleveland accountant by the name of John D. Rockefeller quit his job, started an oil partnership, created Standard Oil, extorted money from the railroads, virtually took over the whole refining industry and eventually was worth about one-thirtieth as much as the nation's gross national product. Castigated by Ida Tarbell and other writers for his greed, this very religious "puritan" (a trustee of the Baptist Church since his young manhood) became the most hated man in America. Recognizing that this was a case of capitalism gone awry, the Supreme Court eventually busted up his monopoly; but he made a fortune all over again supplying fuel for the booming auto industry.

The American spirit was undergoing changes too. Materialistic ambitions and urban concerns were replacing the neighborliness and altruism of earlier days. Middle-class Victorian Americans found some escape from these changing times by hanging romantic Currier & Ives prints on their walls—soothing images of family values with pastoral scenes of sleigh rides, bourgeois family life, joyful children and adoring parents (really not so different from the TV sitcoms of the 1950s and beyond, which encapsuled the traditional family values that were becoming extinct in the real outer world.)

While Americans in mid-19th century had been united by their new political system and by the thrill of becoming a continental nation, they were far from united in other ways. Bernard DeVoto, in his chronicle of the year 1846, called them "a people divided by racial differences, sectional cleavages, cultural antipathies—an enormous disparity of assumption, expectation, hope and philosophy."

Slavery was the divisive issue that smoldered most dangerously, menacing the traditional optimism of Americans. Even Tocqueville had warned that "The most formidable of all the ills that threaten the future of the Union arises from the presence of a black population upon its territory..." With his typical long perspective he had noted the difference between ancient slaves such as the Greeks, who were of the same race, and frequently better educated, than their masters, and American slaves who were uneducated and accustomed only to dire poverty.

Washington and Jefferson had straddled this issue very uncomfortably. Both had their own slaves, acquired principally through their marriages. In the mid-1770s half of Colonial society or more was in slavery, including many whites imported from the United Kingdom and Germany. About half the households in New York City had at least one slave.

Washington freed some of his slaves at the end of his presidency, the rest in his will. Jefferson would have done the same had his hands not been tied up by debts, since slaves were important assets of his bankrupt estate and his creditors brushed aside his pleadings for them. Raised in a state where slavery was such a well-established, unquestioned practice and an integral part of the plantation economy, both of these Virginians were conflicted throughout their lives between their own roles as slaveowners and their intellectual aversion to a practice that collided with their basic belief in freedom and human rights.

All his adult life Jefferson tried to convince his contemporaries that slavery was evil and slaves should be freed. At age 26, as a freshman member of the Virginia House of Representatives, he spoke out for emancipation, but was rebuffed. His condemnation of George III for condoning slave trade was included in the state constitution's preamble, but his proposal for the state to end slavery was rejected.

He volunteered free legal service to slaves seeking freedom, startling the judges in one courtroom by contending that, under nature's law, "we are all free." He had no chance of winning the case but his actions show how early in life the concept of freedom endowed to all men by nature was fixed in his mind. He stirred a fuss when he proposed free public education for all black youths just after resigning as Governor of Virginia. His condemnation of slavery was deleted in the Declaration of Independence by the Constitutional Congress.

Jefferson biographer Noble Cunningham noted that while Jefferson had doubts about the ability of the two races to cohabit successfully (leading him now and then to consider the merits of deporting slaves to Latin America) he "never wavered in his conviction that slavery was an evil that must be extinguished." In his final draft of the Northwest Ordnance Jefferson tried to convince his contemporaries that slaves in the territory should be set free. "Nothing is more certainly written in the book of fate than that these people are to be free", he wrote in his autobiography.

In April 1820, 44 years before the Civil War, Jefferson expressed his worries about the growing dissension over slavery that had flared into angry debate in Congress over the admission of Missouri as a slave state. With remarkable prescience, the 77-year-old Founder said that the unresolved issue of slavery, "a momentous question, like a firebell in the night, awakened and filled me with terror. I considered it the knell of the Union."

A rustic from Pigeon Creek

A short while before Jefferson uttered those prophetic words, a nine-year-old boy on the Midwestern frontier wilderness in Pigeon Creek, Indiana—at a time when bears and other wild animals still roamed those Indiana woods—stood in a one-room cabin in a clearing on his family's $2-an-acre government land listening to the last words of his young mother. She died that day on a bed of poles cleated to the corner of the cabin that was the home of Tom Lincoln and his family. The boy whittled pinewood pegs to go through the hand-hewn planks that became his mother's coffin. No leader of the country before or since ever had a more humble beginning. Yet upon his shoulders was to fall the enormous task of resolving the great questions Jefferson and others had raised about slavery and about the ability of the conflicted Union to survive.

Unlike Jefferson, Lincoln had no brilliant tutors to guide his early education. What he had initially were three books: the Bible, Shakespeare and Euclid. The first two were to influence his taste and style, while Euclid satisfied his yen for intellectual challenges. He was encouraged to read by his stepmother, who had considerably more luck than Aunt Polly had with Mark Twain's Huckleberry Finn. The boy took a path altogether different from his father, a coarse, rootless frontiersman whose world was limited to fishing and hunting (a U.S. senator once disparaged Lincoln as "a man sprung from poor white trash.")

At age 23 this lanky, six-foot-four rustic, virtually uneducated, the son of illiterate parents, took a throw at politics. With less than a year's formal education, and penniless, he offered himself as a candidate for the Illinois state legislature. His qualifications, besides experience splitting rails, included pulling a cross-saw, clearing timberland, milking cows, driving shovel-plows, wrestling, husking corn and killing hogs. He lost the election, became a partner in a general store that went belly up, but succeeded on his second try to become a state legislator. Almost immediately he also became an ardent advocate for the kinds of industrial improvements that might help others escape the economic deprivation of his own youth—the building of canals, railroads and other infrastructure improvements that were about to turn an agricultural nation into an industrial state.

A tautly focused leader

Reveling in politics and full of self-confidence gained not from education and breeding but from pioneer experiences, Lincoln promptly declared his determination to perpetuate the work of the country's Founders, whom he described as a "hardy, brave and patriotic...race of ancestors." He was keenly aware of the work still ahead to implement the Founders' vision. He showed courage in speaking out against the slavery that his family had witnessed and detested— first in the state legislature, then in the Congress to which he was elected in 1846, where he lost no time in drafting a bill to abolish slavery in the District of Columbia.

By February 1856 he decided to join the new Republican Party, which was dominated by abolitionists, and became one of its founders in Illinois. That party had a powerful economic vision, and Lincoln, according to biographer Mark E. Neely, Jr. was an "arch capitalist" who, like Washington and Jefferson, speculated in frontier property during his days as deputy surveyor. Neely wrote that Lincoln believed in a dynamic society where a person who labored for someone ought to have the opportunity one day to labor for himself, and eventually to hire others to work for him. Slavery was inconsistent with such a philosophy.

At the Republican Convention in Springfield in the summer of 1858, where he was chosen candidate for U.S. senator, Lincoln gave a speech as radical in its time as Jefferson's Declaration was 82 years earlier. His speech took its theme from the Biblical passage, "A house divided against itself can no longer stand." Arguing that the nation could not endure any longer half slave and half free, he set the theme that became the keynote of his open-air debates with Stephen Douglas before tens of thousands of people, which followed in the senatorial campaign.

When Lincoln left Springfield for his inauguration as President, on February 11, 1860, a thousand people stood in the brick railroad station or outside in the rain to wish him Godspeed. Recognizing the awesome task facing him, he spoke to them slowly, with a sadness that would mark his visage for the next four years. From his train's platform in the soft drizzle Lincoln spoke prophetic words to the crowd: "I now leave, not knowing when, or whether ever, I may return, with a task before me greater than that which rested upon Washington. Without the assistance of that Divine Being who ever attended him, I cannot succeed." Not long before, Henry Adams had written in a letter that "no man is fit to take hold now who is not as cool as death."

In a sense, the challenge of the war pitting Americans against Americans would actually pose a greater challenge to Lincoln than did the colonies' united war against British tyranny to Washington and his compatriots. Lincoln's White House days took a relentless toll on his life. Most days he would work from seven in the morning until eleven at night, with time out only for brief meals, and with no holidays to break the tension.

While Lincoln was greeted by crowds and artillery salutes as he passed through several cities, and rode in a carriage drawn by six white horses accompanied by brass bands and colorful mounted guards, he was warned, on reaching New York on his journey to the Inauguration, that a plot existed to assassinate him on his way through Baltimore. Pinkerton and others wanted to take him by night straight to Washington. But Lincoln refused, explaining that he had commitments to raise the flag over Independence Hall, Philadelphia and visit that state's legislature. From there he rode in darkened traincars through the night.

Preserving the Union

Lincoln's inaugural address on March 4, 1861, sounded the solemn theme on which he was to stand unequivocally throughout his four years in office. On an outdoor platform, speaking to a crowd of 10,000, he cut a unique figure in his new tall hat, new black suit and boots, with ebony cane in hand, delivering his 271-word address. It was immediately the most widely read statement ever made by an American president. The straight, iron line that was to run through the Lincoln presidency and mark him as a singular, purposeful leader was in these simple, unambiguous words:

"The Union is much older than the Constitution. It was formed in fact by the Articles of Association in 1774. It was matured and continued by the Declaration of Independence in 1776. It was further matured and the faith of all the then thirteen states expressly plighted and engaged that it should be perpetual, by the Articles of Confederation in 1787. And finally, in 1787, one of the declared objects for ordaining and establishing the Constitution was 'to form a more perfect union....'. It follows from these views that no State, upon its own mere motion, can lawfully get out of the Union... I therefore consider that, in view of the Constitution and the laws, the Union is unbroken..."

In his conclusion to this first inaugural, Lincoln's words attained the grace and hopeful sense of history that was to characterize so many of his public utterances:

"The mystic chords of memory," he said, "stretching from every battlefield and patriot grave, to every living heart and hearthstone, all over this broad land, will yet swell the chorus of the Union, when again touched, as surely they will be, by the better angels of our nature."

A group of Southern leaders meeting in Washington on Inauguration night sent word to the Confederacy headquarters, according to Carl Sandburg, that "He is a man of will and firmness. His cabinet will yield to him with alacrity." Relays of ponies rushed off for the week-long ride to carry the President's address across a troubled country.

Whatever hope or optimism there was for the nation to cling to in the Civil War years was rooted in the steadfastness of the leader whom fate had put in charge. Even before his inauguration he was urging governors and key citizens "to maintain the Union at all hazards." His line of thought on the preservation of the Union went straight as an arrow through his public life. His personal commitment was intractable.

In his first message to Congress, in special session July 4, 1861, prefiguring the Gettysburg Address, Lincoln said that "This issue embraces more than the fate of the United States. It presents to the whole family of man the question, whether a constitutional republic, or a democracy—a government of the people by the same people—can or cannot maintain its territorial integrity against its own domestic foes...whether discontented individuals too few in numbers to control administration ...(can) break up their Government and thus practically put an end to free government upon the earth...Must a government, of necessity, be too strong for the liberties of its own people, or too weak to maintain its own existence?"

In his message to Congress in 1862, Lincoln was more explicit about the connection between freeing slaves and the concept of freedom on which the nation was founded: "In giving freedom to the slave," he said, "we assure freedom to the free—honorable alike in what we give, and what we preserve, we shall nobly save, or meanly lose the last best hope of earth."

Civil war was virtually unavoidable after Lincoln's election as President, since he adhered to the Republican platform calling for a 13th Amendment to the Constitution that would abolish slavery. The Southerners fired the first shot on April 12, 1861 after Lincoln had sent food provisions to Fort Sumter. Acting swiftly, with Congress out of session, he gave orders to his cabinet on April 21, 1861 to expand the army and navy, and made arrangements privately to transport and supply his troops.

Set against any presidency before or since, the Lincoln presidency ran headlong into the most incredible obstacles, right from the start. Southerners in Washington were resigning from all branches of government to go south and fight. More than a thousand army officers left their posts to go south. Spies and arms smugglers penetrated north and south. Telegraph wires to the north were cut, mails halted, railroads crippled. Ten-foot barricades of sandbags, cement and iron plate stood at each doorway of the Capitol.

The Confederate flag flying over Alexandria could be seen from the White House windows, and speculation was heard that Lincoln and his cabinet would have to flee to Pennslvania or Ohio, or even to resign, so precarious was their position. "The new pilot was hurried to the helm in the midst of a tornado," wrote Emerson. Editor Horace Greeley, like a nagging magpie, was writing columns and letters describing the "black despair" on every brow in the nation and urging Lincoln to negotiate an armistice with the South.

Emancipation lifts blacks' hopes

When Lincoln, desperately seeking ways to end the insurrection, proposed the Emancipation Proclamation in September 1862 as a measure to weaken the South militarily, various objections were raised in his own cabinet as well as among other Northerners who supported the Union but not necessarily emancipation of slaves. Lincoln's rationale for freeing the slaves, which he had decided to do as early as July 1862, was based not on his moral convictions about slavery but on military concerns, since he believed that "the colored population" was the greatest untapped source for the decisive battle that would save the Union (he recognized later the heroism of black troops in battle.) He thought slavery could be abolished under his powers as commander-in-chief.

On September 24, 1862, two days after announcing the Emancipation Proclamation, he proclaimed suspension of the writ of habeus corpus, believing that anyone who discouraged volunteering or hindered the draft should be liable to military trial. He stirred a violent debate when he suspended the writ, and the Congress tried to avoid a full-fledged flare-up by authorizing him to take this action, thus indicating that the Constitution gave control over the writ to Congress, not to the President alone. One ex-Congressman, Vallandigham, who became a particular thorn in Lincoln's side, called the President "King Lincoln."

Naturally the black population, north and south, lionized Lincoln as their savior. Frederick Douglass, the black leader who knew Lincoln personally, described the President in one of his speeches as "swift, zealous, radical and determined." When, at war's end, Lincoln went to Richmond, the former Confederate capital, the slaves mobbed around him crying and laughing, reaching out to touch "Father Abraham."

In the South the *Richmond Examiner* called the Emancipation Proclamation, officially proclaimed on January 1, 1863, "the most stupid political blunder yet known in American history." The *New York Herald* and the rest of the anti-administration press, as well as the *London Times*, claimed it was a meaningless gesture because it only pertained to slaves in the South, where it could not be enforced. Although public opinion in Britain supported Lincoln, the only European great power that offered a positive endorsement to his administration was Russia, which had recently fought Britain and France in the Crimean war.

Publications like the conservative *London Dispatch* accused the North not only of seeking domination of the South but also of bullying the world. Critics in the northern press heaped scorn on Lincoln as the war dragged on. A *Cincinnati Commercial* writer, calling Lincoln "an awful, woeful ass", claimed that some people felt it would be "doing God service to kill him", except for the fact that his vice-president, Hamlin, "is a bigger fool than he is." Sandburg noted that the *Chicago Times* in the summer of 1863 published "columns of curses on Lincoln and all his works."

Backing Grant against the critics

Longing for military victories after the dilatory bungling of his first military commanders, Lincoln turned to Ulysses Grant, only to endure an outpouring of letters and personal objections to this military chief because of his drinking reputation. "How is it that Grant, who was behind at Fort Henry, drunk at Donelson, surprised and whipped at Shiloh and driven back from Oxford, Mississippi, is still in command?" asked the *Cincinnati Commercial*.

One delegation after another calling for Grant's dismissal failed to shake Lincoln's faith in the one man he felt knew how to fight. On many occasions Lincoln leavened his high- pressure days with a touch of his raw humor, or his backwoods stories. On one such occasion he asked a visiting New York clergyman if he knew where Grant got his liquor; Lincoln said if he could only find that out he would direct the army's chief quartermaster to lay in a large stock of it and supply it to all the other generals who had never won a victory. At another time, in the bleakest days of war losses, Lincoln commented, "I think Grant has hardly a friend left, except myself." Yet he kept Grant in command against the advice and pleadings of friend and foe.

Lincoln was lambasted from one side by Peace Democrats calling for compromise and from the other side by antislavery radicals who called him a poor leader for not going all the way to end slavery. When Horatio Seymour became Governor of New York he claimed that Lincoln's Emancipation Proclamation was meaningless and unconstitutional. The New York Peace Democrats hailed Seymour when he called for an end to the "incompetents" in Washington and claimed that compromise measures could have prevented the war.

Among Lincoln's desperate measures to turn the military tide nothing caused greater turmoil to American spirits than the draft. Congress enacted a conscription law on March 3, 1863, which provoked the tumultuous New York City draft riots of July 13–17, the greatest civil disorders in the republic's history, with over 100 people killed. Ironically, Jefferson and Madison had succeeded perhaps too well in embedding in American minds the idea that fighting tyranny was the highest form of patriotism. Americans were suspicious of federal power, and convinced that power should reside in the states, including the power to raise state militias.

In three days of July 1863 New York city mobs wrecked the rotating drum from which draftee names were drawn, set buildings afire, fought with firemen and police, burned down the draft office and hanged Negroes to lampposts. "To hell with the draft and the war" was their cry. The cry was echoed in other states. Two draft enrollers were murdered in Indiana. Women threw eggs at government officials and men in several states rioted with guns, bricks and clubs.

In a June 1863 Peace Convention in New York the peace radicals denounced the draft and the suspension of habeus corpus and Lincoln himself was hissed by the conventioneers. The chaos of the times was illustrated by New York bartenders who served "Jeff Davis cocktails", while in Ohio speakers excoriated Lincoln at mass meetings that drew thousands of people. Army desertions presented another threat, including border-state soldiers turned off by the Emancipation Proclamation because they had enlisted to fight for the Union "not to free the niggers." According to Sandburg, Illinois had 2,000 deserters arrested in six months.

Lincoln's ratings with the most influential and respectable part of the population sank to new lows in the spring and early summer of 1863. The author-attorney Richard H. Dana wrote that personal loyalty to the president in Washington had ceased to exist: "He has no admirers, no enthusiastic supporters…" Dana said Lincoln might have been a good western jury lawyer but "he is an unutterable calamity to us where he is."

A self-made Commander-in-Chief

Stubbornly, Lincoln stuck to his middle course and his convictions, making enemies on all sides. He saw his simple purpose not unlike that of a policeman bringing criminals to justice. But in the winter of 1862–3 the discontents almost turned into calls for impeachment. For one reason or another—to slow the war, restore human rights or get rid of slavery entirely—parties on every side seemed closer than ever to wanting Lincoln out of public life. These extremes of discontent showed up in many forms, even to the circulation of reports that Lincoln's family engaged in treason.

To meet that charge, a sorrowful, weary president voluntarily appeared before a Senate committee to deny emphatically that any member of his family had communicated with the enemy. Little wonder that the President at his desk in the White House one day was heard to say: "I wish George Washington or some of the old patriots were here in my place so I could have a little rest." In a letter in March 1863, Walt Whitman said that Lincoln "has shown, I think, an almost supernatural tact in keeping the ship afloat at all."

Yet despite all these problems, wrote Sandburg, the late summer and early fall of 1863 "seemed to mark a deepening of loyalties to Lincoln and his vision of where to go and how." Lincoln's secretary, John Hay, working hand in glove with the chief executive, wrote that "there is no man in the country so wise, so gentle and so firm. I believe the hand of God placed him where he is." He wrote that Lincoln "is managing this war, the draft, foreign relations, and planning a reconstruction of the Union, all at once." Gen. William Tecumseh Sherman, after his meeting with Lincoln aboard Grant's steamboat headquarters just before the war ended, said that no man he had ever known possessed such a combination of greatness and goodness.

After the humiliating Union defeat at Bull Run in July, Lincoln issued a call for half a million volunteers and brought General McClellan to Washington to command them. During the following year he felt himself an amateur at war-making. By the time of the Battle of

Fredericksburg, however, largely on the basis of his readings of books on military strategy, he was becoming more confident, and his war strategy was as straight and simple as his political beliefs. He had an instinct, perhaps from his wrestling days, to go for the jugular and to menace the enemy with superior forces at different points at the same time.

On August 11, 1864 he telegraphed Grant, who was engaging Confederate troops in the Shenandoah Valley, to hold on with a bull-dog grip and "chew and choke as much as possible." Grant reportedly smiled when he read this dispatch and commented: "The president has more nerve than any of his advisers." Yet Lincoln combined this tough-ness with great humane concerns for soldiers, including deserters and draft evaders, and his secretary Hay noted in his diary how eagerly Lincoln "caught at any fact which would justify him in saving the life of a condemned soldier."

Lincoln's job as commander in chief dominated his presidency. He met the challenges, from skillful handling of personalities to driving his military commanders, as well as anyone in American history, while remaining virtually a loner. He almost never sought advice about con-duct of the war from his cabinet or other politicians; no cabinet meet-ings were called to make decisions, nor was he influenced by threats made against him or by the draft riots. He used his powers to choose top generals without hesitation or political advice, willing to assume great responsibility, which was a trait he admired most in others dur-ing wartime.

He was frustrated in the extreme by the hesitations of his Northern generals in pursuing the enemy. Repeatedly, Lincoln prodded his gen-erals to be more aggressive, always striving for that elusive battle that could end the war quickly. His conception of commander in chief resembled that of the Founders, who had regarded Washington as a hands-on battlefield commander.

When the war tide was finally turning—when Lee had been re-pulsed at Gettysburg, Grant had taken Vicksburg and the North gained control of the Mississippi—Lincoln wrote a letter aimed at the na-tional and international publics. In rather Churchillian prose he wrote that "the signs look better" and that "It is hard to say that anything has been more bravely and well done than at Antietam, Murfreesboro, Gettysburg and on many fields of lesser note... Not only on the deep sea, the broad bay, and the rapid river, but also up the narrow muddy bayou… they have been, and made their tracks. Thanks to all. For the great republic—for the principle it lives by, and keeps alive—for man's vast future—thanks to all."

While still beset by his critics and dogged by the habeus corpus controversy, he signed a Thanksgiving Proclamation in October 1863. He tried to shift the gloom that had been cast over the first half of the year by inviting his fellow citizens to set apart and observe the last Thursday of the following month as "a day of Thanksgiving and Praise to our beneficent Father who dwelleth in the Heavens." Lincoln was "the most religiously sensitive of our presidents", in the words of historian Arthur Schlesinger Jr.

A speech to lift spirits, for ages to come

Nothing better illustrates the capacity of a great leader to lift a nation's spirit above the agony of national pain and tragedy than Lincoln's brief, three-minute, 271-word address on November 19, 1863 after the horrible sacrifice of 50,000 dead, wounded or missing in the crucial battle of Gettysburgh. Lincoln transformed that historic moment, as historian Gary Wills has written, into "a symbol of national purpose, pride and ideals," transforming an ugly reality "into something rich and strange…"

Without even mentioning the cemetery he was dedicating, the names of fallen heroes, the carnage that lay around him, the issue of slavery or even the people present at the ceremony, Lincoln elevated his message to become a call for people, throughout the world, to move forward into the future by pursuing the still unrealized ideal of the American founding fathers and by completing the great test of government by and for the people, dedicated to the equality of all people, that to him was the whole meaning of the war. He challenged Americans to dedicate themselves to the "unfinished work which they who fought here have thus far so nobly advanced…" so that "this nation, under God, shall have a new birth of freedom—and that government of the people, by the people, for the people, shall not perish from the earth."

With these brief remarks, wrote Wills, Lincoln cast a spell and "distilled the meaning of the war, of the nation's purpose, of the remaining task, in a statement that is straightforward and magical." With typical clarity he stated simply that the dead had given their lives for a single purpose, "that the nation might live." Even though the war was still going on, he refused, as he always did, to vilify the Confederacy or to indulge in self-righteousness. Lincoln's words were "weapons for peace in the midst of war," wrote Wills, "the perfect medium for changing the way most Americans thought about the founding acts." What Lincoln accomplished with these words, one contemporary citizen claimed, was nothing less than a new founding of the American nation.

"The Gettysburg Address has become an authoritative expression of the American spirit," wrote Wills, "as authoritative as the Declaration itself, and perhaps even more influential, since it determines how we read the Declaration." The nation was changed, he wrote, by accepting Lincoln's concept of a single people dedicated to a proposition.

It was a happy surprise to Lincoln, as well as to many others in the fractured nation, when the Union Party swept the field in the elections of the fall of 1863, a sweep in all Northern states except New Jersey. The Governor of Illinois in one of his campaign speeches declared he had visited Lincoln in the White House and Lincoln had told him "It will be all right yet; hold still and see the salvation of the Lord." The New York Herald noted that Lincoln had used this phrase of Oliver Cromwell (known as the "Lord Protector" for winning battles and holding 17th-century England together), and said that the use of the phrase drew immense applause from the Springfield audience to which it was addressed.

By the time Lincoln delivered his second inaugural address in March 1865, the Union troops had taken Atlanta, Savannah and Columbia, South Carolina, but fighting still continued. Lincoln used Biblical references in most of this short, famous address, starting with the irony that both sides "read the same Bible and pray to the same God, and each invokes His aid against the other." The religious fervor on both sides to which he referred explains as much as anything the incredible spirits of the soldiers who fought each other for four tortuous years. Quoting from his own King James version of the Bible, Lincoln connected slavery and "this terrible war" to the Book of Matthew's warning of the heavy consequences of sin, he concluded:

> *Yet if God wills that it continue until all the wealth piled by the bondsman's two hundred and fifty years of unrequited toil shall be sunk, and until every drop of blood drawn with the lash shall be paid by*

another drawn with the sword, as was said three thousand years ago, so still it must be said 'the judgments of the Lord are true and righteous altogether'. With malice toward none, with charity for all, with firmness in the right as God gives us to see the right, let us strive to finish the work we are in, to bind up the nation's wounds, to care for him who shall have borne the battle and for his widow and his orphan, to do all which may achieve and cherish a just and lasting peace among ourselves and with all nations."

A sign of how well Lincoln succeeded in binding together and preserving the nation was the comment of his Secretary of the Treasury two days after Lincoln's assassination. McCullough wrote on April 16: "My hope is, and my belief is, that this great national calamity will teach the world a lesson… that it will show that the assassination of our Chief Magistrate does not affect in the slightest degree the permanence of our institution, or the regular administration of the laws; that an event that would have shaken any other country to the centre does not even stagger for a moment a Government like ours." Nothing would have pleased Lincoln more than to know that "the last best hope of earth" had survived its most awful test.

Lincoln's historic task, and his own role in fulfilling it, were writ with amazing clarity in his own mind, even throughout the four years of agonizing bloodshed that cost the nation some 600,000 casualties. The core of Lincoln's convictions, through the crucial war years—and the explanation for his bold leadership—was his absolute commitment to "the idea" embodied in the Declaration of Independence. As expressed by his good friend, the transcendentalist preacher Theodore Parker, the great political idea behind the nation was in three parts: that each man has unalienable rights; that in respect of these rights all men are equal; and that the government's role is to protect each person in the enjoyment of these rights. From Parker, Lincoln is presumed to have gotten the notion of government of, by and for the people.

Lincoln constantly invoked the founding fathers. He referred to them repeatedly in the Lincoln-Douglas debates. Not a man to hand out praise easily, Lincoln was unstinting in his admiration for Jefferson, "who was, is and perhaps will continue to be, the most distinguished politician in our history." He considered Jefferson the framer of the ideal of the nation, the man who "had the coolness, forecast and capacity to introduce into a merely revolutionary document, an abstract truth, applicable to all men and all times." Like Justice Story, Lincoln held that the united colonies became a nation de facto with the signing of the Declaration of Independence, and that this in effect became a founding document.

Lincoln believed that his own policy began with the origins of the republic, especially with the ideas of equality expressed by Jefferson, who had written the defining assertion that "all men are created equal." In a speech in Peoria, his first great speech, seven years before the Civil War, Lincoln stated that the policy of prohibiting slavery in the new western territory originated with the author of the Declaration, and declared his own hatred of a practice that made hypocrites of believers in the Declaration. Later, he declared that "there is no reason in the world why the Negro is not entitled to all the natural rights enunciated in the Declaration of Independence, the right to life, liberty, and the pursuit of happiness."

Some said that Lincoln virtually made a cult of the Declaration, and indeed he invoked it time and again in almost Biblical tones as one might invoke the gospel for spiritual inspiration. In his 1854 speech on the Kansas-Nebraska Act, he called on his fellow citizens to "re-adopt the Declaration of Independence." If they did this, he declared, they would have saved the Union so that "the succeeding millions of free happy people, the world over, shall rise up and call us blessed to the latest generations."

Guiding a troubled public

Only by understanding these deep convictions of Lincoln can we understand today his perspective on the Civil War and his own iron will and remarkable independent actions as President, over and over again, to steer a straight course when even the people around him were divided by doubts. He saw the Civil War not as a war but as an insurrection threatening the Union created by his revered Founders and the idea embodied in that Union.

As Arthur M. Schlesinger, Jr. has written, the tragedy of the Civil War "showed the possibilities of failure in American society, the miracle of Lincoln showed the possibilities of salvation." Schlesinger said that Lincoln "realized most completely the potentialities of statesmanship in a democracy," marked "by his knowledge that without just and merciful dealing human nature could not be redeemed in this or any other world."

The clarity and simplicity of Lincoln's beliefs derived from his early recognition of Jefferson's Declaration as more important than the Constitution itself (a notion shared by Daniel Webster, the leading constitutional lawyer of his day, and Supreme Court Justice Joseph Story.) This simple belief helped him keep his head when others around him felt confusion and fell into disagreement. The single, unwavering resolve of his thinking stood above, and in remarkable contrast to, the doubts and hesitations of his fellow leaders and countrymen, including even many of his generals.

Lincoln may have been "a man of the people", but he certainly wasn't an ordinary American. It's true that in his early days no one enjoyed a good gab in the country store more than he did, sitting with his feet on the stove swapping stories with loafers. Such time was probably well spent—Whitman would certainly have approved this loafing soul—because it helped him to humanize his wisdom and develop his knack for simple speech and use of dramatic parables to express his thoughts. He was neither a brilliant success like Douglas nor a failure like the early Grant and though he enjoyed having recognition, ambition was not the compelling motive of his life.

Lincoln's pursuit of every chance he got to broaden his mind set him apart from the average western American who was fully preoccupied with the practical tasks and struggles of pioneer life. But the greatness of Lincoln was based on the combination of intellect, and brilliant style of clear communication, with a high degree of moral character. He was probably the most humane statesman who ever led a nation through a bitter war.

His concept of democracy embodied the spirit and principle of brotherhood under God. He could order the killing of those who wanted to destroy the nation while at the same time forgiving them for their error. He showed no resentment against those who did him harm, in fact appearing at times to go out of his way to do them service. Profoundly humble, Lincoln often quoted little verses that questioned whether any mortal had the right to be proud, a universal tenet of the religious. Lincoln had deep religious views all his life, even though, like Emerson, he was put off by the formalities of churchgoing. When a group of black people from Baltimore gave him an *Oxford Bible* as a gift in 1864, Lincoln responded: "In regard to this great book, I have but to say it is the best gift God has given to man."

Unlike Andrew Jackson, who divided the world into friends and enemies, and unlike most politicians, who then and now cordially hate their opponents, Lincoln believed in treating everyone the same, with justice and kindness—including the Confederates, the Negro slaves, his own enemies and the Northern deserters.

It was something of a miracle that this humble man, mixing common sense and patriotism with a fine intellect, did not flinch from leading a nation through its greatest crisis, commanding an army of a million men and spending billions on a civil war. The postwar period surely would have been different if this gentle and forgiving leader had held the helm. When he was assassinated, it was the South as well as the North that lost its best and wisest friend.

Looking back on his saga, one can see that Lincoln's steadiness, and his steadfast commitment to the ideals of Jefferson and the other founders, and his religious faith, all made a transcendent contribution to the spirit of his country. Like Washington, he was a father figure in a troubled time and like the General, standing very tall, he pulled a shaky nation behind him into a new era—nobly, simply, with vision and above partisanship, inspiring Americans with admiration and respect for their "Lord Protector", not just in his time but for generations to come.

THE CONFIDENT YEARS
AND THE VOLATILE 20ᵗʰ CENTURY

With the dawn of the 20th century, the young nation's spirits took wing. Joyous crowds in lower Manhattan celebrated on the eve of the new century by shooting off fireworks, blowing tin horns and ringing bells, while the rest of the country found a thousand ways to show their high hopes for the future. J. Pierpont Morgan played solitaire in the library of his Madison Avenue brownstone, "looking forward with the eagerness of a much younger man to the great possibilities of the century that was about to begin," in the words of a family friend. Within the year he would begin negotiating with Andrew Carnegie to form the world's biggest corporation, the United States Steel Corporation.

"We step upon the threshold of 1900 which leads to the new century, facing a still brighter dawn of civilization", The *New York Times* beamed. One minister got carried away in his Sunday sermon, averring that "Laws are becoming more just, rulers human; music is becoming sweeter and books wiser; homes are happier, and the individual heart is becoming at once more just and more gentle."

At the opening of the 20ᵗʰ century, wrote Henry Steele Commager, "in everything but law, America was a Christian nation... Jurors were required to believe in God, teachers to read from the Bible, and in some states a religious observance of the 'Lord's Day' was a legal obligation." Commager recalled how Tocqueville, a century earlier, had pointed out that in America the Christian religion had more influence over the people than in any other nation. In the United States, remarked this observer, religion "directs the manners of the community, and by regulating domestic life, it regulates the state."

Commager also commented, in *The American Mind,* on the optimism of Americans as they moved into the 20th century. "Nothing in all history had ever succeeded like America," he wrote, "and every American knew it... As nature and experience justified optimism, the American was incurably optimistic."

The years from 1900 to the First World War were tagged "The Good Years" by Walter Lord, who chronicled them in his marvelous book of that name. "These years were good," he wrote, "because whatever the trouble, people were sure they could fix it. The solutions differed of course—Theodore Roosevelt had his Square Deal, Carry Nation had her hatchet— but everyone at least had a bold plan and could hardly wait to try it. To the many varied people who lived through the era—the men and women who wistfully recall marching for suffrage, rebuilding San Francisco, or cheering wildly for Woodrow Wilson—these were, and still are, the Good Years."

Business was good across the country, in part because the country had been united 30 years before this new century by its first transcontinental railroad. On May 10, 1869 a new stage in America's road to superpower had begun when two trains operated by government-chartered corporations, one coming from the East and one from the West, bumped their cowcatchers in the Utah wilderness and linked up the nation, giving homesteaders an easy opening to the West and bringing commerce and wealth to vast prairies and other regions and prosperity to the whole nation.

Another development that knitted the nation together was the telephone, whose staggering implications stirred the popular imagination when Alexander Graham Bell demonstrated his invention in 1876. A popular song then called "The Wondrous Telephone" anticipated two other developments in the upcoming century, the radio and the television, in these prescient lines:

> *You stay at home and listen*
> *to the lecture In the hall,*
> *And hear the strains of music*
> *From a fascinating ball!*

In the so-called Gilded Age after the Civil War, five great railroads were punched through the Rockies, expanding the nation's rail network five times to a total higher than all of Europe's. A downside of these historic events, of course, was that they ended an era for the

American Indian and for much of the prairie wildlife. By the beginning of the new century there were only about 230,000 Indians left, compared with a million in the time of Columbus, and less than a thousand buffalo of the 12 million that had roamed the plains in the 1860s.

As the new century opened, the steel and coal companies were enjoying record profits, exports were up, Kansas had a bumper corn crop, and with holiday sales booming President McKinley's slogan, "The Full Dinner Pail", sounded just the right note. A man's shirt at that time cost 23 cents (nobody remarked that the child who often made the shirt got $3.54 a week, noted Lord.) Glass production was up 52% (nobody noted either that one reason for this was the work of 10-year-old children who each put stoppers on as many as 300 dozen bottles a day.)

One explanation for the era's optimism and confidence was the relative simplicity of life, at least compared to the present. The Federal Government certainly was simple by today's standards. The 1900 Navy budget was $55 million, the cost of a single atomic submarine 60 years later. There was a widespread belief that anyone who was good and worked hard had a good chance of becoming rich. The Boston Herald declared that if anyone hadn't made money in the past year "his case is helpless." Economist John Bates Clark declared: "A certain manly quality in our people gives assurance that we have the personal material out of which a millennium will grow."

The rules of daily life and morals were simple too. Nice people just didn't talk about sex, for instance, and smoking was frowned upon for the young. President McKinley cautioned a photographer, "We must not let the young men of the country see their president smoking." His successor, Theodore Roosevelt, had no use for men or women who were anything but "rigidly virtuous" and he prided himself on his virginity when he fell in love with his future wife, young Alice Hathaway Lee. Sex outside of marriage was unthinkable to him.

One exciting discovery after another raised expectations for an abundant life ahead. Henry Ford, who left the farm at age 16 to join the new industrial age, had two bold ambitions: to enable as many people as possible to enjoy motoring, and to provide as many high-paying jobs as possible for his workers. He introduced his Model T in 1908, offering a new and inexpensive mode of family travel. He created "the

Rouge", the greatest industrial complex in the world. His five-dollar day, the precursor of a minimum wage and profit-sharing plans, made big news across the country in 1914 (as did his five-day work week in 1926) and made it possible for an average worker to afford an automobile. Only two years after Ford's first automobile came on the market there were 8,000 cars bouncing around the country. The first coast-to-coast auto trip was made by a Packard in 52 days, from San Francisco to New York.

The new Xray was revolutionizing surgery. The Caterpillar tractor would lighten farm work. Electricity promised wonders—not just light but help on all sorts of household chores. One of the first electric conveniences was the toaster. A Harvard professor envisaged a nation-wide network of trolley lines binding the country together. Private enterprise rode high, and got respect. Russell Sage commented that millionaires were safe, for "they are the guardians of the public welfare."

At Booker T. Washington's Tuskegee Institute in Alabama, George Washington Carver, the scientist-educator, was beginning agricultural experiments that virtually revolutionized the economy of the South. From his pioneering work came crop diversification, soil-building and more than 400 by-products of peanut and sweet-potato cultivation. In an era when agriculture was still the largest single occupation of Americans, this soft-spoken, modest son of Negro slaves taught rural blacks to become skilled farmers. His work made him a cultural hero and epitomized Booker Washington's conviction that education was the key to improving life for black Americans.

The public was fascinated by inventions such as the subway and the long-distance telephone. The first radio program was broadcast in 1907, a selection of violin music picked up mostly by ships at sea. In 1910 Caruso sang on the radio for a larger though still small audience. By the 1920s barnstorming radio broadcasters roamed the country bringing entertainment ranging from banjo music to hog prices to rural communities that had been isolated from city influences. There was a sense of optimism about this new medium, the "wave of the future," which was to have a huge impact on American life and provide free entertainment for the masses.

The resilience of America's high spirits during this era was sorely tested by a natural disaster. On an early April morning in 1906 San

Francisco was struck by the double demons of earthquake and fire. The size and scope of the fires that broke out everywhere were on the scale of wartime bombings in Europe nearly 40 years later. More than 490 blocks were in ruins, and 225,000 people were made homeless. But the spirits of the San Franciscans, who began rebuilding almost immediately, and of the nation as a whole, which rushed relief to the people of that stricken city ranging from bread and volunteer labor to financial help from rich and poor, turned the disaster into a time of national pride. Americans were more proud of themselves than ever. The disaster was actually given a romantic luster and immortalized in a movie featuring the inspirational song, "San Francisco", starring Clark Gable and Jeannette MacDonald.

The birth of mass entertainment

The first five-cent "nickelodeon" theater opened in a vacant storeroom in McKeesport, PA in 1905, ushering in a revolution in mass entertainment through the motion picture, one of the most important ways of having fun and spreading information. The 20-minute motion picture, "The Great Train Robbery", accompanied by live piano, was the first edited film that told a story, featuring acting and stagecraft. The nickelodeon was an overnight success. Within two years there were about 5,000 of them around the country; they entertained about 200,000 people a day in New York, one third of them children. By 1910, ten thousand movie houses had weekly audiences of ten million people.

Motion pictures brought slapstick comedy, the "Perils of Pauline", Biblical dramas and lots of action and adventure to millions of Americans who had never been able to afford such fun. Zany comedies featuring practical jokes lifted the spirits of more people than the old live vaudeville shows had ever done. In 1914 Charlie Chaplin averaged a silent film a week for 34 weeks. In 1915 "The Birth of a Nation", directed by D.W. Griffith, marked the beginning of the modern "movies". With its Civil War battle scenes and professional photography and editing, it raised the art of the motion picture to the level of literature and the theater and marked the beginning of the "star" system and the emergence of movies as big business.

The new century had rhythm too, as the quickstepping ragtime spread from Negro musicians to dance halls and ballrooms. Popular songs were danceable, and the "bunny hop", the "turkey trot" and the "grizzly bear" became national fads. Thomas A. Edison, whose early Kinetoscope and motion picture projectors led to the movies, also invented the first practical phonograph, his favorite among his many inventions, and that invention brought ragtime, opera and other entertainment right into people's homes.

Not until about 1907 did Washington, if not the public, begin to wake up to the significance of the almost unnoticed experiments in flight by two brothers who ran a small bicycle shop in Dayton, Ohio. In 1900 Orville and Wilbur Wright had built a man-carrying glider; two years later they added a motor and propeller and Orville, wearing his usual starched collar, bowler, tie and dark suit, stayed up in it for 12 seconds. Wilbur managed to stay aloft for 59 seconds and the two brothers made over 50 flights without attracting notice even from the neighbors, much less the local press. During these years the public was more preoccupied with more mundane achievements like the safety razor and modern plumbing. While it would be years before the public realized it, the air age had begun.

One optimist who sprang from nowhere to fan the fires of young men's hopes and ambitions during the years between the Civil War and World War I was a Harvard man and ordained minister by the name of Horatio Alger, Jr. He wrote more than a hundred books selling over 20 million copies—tales of boys who rose from society's bottom ranks to the top through their own ambition and hard work, honesty and thrift. His formula was as simple as that of Ben Franklin's "Poor Richard", who believed that "God helps those who help themselves" and "Early to bed and early to rise" were the keys to every man's riches.

Plenty of real-life stories put flesh and bones on Alger's thesis, even though Alger himself ended his days in the Newsboys Lodging House, a home for orphans and runaways. John D. Rockefeller, who would become the world's richest man, started out working for $4 a week as clerk for a Cleveland merchant. Edward H. Harriman made $5 a week on his first job as office boy to a broker. And Andrew Carnegie pocketed a paltry $1.20 a week when he started out as bobbin boy in a Pittsburgh cotton mill, on his way to becoming the world's leading manufacturer of steel.

With these stories fueling the American consciousness, it's not surprising that as late as the 1960s the chairman of Dun & Bradstreet expressed his belief that poor people are poor simply because they're victims of their own laziness, ignorance or carelessness with money. A great Yale teacher, William Graham Sumner, had told his students back in 1883 that public policy should "increase, multiply and extend the chances" for people rather than trying to redistribute wealth. He felt that "some will profit by the chances eagerly and some will neglect them altogether; therefore the greater the chances, the more unequal will be the fortunes of these two sets of men. So it ought to be, in all justice and right reason."

From the U.S. victories at the 1900 Olympics to the news of J. P. Morgan's ventures into international finance, Americans considered themselves on top of the world. Princeton's president, Woodrow Wilson, observed that expansion was "the natural and wholesome impulse which comes with a consciousness of matured strength." On the Senate floor, Senator Chauncey Depew, chairman of the New York Central Railroad, said: "There is not a man here who does not feel four hundred percent bigger in 1900 than he did in 1896—bigger intellectually, bigger hopefully, bigger in the breast—from the fact that he is the citizen of a country that has become a world power for peace, for civilization and for the expansion of its industries and the products of its labor." President McKinley prayed to God for guidance on the question of whether to annex the Philippines, and the answer came to him: "There was nothing left to do but to take them all and to educate the Filipinos and uplift and Christianize them and by God's grace to do the very best we could by them as our fellow men for whom Christ died."

TR enters, at a run

When Theodore Roosevelt was sworn in as president after a deranged anarchist shot McKinley in 1901, Senator Depew said that the words "I do so swear" at the swearing-in sounded like a salvo of artillery—and that's what much of "TR's" administration sounded like to his millions of admirers. No one was fitter to lead the charge into "The American Century." No one could have brought to the White House such absolute integrity, such zeal for "good" politics and "good" people, and such an effervescent personality that captivated the press as well as the public.

Theodore Roosevelt at 42 was the youngest and most vigorous President the nation had ever seen, just bursting with robust enthusiasms. He was a charismatic man of action, yet able easily to knock off charming prose in his diary as well as books that were distinguished for historical research. He had a fierce curiosity about everything, a first-rate intellect, a solid belief in the merits of hard work and a delight in making big decisions. He had a Darwinian confidence in progress through struggle. He was as quick to urge national shape-up, such as a Navy buildup, as to urge individuals to improve themselves through outdoor life and personal character development. He summoned everyone to a strenuous, moral life. As Herbert Croly later put it, "He preached the doctrine that the paramount and almost exclusive duty of the American citizen consists in being a 60-horsepower moral motor-car."

This exuberance matched the national mood. Yale professor John Morton Blum has written that Roosevelt "contained within him the best and the worst of America, the whole spectrum from practical enlightenment and sound moral judgment to sentimentalism and braggadocio." Compared with Jefferson, "happiness" was not particularly high on his list, not as high as work, although he was an outwardly happy man, cherishing deeply the happiness of his and others' family life, even though he suffered an incredible tragedy when he lost his 22-year-old wife and his mother to illness on the very same night.

Roosevelt's contagious optimism was based on his belief that people "of character" would not be corrupted by power or wealth—and if they were, government had the power to intercede. He was a moralist like his patrician father, a man who put morality ahead of everything else. Throughout his career as a Republican he became increasingly concerned with the need for government action to restrain the powerful, to assist the weak, and to assure order in the country and in the world. Thomas F. Woodlock, editor of The *Wall Street Journal* in its earliest years, had this comment at the time of TR's landslide election victory: "Against such a frank, fearless, honest personality, capital and combination beat as vainly as break the waves upon rock-ribbed shores."

Roosevelt had no fears about the nation's march to industrial power from the agrarian simplicity of Jefferson's time. In response to the anxieties and pessimism of people like Henry Adams over the upcoming twentieth century, he had written a long article in early 1894 expressing confidence in the future. "At no period of the world's history," he wrote, "has life been so full of interest, and of possibilities of excitement and enjoyment." He noted that science had revolutionized industry; Darwin had revolutionized thought; people with ambition had unique opportunities to build, explore, conquer and transform "to bring about immeasurable results."

Visiting the St. Louis exposition of 1904, Roosevelt was fascinated by the inventions displayed there, including a pneumatic process for house-cleaning called the vacuum cleaner, electrical hearing aids and other innovations. He reveled in the rapid industrialization of America in his time, including the expansion of railroads and factories as much as he gloried in the life of the wilds. Against the background of pianolas playing "Meet Me in St. Louis, Louis" Roosevelt's bright smile, his flashing teeth and thick-lensed glasses stamped his image unforgettably on the people who watched him roam the exposition.

In this pre-television era, the general public shared in the sense of good times, even though they could only read in the newspapers about things like fast motor cars and college football festivities, which were still for the rich. But the public was interested in reading about or observing the good times of the fortunate few. For instance, crowds of people went to Grand Central Station in New York to watch society do its thing when 50 private parlor cars brought well-heeled football fans and players into town after the Yale-Princeton game in New Haven.

The generally upbeat mood of the people was reflected in the comment of *The New York Tribune* in its editorial ringing out the old year 1905: "Never did a year close with a better record," wrote the Tribune, "never did a new year dawn with prospect brighter—Good times go marching on!"

The White Fleet and the top of the world

Two events in particular epitomized President Roosevelt's contagious enthusiasms and gave all Americans reason to be proud and confident of their leading place in the world. One was his dramatic act in sending America's Great White Fleet around the world ("Always ready at the drop of a hat, for either a fight or a frolic", boasted Rear Admiral Robley Evans, with Rooseveltian gusto.) The other event of high drama was the President's hearty send-off of Admiral Peary on the heroic adventure to put the American flag on top of the world at the North Pole.

Throughout his public life Roosevelt ardently advocated military preparedness, and his action to send off the fleet, without even consulting his cabinet, was one more expression of his core belief that diplomacy and the protection of America's strategic interests and the preservation of world order depended upon the moral use of power, a belief that later underlay his use of power to establish order in Cuba and Santo Domingo and to acquire the Panama Canal zone. He regarded the building of the Panama Canal—enabling the U.S. Navy to move quickly from ocean to ocean—as the greatest accomplishment of his presidency, and he made the first foreign trip of any U.S. president while in office when he went to Panama to look over the work on the canal.

The sixteen battleships of the U.S. fleet became a new metaphor of American greatness, a source of pride to its citizens and a demonstration to foreigners of both American power and American humanitarianism. "The departure of the fleet was momentous," declared the pastor of New York's Calvary Baptist Church. "It drove me to prayer. I could see in it America's assertion of her right to control the Pacific in the interest of civilization and humanity."

This bold undertaking was concocted by the canny President for maximum suspense and impact worldwide. First, in the summer of 1907, he ordered the fleet to prepare for a cruise to the Pacific Coast, in part as a gesture to impress the Japanese, whose recent aggressiveness had caused some concern. With their white hulls and bright gilt bowsprits, the 16 battleships created a stir wherever they went. Country after country around the world—and city after city on the U.S. West Coast—begged Washington to have the fleet call at their ports. The fleet got a warm welcome with parades in Rio de Janiero. Brazil's foreign minister called the visitors "the pride of the Continent." Another wild celebration greeted them in Peru, before they moved on for a month of target practice in Magdalena Bay.

Roosevelt popped his big surprise March 13, when it was announced that the fleet would return through the Suez Canal—meaning of course that this would be an unprecedented circling of the globe. Again, at every potential stop along the way there were pleas for the fleet to stop at various ports. A half dozen chambers of commerce in

California sought to "capture" the fleet so that their communities could bask in some of the accumulating glory. Even Tokyo sent a cordial invitation, which was promptly accepted, but not without some qualms about whether the Japanese might be planning some sort of trickery.

On the day the battleships sailed through the sunswept Golden Gate and anchored off San Francisco, 60 special trains brought thousands into the city for the wildest celebration of all. Some of the city's natives later recalled the 48-hour ball at the Fairmont Hotel as the best party ever in that partying city. On July 7, the Great White Fleet headed across the Pacific with first stops in Honolulu and New Zealand. They got a huge welcome in Sydney, where 250,000 people who had been awake all night greeted the fleet at dawn. On to the Philippines, and then to Tokyo, where the admirals were welcomed at the Emperor's Palace, the captains in suites at the Imperial Hotel. The visitors were treated to a torchlight parade of 50,000 Tokyo citizens which, in Lord's words, "ended in a near riot of ecstacy."

Crossing the Indian Ocean, this phenomenal procession, which had mesmerized virtually the whole world, went on to Ceylon, picking up the gift of a load of tea, then up through the Suez into the Mediterranean for more rounds of calls winding up at Gibraltar. Finally, with their bands playing "Home Sweet Home", the ships and their proud sailors headed out across the Atlantic bound for Newport News, where, according to Lord, it seemed as if all America had crowded into the city for the welcoming celebration, backed up by the strains of "Strike up the Band" and "There's No Place Like Home." It would be hard to imagine anything that the exuberant American president could do that would arouse the nation's spirits as this enterprise had done.

On July 7, 1908, almost at the time the great fleet moved out from San Francisco, Roosevelt was inspecting a vessel that was getting set to depart from Oyster Bay and was destined to make its own history and headlines around the world. The captain of this stubby black vessel (christened "The Roosevelt"), an ugly duckling compared to the white battleships, was Commander Robert E. Peary, setting forth on just the kind of adventure that aroused the full, gusty enthusiasm of the adventurer in the White House. Like Roosevelt, Peary was virtually fearless, driven by fierce determination to plan and perform great deeds.

The whole country shared the enthusiasm of these two remarkable men. As the Roosevelt pulled out of her pier on July 6, on its way to

Oyster Bay and the final presidential send-off, crowds cheered along the East River shore and endless whistle-blowing on ship and shore was topped off by a shot from the Presidential yacht. Nine months later, Peary led a black companion, Matthew Henson, and four eskimos—Ootach, Egingwah, Seegloo and Ooqueah—to the hummock he had chosen for photo purposes as the North Pole. Henson led three rousing cheers. For a marker, Peary planted a glass bottle with a strip of the American flag, a list of the members of the party and a statement taking possession of the Pole "for and in the name of the President of the United States of America."

The Roosevelt roots

That president was unlike any other before or since. Even when he was a skinny, wiry 17-year-old—an athlete, a scribler and a great talker—one of his female admirers predicted he would one day be president. At the age of 21, a senior at Harvard, he began writing the first of 36 books that he would eventually author, *The Naval War of 1812,* which he finished two years later and which became a classic and a textbook. For his senior thesis he tackled the most controversial topic of the day: the practicality of giving equal rights to women and men. Plucky and fearless, he was runnerup in the Harvard lightweight boxing championship. Raised from childhood on the ethics of the Bible, he was also familiar from his youth with the philanthropies and social work associated with the church.

At 23 he became the youngest member of the New York State Legislature, stating his eager intention "to be one of the governing class." A genuine puritan in politics, and a scrapper in every field he entered, he took on both the Democratic Tammany Hall machine and the miscreants of his own Republican Party in his crusade for reforms. For him, the path of politics was simply to do "the right thing" for the people. The *New York Herald* proclaimed: "Rarely in the history of legislation here has the moral force of individual honor and political honesty been more forcibly displayed."

He did it through sheer force of personality. At a time when corruption was rampant—with politicians accepting bribes from corporate backers even in the lobbies of the legislature—Roosevelt leapt into the headlines and became the darling of the press when he spoke and acted like the defender of the people against the unholy alliance of politics, big business and the judiciary. In the first major speech of his career, on April 5, 1882, he called for an investigation of a Supreme Court Justice and of the late Attorney General who were involved in shabby dealings on behalf of Jay Gould. *The New York Times* cheered his "most refreshing habit of calling men and things by their right names" and predicted a splendid career ahead. One of his former Harvard classmates said, "We hailed him as the dawn of a new era."

Roosevelt reveled in "the excitement and perpetual conflict" of politics and became known as "the Cyclone Assemblyman", according to his Pulitzer Prize-winning biographer, Edmund Morris, who described TR as "an intoxicating conversationalist, very learned." In April 1883, TR moved for passage of his Civil Reform Bill, "to take out of politics the vast band of hired mercenaries" who prevent "pure and honest government." One friend remarked later that "he was in deadly earnest in his consecration to the highest ideals of citizenship." He wanted nothing less than to break the power of the New York City machines, both Democratic and Republican, and he presented three reform bills calling for investigation of corruption in the city government.

During his 1886 run for mayor of New York at the age of 28, Roosevelt was attacked by Labor Party leaders as an upper-class "landlord" without concern for the poor. Roosevelt's frontier philosophy came to the fore in his spirited reply: "If you had any conception of the true American spirit you would know that we do not have 'classes' at all..." The evils of poverty and low wages would disappear, he said, if there were more of "that capacity for steady, individual self-help which is the glory of every true American." He lost the campaign, one of the finest ever in New York, but if anything his spirit further enhanced his reputation and appeal, especially because of the special interest he had shown in black voters.

During his six years as Civil Service Commissioner in Benjamin Harrison's administration he advanced and promoted the merit system for filling public offices, establishing examinations for some jobs and ending the awarding of jobs to friends under the old patronage system. When he became Police Commissioner in New York, he fought dishonesty and corruption and sometimes patrolled the streets himself at night to check on illegal police activity. He gave everything he had to what he called "the grinding labor" at Police Headquarters, while at the same time working on weekends and between appointments on the fourth volume of his book, "The Winning of the West." During his subsequent governorship of New York State, he stirred hearts across the land with his legislation to protect working men and women and consumers, and by his disciplining of errant business leaders.

At the 1900 Republican Convention Governor Roosevelt was nominated to run as Vice President on McKinley's ticket. Later in the year, having succeeded McKinley after his assassination, he helped his party win its greatest victory in nearly three decades. Roosevelt's speech to the party convention proved him an accomplished, confident orator. Radiating pride in his country, he said: "The young giant of the West stands on a continent and clasps the crest of an ocean in either hand. Our nation, glorious in youth and strength, looks into the future with eager eyes and rejoices as a strong man to run a race..." Rather than wasting his time in glad-handing, he spent his evenings just before the convention reading the ancient histories of Thucydides and Josephus.

Besides making many headlines for his political courage, young Roosevelt demonstrated his physical courage also, beyond the frontier of the new nation. In the spring of 1883, at Clark's Tavern in New York, he had met a retired naval officer who described his adventures hunting buffalo in the Bad Lands of the Dakota Territory. Leaving his young wife for a bachelor spree, Roosevelt headed west, taking the night train from Chicago on a jaunt that was to strengthen and refresh him at many intervals in his busy life. The bare, endless Bad Lands then were wild country full of elk, bear and buffalo, a scene of vast emptiness and rough frontier life. Roosevelt said later that it was there that "the romance of my life began", and he captured his feelings in popular books that he wrote later in life. "The sheer immensity of America stirred something in him," wrote Morris. "For the rest of his life 'Big' was to be one of his favorite words."

A spirit of lusty optimism pervaded the Bad Lands and Roosevelt, in his buckskins, on his horse Manitou, responded to it like a native mountain man. On his several trips to the Dakota Territory he spent long wet hours trailing buffalo, rode nearly a thousand miles in a roundup of 4,000 head of cattle, swam and guided Manitou across the frozen Little Missouri River (they actually fell into it), captured outlaws and shot a threatening 1,122-pound grizzly bear at eight paces. One of his fellow hunters later described him as "radio-active... everything about him was force." He combined childlike innocence with great courage and derring-do. Typical Roosevelt remarks overheard by his companions were "By Godfrey but this is fun!" or "By Godfrey, I'd give anything in the world if I could shoot like that". His camp-mates also marveled at his habit of pulling out a book at night on the trail and immersing himself in it.

The young man's bloodthstyness as a game hunter was not unusual among men of his class and generation, wrote Morris, who said Roosevelt had nothing but contempt for the "swinish game-butchers who hunt for hides and not for sport or actual food." The Sioux Indians had been slaughtering many thousands of buffalo during this period—with Federal approval since the government saw getting rid of buffalo one way of getting rid of Indians too. Roosevelt had a typical cowboy's attitude towards the Indians. He once wrote that the Western Indians' claims to lands taken from them were invalid because they never had any real ownership in the first place.

When the little prairie town of Dickinson chose Roosevelt as "orator of the day" for July 4 celebrations in 1886, the event drew the biggest crowd ever in that county (many of whom were "plastered" for the occasion.) Roosevelt's rousing message drew great applause. "Like all Americans", he said, "I like big things; big prairies, big forests and mountains, big wheatfields, railroads, and herds of cattle too, big factories, steamboats, and everything else. But we must keep steadily in mind that no people were ever yet benefited by riches if their prosperity corrupted their virtue… each one must do his part if we wish to show that the nation is worthy of its good fortune. Here we are not ruled over by others, as is the case in Europe; here we rule ourselves…"

Roosevelt's love affair with the great outdoors was to account later for his considerable efforts to protect the wilderness. Appalled by the waste of natural wealth, especially by railroad, lumber and mining interests that were cutting down forests and leaving them desolate, he began a program of conservation and reclamation from the time he took office in 1901. The nation then had 47 million acres of national forests; by the time TR left office it had 195 million acres.

The joys of outdoor life were opened to millions of Americans after TR doubled the number of national parks (creating them by edict when Congress wouldn't cooperate—by calling them "national monuments".) Grand Canyon was just one of the parks spared commercial exploitation. He got Yosemite Park returned to the federal government after it was mismanaged under state rule. He established 51 bird reservations and four big-game refuges.

Roosevelt's concept of Americanism was spelled out in the volumes of "The Winning of the West", which he worked on for nine years. In his writings he portrayed the white settlement of Indian lands in the 1700s as part of an epic racial saga, part of a continuum of Anglo-Saxon history going back to King Alfred. "Never in history," he wrote, "has a race ever expanded over so wide an area in so short a time; and the winning of the American West may be counted as 'the crowning and greatest achievement' of that mighty movement."

The friends and admirers Roosevelt acquired in his days on the frontier, and the figure he himself cut as a fearless outdoorsman, accounted in large part for the outpouring of support he received when he resigned as Assistant Secretary of the Navy in 1898 to head up the "Rough Riders" who fought in Cuba. Roosevelt, as described by Morris, was "congenitally unable to function unless he had some symbols of evil to attack", and the brutal treatment of Cuba's peasants by Spain's occupying troops—including brutalizing concentration camps for peasants and their families—provided just such an electrifying symbol.

Cowboys to Cuba

The Explosion on the U.S. battleship Maine in Havana Harbor with a loss of 254 men (which jingoist American newspapers attributed to a Spanish submarine attack, but which later was thought to be an accident) was reviled by Roosevelt as "dirty treachery". He had worked as Assistant Secretary of the Navy within McKinley's administration for a year to prepare the country for a war to liberate the Cuban people ("a man of unbounded energy and force," the Navy Secretary called him.) Fixing his image forever as a fearless, dashing, highly popular fighter, he rounded up one of the oddest battle groups in history—expert horsemen and marksmen including rugged cowboys from the frontier wearing sombreros and carrying their own guns, a Harvard quarterback, the U.S. tennis champion, the world's greatest polo player, high-jumpers from Yale and football men from Princeton.

After his colorful troops won their victory—ending the imperial rule of Spain that dated back four centuries to Columbus—the Rough Riders got a tumultuous reception when they disembarked at Montauk Point, Long Island. Roosevelt, now the most famous man in America, and still only 40 years old, modestly declared they'd had "a bully fight." In longer perspective, the war with Spain, which he had worked hard to precipitate, propelled the United States into a new role as a responsible world power.

As a military hero, Roosevelt received the adoration of the public, who flooded him with letters and telegrams urging him to run for the governorship of New York. Like General Eisenhower when he returned as a "reluctant candidate" for president after European victory in World War II, Roosevelt had the country in the palm of his hand, and the suspense was building. Everywhere he went a color sargeant and a group of Rough Riders went with him as if they were still scrambling through the Cuban jungles.

When he became President, TR had more real fun on the job than any of the nation's chief executives before or since. When he left the highest office in 1908, he wrote, "I do not believe that anyone else has ever enjoyed the White House as much as I have". The stream of visitors to the White House, Morris reported, reflected the enormous variety of Roosevelt's interests. He loved matching wits with historians, zoologists, inventors, linguists, explorers, sociologists, actors and statesmen. Except for Jefferson, he was without doubt the most impressive intellectual ever to hold the presidency, the first real intellectual since John Quincy Adams. He spoke several languages and was reputed to be able to read two books a night. When Mrs. Henry Cabot Lodge invited him to dinner in March 1906 he asked, tongue in cheek, if she would invite some people with whom he could discuss "the Hittite empire, the Pithecanthropus, and Magyar love songs, as well as the relations of the Atli of the Volsunga Saga to the Etzel of the Nibelungenlied, and of both to Attila..."

Throughout his Presidency Roosevelt welcomed visitors of all stripes. He gave important posts to a broad variety of labor leaders, Catholics, Jews and Methodists and people of other races and backgrounds. In October 1901, to the surprise of many, and taking criticism for an unprecedented initiative, he invited Booker T. Washington, the nation's most prominent Negro, to dine at the White House and help him broaden the Republican Party and the ranks of federal officeholders.

As a world peacemaker during his two terms Roosevelt became the first American to win the Nobel Prize, for his part in mediating the

Russo-Japanese war. King Edward VII and former British Prime Minister Balfour called him "the greatest moral force of the age", and British papers ranked him right up there with Washington and Lincoln. "It is not hard to covet such a force in public life as our American friends have got in Mr. Roosevelt", said the London *Times*.

TR and business

Roosevelt admired and respected the productivity of big business and entrepreneurs and, coming from the top of the New York aristocracy himself, he was not put off by great wealth. But he deplored the "malefactors of great wealth." He recognized the bad and the good of industrial consolidation and believed that the president had a role to see that concentration of power—by any company or group—did not lead to excesses and harm the public. His notion of positive government—more positive than Jefferson had ever envisioned—was to promote the national strength and assure individual liberties.

His economic policy could be summed up in four words: "doing what was right" for the people. He was a president of the whole people, unafraid to take on any individual or group he considered at odds with the public interest. This attitude in the White House doubtless was no small factor in inspiring public confidence and optimism during the early decades of the new century.

Roosevelt wasted no time in taking on the most powerful interests—the bankers and the railroad kings who had enormous power in the days before air travel, highways and interstate regulations. Right off the bat, in his first Message to Congress, he startled moguls like Mark Hanna by suggesting the need for tighter anti-trust control by the federal government. Up until his time, the idea of government having any control over corporations had not been accepted.

He wielded his big stick by telling his Attorney General to challenge the Northern Securities Company for violating the anti-trust act by planning to merge with U.S. Steel. J.P. Morgan and the Western railroaders were taken aback at this first attack. "The little group at the top", wrote Lord, "saw nothing wrong with any of this. To corner a market, to juggle prices, to manipulate stocks, to subsidize a Senator were all part of the game, part of what Boss Platt of New York called, 'the right of a man to run his own business in his own way, with due respect of course to the Ten Commandments and the Penal Code.'"

Roosevelt recognized that in a rich and complex industrial society some corporations and consolidations could become so big, and some individuals so wealthy, that power in greedy hands could work against the interests of small businessmen and ordinary citizens, whom he once called "Abraham Lincoln's plain people". That's why he believed in a strong executive and the creation of Federal agencies to ensure fair play. He wanted a "moral regeneration" of the business community. Indeed he led a revolt of the American conscience that was to dominate the American spirit right up to the First World War.

Before he was through, this Republican president settled a nationwide coal strike by using his Big Stick to get labor and management together and settle their dispute by arbitration in Washington, something no president had done before; got anti-trust legislation passed; began 40 suits against various trusts; ended discriminatory fees and rebates and other abuses by the railroads; achieved legislation to end unsanitary conditions tolerated by the beef trust. He established the Interstate Commerce Commission to ensure truly free markets, established the departments of Commerce and Labor and the Bureau of Corporations—all in the spirit of protecting the common folk against those with power to oppress them.

His vivacious leadership in many of his early roles—as reform Assemblyman, reform Civil Service Commissioner and reform Police Commissioner—and his work on reclamation and Federal irrigation projects—reinforced the reform movements of the early 1900s that had been kindled by the Muckrakers. The effect of TR's legislative initiatives, as Frederick Lewis Allen wrote, "was minor compared with the effect of his personality and his preaching upon a great part of a whole generation of Americans. He struck a new keynote for the times, and it resounded all over America."

After promising to continue fighting for "a square deal" for every American, Roosevelt was reelected in 1904 with the largest popular vote in the nation's history. His square deal was really not much more than a declaration to voters that he would continue using his power to fight for honesty and fairness. But that image of this St. George battling with powerful dragons captured the hearts and minds of ordinary people, who roared their appreciation at every opportunity.

The year 1907 was a mixed bag of joys and fears for America, but it certainly began on a high note. Trumpets sounded in the White

House to herald the first day of the new year. In the sunshine outside, lines of citizens four deep were waiting to wish a "happy New Year" to the President. This amazing queue of men in bowlers and ladies in dress hats and long dresses stood four abreast and extended for more than a mile down Pennsylvania Avenue and beyond.

Roosevelt, who had a reputation as the world's greatest hand-shaker, greeted his loving citizens that day with 8,150 hand-shakes, plus many smiles and quips. Elsewhere across the land Americans were congratulating themselves again. The *Washington Post* boasted: "On this day of our Lord, January 1, 1907, we are the richest people in the world." The paper calculated that the national wealth had been rocketing up at a rate of $4.6 billion a year during Roosevelt's two administrations. "Never have American farmers harvested such tremendous crops; railroads are groaning under the weight of unprecedented payloads; shipyards throb with record business; the banks are awash with a springtide of money."

TR had good words for Congress, saying "No Congress in our time has done more good work" (he had fairly trampled the Congress with his stampede of social legislation.) His Pure Food Act went into effect the very first day of the year. He was proud of the Panama Canal, which he'd visited recently on the first trip out of the country by a president. Abroad, he was lionized as an extraordinary diplomat—thanks to the peace that ensued from his negotiations of settlements in Eastern Asia and Europe and his handling of the Cuban insurrection, where he had taken charge swiftly to save the population from its foreign oppressors.

But on the domestic front, a shadow was cast over the heady events of early 1907 when that year became the first bad year for the American economy in a long while . As this situation played out, the financial crisis that occurred became one more example of the power of a strong leader to inspire public confidence when storm clouds threatened. However, in this case the strongman was not the President who, like most American presidents had little interest in or knowledge of the "dismal" subject of economics. In fact, he romped off to hunt bear in Louisiana just when a major dust-up in the financial markets occurred.

Recent events had choked off the capital needed for continued American expansion. The big railroads had soaked up capital for their own expansion, the farmers were stretched by a late crop season, the industrial tycoons had been using other peoples' savings to plunge into their own huge speculations, the Russo-Japanese war had drained capital abroad and on Wall Street stocks were falling for lack of buyers. Everyone who had money in a bank became alarmed, and runs started on the banks in places as remote as Butte, Montana.

The strongman who rescued the country from panic was from the private, not the public, sector. After mulling over the crisis while playing solitaire (his customary way of concentrating on a big problem) J.P. Morgan swept into action from his Madison Avenue "White House" on every possible front. He pressed into service the brightest young bankers in New York, putting them to work examining the books of all the financial institutions. He forced the trust company presidents to form an association. He summoned presidents of all the Wall Street banks to his office and by sheer force of personality made them come up with $27 million in pledges to restore financial order.

When New York's mayor sounded the alarm that the city was about to go broke, Morgan, in a remarkable display of bravura, wrote his own pledge of $30 million, without knowing how he could collar such a sum. He arranged for U.S. Steel to save the Tennessee Coal and Iron Company from bankruptcy, and he corralled 125 bankers, locked them in his library and brow-beat them into pledging $25 million to save the trust companies that held TC&I stock and other securities that were cascading. Using his powerful influence, this bigger-than-life-size financial wizard improvised brilliant solutions to the crisis and rescued the nation's economy. On New Year's Day 1908, with the crisis having passed, one of the bankers sent Morgan a richly bound copy of Shelley's "Prometheus Unbound", praising the old man as "our financial Prometheus."

President Roosevelt, the *political* Prometheus, had returned to Washington with his own triumph of sorts, boasting to the press that he had "got a bear" on his hunting trip in Louisiana. As the Christmas season approached, the President prepared for a gala holiday at the White House. Roosevelt's love of family resonates into our present day, when "family values" are having something of a revival, at least in political campaigns. His White House years included pillow fights, wrestling matches and hide-and-seek romps with his children. He considered "happy family lives" to be "the greatest happiness which there can be on this earth…The highest idea of family is attainable only where the father and mother stand to each other as lovers and friends. In these homes the children are bound to father and mother by ties of love, respect and obedience, which are simply strengthened by the fact that they are treated as reasonable beings with rights of their own, and that the rule of the household is changed to suit the changing years, as childhood passes into manhood and womanhood."

Morris took this passage to be symbolic of Roosevelt's attitude towards his country and the world. Transposed to public policy, government was strength in America—and in the world—just as the father brought strength to the home; mother represented upbringing, education, the spread of civilization. Children were to be "brought to maturity and then set free."

To the general public, TR remained an ever-present inspiration. Even in the year after he left office, on a tour of New York City he was treated to the first confetti and ticker tape parade up Broadway, showering him all the way on the triumphal mile to City Hall.

Roosevelt was not without his faults and failures. Particularly in later life, when he had lost the power he loved, his combative nature led to excesses of intolerance for other public figures, blind opposition to Wilson's programs including the League of Nations and a chauvinistic call for Germany's unconditional surrender. And, in opposing Taft in 1912, he bolted the Republican Party to form a third party, the Progressive or "Bull Moose" Party, shattering the party to which he had devoted his political life. Great crowds of TR-worshippers were still cheering for him, singing "Onward Christian Soldiers" and respectfully listening to his hearty preaching on The Ten Commandments. TR's third party, whose visionary platform called for reforms like social security and the minimum wage (which the nation adopted later) got more votes than any independent party in history. But it also assured that a Democrat, Woodrow Wilson, would become President.

But these failings notwithstanding, TR throughout his political reign was the most charismatic, exciting, entertaining and inspiring figure on the world stage. After Wilson succeeded TR in the White House, as Blum wrote: "Even the most partisan, most loyal supporter of Woodrow Wilson confessed unashamed when Roosevelt died that America loved him." America missed Roosevelt, wrote Blum: "It missed his spirit. It missed his fun. Even his critics knew when he died that there was no one quite like him to take his place."

The feminine revolution

While the history of "The Good Years", like the rest of American history to that time, was largely a story of many men and their achievements, at the start of the century the opening gun was fired in a revolution that was to lift the spirits—and ambitions—of the women of America. The plucky Texas schoolmistress who shot over Niagara Falls in a barrel in August 1901 was one of the pioneers of a revolution that would change forever the attitudes of the male-dominated society towards women, who had been bearing the status of a non-voting weaker sex whose opportunities for careers were not just limited but actually frowned upon.

To many men of TR's era, a "girl" who worked was sure to lose her "peach blossom" of innocence by mixing into the rough workaday world. Upper class women lived a cocoon-like existence guarded by servants, chaperones and patronizing older men. Middle-class housewives were expected simply to provide admiration and support for their hard-working mates. Working-class women filled the most menial jobs in manufacturing and services, at what would be regarded today as slaves' wages.

But the revolution was underway, and nothing could stop it. The "Gibson girl", artist Charles Dana Gibson's vision of the ideal, long-skirted society woman, appeared on golf courses and tennis courts, and even behind the wheels of the new automobiles. A few grand dames started riding their horses cross-saddle instead of side-saddle. The trend to bloomers shocked society's elders. Six-foot-tall Carry Nation, former wife of an alcoholic, was smashing saloon windows in Kansas and New York, convinced that she was divinely appointed to destroy that hardy American institution . "Muckraker" Ida Tarbell wrote blistering articles about errant business managements in McClure's Magazine. Emma Goldman, an immigrant from Lithuania, was preaching anarchy, and Jane Addams at her Hull House in Chicago was busy building one of the first social settlements for the poor and for social reform activities.

As for women's voting rights, Grover Cleveland proved to be way off base when he wrote in the October 1905 *Ladies' Home Journal* that "Sensible and responsible women do not want to vote. The relative positions to be assumed by man and woman in the working out of our civilization were assigned long ago by a higher intelligence than ours."

The fact was that women were clamoring for the right to vote, and that clamor grew louder year by year.

The first public convention on women's issues had taken place in a Seneca Falls, New York chapel on a hot July day in 1848. The 300 women attending, led by Elizabeth Cady Stanton, issued a feminist version of the Declaration of Independence called the Declaration of Sentiments. In this first salvo of the women's movement, they listed their grievances including the radical demand that women be given the right to vote (a right that was won after 72 more years of efforts.) They decried the legal and social status of women in the new republic, listing 18 areas of life where women's rights were denied. Two years later, at the anti-slavery convention in Boston, a small group of delegates called for a national women's rights convention, and this resulted in such a meeting in Worcester that fall. The first federal proposals for women's suffrage had been presented to Congress in 1868. The territory of Wyoming gave women full suffrage the following year, followed by Utah, Colorado and Idaho by 1896. The women's suffrage organizations had their own pavillion at the 1893 Chicago World's Fair.

One irrepressible optimist who virtually gave her life to this movement was a remarkable woman of Quaker stock, Susan B. Anthony. A brilliant and energetic organizer who held meetings in no less than 54 of New York's 61 counties in 1854 alone, this tireless leader founded the Working Woman's Association in 1868, led the women's movement for more than 50 years, worked tirelessly for women's rights worldwide and among other things pressed TR and Congress for a Constitutional Amendment for women's suffrage. In her 86th year this happy warrior attended the 1906 convention in Baltimore of the National American Woman Suffrage Association, the sisterhood she had led for nearly 40 years. After being acclaimed there, she took a train to Washington for her last birthday celebration.

This woman who had been laughed and scoffed at in her early days received homage from public officials and others, and a letter of congratulations from TR. With characteristic pluck she rose to say, "I wish the men would do something besides extend congratulations," reminding the cheering crowd that she had asked TR to push harder for the Constitutional amendment (the 19th Amendment guaranteeing women's suffrage finally passed in 1920, 14 years after her death.) But optimistic as ever in her final public words, she praised the many women who had worked for the cause, remarking, as Lynn Sherr wrote later, that "with such women consecrating their lives, failure is impossible!"

In the beginning, the suffragettes had been disappointed that so few women were willing to stand up and fight. Only a few hundred ladies marched down New York's Fifth Avenue through a drizzle with the Women's' Political Union on May 21, 1910 in the first suffrage parade. The next year about 3,000 women marched, but hecklers' jeers from the sidelines were even louder than the year before. The tide began to turn in 1912, when 50 women on horseback wearing three-cornered hats led 15,000 marchers past half a million cheering spectators. The marchers this time were a cross-section of female America—clerks and housewives, factory and shop girls, artists, nurses and society dames. When this march ended at Carnegie Hall one speaker after another heralded the new age of emancipation. "Never was the outlook brighter for the welfare of humanity", proclaimed one WPU speaker.

"The situation is dangerous", warned an old-guard editor of *The New York Times*. But the tide was turning, and would spread across the country. When Kansas became the eighth state to vote for suffrage the following November, the women there celebrated with a great community bonfire. At a signal they threw their old bonnets into the blaze. "As the flames rolled skyward," wrote Lord, "all of them could plainly see the passing of the old and the coming of a golden new day."

The women's liberation movement continued moving forward when Margaret Sanger opened the first family-planning clinic in Brooklyn, New York in 1916. During her 50-year career she coined the phrase birth control, founded the American Birth Control League (precursor of Planned Parenthood) and helped to develop the first contraceptive pill to be marketed in America. Defying church and state, she fired the spirits of women in this country and abroad to fight for control over their bodies and their destinies. One year after Sanger's clinic opened, well-organized suffragettes marched down New York's Fifth Avenue carrying placards bearing the signatures of over one million women demanding the right to vote.

Wealth and poverty, side by side

With progress underway on so many fronts, and the American economy running in high gear, there was still, however, one big festering sore on the belly of prosperous, hopeful America. The antithesis of American optimism, it went all the way back to the Spaniards' en-slavement of native Americans and to the anguish of Jefferson, Washington and others over the importation of African slaves and the unequal treatment of slaves and freemen. And to the present day it represents the greatest enduring blemish on the American character and on the American republic.

"At the turn of the century the gulf between wealth and poverty was immense," wrote Frederick Lewis Allen, who described the country as "an America in which such gaudy wealth was contrasted with such inhuman misery, especially among black citizens and immigrants." The lords of industry, a relatively small group of very rich men, wielded immense power, paid no income taxes and conducted their affairs without any regulatory agencies to interfere. The public loved to follow the doings of William K. Vanderbilt, whose Long Island palace had a garage for 100 cars; Mrs. Jacob Astor, who splashed about in a two-ton marble bathtub and James Hazen Hyde, whose masquerade ball, with costumes from the Court of Louis XV, was held in a replica of the palace of Versailles built for the occasion.

The public didn't seem to mind that the upper classes for the time being monopolized things like fast motor cars and college football; in fact, in the absence of television, ordinary citizens took pleasure in keeping track of such things in the press, and sometimes as spectators. When those 50 private parlor cars brought well-heeled football fans and players back to Grand Central Station from the Yale-Princeton game in New Haven, crowds were there just to gawk at society doing its thing. The majority of the public who merely read about the grand time being had by the rich shared the sense of good times, according to newspaper reports. The *New York Tribune* rang out the old year in 1905 with this cheery comment: "Never did a year close with a better record—never did a new year dawn with prospect brighter—Good times go marching on!"

The gap between the privileged few and the millions of people who worked for them, however, was enormous. The average wage of the roughly 30 million Americans in the workforce at the time was about four or five hundred dollars a year—less than $10 a week—and the average workday was 10 hours, six days a week. In the steel industry, the work week ran as high as 84 hours. In textile mills, 75 cents for a 10-hour day was not uncommon.

The annual income of the little steelmaster Andrew Carnegie was more than 20,000 times greater than that of the average American jobholder. Rich Americans like the Vanderbilts built themselves palatial houses, and the society dames of New York and Newport thought nothing of setting dinners for a hundred or more people on a whim or a fancy (this was easier then, when house servants worked for $3.50-4.00 a week and were willing to nest in tiny rooms many flights up from where they did their chores in the great houses.)

Workers in the mill and factory towns expanding in the East and elsewhere had little of the independence of the Americans of frontier days. They were wholly dependent on their employers; they didn't own the tools they worked with and they couldn't earn enough to make a move. By 1900 the "good American land" was filling up, as Allen put it, and the America of farms and villages had been transformed into a land of factory towns and cities.

A newspaper reporter and immigrant, Jacob Riis, wrote a book called *How the Other Half Lives* in 1890, one of the first exposés that awakened Americans to the horrors of the ghettos. Roosevelt read the book and offered his help; he also coined the term "muckraker" and befriended another muckraker, young Lincoln Steffens, during his tour of duty as New York police commissioner. A book called *Poverty* in 1904 estimated that there were ten to fifteen million Americans without the "basic necessaries" of life. Although places like New York had begun to provide playgrounds, parks and gyms for the poorest neighborhoods, the human misery of people at the bottom of the social scale included not only sickness but overcrowding, filthy living conditions and financial insecurity. No props existed such as Social Security, pensions or welfare. Labor unions were not yet defending the interests of lower-rung Americans.

Most of those imprisoned in the ugly urban and factory conditions were immigrants who streamed into the factory towns and slums of New York, Boston, Philadelphia and Chicago. Half a million of them landed in 1900 alone, and their numbers increased through most of the decade. Immigrants led some major strikes including 20,000 New York apparel workers who went on strike for three months in 1909 to protest low wages and to protest because employers made them pay for their own needles and thread. This was the first mass strike by women and it drew support from a Carnegie Hall benefit sponsored by J.P. Morgan's daughter and several other socialites.

Child labor was a sorry story. The 1890 census said nearly two million children aged 10–15 were working; by 1913 one in five of all American children were earning their own living, frequently working a 60-hour week and, in the cotton mills, working 12-hour days without time off for lunch. Twelve-year-olds were working in West Virginia coal mines and Georgia factories; in Pittsburgh a little girl rolled 1,000 cigars a day. In New York little children labored in tenement sweatshops. A bakery in the garment district handed out little apple turnovers as overtime pay for teen-agers working 80-hour weeks during the rush season. Five thousand little girls between 10–12 worked the cotton mill spindles in Southern cotton mills.

Reform, and war clouds

The reforming American spirit finally came to the rescue of the nation's underpriviledged children, just as it was to lift the lives of America's adult women. Reformers set up the National Child Labor Committee in 1904. Massachusetts passed a bill in 1913 setting an eight-hour day for anyone under 16. In the summer of 1914, a bill forbidding most children under 14 from working in mills and factories was passed in Georgia. A spate of new laws also governed factory safety, minimum hours for women and workmen's compensation.

The reform movement was part of a moralistic revival taking place around the country. The Progressive movement had been active at the state level ever since Robert M. LaFolette had been elected governor of Wisconsin in 1900. By the time that reformer went to the Senate in 1906, his state had set up a railroad commission to protect the public, required lobbyists to register and required examinations for civil service. The reform movement took some puritanical turns (the Bishop of Nashville forbade the tango.) But in January 1914 *Collier's Magazine* declared: "Fifty years from now the future historian will say that the ten years ending about January 1, 1914, was the period of the greatest ethical advance made by this nation in any decade."

But these positive changes, still very much short of broad and full social justice, were soon to be eclipsed by far-away events, before they could make major inroads on the serious domestic problems. In fact, on the very summer day when a Senate committee approved the child labor bill, Germany unexpectedly invaded Belgium. Within a few years the tramp of marching feet was heard around the world.

The summer of 1914 brought to a close a glorious chapter of American history. The new year was expected to usher in more happy times. "Sunshine movements and Prosperity Leagues were still blossoming", wrote Lord. "Nickelodeons winked on every side street, and in a burst of enthusiasm the press referred to them as 'the university of the poor'". On Broadway the first Ziegfeld Follies captivated the more affluent scions of society.

The languid summer had begun quietly. The Chatauqua arrived in Cheyenne, Wyoming with its popular spectacle of education and entertainment. The tango was catching on, from Coney Island to Denver, where thousands of people danced this high-toned step in the streets on the last night of the Elks' jamboree. Lavish parties were still being given in Newport, including Mrs. Belmont's Chinese Ball, for which she converted her marble house into the Imperial Palace of Peking. The sporting crowd was making bets on the America's Cup.

"So America continued to drift—another untroubled day of Eskimo Pies... droning electric fans... open-air trolley rides... winding up the Victrola to hear 'Sylvia' just once more," wrote Lord. On July 28, when Austria declared war on Serbia, that faraway scuff-up between foreign kings and princes, between the Kaiser and the Czar, at first seemed remote and dreamlike to a nation that was hitting its stride with all kinds of progress.

"Almost overnight, Americans lost a happy, easygoing, confident way of looking at things," wrote Lord. "Gone was the bright lilt of 'When You Wore a Tulip'; already it was the sadly nostalgic, 'There's a Long, Long Trail a-Winding' or the grimly suggestive, 'I Didn't Raise My Boy to Be a Soldier'.... Nothing seemed simple any more. Nothing was black and white. Nothing was 'right' or 'wrong' the way Theodore Roosevelt used to describe things."

Something had been lost, "a touch of optimism, confidence, exuberance, and hope. The spirit of an era can't be blocked out and measured, but it is there nonetheless. And in these brief, buoyant years it was a spark that somehow gave extra promise to life. By the light of this spark, men and women saw themselves as heroes shaping the world, rather than victims struggling through it."

A CENTURY OF WARS

The "Great Wars"

The century that began so confidently in peace was to wear a different face in history. It became an extraordinary century of warfare. The ebullient years of TR were all but swept from memory by the turbulence that followed. Within 75 years—just one lifetime—nearly 640,000 Americans would lose their lives in five wars, not counting about 1.4 million who suffered battle wounds. In the aftermath of each of these periods of war the incorrigible optimism of Americans re-asserted itself, phoenix-like, with various postwar intermissions featuring entertainers as different as flappers and hippies.

America's moral affirmations that began with the Puritans and were manifest in leaders such as Jefferson, Lincoln and the first Roosevelt were extrapolated into foreign affairs via the three major wars that were to dominate the 20th century. America entered the two "great" wars—World War One and World War Two—with the same moralistic spirit and enthusiasm that TR had brought to his era. The Korean War and the Gulf war, with far fewer casualties, also drew broad public support, because the public generally accepted the arguments of Harry Truman and George Bush that American national interests were imperiled. The Vietnam War was a wholly different story. It was the greatest jolt to Americans' traditional confidence and optimism since the beginning of the Republic.

The spirits of Americans have been lifted over two centuries by many things—by good times, popular political campaigns, by the experience of buying first homes and thus raising their living standards, by the exploits of national heroes and by their materialistic gush over forward-leaping products and services like Macintosh Powerbooks and Chrysler minivans. But their spirits have also been roused by warfare when it had a clear and moral national purpose.

Usually the public in a democracy abhors the thought of war and doesn't hesitate to say so. But strong, articulate leaders with firm vision can turn reluctance to resolution and action, if they convince people that theirs is an honorable cause worth the shedding of American blood. The Revolutionary War had such a leader in Washington, the Civil War in Lincoln. Later, Wilson and Eisenhower demonstrated again in their times how strong leaders, sure of their bearings, embodying high principles respected by the public, can maintain public morale and optimism, even enthusiasm, through periods of the most tragic warfare and destruction.

Idealism externalized

American idealism was externalized by Wilson, and later by Eisenhower, so effectively that millions of Americans went to battle with the same high spirits that had propelled them in peacetime to create the world's greatest industrial power. "People call me an idealist," said Wilson in one of his many speeches; "well, that is the way I know I am an American. America is the only idealistic nation in the world."

Wilson embodied the idealism founded on moral principles that had run through the Puritans, the founders, Lincoln and TR. Son of a Midwestern Presbyterian minister, married to the daughter of a Presbyterian minister, he grew up in a pious, scholarly family that read the Bible every day and sang hymns together on Sunday evenings. But in the grain of Jefferson and TR, he was also a true intellectual, with superb accomplishments behind him when he entered the White House in 1912.

Wilson's "resumé" for America's top job was remarkable. He had been scholar, professor (Bryn Mawr, Wesleyan and Princeton), Ph. D (Johns Hopkins University), college football coach (developing some of Wesleyan's best teams) and president of Princeton University, which he shook up completely and made into a major institution by leading it away from its snobbish, clubbish ways and introducing changes that influenced the course of education throughout the nation. Elected Governor of New Jersey in 1910, he turned his back on machine politics and politicians, just as TR had done. He pushed one reform after another through the legislature—reform of election primaries, schools and public utilities and reform of employers' liability as well as corrupt practices reform. One reporter of the time summed it up: "He licked the gang to a frazzle."

The public voted for reform and for progressive leadership when it elected Wilson to his first term as president. This was the culmination of years of progressive efforts to reduce the grip of a privileged elite on local and national affairs and to address social needs, to end graft in government and clean up slums. Wilson's reputation for reform rested on the name he had made for himself as governor defending public interests against the concentration of capital and other problems arising from the mushrooming growth of cities and the accumulation of power by big corporations.

His landslide election victory electrified the nation. He was an open and proud leader, the first president to hold a press conference, and the last to ride to his inauguration in a horse-drawn carriage, top-hatted beside outgoing President Taft. Starting right off at his inauguration ceremony he showed he had TR's gift for identifying with the people. He ordered the police to "let the people come forward" to fill the empty seats in front.

In his moving inaugural address Wilson called for a new era dedicated to meeting the needs of humanity. "I summon all honest men," he said, "all patriotic, all forward-looking men, to my side. God helping me, I will not fail them, if they will but counsel and sustain me!" His address was a high-toned ode to America and its moral force, as well as an admission of the country's problems still to be resolved. "Nowhere else in the world have noble men and women exhibited in more striking forms the beauty and the energy of sympathy and helpfulness and counsel in their efforts to rectify wrong, alleviate suffering, and set the weak in the way of strength and hope," he said. "We have built up, moreover, a great system of government, which has stood through a long age as in many respects a model for those who seek to set liberty upon foundations that will endure against fortuitous change, against storm and accident. Our life contains every great thing, and contains it in rich abundance."

Like others before and after him Wilson honestly believed, as his biographer Lord Devlin put it, that America had a moral mandate, that "what America touches, she makes holy." He was convinced that God had created one truly free and democratic nation, and that all other nations should study and learn from her.

Democratic President Wilson was at first more laissez-faire than Republican TR, who had been a firm believer in enlarged federal authority. Wilson advocated a "New Freedom", a Jeffersonian concept meaning that the federal government should ensure free competition among relatively small economic units and limit itself to enforcement. He wanted to set business free of monopolies and special privilege. Within a few months of his election he virtually killed protectionism, authorized the first (minuscule) income tax, got a historic act passed creating the Federal Reserve System, strengthened the Interstate Commerce Commission's authority to deal with unfair trade practices and in fact to oversee and restrain big business in general. Like Lincoln and TR, he stood rock-firm against a flood of abuse and criticism from special interests.

All was not peaceful on the domestic scene during Wilson's first term, however. Unions were seeking recognition,. unemployment and strikes disrupted many industries, homeless and hungry people demonstrated for attention and references were rife to "class struggle" over the disparity of wealth in the country.

But by 1917 much of the power that wealthy members of American society held at at the start of the century was subject to oversight by public officials. J.P. Morgan was dead, and his house had lost its control of 30 banks and corporations. City, state and federal administrations were expanding their services—operating public utilities, enforcing tenement laws, regulating transportation charges, policing business competition and sometimes deciding on hours of labor.

Wilson's re-election in 1916 more or less completed the triumph of such "progressivism". With a shrewd shift away from his former conservatism, he campaigned for liberal measures like a series of welfare acts for farmers including farm loan banks, a workman's compensation law for federal employees, an eight-hour day for railroad employees and a ban on interstate goods made by child labor. But he knew that his hairbreadth win was mostly based on the fact that many of the millions who voted for him had done so trusting that he would keep the country out of war. Americans were so much opposed to involvement in Europe's gruesome war that they raised Wilson to power on the theme: "He kept us out of war."

As for foreign policy, probably no other American president ever put the interests of other nations and people on such equal balance with those of his own country. He had the support of that silver-tongued champion of peace, William Jennings Bryan, who became his Secretary of State. Wilson believed the country's only international interest was to serve humanity and guide other nations to true democracy. The idealism and moral force that had run through American history since the Puritans virtually turned this Calvinist leader into a world missionary, putting his moral stamp on foreign policy.

The European powers of the time had no such altruistic bent. It was their nationalistic belligerence during three years of conflict that forced Wilson, and the American people, to see finally that preservation of American democratic values would require bearing arms again. When war had begun in 1914 Wilson proclaimed neutrality. There followed his long, excruciating period of efforts as peacemaker, even as German submarines were already sinking passenger liners. Brushing off his appeals on behalf of "the rights of humanity", the Germans made it increasingly hard for him and for his public to avoid entanglement. Evidence of German espionage in the U.S. was mounting, and the final straw was Wilson's disclosure of German plans to urge Mexico to attack the U.S. if it entered the war. In 1917 the Germans began unlimited submarine warfare against all merchant ships. Wilson immediately broke relations with Germany, and enraged Americans began demanding that America join the fight.

American public opinion did an about-face within a year after Wilson's election. The German submarines had fired at American as well as other merchant ships. After agonizing all through 1916, Wilson decided early the following year to scrap neutrality and to join the Allies, who had already been fighting on bloody battlefields for three years. He believed his neutrality policy had been right; but the war and the world had changed. Personally convinced that God was on his side, and had appointed him to do the right thing, he resolved to plead heart and soul for immediate American military action. Wilson quickly became an eloquent spokesman for his angry public, a leader fully in tune with his citizens and fully prepared to execute programs that would finally engage American power and turn his idealistic words into action.

Uniting U.S. power and moral conviction, he made the war his personal mission. On April 2, 1917 he drove to the Capitol with a cavalry escort. He spoke emotionally to a joint session of Congress, charging that German actions were in fact "nothing less than war against the government and people of the United States." To thunderous applause, he asked Congress to declare war on Germany, saying: "The world must be made safe for democracy." He said: "It is a fearful thing to lead this great peaceful people into war, into the most terrible and disastrous of all wars, civilization itself seeming to be in the balance. But the right is more precious than peace, and we shall fight for the things which we have always carried nearest our hearts—for democracy, for the right of those who submit to authority to have a voice in their own governments, for the rights and liberties of small nations, for a universal dominion of right by such a concert of free peoples as shall bring peace and safety to all nations and make the world itself at last free. To such a task we dedicate our lives and our fortunes…"

"From the halls of Congress the deafening thunder of applause reverberated round the world," wrote historian Arthur S. Link. With Wilson leading the way, stirring people throughout the country with his speeches, Americans rallied with great loyalty and patriotism. They had distrusted the Kaiser and the military clique running Imperial Germany; now distrust flamed to anger. An almost crusading spirit swept the nation. People were singing, "I'm a Yankee Doodle Dandy", "Over There" and other war songs and Charlie Chaplin, Douglas Fairbanks and Mary Pickford were among the film stars who drew huge crowds to liberty-bond rallies.

Movies like "The Fall of a Nation" imagined an attack on the U.S by goose-stepping invaders. A great Preparedness Parade of 150,000 men marched up New York's Fifth Avenue carrying American flags. Americans really had gone war-mad. "There has probably never been a war in history so passionately embraced in a flush of naïve patriotic ecstasy as America's war against the Kaiser," wrote the American Heritage editors.

Beginnings of Big Government

As Robert Nisbet was to write years later, "Rarely has the sense of national community been stronger than it was in America during the Great War. True, that sense had to be artificially stimulated by a relentless flow of war propaganda from Washington and a few other pricks of conscience, but by the end of the war a stronger national consciousness and sense of cohesion was apparent." Perceptively, Nisbet added: "But as we know in retrospect, with these gains came distinct losses in Constitutional birthright."

Wilson made the war "his road to salvation for not only America but the world," Nisbet said, "and in the process he made the war the single most vivid experience a large number of Americans have ever known. Even the casualties (not many compared to those of France, Britain, Russia and Germany) didn't dampen enthusiasm at home; nor did the passage of legislation which put in the president's hands the most complete thought control ever exercised on Americans."

To lift all Americans up to his lofty perspective on the war, Wilson set up a former newsman, George Creel, as head of a ministry of war information. One of the canny innovations of this propaganda czar was the mobilization of "four-minute men"— volunteers who could speak for four minutes at public forums, clubs, schools and other places to encourage support of the government and its war mission. Besides this force that grew to 70,000, another several hundred thousand citizens volunteered to be "neighborhood watchers", reporting to government agencies anything that smacked of dissent from the nation's new course.

"Home Front Awards", honors and decorations were bestowed on "The Worker of the Week", "The Farmer of the Week" and "The Surgeon of the Decade", among others. A virtual police-state atmosphere was created by government agents' raids on private homes, businesses and other places where dissenters gathered. Defense societies were swamped by volunteers offering their support.

The Congress, which declared war on Germany in April 1917, swung as radically from neutrality to a war temper as Wilson had done. In its fervor it granted war powers to the Wilson regime that went beyond anything the nation had ever experienced. "In a series of the most remarkable laws ever enacted in Washington," wrote Charles and Mary Beard, "the whole economic system was placed at his command."

Among the new Washington agencies and boards that were created one of the most powerful was the War Industries Board, whose powers to grant licenses and authorizations for various forms of economic activity gave it authority over the whole economy. The most lasting impact on American society of World War One, and the second world war as well, was the expansion of the federal government's role beyond anything ever imagined by the Founders or by the succeeding generations.

Wilson's political, economic, social and even intellectual reorganization of America during the 1917–1919 period was described by Nisbet as "one of the most extraordinary feats in the long history of war and polity." Through "artfully created" boards, commissions and agencies, "he and his worshipful lieutenants, drawn from all areas— business, academia, law, even entertainment—revolutionized America to a degree never reached in such a short period of time by either the French or the Russian revolution." Within only a few months Wilson had transformed a basically decentralized America, having a constitutional system providing separation of powers and devolution of considerable powers to the states, into a war state that reached into the lives of virtually all Americans. The momentum of this upheaval, and the benefits such as high wages for many Americans, assured public support and even enthusiasm for the new nationalism.

Although Wilson demobilized the country after the war, an enormously important precedent had been set for expansion of federal power. Reflecting this sea change in American economic policy, and presaging America's swings to the left, was a truly seminal book published in the last of TR's White House years. It emerged from the progressive ferment that provided an intellectual structure for the policies first undertaken in TR's "New Nationalism", then in Wilson's creation of a war state, and finally was taken to full term in the second Roosevelt's "New Deal."

The book was *The Promise of American Life* by Herbert Croly, who, with Walter Lippmann and other writers, founded the New Republic magazine. TR called the book, published in 1909, "the most powerful and illuminating study of national conditions" that had appeared in years. The book made Croly one of the foremost political philosophers in America. Croly's passion for political programs to benefit the less fortunate members of society, together with the philosophy of John Dewey, were the underpinnings of the golden age of liberalism and its optimistic hopes for improving American life.

Croly started this sweeping study with the upbeat observation that "never has it been our fortune to catch the slightest whisper of doubt, the slightest want of faith, in the chief God of America—unlimited belief in the future of America." He wrote: "The faith of Americans in their own country is religious, if not in its intensity, at any rate in its almost absolute and universal authority. It pervades the air we breathe. As children we hear it asserted or implied in the conversation of our elders. Every new stage of our educational training provides some additional testimony on its behalf."

Then he pointed out that all the conditions of American life had tended to encourage an easy, generous, and irresponsible optimism. "Had it not been for the Atlantic Ocean and the virgin wilderness," he wrote, "the United States would never have been the Land of Promise." The country, he said, was virtually free from "alien interference" and could experiment with political and social ideals as no nation had done before.

The American past, Croly wrote, "compared to that of any European country, has a character all its own. Its peculiarity consists in the fact that from the beginning it has been informed by an idea. From the beginning Americans have been anticipating and projecting a better future for themselves. From the beginning the Land of Democracy has been figured as the Land of Promise, the promise of a better future." However, after much reflection, he concluded that "this better future… will have to be planned and constructed rather than fulfilled of its own momentum."

Croly saw that American life had changed radically as a result of industrialization, technology, the unfettered growth of big corporations, the shift from an agricultural to an urban society and, above all, by the very uneven distribution of wealth and opportunity that had resulted from these changes. He decided that the freedom and individualism promoted by Jefferson's philosophy had led American society into excesses of greed and income disparity, putting a cloud over the American dream. He charged that the public had misused democracy as "a happy device for evading collective responsibilities by passing them on to the individual." He felt that the public wrongly assumed that the "promise" would be fulfilled automatically, simply through free-wheeling competition.

Croly's book pinpointed a big question that haunts Americans to this day, perhaps the most important issue in the nation's future: that is, the increased insecurity and in some cases poverty of those left hanging on the lower rungs of society as the nation drives forward. "American energy has been consecrated to economic development," he wrote. "The businessman in seeking to realize his ambitions and purposes was checked neither by government control nor social custom.... No great intelligence is required to detect in this situation the evidence of a vicious circle. The absorption of Americans in business affairs, and the free hand which the structure and ideals of American life granted them, had made business competition a fierce and merciless affair, while at the same time the fluid nature of American economic conditions made success very precarious."

Croly's prescription for restoring the American dream was for the nation to steer in a Hamiltonian direction to a more "professional" approach to the problems of modern life, in short to an assumption of "national responsibility." He accused corrupt state and city governments of failing the public in part because they lacked "centralized, responsible organization." The central government, therefore, should take responsibility for beneficent planning for social improvement. He summoned the nation to experiment with collective action and "constructive" regulation, in pursuit of a "collective purpose."

This challenge was met by Wilson and his czars, such as Bernard Baruch, Hugh Johnson, Herbert Hoover and Gerard Swope, in their planning and managing of the wartime economy. Croly's intellectual arguments were reflected also in Wilson's other expansions of federal intervention, in Franklin D. Roosevelt's programs in the '30s to crank up a stalled economy and indeed to this day in the prescriptions of liberal lawmakers and bureaucrats for federal answers to the social problems that began undermining American life in the '60s.

Wilson never lost his optimism, though his dream of a world order based on moral principles, on the principle of Christian love rather than power politics, was never fulfilled. In the best of his many great speeches, he had proposed his "Fourteen Points" to the Congress, a high-minded, clear-thinking guide for world peace. Five of the points expressed general ideals, calling among other things for free trade among nations. His last point called for a League of Nations to ensure the peace. Two months after that speech an armistice negotiated by Wilson was proclaimed.

The State Department released the news early on November 11, 1918 and by late afternoon horns, bells, sirens and whistles were sounding off across America. Newsboys handed out the good news to a public first skeptical, because only four days before they had heard a false report of peace, then wildly jubilant as they realized this time it was for real. People flooded the streets, offices closed for the day. Young women kissed every soldier in sight. Crowds burned effigies of the Kaiser. And within days the fuel-saving blackouts ended, Broadway lit up again and families prayed that the names of their fighting men would not be on the war casualty lists still being published daily.

Leading the U.S. delegation to the Paris Peace Conference, Wilson became the first American President in office to cross the Atlantic. On December 14, 1918 he rode in his carriage through the streets of Paris, where he was greeted with a tumultuous welcome and banners celebrating "Wilson le juste", an acclaim greater than anything ever seen before. Everywhere he went in Europe streets were mobbed with crowds who cheered him as the peacemaker and the hope of all humanity. He toured France, Italy and England in a glow of triumph. His passage through the streets of London was compared to a Coronation procession. And, for his efforts, like TR before him, Wilson was awarded the Nobel Peace Prize for seeking a fair peace agreement and for proposing the League of Nations. Winston Churchill said of him: "He played a part in the fate of nations incomparably more direct and personal than any other man."

But while the world recognized his pivotal role in history, and his leadership in drafting the Versailles Treaty at the 1919 Paris Peace Conference, the American Congress was turning to domestic affairs. The peace treaty was defeated in the Senate. The victorious Allies and most neutral nations joined the League, but not the U.S. The League went on to accomplish many peacekeeping missions as Wilson had envisioned. It set a pattern for international organization on which much of the United Nations was later modeled long after the League collapsed in the face of wars among its members and the rise of Hitler.

Against his doctor's advice, Wilson had campaigned vigorously for the League across the country, finally collapsing with a stroke in Wichita, Kansas. In his last public speech, outside his home, still sounding like a good Presbyterian preacher, his dauntless optimism still rose above his setbacks:

"I cannot refrain from saying it," he said, "I am not one of those who have the least anxiety about the triumph of the principles I have stood for. I

have seen fools resist Providence before and I have seen their destruction, as will come upon them again... utter destruction and contempt. That we shall prevail is as sure as that God reigns."

UP AND DOWN: FROM THE TWENTIES TO THE DEPRESSION

The era known as "The Twenties", while it lasted, for eleven years between the end of the war with Germany and the stock market crash on November 13, 1929, had an impact on the American spirit far out of proportion to its brief life. It was a joyride, at least for the growing minority who could afford it. F. Scott Fitgerald called it the "greatest, gaudiest spree in history."

From boom to bust in one decade, it began with the inevitable unleashing of spirits and behavior that follows the harsh discipline of war. It ended with the equally inevitable crash that occurs when joy-riders drive too fast, flout time-honored rules of the road, drink too much and don't look where they're going. All in all, though, it left a major imprint on American character. Many of its influences are visible today, in fact are driving some of the most promising and some of the most disturbing developments in America's evolving culture.

After the patriotic ecstasy of the war against the Kaiser, after the battle victories of the Yanks who came to the rescue of their European allies and after the enormous celebrations set off by sirens, whistles and bells announcing the signing of the armistice on November llth, America turned its mind back to the pursuit of pleasures at home—material, sensational and even spiritual. The doughboys enjoyed the brief acclaim of cheering crowds but then turned somewhat cynical when memories of their brave deeds were eclipsed by a very different kind of excitement in one of the wildest decades in American history. Among other things the nation, tired of war and its demands, cast off old moral and ethical restraints.

As for American women, who had been spending their time knitting socks and making wartime sacrifices, they were finally ready to claim—and demonstrate—their own independence. Their long fight for the vote ended with ratification of the 19th Amendment in August 1920. But the postwar American woman's emancipation went far beyond that. She sheared her locks, shortened her skirts to a daring inch above the knee, dabbed on cosmetics, flattened her hips, affected a new poise, a new sleek chic, and discarded many if not most of her old scruples. Once regarded as the guardian of morality and proper behavior, the model for the morally weaker sex, the new American woman started smoking cigarettes, cutting her hair short in a "bob", rolling her stockings to just above the knee and sometimes even putting a foot on the old brass rail at the speakeasy bar and drinking with the men.

The high spirits of the times were a far cry from the simple pastoral pleasures of that happy farmer, Crevecoeur, and his concept of happiness. The gospel of Vienna's Sigmund Freud convinced the trend-setters of a new generation that sex was the central and pervasive force in human life. Their way to pleasure was to have an uninhibited sex life.

A new crop of sex and confession magazines, and the new "realism" of film and stage, together with the combined influence of Prohibition, cocktail parties and the new freedom afforded by automobiles, almost swept the old, established notions of family and matrimonial fidelity into oblivion. The word "puritan" had become a term of ridicule. Just as rebel spirits of future times would express themselves in rock, pop and grunge, the rebels of the '20s flourished their gin flasks and their raccoon coats at football games and shed their inhibitions, on the supposition that *they* had found the good life.

The upper-class role models deliberately cultivated whatever was new, shocking and frequently vulgar. The old inherited modes of behavior were passé. "Boiled", "stewed" and "fried" joined the new vocabulary. On the New York stage, a character's "damn" or "hell" got no rise at all. "In fact," the editors of *American Heritage* wrote, "anything that inhibited self-expression was deemed intrinsically bad. Even the old respectable *Saturday Evening Post* succumbed and allowed drinking, petting and unfaithfulness to be mentioned in its stories, whose illustrations showed women smoking." One reflection of the new status of infidelity was the climbing divorce rate, rising from less than one in eleven in 1910 to one in six by 1928.

Fast beat of the Jazz Age

Nothing caught the '20s spirit more dramatically than the syncopated beat of jazz, a Negro creation that answered the age's hunger for fresh pleasures. The big bands of Duke Ellington, Fletcher Henderson and Paul Whiteman, blues performers like Bessie Smith, Ma Rainey and Cab Calloway and instrumentalists like Jelly Roll Morton, Bix Biederbecke and Louis Armstrong were on their way to becoming legends. New Orleans-born jazz, elaborated on by Chicago's Louis Armstrong, flowered in Harlem and became the rage of the upper-set "flaming youth" and by 1922 gave the exuberant "jazz age" its name.

Fads swept the country, among them the Charleston, which moved down from Harlem to the New York stage when a male chorus line danced it in the Broadway musical, "Runnin' Wild"; the shimmy; dance marathons; the Chinese game Mah Jong; miniature golf; Eskimo Pies; Stutz Bearcat races and crossword puzzles (*The Cross-Word Puzzle Book* was a 1924 best seller.) And Hollywood ballyhoo turned a little Frenchman, Emil Cóue, into the most talked-of person in the country: the institutes established in his name taught Americans to repeat his dictum: "Day by day in every way I am getting better and better."

In the White House, from 1921 to his death in the summer of 1923, Warren Gamaliel Harding—an affable, handsome, poker-playing, horseshoe-pitching small-town pol who led the "return to normalcy" and was probably America's all-time least qualified chief executive—set a loose tone of behavior compared with anything seen in Washington before him. He brought scandalous sex to his high office by coupling with his 20-year-old mistress in the White House coat closet. His White House study typically was filled with trays of whiskey, poker chips and cards and an entourage of assorted cronies made themselves at home there. His highest aim was to become America's best-loved president, and despite his failings this good-natured man was loved by his people and mourned when he suddenly died.

Harding was betrayed by friends who used their Washington connections for personal gain. But he didn't live to witness the full scale of his administration's scandals. He was succeeded in the White House by Calvin Coolidge, a flinty New Englander famous for his four-hour workday, his frequent naps and his devotion to pro-business, laissez-faire policy-making.

The most gifted chronicler of the hell-raising '20s of course was the young writer Scott Fitzgerald, whose novel, *This Side of Paradise*, published at the start of the decade, ushered in the new era, haunting the decade "like a song, popular but perfect", as critic Glenway Wescott put it. The novel's wholesome hero left his Midwestern town to go to Princeton, as Fitzgerald had done, where he watched libertine girls doing "impossible things like eating three o'clock after-dance suppers... talking of every side of life with an air of earnestness, half of mockery, yet with a furtive excitement" that the young man considered "a real moral let-down" compared with his conservative small-town boyhood.

Yet this impressionable young character, Amory Blaine, personified the preoccupation of his generation with keeping up with new modes of conduct and dress and with the sensations and pleasures of the moment—as, for example, the moment when Amory, in a haze of first love, looks at himself in his mirror with satisfaction. "As he put in his studs," wrote Fitzgerald, "he realized that he was enjoying life as he would probably never enjoy it again." The generation pictured in Fitzgerald's novels was actually the top cut of the postwar generation—the young, monied crowd that equated success with money, lived high on the hog, wasted their money and eventually burned themselves out. But while the party lasted they raised a lot of hell and had a lot of fun.

The motor car changes everything

Nothing changed society more profoundly during the '20s than the "motor car", which brought with it new thrills and profoundly changed America's social scene. By 1923 the Ford Motel T "Tin Lizzie" ruled the road. It leapt forward with a roar at the driver's command and bounced like mad over the rough, muddy roads that were unprepared for it. Affluent citizens bought stunning Pierce-Arrows or Cadillacs. Ford's first pickup, the Model T Runabout, came out in 1925. Indifferent to the lack of good highways, automobiles soon were everywhere, providing youngsters with an escape from parental supervision (a new sanctum for courtship on country roads instead of on the front porch or in family parlors) and opening up new adventures for vacationing families, providing a boon to housewives running errands and a new opportunity for everyone to enjoy new sports and speed.

Between 1920 and 1929 the auto population exploded from eight million to more than 23 million. The price of Ford's "Flivver" was within reach of most wage earners by 1924. These buggies pulled city

146

and country together, and as cars multiplied so did jobs, creating still more demand for cars. And as road builders laid new trails across the country new businesses sprang up along the way to serve the motorists. Humorist Will Rogers, while tipping his hat to Henry Ford for starting all this, declared that "it will take a hundred years to tell whether you have helped us or hurt us, but you certainly didn't leave us as you found us."

President Coolidge's trademark statement that "the chief business of the American people is business" typified the laissez-faire atmosphere that accompanied the loose government of the Harding-Coolidge years. Industrial production jumped nearly 50% from 1920 to 1929. American industrialists developed new manufacturing techniques and American architects had contests for skyscraper design. There were more things for Americans to buy than ever before—not just cars but also cheap electric and mechanical devices that lightened housekeeping, a wide range of foods that could now be kept fresh in refrigerators, new clothes to match the new, jazz-age styles, beach pajamas, cosmetics, vacation bungalows, Florida real estate speculations and many other things that most people had never indulged in before. The consumer economy went on a tear.

Of course the '20s was a golden age only for a privileged part of the public. Wage increases in general were relatively small, income distribution became more unequal and some industries—farming, coal mining, shipping, textiles and railroads—were downright sick. Some 60% of the population had incomes that the Brookings Institution called below the poverty line. "There has been a tendency," observed Brookings' economists, "at least during the last decade or so, for the inequality of income to be accentuated."

Still, the bankers and brokers walked like kings and the rich kept getting richer. The era was big on heroes and, since business had become god, among the biggest heroes were businessmen like Henry Ford and Samuel Insull. Ford had became a virtual folk hero when he announced in 1914 that the basic wage for his workers would be $5 a day, considerably above the national average. While this had helped him win esteem as a friend of labor, it was most likely intended to keep out the unions. Ford's antipathy towards unions, his lack of sympathy for assembly-line workers who put in grueling hours at repetitive jobs, his ugly battles against strikers and his practice of putting ex-FBI men and ex-cops in the plants to oversee workers was only modified when his wife Clara threatened to walk out on him if he didn't recognize the unions he had battled so viciously.

The enormous success of Ford cars enabled the company to keep on producing more or less the same simple, all-black models until 1925 when Chevrolet offered consumers a choice of colors. By 1926 Chevrolet's sales were overtaking Ford and a promoter and carriage-maker by the name of William Crapo Durant was buying up one car company after another to create the giant General Motors empire. These two men, Ford and Durant, two great entrepreneurial dreamers, were mainly responsible not only for putting Americans on the road but also for the huge auto industry that was fueling the boom and the construction of new highways and new suburban communities all over America.

Radio and motion pictures

Also affecting the traditional habits of Americans, and offering them a new dimension of cozy pleasure, was the development of radio. By the winter of 1921–22, only a year after the opening of the first broadcast station in Pittsburgh, radio music including a lot of dance music and classical music was being listened to by millions. By 1925 some 50 million Americans were tuning in on their Crosleys or on fancy consoles or radio sets made from mail-order kits.

Radio sales soared as broadcasts like the Democrats' '24 convention at Madison Square Garden, the famous Scopes trial in '25, the crooning of Rudy Vallee and the sportscasts of Graham McNamee as well as Sunday sermons and morning exercises brought new life into living rooms across the country. By the end of the decade 40% of American homes had radios. Broadway stars like Eddie Cantor and Al Jolsen brought vaudeville to this new medium, and in the summer of 1929 two white minstrel players introduced the first and most famous sitcom, the "Amos 'n Andy Show", which enjoyed immense popularity as listeners, glued to their sets, followed nightly the trivial doings around the Fresh Air Taxicab Company and the fraternal lodge of the Mystic Knights of the Sea.

Another society-changing industry was the motion picture business, which reached new heights in the '20s. Idols of the silent screen like Valentino, Fairbanks, John Barrymore and Mary Pickford, Gloria

Swanson and Clara Bow, brightened ordinary lives with vicarious excitement and glamour. In their films and in their lives the '20s stars maintained a reputation for wickedness that seemed to stick to them. Hundreds of films depicted a high society that featured loose affairs, fast cars and hip flasks. Divorces, drug addictions, even murders gave a scandalous tone to the Hollywood scene, prefiguring the preoccupation with crime and misbehavior that was to dominate so much of the movies and, later, so much of television.

But if Hollywood gave crime a new cachet, Prohibition did so in spades, and made law-breakers of a large part of the general public. The 18th Amendment to the Constitution, passed at the start of the decade, outlawed manufacture, sale or transport of intoxicating liquors. It was a fruitless effort by government to defend the conservative ideals of rural America against the threats of radical social change precipitated by industrialism and the rapid growth of the wicked cities and their amoral cultures.

The practical effects of this effort to legislate morality were to increase drinking among the prosperous classes (it did reduce drinking among the common folk) and to explode the prices paid for illegal alcohol, thus creating a whole new world of adventure, crime and excitement built around ingenious efforts to circumvent the law. Bathtubs became mixing vats for gin, speakeasies with peephole doors became dramatic rendez-vous, bootleggers sold whisky and bourbon for as much as ten times pre-Prohibition prices and smuggling became big business. All this produced enormous wealth for underworld bosses who smuggled the booze and ran the speakeasies (32,000 in New York alone) and elevated crime and gang wars to front-page news all over the country. The gangsters carved up their "territories" and Al Capone and his seven-ton bulletproof limousine, surrounded by bodyguards' cars, became a tourist attraction in Chicago.

The New York Daily News, whose lead stories were usually about crime or sex, became the largest daily circulation newspaper by 1924. Other newspapers and tabloids also found that crime "sold". Grisly murder trials like the trial of Leopold and Loeb for the "thrill crime" of murdering a 14-year-old boy, and the trial of Frances Stevens Hall for the murder of her minister-husband and his mistress, were splashed across front pages nationwide.

But all the heroes and celebrities were by no means criminals. At the other end of the moral compass, so to speak, a new breed of back-to-the-Bible religionists were stirring the spirits of vast throngs of followers who abhorred Jazz Age sinfulness. Preachers like Billy Sunday and Aimee Semple McPherson became big-time operators, whipping up a fundamentalist fury with their showmanship and mass soul-saving. In a gaudy Los Angeles temple, to the accompaniment of a carnival of lights and wailing sirens, "Sister Aimee" praised Jesus as "the greatest scrapper that ever lived" and called her followers to redemption.

Billy Sunday, a major league baseball player turned flamboyant evangelist, preached to over 100 million people and was said to have converted over a million in his high-powered campaigns. The odd embracing of religion by business reached a peak when an advertising man, Bruce Barton, gave the pop-religion trend an especially vulgar turn when he published *The Man Nobody Knows*, the nonfiction bestseller of 1925–6, depicting Jesus and his disciples as go-getting businessmen who had staged the world's greatest sales campaign.

Most of the intellectuals of the era naturally turned against the grain of this kind of ballyhoo, rebelling equally against the huckster-ism of businessmen and preachers on one hand and, on the other hand, against what they considered the phony prudishness of the age and the emphasis on material things. In so doing they created a lot of excitement in society's upper circles by upsetting sacred apple carts. Sinclair Lewis, who actually believed in the old virtues, ridiculed the small town boosters who didn't live up to the old ideals in his books like *Main Street*, a devastating satire of the small town Gopher Prairie as seen through the eyes of his sophisticated heroine. Journalist H.L. Mencken ridiculed practically everything "respectable" and averred in his essay "On Being an American" that the American people "constitute the most timorous, sniveling, poltroonish, ignominious mob of serfs and goosesteppers ever gathered under one flag in Christendom since the end of the Middle Ages..."

The most wholesome heroes of the times were in sports, as the '20s kicked off America's long and passionate love affair with star athletes. Sports helped to erase some of the divisions of race, class and other cultural differences in what had become a very heterogeneous society. The '20s was the golden age of baseball. Tens of millions of Americans were thrilled as they counted Babe Ruth's 714 home runs, grinned

150

at the fierce temper tantrums of Ty Cobb and developed the habit of opening their newspapers first to the sports section to find out how their favorite teams were doing. Sports fans themselves got into the action too: on golf courses in their baggy plus-fours and checked stockings, in tennis clubs and on crowded beaches.

Nearly 75,000 people watched Jack Dempsey knock out Georges Charpentier in Jersey City in 1921, the first of the huge million-dollar boxing bouts of the decade. In football, Knute Rockne, Red Grange ("The galloping ghost") and the "Four Horsemen" (also known as "The Cyclone from Indiana") became household names, as did the names of Johnny Weismuller, the fastest swimmer of the age, Bill Tilden and Helen Wills who dominated the tennis courts, Barney Oldfield, the auto racer, Gertrude Ederle, the swimmer and the amazing Bobby Jones in golf. Among the great sports writers were Grantland Rice and Heywood Broun (Broun was the one who wrote "The Ruth is mighty and shall prevail" in his reporting of the Yankees' win over the Giants at the Polo Grounds.)

A youthful hero

But of all the '20s heroes one stood out on the scale of Columbus, a lone genius defying the skeptics of the time, whose feat of courage had almost mystical vibrations for generations afterwards. That hero of course was the 25-year-old former St. Louis-to-Chicago mail-running pilot who made history traveling in the opposite direction of Columbus but, like the admiral, opened a new era for all mankind.

At 3 a.m. on May 20, 1927, the year Babe Ruth hit 60 home runs for the Yankees, in driving rain and darkness over Roosevelt Field in Long Island, New York, Charles Augustus Lindbergh gunned the engine of his little shiny silver monoplane and took off for what would be the most celebrated flight in history. At nearby Yankee Stadium that night 40,000 people waiting for the start of a heavyweight boxing bout between Jack Sharkey and Tom Maloney rose to their feet when the referee, Joe Humphreys, pointed his arm to the sky and asked them to "think about a boy up there tonight who is carrying the hopes of all true-blooded Americans. Say a little prayer for Charles Lindbergh!" Nothing could better illustrate the suspense and excitement that swept the nation as the little plane made its way jerkily across the skies.

The whole nation, listening to hourly radio bulletins, held its breath as Lindbergh piloted his craft past Newfoundland through sleet and fog and disappeared into the stormy North Atlantic. The young pilot had nothing to guide him over the ocean but a compass, a sextant and a chart on his knees. Sitting in a wicker seat, he was forced to use a small periscope to peer ahead because his gasoline tank was directly in the line of view. He read the stars by tilting his head backwards. A couple of times he flew as low as 50 feet above the water. The flight lasted 33½ hours and defied many observers and experts, including the French newspaper *Paris-Soir,* which had considered it doubtful "that a single flyer can stay awake and alert long enough to challenge successfully the dark forces waiting to do battle with him over the Atlantic."

The extraordinarily cool and confident young man brought his plane down at Le Bourget airport. He received a fantastic welcome from the French public. Europe's kings and presidents opened their doors for this most admired man in the world. He rode before half a million people though the streets of Paris, received the Cross of the Legion d'Honneur from the president of France and the Gold Medal of the Municipality of Paris, after which he addressed the French National Assembly. President Coolidge sent a navy cruiser to bring him and *The Spirit of St. Louis* back from France.

On his return to Washington the U.S. Armed Forces put nearly every aircraft they had into the air to greet him and he was saluted by guns ashore and from an offshore cruiser. The hillsides were jammed with people as he proceded in a parade to the Washington Monument. Coolidge presented him with the Distinguished Flying Cross and Congress awarded him the Medal of Honor. In New York on June 13 he was greeted by 200 boats, 75 planes and close to five million people. He was showered with 1,800 tons of ticker tape and paper in a spectacular parade up Fifth Avenue.

His air tour across the country fanned further "the Lindbergh religion" as adoring crowds greeted him everywhere. Young women particularly swooned at the sight of him and even purloined pillow slips from hotels where he slept and pinned them to their walls. Among the many tributes to the daring pilot was a carefree new dance called the Lindy Hop, which started in Harlem and in a few years would become therapy for depressed spirits in depression times. The song "Lucky Lindy" celebrated his feat.

Throughout all this he maintained an uncorrupted modesty and quiet dignity that was totally out of sync with the Age of Ballyhoo. A spiritually starved nation, Frederick Lewis Allen declared in *Only Yesterday*, a nation which had been feeding on cheap heroics and scandal and crime, "was revolting against the low estimate of human nature which it had allowed itself to entertain." No other American, except perhaps Lincoln, had ever commanded such respect from the public, remaining a national idol for years after his time. The roads to Lindbergh's New Jersey farm were filled with weekend crowds of admirers for several years after his flight, and his picture was hung in thousands of homes and hundreds of schoolrooms.

America's fascination with qwirky mavericks was to be re-ignited by another aviator known as "Wrong Way Corrigan", who took off from Brooklyn ostensibly on a nonstop solo flight to Los Angeles but landed instead in Dublin, Ireland. Having failed to get permission for a trans-Atlantic flight in his jerry-built plane, he fooled the authorities by claiming to have mistakenly gone in the wrong direction. When he returned to New York, he got a tumultuous welcome; a crowd of a million admirers lined lower Broadway for a ticker-tape parade even bigger than the one New York had given Lindbergh.

The Jazz Age ended in 1929, Fitzgerald wrote in "Echoes of the Jazz Age", because "the utter confidence which was its essential prop received an enormous jolt, and it didn't take long for the flimsy structure to settle earthward... It was borrowed time anyhow—the whole upper tenth of a nation living with the insouciance of grand dukes and the casualness of chorus girls... Even when you were broke you didn't worry about money, because it was in such profusion around you."

In a later reminder that high spirits don't necessarily equate with true happiness, Frederick Lewis Allen wrote that "with the old order of things had gone a set of values which had given richness and meaning to life, and substitute values were not easily found." There was no equivalent to replace the codes of values and manners of older times. For a large part of the tone-setting classes of society, almost everything had become meaningless and unimportant. "And so the saxophones wailed," wrote Allen, "and the gin flask went its rounds and the dancers made their treadmill circuit with half-closed eyes, and the outside world, so merciless and so insane, was shut away for a restless night." At the decade's end, Walter Lippmann, in *A Preface to Morals*, tried to lay a new foundation for a system of ethics and morals to counter the disillusionment that followed the era's high jinx.

It was certainly a different kind of spirits that stirred the hearts and minds of Americans in the '20s, compared with any previous period in American history. But no one can deny that it was indeed a spirited time.

The Roosevelt Era and World War Two

The Great Depression

The national trauma of the Great Depression, which savaged the country for 12 years starting in 1929, is inseparable from the man who presided over it, Franklin Delano Roosevelt. The interaction of the man and the misery of the nation during this period was as important to the preservation of the nation's spirit—in fact, to the preservation of the republic itself—as was the interaction of Lincoln and the Civil War in the first near-breakup of the union a generation earlier.

Like Lincoln, "FDR" was vilified, and still is, by many who viewed him as a dangerous power-seeker. He sought and was given more power than any president before or since. But according to those closest to him it seems clear, in hindsight, that this unique leader, elected President four times, had only one motive for seeking unprecedented power. That was to deal with an unprecedented national emergency. Shortly before he took the nation's highest office he expressed his opinion that the presidency is pre-eminently a place of moral leadership, according to his biographer, James MacGregor Burns.*

By wielding power boldly, as the vast majority of the public and most business leaders wanted him to when he first took the reins, he

---

* In Professor Burns' book, *Roosevelt—The Soldier of Freedom.*

maintained the nation's stability and sustained the spirits of the people through the kind of distress that might have shattered a weaker democracy. Had it not been for the leadership qualities of Lincoln and FDR the American experiment might well have been wrecked on the rocks of either of those two terrible times of testing.

The causes of the depression are clear today. For one thing the prosperity of the '20s had not trickled down to important sectors such as farmers and unskilled workers. Even Hoover later agreed that "a margin of some thousands... got too much of the productive pie for the services they performed... Another margin of some 20% got too little." The nation was producing more than it was consuming. Buying from abroad was impeded too by high U.S. tariffs and tough war-debt policies, and farm prices had been weak for most of a decade. A major factor was the huge expansion of credit—especially for stock market speculation and installment buying and wild speculation in Florida real estate.

Masses of ordinary citizens were buying stocks by the bundle, carrying the Dow Jones Industrial Average from about 100 in 1924 to 400 by mid-1929, until the steam started escaping from the bloated market in harrowing gasps, destroying the savings of millions. Banks and other financial institutions contributed to the blow-off both by over-extending credit and indulging in speculations and greedy market-manipulations themselves. A series of bank panics began in the fall of 1930; depositors withdrew their money and more than 9,000 banks closed their doors, and the panic continued until 1933, when the government established deposit insurance. Ordinary Americans, and most of the New Dealers, had their own simple explanation for the depression: capitalism had run amok because of the monopolies and manipulations of big banks and big business.

Many Americans actually feared revolution during the last months of President Hoover's administration. The federal government helped ignite such fears by the way it handled rising protests. In the summer of 1932 the U.S. Army, under General Douglas MacArthur, routed 25,000 penniless, American flag-carrying war veterans who had encamped in the nation's capital with wives and children. Suffering from almost three years of depression, they demonstrated asking for prepayment of small bonuses due them in 1945.

Declaring "There is revolution in the air", MacArthur sent into the crowd of unarmed men and women civilians a force of cavalry troopers with drawn sabers, soldiers throwing tear gas bombs and a machine gun group and six tanks. Disobeying Hoover's order for restraint, the troops drove the ragged protesters back to the parks and dumps and empty buildings where they had encamped, trampling their vegetable gardens and torching their shacks and tents. In Albany, New York Governor Franklin D. Roosevelt chided Hoover for not offering coffee and sandwiches to the pitiful veterans instead of setting troops after them.

The first point to make about the Great Depression is that practically no one, including President Hoover, had any solution for dealing with it that appeared to have a chance of restoring public confidence. Hoover believed that a balanced budget and reduced taxes would induce economic recovery, whereas cutting the $4 billion federal deficit would have simply reduced the puny help that Washington was offering to a suffering populace. Hoover reasoned that private charities and state and local governments were the proper agencies to help the poor. His posture at the darkest hour was not what one might have expected from the great humanitarian and aid administrator who had rescued starving postwar Belgium. His public bearing was aloof, his habits, including his nightly black-tie dinner, contrasted starkly with the plight of a large part of the general public. He avoided personal contact with the suffering that had brought the world's richest nation to its knees.

Like Hoover, businessmen and other establishment leaders put their emphasis on law and order and deplored the loss of faith in private enterprise. They accused demonstrators of being unpatriotic or Communist-inspired. The president of Columbia University commented wishfully that "courage will end the slump." Even Little Orphan Annie shared the dream world of the privileged members of society. "Leaping Lizards! Who said business is bad?" she asked innocently in one episode of Hoover's favorite comic strip.

The reality was starker than government or business leaders recognized. Few Americans living today can imagine the state into which the nation had fallen, or the despond of the public. One big-city mayor described conditions in 1932 as "a spectacle of national degredation." In that year about one-quarter of the labor force—some 13–15 million men—were out of work. Nearly 28% of the population—34 million men, women and children by Fortune's estimate—no longer had any income, not counting 11 million farm families who were experiencing their own heartbreaking tragedies.

In that summer of 1932, while Rudy Vallee was singing "Brother—Can You Spare a Dime?", hundreds of thousands of desperate men, trying to move around the country seeking work, were tossed off freight cars. U.S. Steel, the kingpin of heavy industry, slashed operations. By 1933 over 250,000 families lost their homes and foreclosures of farms were running at more than 1,000 a day.

More than a quarter of the labor force was on relief by Inauguration Day, 1933, in some states more than that. National income in March that year was less than half of what it had been four years earlier. Almost every bank in America had locked its doors, and 5,500 banks had gone under. Everywhere funds were running out. The Treasury was too short to meet the federal payroll or make payments to government bondholders.

Farmers in the upper Midwest had been picketing highways and building campfires to protest the eastern "banking interests" whom they blamed for the crisis. They laid siege to cities and blocked roads, virtually isolating Des Moines, Council Bluffs and Omaha. On the opening day of Congress in the winter of 1932 three thousand hunger marchers, most from the industrial centers, arrived in Washington chanting at the Capitol steps, "Feed the hungry, tax the rich."

In New York preacher Norman Vincent Peale demanded that bankers and corporate heads get down on their knees before God and confess their sins. Dorothy Day set an example for many others when she opened a soup kitchen. Woody Guthrie sang about depression victims and in support of unions, migrant workers and social justice, hanging on to his hopeful view on life despite the troubles and setting a folk music style that Bob Dylan and others were later to follow.

Public spirits were crushed under the heel of unemployment. Daily life for millions of Americans had become grimmer than at any time in the country's history. Men, women and children were combing refuse dumps for food; men re-sharpened old razor blades, put in 25-watt bulbs to save electricity in their homes and stood night-long vigils at employment offices. Women lucky enough to have jobs got as little as $2.39 a week for a 52-hour workweek (25 cents or even 10 cents an hour for working girls in Chicago.) Teen-agers worked in Brooklyn sweatshops and children turned in old pop bottles for two cents each and stood in lines at bakeries for day-old bread.

Across the nation millions of unemployed people couldn't make rent payments, canceled their insurance and, in order to qualify for what relief there was, sold homes and possessions. Some 4,000 men occupied the Nebraska state-house; 5,000 took over Seattle's County-City Building and 500 Chicago teachers stormed that city's banks. Among those who qualified for relief payments for food and fuel, a family of four got as little as $2.39 a week in New York, $5.50 a week in Philadelphia. New York's city workers, who were closely exposed to the poverty, voluntarily gave one percent of their salaries so that food could be distributed by the police. In Chicago school teachers hitch-hiked to work without pay and were appalled to see students suffering from malnutrition.

Articles debating the immanence of revolt appeared in *Harper's, The Atlantic, Scribner's* and the *Yale Review*. In his classic, *The Glory and the Dream*, William Manchester listed the writers who were flirting with Communism and the notion of revolution, including John Dos Passos, Sherwood Anderson, Erskine Caldwell, Malcolm Cowley, Lincoln Steffens, Granville Hicks, Clifton Fadiman, Upton Sinclair and Edmund Wilson. Even Scott Fitzgerald was reading Marx and speculating about working in the Communist Party to bring on a revolution. Nothing better illustrates how low spirits had sunk throughout the early thirties than the fact that more people were leaving the country than entering it, including many fleeing to Communist Russia.

Of course many fortunate Americans continued working at their jobs right through the depression, and some businesses flourished. Business was thriving at New York's Stork Club, originally a front for Jazz Age gangsters, where one customer ended a late night out by giving the headwaiter a $20,000 tip. In 1934 Sherman Billingsley moved the Stork to bigger quarters off Fifth Avenue on East 53rd Street, where, among other members of café society, Alfred Vanderbilt, Jimmy Durante, J. Paul Getty and Charlie Chaplin all met the women they married.

The disparity between the wealth of the small fortunate minority and vast numbers of less fortunate people at this time was striking. In 1932 one percent of the population owned 50% of the wealth and 600 companies owned 65% of American industry. Jobless men hovered over scrapwood fires burning within sight of the high-rise offices in Chicago which were the headquarters of Samuel Insull, one of the greatest industrial magnates of America. Insull had come to America from London at age 22 and worked his way up from his first job as secretary to Thomas A. Edison to become boss of a mammoth interlocking holding-company directorate controlling public utilities that included hundreds of power plants throughout the country. His corporate-Cinderella story ended, however, when his public utilities empire collapsed in 1932 with the failure of three of his companies. Accused of fraud and toppled from the corporate heights of wealth and success, this mogul of industry fled to Greece. He was later brought to trial and acquitted, but his reputation was ruined and one of the great corporate success stories of the 1920s was brought to a most unseemly end.

The Great Improviser

The only leader in either party who spoke up confidently for new plans to help the forgotten man at the bottom of the economic pyramid as the depression began to tighten its grip on America was the man in the governor's mansion in New York, who during his governorship was suffering his own abuse not only from Republicans who called him "wishy-washy", among other things, but even from liberals like Walter Lippmann, who called him "an amiable boy scout" and Heywood Broun and the liberal journals, which dismissed him as a weak and uninspiring leader.

FDR's career and principles paralleled those of his elder cousin Teddy right down the line; in fact TR was his cousin's model. Although so different in looks (except for the pince nez glasses), intellect and even their political parties, these two exuberant thoroughbreds were the most activist, optimistic presidents in American history, in terms of their faith in the federal government's capabilities to serve public needs and their willingness to seize executive power to right what they saw as the wrongs of the system.

Their careers in public life proved that optimism trumps pessimism in American politics. Taken together, the collective impact of these two stalwarts on American spirits in their times was tremendous. Each in his own way gave a huge boost to national confidence in the country and its future.

Each of them believed that the central government could accomplish great things and should take responsibility for the economic security and growth of the nation. Uncannily, each of them took the same steps up the ladder after Harvard and Columbia Law School, becoming in succession: reform leader in the New York legislature, governor of New York, Assistant Secretary of the Navy and finally President.

Perhaps most remarkable, each of them drew strength—and empathy for people with disabilities— from overcoming their own major handicaps early in life. TR turned a weak and sickly asthmatic constitution into robust strength by throwing himself into the rough life of a cowpuncher in the Dakota Territory. FDR mastered his paralysis from polio through sheer strength of will, and arduous rehabilitation. Each of them displayed the same sang-froid in the face of a would-be assassin's bullets. Each of them was brilliant and outgoing in handling the press.

Each of them liked people of all classes (FDR even invited the janitor of his old Harvard residence hall to visit him on one of his return visits to his alma mater.) Each of them was a moral idealist as well as man of action, devoted to public service. Each of them took on powerful business and financial giants whom they considered immoral, yet both remained loyal to the capitalist system. Each of them had a special interest in preserving natural resources, which FDR acquired growing up as son of an aristocratic country squire in the upstate Hudson River community and TR acquired during his frontier adventures out west. Each of them, through thick and thin in the White House, considered the presidency the most fun job in the whole world.

After his nomination at the Democratic presidential convention in Chicago, FDR stood before the delegates, with steel braces supporting legs that had been crippled for 11 years by polio, and pledged himself and his supporters to "A New Deal for the American people." He had borrowed two phrases ("the forgotten man" and "a new deal") from a speech and a book written recently by others, which in itself was a sign of his eagerness to grasp new ideas from any quarter, and to improvise programs.

After winning the biggest election victory in a two-party race since Lincoln whipped McClellan, FDR immediately transfixed the country. "He has been all but crowned by the people," said William Allen White. The new president felt he had a mandate for quick and drastic change and his mind was full of ideas that had sprung up starting in his days as governor, from discussions with his brainy, expanding group of advisors. He was totally unafraid to take chances and convinced that the country could be saved only by striking out in new directions. "The country needs, and unless I mistake its temper, the country demands bold, persistent experimentation," he said in one speech; "Above all, try something."

To help him decide what to try, he gathered about him an extraordinary, diverse group of intellectuals, chosen for their drive and new ideas. Many of these chain-talking teammates were idealistic people with a near-religious fervor—especially Harry Hopkins, the ex-social worker, and Hugh Johnson, Harold Ickes, Rex Tugwell and the economist Aldolf Berle, all of whom wanted to create a new moral climate. They shared a passionate belief, as Arthur Schlesinger, Jr. put it, that "the economic order had to be conceived as an organism, and not as a battlefield." Roosevelt himself, Manchester noted, "thought of economics as a moral problem." Somehow he managed to hold the reins, master the details and avoid pandemonium as program after program was launched in the greatest blizzard of government innovations in history.

On Saturday morning, March 4, 1933 Roosevelt and his cabinet members began the day with services at St. John's Episcopal Church across the street from the White House. Leading the services was Endicott Peabody, who had been FDR's headmaster at Groton, the prep school where young Roosevelt had his early lessons in moral values. Later that morning the new President stood hatless and coatless in a windy mist before a mass of people huddled in front of the Capitol. He read from a longhand script he had written at Hyde Park. He began this, his first inaugural address, on the note of confidence and candor that was to mark his public statements during his long tenure in the White House. It was to be the secret of his success in raising national spirits. Declaring that it was time to speak "the truth, the whole truth and nothing but the truth", he then uttered these famous words:

"This great nation will endure as it has endured, will revive and will prosper. So, first of all, let me assert my firm belief that the only thing we have to fear is fear itself—nameless, unreasoning, unjustified terror which paralyzes needed efforts to convert retreat into advance."

He called on the nation to "apply social values more noble than mere monetary profit." He castigated "unscrupulous" money changers who "stand indicted in the court of public opinion, rejected by the hearts and minds of men." He outlined his lines of attack:

Our primary task is to put people to work. This is no unsolvable problem if we face it wisely and courageously. It can be accomplished in part by direct recruiting by the government itself, treating the task as we would treat the emergency of war, but at the same time, through this employment, accomplishing greatly needed projects to stimulate and reorganize the use of our natural resources.

He demanded that federal, state and local governments reduce their costs, and referred twice to the reprehensible unbalanced budget. He called for "a recognition of the old and permanently important manifestation of the American spirit of the pioneer." This spirit, he said, "is the way to recovery. It is the immediate way. It is the strongest assurance that the recovery will endure." While lauding the Constitution as "the most superbly enduring political mechanism the modern world had produced," he made clear he would not hesitate to ask for broad executive power "to wage a war against the emergency" if Congress failed to take the recovery measures he would recommend. And he concluded:

"In this dedication of a nation we humbly ask the blessing of God. May He protect each and every one of us. May He guide me in the days to come."

The spirits of the millions listening to this speech on their radios soared. Manchester wrote that "in the three-decker tenements with radios the hungry children looked up; housewives patching threadbare clothes looked up; there was a kind of magic in the air." And in Santa Monica Will Rogers' typewriter clicked out: "If he burned down the Capitol, we would cheer and say, well at least he got a fire started somehow". FDR's former Harvard roommate later wrote: "In a few weeks the nation was lifted from the pit of despair to the high ground of confidence. It was no small thing that within one man could be contained enough of faith to restore the lost morale of a great nation".

David McCullough later pointed out the irony that "a man who couldn't walk would begin to lead a crippled country," adding, "Americans love people who are good at what they do, and he was as good as they get." The public had been captivated and persuaded by a president who seemed to believe in them and was giving them action, action, action wrote Frederick Lewis Allen, comparing FDR to a physician who had a lot of medicines in his bag and "an air of authority and an agreeable bedside manner; and the American people hailed him with delight." In the several days following the speech nearly half a million people wrote the White House to praise it, some as if welcoming a new Messiah, some as if writing to a new friend.

The "One Hundred Days"

FDR's "One Hundred Days" took off at full gallop. Skipping the Inaugural Ball, the president rose Sunday morning and had himself wheeled down a newly built ramp to the quiet oval office. By evening he was ready to act. He declared a four-day holiday for all banks and called for a special session of the 73rd Congress within four days, when emergency legislation would be ready. He improvised a barrage of legislation. His bank bill was ready as promised. Eleanor Roosevelt sat knitting in the gallery while the Congress rushed it through. Roosevelt signed it before even unpacking his belongings that had been sent down from Hyde Park.

The bill was tough medicine. It provided prison terms for hoarders (who in one week had taken 15% of the nation's currency out of circulation), appointed receivers for weak banks and authorized the issue of two billion dollars in new currency based on assets of the sound banks. Faced by a Federal Reserve threat to announce names of people who had withdrawn gold, hoarders turned in $300 million in gold and gold certificates by Saturday night. Within a week three-quarters of the nation's banks were back in business, and the business and financial panic subsided. In New York stocks took off and the Dow Jones ticker crowed: "Happy Days Are Here Again."

Winston Churchill described Roosevelt as "an explorer who has embarked on a rough voyage as uncertain as that of Columbus, and upon a quest which might conceivably be as important as the discovery of the New World." In the same vein Schlesinger later wrote that Roosevelt "lived by his exultation in distant horizons and uncharted seas. It was this which won him confidence and loyalty in a frightened age... this and the conviction of plain people that he had given them head and heart and would not cease fighting in their cause."

The day before Congress convened for the special session FDR held the first of many press conferences. Playing the role of educator even with the media, he discussed frankly the banking crisis that had

164

been choking the nation. The news reporters broke into spontaneous applause, and the president resolved to meet with them twice a week. In his first term he held 337 press conferences.

In these salad days of the New Deal there was plenty of excitement and little resistance or criticism. FDR had electrified the public. "People drew strength from the very cock of his head, the angle of his cigarette holder, the trademark grin that was a semaphore of hope," wrote Garry Wills. Friend and foe, for the moment, stood by him as they were later to do in war. He drove 13 major new laws through the legislature. He gave ten key speeches and presided over twice-weekly cabinet meetings and press conferences. He took the country off the gold standard, crafted a new foreign policy and got Congress to legalize beer. But most important of all, he radiated confidence. "Meeting Roosevelt," Churchill said later, "is like uncorking your first bottle of champagne."

What Roosevelt's audiences saw in those wrenching days, Manchester wrote, "was a magnificent leader—his leonine head thrown back, his eye flashing, his cigarette holder tilted at the sky, his navy boat cloak falling gracefully from his great shoulders. He was the image of zest, warmth and dignity; he was always smiling; he always called people 'my friends'."

Roosevelt sensed that the main thing was not any particular program for recovery but rather the public's need for a psychological lift that could restore spirits and hope for the future, even if it didn't immediately put bread in the hands of the needy. And his own buoyant nature, fire-tested by his personal battle with polio, told him that the way to lift spirits was to dive boldly into all kinds of action, scooping up ideas from every quarter and, by communicating honestly and often with the public, to educate everyone willing to listen about the steps he was taking to bring them relief. Wrote Eleanor Roosevelt in her autobiography: "I never heard him say there was a problem that he thought was impossible for human beings to solve."

The calming fireside chat

Roosevelt was a virtuoso in knowing instinctively how to communicate with, and educate, the entire American public at this time of trouble. As James MacGregor Burns put it, "He took the role of national father, of bipartisan leader, of president of all the people."

Drawing on a skill he had honed as governor, he turned to the radio as his prime medium for reaching the people and dispelling the unease that had dampened the national spirit; it was a way for him to speak to the people without letting them see that their president could not even stand up on his own. Wheeled into a room in the White House carrying his copybook and his trademark cigarette, he would sit behind a desk, facing three or four microphones and a few friends and officials on folding chairs, and send his message of hope into some 30 million homes.

Almost all of these fireside chats took place in the evening, usually a Sunday evening, and almost all of them began with the words, "My friends." He often made historical allusions—references to the American revolution, to Lincoln and other admired leaders of the past—and frequently he ended his talk with an appeal to God. After each talk, the playing of "The Star-Spangled Banner" gave the performance a patriotic tone.

The smooth, confident voice spoke with extraordinary clarity, using simple words to discuss complex problems and momentous issues and sounding as if he were right there in the living room speaking casually but earnestly with close friends, which is exactly the effect he wanted to create. He took the listeners into his confidence, offering them hope. He grafted his own optimism and confidence onto the huge radio audience. This was the magic that gave Americans the confidence to choose him over and over again to lead the nation. He developed a closer rapport with the public than any president before or since. Just one week after the Inauguration, on March 12, 1933, he began his first fireside chat with these frank, simple words:

My friends, I want to talk for a few minutes with the people of the United States about banking."

He explained the bank holiday as the first step in economic reconstruction, the broadening of his presidential powers as the second step, and the plans for the 12 federal reserve banks to issue additional currency so that banks could reopen for business. When the people realized they could get their money, he said, "the phantom of fear will soon be laid." He said he had caught "a note of confidence from all over the country." And he concluded that "confidence and courage are the essentials of success in carrying out our plan... Let us unite in banishing fear."

When Congress passed the bill declaring a bank holiday and controlling gold deposits five days after Inauguration, confidence returned to the markets and gold and bank deposits started returning home. Passage of bills to reduce federal and Congressional salaries and veteran pensions, and legalize beer and light wines, also were well received. "In one week," Walter Lippmann wrote, "the nation, which had lost confidence in everything and everybody, has regained confidence in the government and in itself." Wrote Anne O'Hare McCormick in *The New York Times*: "No president in so short a time has inspired so much hope." Responding to the fireside chats as he hoped they would, the public sent FDR between 5–8,000 letters a day, many of them in the same "friend to friend" language that FDR had used in addressing them.

The index of industrial production jumped about 70% during FDR's first four months in the White House, according to the Federal Reserve Board. The first issue of Treasury securities since 1931, which took place in the first summer of his administration, was oversubscribed six times over, giving a strong signal of revived business confidence. The Dow industrial stocks rose 39 points in 1933, six points more in 1934 and 40 points more in 1935.

Eight weeks after his first fireside chat FDR went on the air again, "to tell you about what we have been doing and what we are planning to do." Reassuring listeners that he had no desire to change the balance of power between President and Congress, he said that Congress had simply designated the President as the agency to carry out certain of its purposes. First, he announced creation of the Civilian Conservation Corps (CCC), a new government agency to employ a quarter of a million young, unemployed men as volunteers in forestry and flood prevention projects. This, his biggest program, was to be organized and overseen by the long-neglected U.S. Army (helping to prepare it for a future war mission no one foresaw at the time.) The CCC set the precedent for creation of a whole bevy of emergency agencies, which was FDR's favorite strategy for dealing with the crisis. In the state of Washington alone, the CCC erected 260 forest-fire lookouts, strung 4,000 miles of telephone line through forests, cut in half the annual acreage burned by forest fires and created or improved more than a dozen state parks.

Roosevelt unveiled a broad plan for improvement of the whole seven-state Tennessee Valley; a law to ease mortgage distress among farmers and homeowners; a grant of half a billion dollars to help states and counties care for people who needed direct and immediate relief. He gave his radio audience a preview of other upcoming plans—for public works, farm relief and railroad reorganization—all under the rubric of new partnerships between the government and farmers, industry and the transport industry. He expressed his "profound debt of gratitude" to the public for its patience during the depression and pledged that their confidence would be rewarded.

FDR had a lofty idea of politics as education of the public. He wanted to be a "preaching president" like TR, and one thing he prized about the New Deal was the way it provoked public thinking about public policy. Charles A. Beard went so far as to say that he "discussed in his messages and addresses more fundamental problems of American life and society than all the other presidents combined." Later criticism of FDR as a "socialist" was undeserved; "pragmatist" would be closer to the truth. He was basically conservative in spirit. He had no scheme to found a welfare state—he was not an ideologue or a philosopher or even a true intellectual like TR.

He was a man of action, political action. He said he feared welfare as a narcotic, a destroyer of the human spirit. He felt that federal direct relief should be ended at some point, leaving pauper relief to state and local governments. But in the emergency, he believed that Washington should concentrate on giving every employable worker a job through massive public works. He never lost faith in the capitalist system nor his own sincere belief in balanced budgets and his preference for private over public enterprises. But he believed the federal government had a duty to help the helpless, and to curb abuses by using new agencies like the Securities and Exchange Commission, set up in 1934 to regulate banks and stock exchanges.

On July 24, in his third fireside chat, the President assessed the work of his first hundred days. He reported that 300,000 young men were doing useful work in the nation's forests and on projects to prevent flood and soil erosion. He described the great public works program "for highways and ships and flood prevention and inland navigation and thousands of self-sustaining state and municipal improvements." The CCC corps, working out of 2,000 camps, had among other things put slum youths to work planting 200 million trees from Texas to Canada. FDR considered this one of the New Deal's most successful programs.

More than two and a half million single young men from relief families, between 18 and 25, worked in the CCC camps starting in the winter of 1933, building dams, bridges and fire towers, clearing campgrounds, restoring historic battlefields and improving parks, forests, beaches and watersheds. Additional relief was provided through three other new agencies (the Civil Works Administration or CWA, the Works Progress Administration or WPA, and the Public Works Administration or PWA (which undertook in all 30,000 construction projects, financing the building of waterworks, dams, bridges, hospitals, offices, airports, sewers, playgrounds and power systems.) To bring relief to agriculture FDR got Congress to raise prices by paying farmers to create scarcity of supplies, a policy that remained controversial for more than half a century.

In his calming, avuncular style, FDR insisted in the July 24 radio talk that the New Deal schemes represented "the orderly component parts of a connected and logical whole," which of course was quite a stretch considering the variety of academics, economists, social workers and others who had been feeding him ideas. But the programs did, as Frederick Lewis Allen noted, put "a new emphasis on the welfare of the common man, a new attempt... to build prosperity from the bottom up rather than from the top down." FDR spent more than half of his July radio talk trying to stir up enthusiasm for his program to enroll the business and industrial community in the New Deal, via the National Industrial Recovery Act and the National Recovery Administration (the NRA) that it set up.

He appealed to balky employers to hurry and back up the voluntary industry codes, as all the basic industries had done, "in the name of patriotism and humanity." Those who joined this government-industry partnership signed on to mutually agreed standards that limited working hours to a 40-hour week and met a minimum hourly wage— the idea being that such measures would help get people back to work with decent jobs and reduce exploitation of workers. As an example, he cited the cotton textile industry code, which had abolished child labor.

Over two million employers heeded this call, earning the right to display everywhere the "Blue Eagle" NRA symbol. The initial success of the program was dramatized in early September by the "Blue Eagle Parade" in New York. A quarter of a million men and women marched down Fifth Avenue in the greatest ticker-tape parade in the city's history, with General Hugh Johnson, the evangelistic head of the program, on the reviewing stand with Governor Herbert Lehman and W. Averill Harriman. CCC workers, business people, stock brokers, brewers and even chorus girls strode past more than a million New Yorkers while the band played "Happy Days are Here Again." For a brief moment—about six months to be exact—the Blue Eagle campaign created a sense of national solidarity and lifted the business mood from despair to affirmation.

By the end of October 1933 the principal early New Deal projects were underway. In his fireside talk of October 22, FDR recapped the progress being made, overlooking some disappointing news on sliding production. He described the new machinery set up for farm credit and home credit in more than 3,000 counties, using federal credit to stop foreclosures. The Home Owners Loan Corporation, which rescued the collapsed real estate market, probably did more than any other single measure to bolster middle-class support for the Administration, while the Reconstruction Finance Corporation lent large sums to ease the credit squeeze on industry and finance.

Although business leaders increasingly objected to the NRA's intrusion of bureaucratic control, and the Supreme Court later found it unconstitutional, this greatest of all New Deal efforts was not a total failure because, like FDR's other programs, it did succeed in raising morale for a time, lifting the hopes of organized labor especially in this period of management-labor violence and inspiring civic pride as communities across the country held their NRA parades and flaunted their Blue Eagles. "The country just lifted itself up," said Alistair Cooke. "All the world's on the way to a new sunny day, 'cause the road is open again," sang a song of the period. In some places public schoolchildren started the school day with a song that went: "We're out to finish what we began in 1933/ from millionnaire to forgotten man we're all with Franklin D/ Marching along together, proud to be with the NRA."

But the early euphoria over this mammoth effort to regulate business soon gave way to growing fears of excessive centralization of power and bureaucratic control of the economy. It did result in important progress, such as elimination of sweatshops, the banning of unfair trade practices and the first steps in consumer protection. And perhaps it helped prepare the nation for the united effort that was to be required in the war that was soon to come. But neither the NRA or the other New Deal programs solved the basic problem, which was that millions of people who wanted to work still could not find jobs.

Ways of escape: movies and radio

One thing that helped Americans keep up their spirits during these terrible thirties was the pervasive influence of the movies and radio, offering a romantic escape from reality. It cost only 20 cents to go to one of the 17,000 movie theaters around the country and 85 million Americans went to the "shows" once a week. The style of movie-going and the content of movies was in sharp contrast to today's electronic entertainments. The viewers of the '30s escaped into a celluloid dream world where they could forget about the grim times outside by watching screen romances that buoyed their spirits.

Mostly, Americans went to the movies as families, including their teen-agers (who were just called "our young folks" in those days.) The uplifting shows they saw transported audiences on a magic carpet to Hollywood's version of wholesome American life. In the year that FDR took the oath of office, Fred Astair and Ginger Rogers were paired up in "Flying Down to Rio" and, while they weren't the stars of the picture, the sophistication, grace and energy of their dancing wowed audiences and their careers took off. Other wholesome family fare included Shirley Temple in "Little Miss Marker", Charles Laughton in "Mutiny on the Bounty" and the Busby Berkeley musicals.

Throughout the depression years, an extraordinary movie personality helped to lift spirits of ordinary American families, a fanciful character who was a symbol of American pluck and resilience that helped people survive and overcome adversity in a society riddled with danger and insecurities. A creation of Walt Disney, whose first studio was in a Los Angeles garage, Mickey Mouse starred in the cartoon series "Silly Symphonies", which ran for ten years starting in 1929. Donald Duck, Goofy and Pluto joined Mickey as the series progressed, and in 1938 Disney produced his first full-length animated film, "Snow White and the Seven Dwarfs", which also transported audiences into a make-believe world.

During these times a new sound of music got people humming or tapping their feet. Benny Goodman, who had studied clarinet at Hull House in Chicago, started his orchestra in 1934 in New York. The next year "swing" became the sound of the '30s as Goodman and his band did wild improvisations and sold their music on 35-cent or 50-cent Bluebird, Decca and Columbia records. Cole Porter's "Night and Day" began its immortal life in the movie "The Gay Divorcee" in 1934. Irving Berlin's "Top Hat, White Tie and Tails", the big hit of 1935, and "Cheek to Cheek" accompanied Astair's brilliant dancing. Jerome Kern's "Lovely to Look At" and "A Fine Romance" came along in "Roberta" and "Swingtime" in 1935 and 1936. And perhaps the greatest escape song of the era was Berlin's ballad sung by Astair in 1936's "Follow the Fleet":

"There may be troubles ahead
There may be teardrops to shed
So while there's moonlight and music
And love and romance
Let's face the music and dance."

Like another Berlin tune the following year, when Astair and Judy Garland in "Easter Parade" sang these cheery if poignant lines:

"We would ride the trolley car
But we haven't got the fare
So we'll walk up the Avenue
Yes we'll walk up the Avenue
Till we're there."

Topping off the decade was Berlin's song of hope, "It's a Lovely Day Tomorrow" in his hugely successful musical, "Louisiana Purchase", which opened in Broadway's Imperial Theater on May 28, 1940. It was full of romantic songs that audiences went away singing—for the most part oblivious to the fact that, across the Atlantic, Hitler's armies were just then rolling through the Netherlands and Belgium.

Claudette Colbert won the Academy Award in 1934 playing a runaway heiress opposite Clark Gable in Frank Capra's "It Happened One Night" and in the same year proved her versatility as an actress in "Cleopatra." She told an interviewer later that "the depression killed the theater, and the pictures were manna from heaven." In three years, starting in 1938, the handsome young actor Ronald Reagan starred in 22 gung-ho, uplifting films, playing the all-American hero in a military academy, on the college football field, in the cavalry and in the navy.

The other '30s shows that soothed troubled spirits were the free ones on radio, as that medium enjoyed its golden age. Radio was a simple, innocent source of pleasure that stirred the imagination as listeners tuned in regularly to follow the fortunes of radio families or virtuous adventurers like the Lone Ranger or Buck Rogers. One of the most durable shows was NBC-Red's "One Man's Family", which came on every Wednesday night, "dedicated to the mothers and fathers of the younger generation and their bewildering offspring." Among the other regulars that drew the family around the locus familia, the old Philco console, were "Amos 'n' Andy", Morton Downey's "Carolina Moon", "The Major Bowes Amateur Hour" and Edgar Bergen and Charlie McCarthy. One highly popular soap opera starting in 1935 was the long-running comedy show, "Fibber McGee and Molly", which followed the fun and foibles of the McGee family living at 79 Wistful Vista in a fictional Midwest town.

In literature, the popular favorite in 1936 and 1937, Margaret Mitchell's *Gone With the Wind*, starred a scheming, hot-tempered, self-centered young woman who survived the hard knocks of the Civil War and the loss of both lovers, Clark Gable and Leslie Howard, but clung to her hope for a better "tomorrow." And in 1937, readers could escape into history with Kenneth Roberts' *Northwest Passage* and a number of other books that glamorized the past. Other leisure activities such as amateur photography, bowling, golf, tennis and softball also were distracting the public.

One uplifting influence on women during these years, in what was still very much a man's world, was the example set for them by the President's wife, which had an enormous impact. In her refreshingly open style, Eleanor gave coffee and sandwiches to anyone who came to her door. Her self-made role was to be the eyes and ears of her crippled husband and in that role she traveled some 40,000 miles a year visiting schools and playgrounds, hospitals and hovels, slums and sharecroppers, becoming an advocate not only for women but also for blacks and other minorities. She flooded FDR's office with memos. She lectured, held weekly press conferences for women reporters, encouraged women's organizations and youth movements and, starting in 1935, penned a widely read daily syndicated newspaper column called "My Day". She campaigned against child labor and for public housing and unemployment insurance.

During the war Mrs. Roosevelt was a morale-builder in faraway theaters of war and she filled in for FDR on ceremonial occasions.

These and other activities (finally, as U.S. delegate to the United Nations and chair of the Commission on Human Rights) made her the world's most popular woman, but most importantly, for several generations, the "most admired" among women of her own country. Many of these women, thanks to the war, were graduating at least temporarily from housework and daytime soap operas into jobs in factories, airplane assembly lines and shipyards, where they became indispensable to the all-out war effort.

Another influential figure during this period was that "preacher of the gospel of optimism", as the *New York Times* called him, Norman Vincent Peale. In his sermons as pastor of Manhattan's Marble Collegiate Church, and in his radio ministry starting in 1935, his column, "Confident Living" published in more than 200 newspapers and his 41 books, this enormously successful preacher told millions of Americans that "positive thinking", induced by simple prayer, was the secret of both spiritual and material success. He was one of the first clergymen to marry psychiatry and counseling with religion.

One theologian-writer from Yale University, while mocking the simplistic pop culture of Peale and his followers, acknowledged in an essay that the preacher had tapped into the characteristic American confidence, the "triumphant power of mind or faith over all external limits," and that the roots of "positive thinking" were the characteristics that observers had always considered typical American characteristics: "Our self-confidence and optimism, our worldly practicality and our individualism and striving for success, concerned more with private careers than public problems."

Back to reality: limited progress

By the winter of 1934 one out of seven Americans—more than 18 million people—were still on relief. Some seven million were still looking for work two years later, and the programs that were supposed to rescue them were running into Constitutional challenges in the courts. But the people hadn't lost faith: they re-elected FDR in 1936 with 61% of the popular vote and gave the Democrats overwhelming majorities in both houses of Congress.

Roosevelt acknowledged the continuing travails of the people in his January, 1937 Inaugural Address, delivered in a snowstorm, when he referred to "one-third of a nation ill-housed, ill-clad, ill-nourished."

174

By the spring of 1938, five million workers who had found jobs over the preceding five years were jobless again and nearly 14% of the population was still on relief. By 1938 the Dow industrials had fallen below 100, about one-quarter of their peak level before the 1929 crash. Even in 1940, seven years after the first New Deal program began, 8–10 million people remained unemployed.

FDR's programs, while they provided much experience and many lessons for the future, did not cure the depression. But it must be admitted that they ended the perilous slide of the economy, gave jobs to millions of desperate unemployed men and lifted the spirits of the majority of Americans out of the awful funk into which they had fallen. One can safely speculate that four more years of Hoover's inertia would have led to colossal human misery and tragic consequences for the nation. By the end of October 1933, homes and farms were being saved from foreclosures and banks were gaining strength.

Before they were done the New Dealers had a great many permanent, worthwhile improvements to show for their efforts. Among them was the Social Security Act signed by FDR in 1935, a cornerstone of New Deal social agenda, with its posters proclaiming "Old Age Should be the Harvest of a Fruitful Life." The Social Security system was a tremendous break with the past and its champion was the first woman cabinet member, Frances Perkins. Promising citizens for the first time some protection from life's hardest knocks, the act provided unemployment insurance and help for the sick and aged, the regulation of securities markets and the establishment of minimum standards for working pay and conditions.

Five weeks before the congressional elections of 1934, at a time when businessmen had become increasingly critical of the New Deal and the President, FDR used a fireside talk to discuss the relations between capital, labor and the government. He argued that unregulated free enterprise capitalism had shown its inability to manage without government assistance and regulation. He said his administration had regulated "only to meet concrete needs, a practice of courageous recognition of change." And he closed with these words:

"I believe, with Abraham Lincoln, that 'The legitimate object of government is to do for a community of people whatever they need to have done but cannot do at all or cannot do so well for themselves in their separate and in their individual capacities."

The last New Deal reform measure, the Fair Labor Standards Act in June 1938, was welcomed by the industrial working class. It established a 40-cent minimum wage and a maximum work week of 40 hours for non-farm workers in interstate commerce, and it forbade labor by children under 16.

While the New Deal programs in general caused an enlargement of government in their efforts to remedy unemployment, they also, to some extent unconsciously, were a response to a changing society. The nation was no longer a rural economy, where each new generation took care of its own older people on the farm and there were always jobs when people worked to raise their own food. Urbanization and the great migrations of people to the cities changed all that. These changes, together with the rise of big, concentrated mass-production factories, spawned new issues such as welfare and environmentalism.

The behavior of business leaders who exploited the new economy without regard to public consequences also was a factor. FDR made bitter enemies in business, because he identified with a popular, well-founded conviction that greedy excesses of bankers and big businessmen were among the devils to blame for the depression, and the federal government had to step up to the middleman role as monitor and regulator of these excesses.

The Senate hearings that had been guided since January 1933 by a tough Sicilian immigrant by the name of Ferdinand Pecora, left no doubt that even the heads of prominent financial institutions were guilty not just of speculation but of favored treatment for their own crowd and for other special interests. (Congress followed up with important legislation prying banks away from the securities business and legislating federal insurance of bank deposits, one of the most successful achievements of FDR's first 100 days.) The moral authority of banking was hacked down rather brutally during this period, compared with those early days of J.P. Morgan, and the unethical manipulations of stock traders were dealt with by new securities laws and the new Securities and Exchange Commission. But FDR's faith in the capitalist system and his preference for private over public enterprises remained unshaken.

So in hindsight, FDR was both a success and a failure in dealing with the depression. He was a success beyond anyone's expectations in averting anarchy and lifting the sunken spirits of a desperate nation that had been at wit's end. Through superb communications with the public, aided by his team of experts (as distinguished from today's more familiar presidential "handlers" and pollsters), he not only conveyed a strong sense of his own self-confidence but also persuaded a great part of the public that he was unfolding a broad, coordinated program of recovery that would lift the nation out of its morass, which was quite a stretch of imagination.

On this psychological level he charmed the public and raised its hopes even as their miseries persisted. "Roosevelt unlocked new energies in a people who had lost faith, not just in government's ability to meet economic crisis, but almost in the ability of anyone to do anything", wrote Schlesinger. And far from destroying the capitalist system, Schlesinger maintained, FDR had probably saved it.

On the realistic level of daily lives, however, joblessness continued at perniciously high levels, relief reached only part of the destitute masses and the engines of production did not accelerate enough to produce a gross national product that was much higher in 1940 than it was in 1930, comparing in constant dollars. FDR's era was characterized both by extremes of suffering and pessimism on one hand, and extremes of faith among those who virtually worshipped their strong leader. The best that can be said is that FDR's make-work programs, and his efforts to restore the financial system and pull farmers and industrial workers out of debt at least put the brakes on in time to stop the slide to total disaster and lifted the hopes of most Americans for better times.

But his New Deal hadn't cured the basic problem, and there began to be signs that Americans wanted a limit placed on the expansion of federal power and influence. The federal government assumed responsibility for the economic security of the people and the economic growth of the nation, but this came at a price. The New Deal cost more than the nation received in tax revenues, so it was financed largely by borrowing through the sale of bonds, which nearly doubled the federal debt over six years (from $22.5 billion in 1933 to about $40.5 billion in 1939.)

Finally, there was disagreement about FDR himself. As early as 1935 Charles A. Beard wrote that "Roosevelt's spell of leadership is definitely broken." In 1936 his popularity hit bottom. By May of 1936 columnist Marquis Childs wrote that the upper-class hatred of FDR that started spreading in 1935 and became acute in 1936 "was beginning to permeate the whole upper stratum…"

In the upper reaches of conservative society—in cocoon-communities like Greenwich, Connecticut and Grosse Pointe, Michigan—anti-Roosevelt sentiment was rampant. People of FDR's own class, including most of his college classmates, opposed him and many loathed him—even to the point of canceling subscriptions to magazines that profiled him. Jokes and slurs about "that man" and "Eleanor" went from gross to grosser. On commuter trains, in county club locker rooms and on the golf course such sentiments were so widespread that these affluent Americans scarcely dared say a good word for this President lest they alienate themselves from their peers. All this while the ordinary public was accepting him as savior and hanging his picture in homes and stores and businesses everywhere.

FDR's virtuosity would always be seen by some as simply the brilliance of a political tactician and a consummate actor (he once told Orson Welles "You and I are the two best actors in America.") He was not a particularly deep thinker, and some of the criticism leveled against him has stood the test of time. Although he built a party of ordinary people and reached out to minorities, he was criticized for showing contempt for Congress and the Supreme Court, for disregarding Constitutional constraints in the way he handled some issues furtively, even deceivingly at times, for not doing enough for blacks, for allowing the wartime internment of Japanese Americans and for not rescuing European Jews from the Holocaust, not to mention his indifference and infidelity to a wife who made heroic efforts to support him.

As for the American people, they did not lose their spirit altogether during those dark pre-war days. Among other things, the release of uplifting motion pictures that marked Hollywood's heyday continued to give them a cheap escape from reality. Among these were such hits as "Young Mr. Lincoln", "Mr. Smith Goes to Washington", "Gone with the Wind", "Stagecoach", "Babes in Arms" and "The Wizard of Oz", which has been called "the quintessential American family film."

Probably the most inspiring metaphor for hope in the future during the latter part of the thirties was The New York World's Fair in 1939 and 1940, with its theme, "The World of Tomorrow". Even though the depression still lingered and the flame of war was licking at Europe, this great fair embodied dreamlike optimism and an almost childlike belief in the perfectibility of modern life. "To go to this fair was to have your life changed forever," wrote the site's creator, a professor of philosophy and religion in Milton, Massachusetts.

The fair's opening ceremony featured a speech by FDR. Presiding over the fair was New York City's ebullient, five-foot-high mayor, Fiorello H. La Guardia, who spoke seven languages (including Croatian and Yiddish) and lifted spirits through the depression and the war that followed, especially with his regular Sunday radio show. Uptown in New York during this period another boisterous leader, the Rev. Adam Clayton Powell had an enormous, positive influence on the morale of the city's black community.

Conceived by New York's official greeter, Grover Whalen, the World's Fair's exhibits pictured a virtual utopia that technology promised for the future. Robotics, FM radio, fluorescent lighting and a crude fax machine were among the wonders of tomorrow on display. Riders at General Motors' "Futurama" sat in conveyor-belt-driven armchairs and gaped at the imagined American landscape of 1960, criss-crossed by wide highways bearing futuristic cars as envisioned by Norman Bel Geddes. At the end of the ride visitors received a button declaring "I have seen the future". They also trooped around the Lagoon of Nations, took a scary 10-second parachute jump, strolled wide-eyed around the Trilon and Perisphere and through exhibits of folk arts and folk dancing from foreign lands, and watched Johnny Weissmuller and Eleanor Holm and the gorgeous precision swimmers in the Billy Rose Acquacade. They marveled at the new technology of television. NBC's David Sarnoff announced the birth of this new consumer wonder, predicting that one day there would be a TV in every home, though at that time there were only 200 small-screen, black and white TV sets in New York City.

The teen-agers who went with their parents and friends to this inspiring panorama of wonders-to-come could not have imagined that only two years after the fair closed down they would be putting off their dreams of a glamorous "World of Tomorrow" and instead marching off to war. They had seen the future all right, and many futuristic visions—of new technologies, streamlined products , gadget-filled new homes and television for the masses—would indeed come within their reach later on. But first they would have to make an enormous effort to defend the very life of the American nation.

FDR and World War II

The Great Improviser performed his alchemy on the American spirit not only through the nation's worst depression but also through its ordeal in the longest and costliest war in history, which came only a bare two decades after the great "war to end all wars". The President who had fought depression for eight years with mixed results achieved a more clear-cut success in leading the nation through six years of worldwide war. As Alan Brinkley wrote, this great war was a paradoxical experience, "simultaneously horrifying and exhilarating." But it was "a good war" in the sense that at its beginning and at the end Americans regarded it as a just and necessary war against tyrannical, threatening enemies. It began and ended in idealism, compared to the first great war, which ended in disillusionment.

The government spent $380 million to arm for the world war—six times the cost of the New Deal—and the country achieved its highest state of solidarity. Never before or since has the nation been so united in spirit, so powerfully driven to accomplish great things together. And finally, everyone who wanted a job had one and the awful experience of the depression could be put behind them. The war demanded the labor—the dedicated, seven-days-a-week labor—of nearly every man and woman in the nation.

Just as FDR used his fireside chats to condition public thinking about his domestic programs, he used a new series of firesides beginning in September 1939, two days after the Nazis invaded Poland, to educate the public about foreign policy. Most Americans wanted no part in Europe's war at that time. They were no more aware of what was happening in Germany than was the black sharecropper's son, Jessie Owens, who won four gold medals and dominated Adolf Hitler's 1936 Olympic games in Berlin. But FDR got a Special Session of Congress to authorize sale of U.S. munitions to belligerents on a cash and carry basis. As events progressed on the European battlefields public awareness of events in Europe began to rise, and movie houses began playing "The Star-Spangled Banner" at the end of each evening's show.

FDR's radio monologues during this time attempted at first to still public fears of involvement in foreign wars. Referring to the first American president's admonitions to keep the country out of foreign wars and entanglements, in his September 3, 1939 chat FDR took a high moral stance, but he laid the way for support of the Allies against the Axis powers, arguing that even neutrals must have a conscience. He said:

"In spite of spreading wars, I think we have every right and reason to maintain as a national policy the fundamental moralities, the teachings of religion, the continuation of efforts to restore peace because some day, though the time may be distant, we can be of even greater help to a crippled humanity... Most of us in the United States believe in spiritual values. Most of us, regardless of what church we belong to, believe in the spirit of the New Testament—a great teaching which opposes itself to the use of force, of armed force, of marching armies and falling bombs."

But eight months later, after Hitler had overrun the Netherlands, Belgium, Luxembourg and France, FDR said in a second foreign-policy chat that Americans had "lost the illusion that we are remote and iso-lated." He outlined the buildup underway of the U.S. Army and Navy and the passage in Congress of the largest appropriations ever asked for these forces in peacetime. He emphasized that underlying the strength of these forces "are the spirit and morale of a free people." And he pledged that "There is nothing in our present emergency to justify a retreat—any retreat—from our social objectives, from conser-vation of natural resources, assistance to agriculture, housing and help to the underpriviledged." The moral foundations laid down by the country's forefathers, he said, must be preserved despite the military preparations.

FDR's victory in the 1940 election, earning him an unprecedented third term, was the closest of his career. But his adversary, Wendell Willke, pronounced him still "The Champ". The president rode down Pennsylvania Avenue savoring his third presidential triumph and doff-ing his fedora to 200,000 people cheering along the route to the White House. It was clear that the general public still adored him.

Just as Lincoln and Wilson had done, FDR was moving quickly and quietly to prepare for a war from which, he'd become convinced, the U.S. could not stand aside. He was sending Britain P-40 fighter planes, mobilizing industry and arming the country to the teeth. In late 1940, relaxing in the Caribbean on a cruiser after his third presidential cam-paign, he received by seaplane a very desperate note from Churchill. Two days of lonely brooding at sea produced an idea for a life-pre-server for Britain that showed he could improvise in war as well as he had done in peace. The idea was Lend-Lease and he described it at a press conference on December 17, using the simple metaphor of a citizen loaning a garden hose to a neighbor. Like a patient and earnest teacher, he expounded on this new concept for 45 minutes.

He followed this up December 29 with one of his most important radio addresses to the American people. The pact between Germany, Italy and Japan had been signed two months earlier in Berlin, and FDR proclaimed that "Never before since Jamestown and Plymouth Rock has our American civilization been in such danger as now." He said:

"I want to make clear it is the purpose of the nation to build now with all possible speed every machine, every arsenal, every factory that we need to manufacture our defense material..."

He appealed "to the managers, to the workers, to our own government employees, to put every ounce of effort into producing these munitions swiftly and without stint... We must be the great arsenal of democracy. For us this is an emergency as serious as war itself... We have no excuse for defeatism. We have every good reason for hope— hope for peace, yes, and hope for the defense of our civilization and for the building of a better civilization in the future." Letters and wires supported his call 100 to one, and polls showed 71% of the public stood with him.

On May 27, 1941, after Nazi forces broke through Greece, Yugoslavia and North Africa, the President, in another fireside chat, announced that he had issued the proclamation of "an unlimited national emergency." He still had no real plan for direct American entry into combat but he spoke vehemently of the threat of Nazi domination. Recalling the odds against which America's first patriots fought, he repeated the words of the signers of the Declaration of Independence: "With a firm reliance on the protection of Divine Providence, we mutually pledge to each other our lives, our fortunes, and our sacred honor."

Pearl Harbor zings up American spirits

On December 9, 1941, two days after Japan's surprise attack at Pearl Harbor blasted the U.S. Pacific Fleet, and the day after getting Congress to vote a declaration of war with Japan, he used a fireside chat to condemn the Japanese attacks in the Pacific as "the climax of a decade of international immorality." Preparing the country for the ordeal to come, he summed up the succession of Axis invasions that had made the whole world "one gigantic battlefield." He called for seven-day-a-week production in every war industry, and warned of the sacrifice (which he called a "privilege") that every citizen would have to make in the diversion from civilian to military effort. He said:

"We are now in this war. We are all in it—all the way. Every single man, woman and child is a partner in the most tremendous undertaking in American history."

The spirit in which the American public responded to this challenge was as extraordinary as the spirit of American fighting forces on global battlefronts. Never before or since has the nation been so united in spirit, so powerfully driven to accomplish great things together and feel so proud of themselves. American industry went into high gear around the clock, with Ford's Willow Run plant producing 30-ton B-24 bombers at a rate of one an hour, Chrysler churning out tanks, Kaiser turning out Liberty Ships.

Typewriter factories were making machine guns and Boeing produced Flying Fortresses. A ripple of pride swept the nation as workers, including "Rosie the riveter", the young woman recruit at plants of General Electric and other manufacturers, joined this huge effort. Spirits on the home front ran high. After some initial industry fits and foibles, a volcanic output of nearly 300,000 warplanes, over 1,000 tanks, nearly three million trucks and close to a million tons of aircraft bombs streamed out of the great American industrial furnace within five years after the fall of France.

The Allies took one defeat after another in battles throughout the world in 1941 through February 1942, and in his fireside chat on Washington's Birthday of that latter month FDR called on his fellow Americans to remember how Washington and his Continental Army had weathered recurring defeats for eight years against formidable odds. He urged Americans to emulate Washington's "moral stamina". And he concluded with the ringing words of Tom Paine that Gen. Washington had ordered to be read to every regiment in his army in 1776:

"The summer soldier and the sunshine patriot will, in this crisis, shrink from the service of their country, but he that stands it now deserves the love and thanks of man and woman. Tyranny, like hell, is not easily conquered; yet we have this consolation with us, that the harder the sacrifice, the more glorious the triumph."

Roosevelt used his fireside talk of April 28, 1942 to call for further sacrifices and to recount heroic acts of servicemen as American forces continued fighting against overwhelming odds. Not until his talk of September 7 that year was he able to report some progress in the war—the halt of the German advance into Russia, the American victory at Midway (that turned the tide of the Pacific war when outnumbered U.S. Navy fliers sank all four Japanese aircraft carriers) and the hint of plans afoot to launch attacks in Europe. He concluded:

"This is the toughest war of all time. We need not leave it to historians of the future to answer the question whether we are tough enough to meet this unprecedented challenge. We can give that answer now. The answer is yes."

In the fall of 1942, when the U.S. had been at war for ten months, FDR toured the nation on the presidential train, stopping at war factories and making surprise visits from San Francisco and Seattle to Texas and New Orleans. He returned to Washington in high spirits, optimistic, full of praise for his fellow citizens and sufficiently relieved to show a trace of humor. His radio address of October 12, celebrating Columbus Day, bolstered the spirits of the radio audience:

"That is the main thing I saw on my trip around the country—unbeatable spirit. If the leaders of Germany and Japan could have come along with me, and had seen what I saw, they would agree with my conclusions. Unfortunately they were unable to make the trip with me. And that is one reason why we are carrying our war effort overseas—to them."

One of the things that impressed FDR on his trip across the country was the large number of women working at skilled manual labor, running machines and generally playing a vital part in war production. "Within less than a year," he predicted, "there will probably be as many women as men working in our war production plants." He also praised the more than ten million people who were working hard as volunteers in civilian defense.

After noting that Americans were celebrating on this day that bold and adventurous Italian, Christopher Columbus, he added: "Today, the sons of the New World are fighting in lands far distant from their own America. They are fighting to save for all mankind... the principles which have flourished in this new world of freedom." He concluded by declaring that the country was united "in seeking the kind of victory that will guarantee that our grandchildren can grow and, under

God, may live their lives free from the constant threat of invasion, destruction, slavery and violent death."

In the fall of 1942, when FDR was making his tour of the country, a highly original and ambitious play appeared on Broadway that mirrored the president's tributes to the spirits of Americans as they shouldered the burdens of world war. It was Thornton Wilder's "The Skin of Our Teeth," starring Fredric March and Florence Eldridge as Mr. And Mrs. Antrobus— parents of an archetypal American family who virtuously carry on through the ups and downs of the Ice Age, the Great Flood and the chaos of war. Wilder saw Americans, as a *Times* critic noted, "as a species in love with life and infatuated with hope", which was a hopeful message for a country newly thrust into war.

For black Americans, the war was a seminal turning point of spirits. Nearly two million African-Americans left the rural South in the 1940s, mostly to take war jobs in the North. In 1941 the Fair Employment Practices Committee aimed to guarantee blacks access to work in war industries. Blacks displayed loyalty and courage in military service, setting the stage for integration of the military, one of the most significant steps forward in racial justice. While these positive developments did not end the "American Dilemma" (the title of Gunnar Myrdal's 1944 book describing America's failure to give blacks a fair chance at economic rewards), they certainly helped to rock the system of segregation that had persisted as the nation's major social problem.

FDR was in high spirits again on July 28, 1943 when he celebrated the fall of Mussolini, "the first crack in the Axis", and looked forward to Allied victory in Sicily. In this same fireside chat he outlined his proposed postwar G.I. Bill of Rights. Two months later, in a brief radio talk, he announced the Allied armistice in Italy and the launching of the first of six war loan drives. On Christmas Eve that year he reported on his conference with Churchill in Cairo, and his conference with Churchill and Stalin in Teheran, where the leaders agreed on an Allied cross-channel invasion of Europe the following May or June. By this time there were over ten million men in the U.S. armed forces. He sent this Christmas message to these soldiers, sailors and airmen:

"We ask God's blessing upon you... We ask that the comfort of God's grace shall be granted to those who are sick and wounded, and to those who are prisoners of war... And we ask that God receive and cherish

those who have given their lives, and that He keep them in honor and in the grateful memory of their countrymen forever."

Dreamy music and romance

At home and abroad, one of the distinctively American influences on the nation's younger generation during the forties was the mesmerizing romantic music and jitterbug beats of big bands and the spirited high jinks of the new screen idols. Bob Hope, Bing Crosby and Dorothy Lamour starred in five road movies during the 1940s. Ms. Lamour, who entertained servicemen at the Hollywood Canteen and became one of the GIs' favorite pin-ups, was such a great promoter of war bonds that the government put a private train at her disposal. Hope and Crosby, with various starlets on their arms, traveled to the war fronts to raise the spirits of the fighting forces. On stage, "Oklahoma" in 1944 introduced the team of Rogers and Hammerstein, who came to stand, in the words of a recent critic, "for a corn-fed American goodness and the more saccharine forms of optimism", but their shows brought enormous joy to young and old audiences in worrisome times.

Everywhere the young people in uniform, and thousands of others soon to join them, listened to "music for dreaming", mood music usually composed and directed by one of its inventors, Paul Weston, and crooned by Frank Sinatra and other singers like Dinah Shore, Jo Stafford, Rosemary Clooney and Frankie Laine. Because of the gas shortage, young Americans rode bicycles or took the trains to hear and slow-dance or jitterbug to the sounds of the Big Bands, especially the smooth saxophones of Glenn Miller's "In the Mood", "Moonlight Serenade" and "Sunrise Serenade" and the music of Claude Thornhill, Harry James and others.

In January 1944, as the U.S. entered its third full year in the war, FDR gave what historian James MacGregor Burns has called the most radical speech of his life. Burns called it "a dramatic reassertion of American liberalism even at the height of war." Roosevelt proposed, and asked Congress to explore, an economic Bill of Rights to supplement the political rights defined in the Constitution's first ten amendments. After the war, he proposed, the nation should move forward to implement these rights, which would assure the economic security without which "individual freedom cannot exist." Among these broad new rights would be the right to a "useful and remunerative job", the right of every family to a decent home, the right to a good education and the right to protection from fears of old age and sickness and accident and unemployment. These prophetic words were the seeds of the welfare state, which was to grow piece by piece under his successors but particularly in the Great Society programs of future President Lyndon Johnson.

Allied forces were moving across the English Channel when FDR spoke to the nation on June 5, 1944. The President had been visiting with a military aide in Virginia, praying and re-reading the Book of Common Prayer to find appropriate D-Day comments. On D-Day an estimated hundred million of his countrymen gathered about their radios awaiting news from the Continent. FDR told them that Rome had fallen to American and Allied troops the previous day. "The first of the Axis capitals is now in our hands," he said. "One up and two to go!"

He lauded the generals and admirals and "all of our gallant, fighting men" who were leading the way to victory. That night he led the nation in prayer, assuring Americans that "...by the righteousness of our cause, our sons will triumph." On the day of his radio talk the Allies landed 132,000 men in Normandy, including 57,500 Americans, and in the Pacific over 500 ships and landing craft were getting ready for the invasion of Saipan. To pay for these immense and far-flung undertakings, FDR used this talk to launch the fifth war bond drive. He urged all Americans to buy these bonds to "swell the mighty chorus to bring us nearer to victory!"

The spirits of the American public at home mounted steadily as the U.S. fighting men proved their mettle and skill on distant fronts. Even Field Marshall Montgomery paid tribute to the fighting qualities of the American soldier. "I take my hat off to such men," he said. "I salute the brave fighting men of America—I never want to fight alongside better soldiers." The conservative London Express chimed in: "Americans have proved themselves to be a race of great fighters, in the very front rank of men at arms." In the Pacific, U.S. Marines were planning Okinawa, to becomethe bloodiest battle of all in that region, and U.S. Superfortresses were flying daylight raids over Tokyo. The U.S. Navy gained the offensive and, in the air, Hellcats from U.S. carriers triumphed in the Battle of the Philippine Sea. The fighting forces got a particular lift when several thousand Banzai were decisively defeated on Saipan.

In his final fireside chat of January 6, 1945—just three months before his death, and after the Allies had been battered by German counter-attacks in the Battle of the Bulge before resuming their offensive—FDR once again told how "Our men have fought with indescribable and unforgettable gallantry under most difficult conditions." He had high praise for the "admirable calm and resolution" of Supreme Allied Commander Dwight Eisenhower, and he added that the final, "toughest" job was being performed "by the average, easygoing, hard-fighting young American who carries the weight of battle on his own shoulders." He quoted from a Stars and Stripes editorial: "For the holy love of God let's listen to the dead. Let's learn from the living. Let's join the ranks against the foe. The bugles of battle are heard again above the bickering." And then, in his last hopeful words spoken to his great radio audience, he said:

"This new year of 1945 can be the greatest year of achievement in human history... We Americans of today, together with our allies, are making history—and I hope it will be a better history than ever has been made before. We pray that we may be worthy of the unlimited opportunities that God has given us."

FDR'S public persona was anything but modest throughout all his many ordeals, but the private man within had a humility witnessed by only a few intimates. At no time was he absolutely sure that any one of his prescriptions would be a cure. Even on the night after coming to power he confessed to his 25-year-old son, Jimmy: "I'm just afraid that I may not have the strength to do this job." But his patrician background, and an intelligence symbolized by the Phi Beta Kappa key he wore with pride helped him to call on bright and knowledgable people from whom he sought bold new ideas. The nation's way out as he saw it was in experimenting with new initiatives by the federal government which, even conservative Republicans were admitting at the time he rose to power, had become the nation's last resort.

The sources of FDR's optimism

The sources of FDR's own self-confident optimism, idealism and sense of ethics are not hard to find. His parents, both from wealthy families, instilled in him a noblesse-oblige sense of duty to community and nation. Like Jefferson and TR, his early education was in the hands of excellent tutors, including a Frenchwoman who taught him humane values as well as history and languages, according to Schlesinger. At 14 he bicycled through the Black Forest in Germany with a tutor.

His education and his sense of moral values was polished further at Groton, the most exclusive school in the country, known for producing well-educated Christian gentlemen. At Harvard, where he took his degree in three years, he encountered great teachers including Edward Channing, Frederick Jackson Turner and A. Lawrence Lowell in history and government, William Z. Ripley in economics and George Pierce Baker in public speaking.

Perhaps starting with the influence of his church at Hyde Park, and his Episcopal headmaster at Groton, FDR had a strong religious faith and assurance at his core, even though he did not manifest it in formal or public ways. The playwright Robert Sherwood, who wrote speeches for FDR, observed that "his religious faith was the strongest and most mysterious force that was in him." Schlesinger wrote that "if nothing ever upset him, if his confidence seemed illimitable, it was because he deeply believed, with full reverence and humility, that he was doing his best in the eyes of God, and that God was blessing his purposes, that he was at one with the benign forces of the universe." FDR himself once wrote: "I doubt if there is in the world a simple problem, whether social, political or economic, which would not find ready solution if men and nations would rule their lives according to the plain teaching of the Sermon on the Mount."

America was fortunate to have a leader who, while seeking maximum power for himself to do his experimenting, never had the ambition to become a tyrant that was so often ascribed to him. And the country was fortunate to have a people who remained essentially loyal to their system even when it nearly broke down, abhorring either of their obvious alternatives—anarchy or revolution—that might well have been chosen in another country.

FDR performed a feat of virtual magic in keeping the public almost unaware that he was a paraplegic, dependent on others to move his crippled body about throughout his busy reign, and "remained his funny, joyful, ebullient self, laughing, joking and teasing" right through his final months, wrote James MacGregor Burns. He was an unquenchable optimist right to the end. The last words he wrote, for a Jefferson Day address, were: "The only limit to our realization of tomorrow will be our doubts of today. Let us move forward with strong and active faith."

FDR died, still young at 63, in Warm Springs, Georgia of a cerebral hemorrhage on April 12, 1945, just 85 years after the death of

Lincoln, in both cases after pronouncing victories in great wars. As the news of his death was flashed around the world, "Americans were incredulous, shocked, and above all, afraid", wrote Manchester. "He had been leading them so long." On the radio, the afternoon broadcasts of "Tom Mix" on Mutual and "Captain Midnight" on ABC were interrupted by the simple, heart-stopping bulletin: "FDR Dead", and the weeping began across the nation.

Doubtless millions of Americans shared the feelings of one nameless soldier who, when informed of the President's death, said that "America will seem a strange, empty place without his voice talking to the people whenever great events occur". For whatever judgment individual citizens made about FDR and his policies, no one could doubt that his confident voice on the radio, and his confident, smiling appearance in public, kept up the spirits of the nation during these strenuous, trying years. In the cool hindsight of history, even the most conservative American can appreciate today, simply by reading FDR's fireside chats to the American public, that this president knew instinctively how to rebuild confidence and knew how to find the words with which he could explain both the crisis and his proposed cures of the nation's many problems.

As the train carrying FDR's coffin proceded slowly from Warm Springs to Hyde Park on the evening of April 12, thousands of Southerners knelt and prayed by the tracks along the route or sang religious hymns such as the one ("Onward Christian Soldiers") that FDR and Churchill had once sung to buck up public spirits in a much darker time four years earlier. Mourners stood on rooftops, gazed from windows and waited at grade crossings and stations throughout the night to pay their last respects.

Men took off their hats, women fell on their knees, trains were halted, movie theaters were closed, department stores were draped in black, newspapers dropped advertising and even phone service was discontinued. For the first time since Lincoln's death in 1865, Carnegie Hall cancelled a concert of the New York Philharmonic. Eleanor Roosevelt said later that this was when she realized for the first time just how direct and intimate FDR's dialogue with the American people had been. The emotional, nationwide sorrow at his death reflected the bond this unique leader had created with his people and the confidence he had given them in themselves.

Many national and world leaders expressed their shock, and the tributes rushed in. In London, Churchill said he felt as if he had been struck by a physical blow, and the British Broadcasting Company called it "the darkest night of the war." Lyndon B. Johnson described FDR as the only person he ever knew who was never afraid. John Gunther, who said he felt as if he'd lost his best friend, paid tribute to "FDR's belief in the basic goodness of man, his work to better the lot of humble people everywhere, his idealism and resourcefulness, his faith in human decency, his unrivaled capacity to stir great masses and bring out the best of them..."

With the war not yet finished and the peace yet to be secured, FDR left to his successor, Harry Truman, a host of major global problems. But he left Americans in far better spirits than when he had taken the reins twelve years before. Like several other great presidents he had wanted to retire many years before his rule ended, but he served longer than any other holder of the highest office. During that time he held up the nation's morale, first in the time of its worst depression, then in the time of its greatest war and its greatest, herculean effort to produce the ships, planes and other materiel needed to win that largest-scale war in history.

Once again all Americans had received a lesson on the value and importance of strong leaders who can meet recurrent challenges to national survival and social progress while maintaining their fealty to the principles of republican government and individual rights and liberties. Perhaps no other lesson of history is more important than that for American citizens to learn and to teach.

The behavior of Americans fighting World War II abroad and at home confirmed the traits that have been distinguished as peculiarly American and didn't really change them. "It confirmed Americans in their optimism, their self-confidence and their sense of superiority," wrote Commager. "They had been sure that America was the best and happiest of nations, and what they had seen overseas had strengthened this conviction."

The two "Great Wars"—Wilson's war and Roosevelt's war—far overshadowed two other American wars of the century. Both of these smaller wars—in Korea and the Persian Gulf—were victories for presidential leadership, in the sense that Truman's leadership halted the Communists' advance in Korea and George Bush's leadership in the

Gulf War repulsed Saddam Hussein's attempt to seize Kuwait. Each of these wars reinforced public confidence in international action to preserve peace.

But another war during this century of wars was far different from the others in terms of both public support and ultimate outcome. The Vietnam War was the biggest jolt to the naturally optimistic spirit of Americans in all their history.

PART THREE

AGE OF ANXIETIES

Bearing the Superpower Mantle

In the 1900s a literature of disillusionment mirrored the public anxieties that were growing in the postwar years. From the '20s on, much of the work of major writers exemplified the droop of American spirits—the "dispossession from paradise", as Prof. Charles Sanford put it in his Middlebury College lecture, later an important book, *The Quest for Paradise*. The core of this disillusionment, wrote Sanford, was in the heartland of the Middle West, where "the self-reliant pioneer farmer, driven ever westward in quest of the New Jerusalem, had lost his momentum, become weighted down with mortgages and surrounded by skyscrapers."

Although still believing that America was the best of all countries, "the American of the mid-20th century was by no means so sure that his was the best of all times, and after he entered the atomic age he could not rid himself of the fear that his world might end not with a whimper but a bang" wrote Commager. "His optimism, which persisted, was instinctive rather than rationalized, and he was no longer prepared to insist that the good fortune which he enjoyed, in a war-stricken world, was the reward of virtue rather than of mere geographical location. He knew that if there was indeed any such thing as progress it would continue to be illustrated by America, but he was less confident of the validity of the concept than at any previous time in his history."

Literary malaise

The myth of Eden survived in the moral indignation of 20th century writers, who mourned the lost innocence of the past when industrialism and materialism replaced old simple virtues with a new commercial ethic. Among the American writers who felt the individual had gotten lost in barren modern life, one of the first who saw the Edenic garden turning into a wasteland was T.S. Eliot, born in St. Louis, Missouri, who withdrew to England where he found life more civilized.

Among others similarly affected by change in America just before and after the turn of the century were Mark Twain, whose sympathies, as he satirized adult America, were with youth, the remembered youth of his own boyhood on the Mississippi; Sherwood Anderson of Camden, Ohio, whose *Winesburg, Ohio* and other books showed the conflict between the instincts of the individual American and the new organized industrial society and the sterility of the success-oriented machine age; Sinclair Lewis of Sauk Centre, Minnesota, the great satirist whose *Babbitt,* one of his 22 novels, showed how conformist values erased individuality in his protagonist, an average American businessman-Republican-Rotarian; and Theodore Dreiser, of Terre Haute, Indiana, who portrayed ruthless industrialists and, in *An American Tragedy*, told a depressing story of a young man's futile effort to climb to financial and social success, finally meeting a tragic end.

Chicago's James T. Farrell and John Dos Passos; Oak Park, Illinois' Ernest Hemingway; Michigan's Ring Lardner and Ohio's Hart Crane were among the other disenchanted Midwest voices. Crane, perhaps the most disillusioned of American writers, ended as a suicide, as did Vachel Lindsay, another Midwesterner, whose death in poverty contrasted with his poetry's early idealism and hope. In the South, William Faulkner, immersed in the scents of honeysuckle and wisteria that expressed for him the undefiled beauty of nature, saw a country rendered into a desert "by the iron and fire of civilization" and described a people "dispossessed of Eden."

Archibald MacLeish of Glencoe, Illinois, whose early poems celebrated the promise of nature in the grasses of Iowa, Illinois and Indiana, wondered whether the American dream of liberty was fading, "...the generations up, the years over." Among the Midwestern writers only Carl Sandburg continued the hopeful tradition of Whitman, wrote Sanborn, "celebrating with indiscriminate democratic rapture sunsoaked cornfields and grubby tenements, cornhuskers and convicts, redwood trees and skyscrapers, little people and empire-builders... and even he... turned with increasing nostalgia to a heroic past."

196

The myth of Eden did remain alive more or less in the "beat generation" of Jack Kerouac, the poet-essayist Lawrence Ferlinghetti and the poet Allen Ginsberg. In 1955 Ferlinghetti, sounded this plaintive note: "I am waiting for a rebirth of wonder... I am waiting for the discovery of a new symbolic frontier... I am waiting for the Second Coming... I am waiting for them to prove that God is really American..."

The Truman era

In the political life of the nation, another man from the Midwestern heartland, Harry Truman, tried to keep alive the nation's pride and spirits through years when its traditional ebullience was checked by troubling events far from its shores. Ever since the first emigrants turned their backs on Europe and sought to create their own new world, America's leaders, from Washington on, tried to avoid entanglements in the old world's conflicts.

After Wilson tried and failed to avoid involvement in World War I, and FDR tried and failed to avoid involvement in World War II, Americans hoped that they could finally turn inward again, hopefully to continue their pursuit of Eden.

One postwar development that was to have an enormous influence on American home life was the rapid spread of the postwar TV sets that went on sale during the first term of Harry Truman's presidency. The first TV broadcasts of a presidential inaugural and of the national party conventions took place during the Truman administration. But the increasing time spent by Americans in TV-watching drew them more and more into awareness of problems and crises far beyond their shores—giving immediacy and intimacy to events and people who were a very long way from America, enlarging what Boorstin called Americans' "sense of the contemporary" to a world scale and compounding their anxieties as the postwar era came up with new things to worry about. TV brought tragedies, crimes and suffering worldwide, to which earlier generations would not have been so directly exposed, right into the living room. What a contrast this was to the peaceful farmhouses of Crevecoeur and his neighbors—or the games of whist at Puritan hearthsides!

In fact, Harry Truman's ascent to the Presidency in 1945 marked the beginning of nearly four decades of underlying anxieties and confusion of American spirits as the country was drawn, like it or not, into complex foreign problems and erupting foreign controversies. This long period of anxious spirits came to a crest when President Jimmy Carter, in a speech on July 15, 1979 referred publicly to the national "crisis of confidence" and the "malaise" of the American spirit.

Though the American public had hoped for friendly postwar relations with its wartime ally, the Soviet Union, Stalinist Russia's postwar imperialism smashed these hopes, produced the global Cold War and forced America to wear the superpower mantle and remain, more than ever, intricately involved with conflicts far from home. Truman called the Soviet Union's refusal to cooperate on peace with its old allies "the most bitter disappointment of our time." On Truman's shoulders, from the moment he took office, fell the greatest range of challenges and responsibilities for preserving peace ever borne by any president before or since.

Samuel Eliot Morison called Truman, then almost 61 years old, an inconspicuous-looking president who "could easily have got lost in a crowd", but "one of the most conspicuously successful." Jonathan Daniels, the North Carolina editor who worked with Truman in the triumphant campaign of 1948, saw Truman as a "Ulysses", a symbol of the "everyday man" and the aspirations of ordinary people intuited by Jefferson, people capable of rising to the occasion.

Until his presidency, the main accomplishment of this amiable man from Missouri was the chairing of a U.S. Senate committee that had conducted a vigorous investigation of World War II spending, an investigation that startled the country by exposing inefficiencies and bungling on war contracts. With slim experience for the highest office of the land, Truman became the nation's chief executive by the fluke of FDR's premature death, and as chief executive he had to make decisions that had enormous effects on the nation's course and the peoples' spirits for decades to come. Max Lerner, one of many liberals like Walter Lippmann who doubted Truman's intellectual capacity to handle the job, called him one of history's "wild accidents."

Truman's background was humble. Growing up on a farm near Independence, Missouri (one of the old pioneer jumping-off places for both the Santa Fe and Oregon trails) he learned early to sow a 160-acre wheatfield with four mules and a gangplow. He was especially close to his grandfather, a big man with a big white beard, a Kentucky farmer who had migrated with his and many other families to what was then the far frontier, seeking the "New Eden." His grandfather, mother and other members of the big family talked a lot about their past and their politics and fanned young Harry's interest in history.

Though Truman read avidly, he never went to college. By the time he was 12 he had read the Bible through several times, memorized many of its passages and become enough of an expert on Biblical history to help settle religious disputes between various branches of the family, who were divided among Baptists, Presbyterians and Methodists (and, much later, to make up his mind about supporting the idea of a new Jewish homeland in Palestine.) In his early years he licked up American histories and biographies like a cat licks up discovered milk. Politically, Truman became a product of the crooked Pendergast machine. But from family, school and his rural Missouri community he inherited middle-class, middle-American, Bible-based religion and earnest patriotism, as well as habits of plain talk and the skill to play a mean hand of poker, his favorite pastime, which he taught later on to Winston Churchill.

On Monday, April 16, 1945, twenty-seven years after he had landed at Brest as a young artillery officer in the American Expeditionary Force, Truman strode down the aisle to deliver his first address to an anxious Congress. His 15-minute speech, carried to a huge radio audience, exemplified the determination, straightforwardness and humility that were to characterize his two extraordinary terms of office. In the conclusion of his speech, like the good true-believer Baptist that he was, he raised his hands, looked up at the audience and said, sincerely:

"I humbly pray Almighty God, in the words of King Solomon: 'Give therefore Thy servant an understanding heart to judge Thy people, that I may discern between good and bad: for who is able to judge this Thy so great a people?' I ask only to be a good and faithful servant of my Lord and my people."

The applause of Congress was echoed across the country, as Americans heaved a sigh of relief. "People everywhere felt relief, even hope, as they listened," wrote Truman biographer David McCullough. "He seemed a good man, so straightforward, so determined to do his job", promising to prosecute the war, work for a lasting peace and improve the lot of the common people. At his first press conference, the day after inauguration, Truman gave quick, forthright answers to questions, impressing the record turnout of 348 reporters.

The spirits of a people reflect to a large extent the popularity of their top leader, and Harry Truman's popularity chart was a running commentary on his times. He pulled off two of the biggest political surprises of all time and the American populace loved him for both of them. First of course was his immediate display of vigor and spunk upon taking the reins that had been held for so long by FDR; this performance won immediate public acclaim. In the months after FDR's death Truman's approval rating in the Gallup poll hit 87%, higher than FDR himself had ever scored and the highest Truman would score in the extraordinary years of crisis that lay before him. The second big surprise was his incredible landslide win of a second term on his own merits and against all odds.

"Everyone has been going at a terrific gait," Truman wrote to his mother at the end of his first few months, just after the surrender of Japan, "but I believe we are up to the parade now." The previous day Washington had seen its biggest celebration in history. Half a million people choked the streets as the bands played "I'm Just Wild About Harry." Fifty thousand or more pressed around the White House. Bells were ringing, people were cheering, car horns blaring and the crowd chanted: "We want Truman! We want Truman!" So with wife Bess beside him, Harry Truman stepped out on the White House porch and spoke these impromptu words:

"This is a great day, the day we've been waiting for. This is the day for free governments in the world. This is the day that fascism and police government ceases in the world." Speaking of the task ahead to restore peace and help spread free government around the world, he got another roar of approval when he said: *"We will need the help of all of you. And I know we will get it."*

Nothing sent the nation's spirits up and down more, after the two great wars, than the seesawing prospects for world peace, and Harry Truman earned a high place in history for his resolute efforts to secure that peace. He had a shaky start in foreign affairs, mainly because, being an amiable, trusting man, he was beguiled for a time by Stalin at their initial meetings. He took the heat at home for this naivete when the Red Scare raged like an epidemic through the American public. But his soft side towards the former Russian allies was not the side of this President that history would remember.

Fateful decisions

With incredible composure, and a display of remarkable vitality, Harry Truman navigated his way through some of the most epochal changes of his or any other era. His fateful decisions over the seven years starting in 1945 might be seen retrospectively as examples of William James' construct of will converted to action—heroic action in this case, because Truman not only was ahead of the public in judging American interests in the world but he also frequently, and correctly, overruled the advice of some of the nation's most distinguished leaders and experts.

In his first three months in office, as McCullough wrote, Truman faced "a greater surge of history, with larger, more difficult, more far-reaching decisions than any psresident before him." Riding high on his initial popularity, he made his first presidential public appearance in San Francisco, less than three months after being sworn into office. Cheered on by a million people, he rode in an open car leading a 75-car procession to the Opera House for the signing of the United Nations Charter. The next day he flew to Kansas City, which gave him the biggest welcome home Jackson County had ever given to anyone.

Truman rose to his challenges with immediate aplomb and decisiveness that no one could have predicted. A very early riser, he set a brisk pace for everyone. Just in that first year as President he got the Senate to ratify the U.N. Charter, played an active role in the last "Big Three" meeting with Churchill and Stalin, ordered the first use of the atomic bomb (which was dropped on Hiroshima on August 5, after he had agonizingly weighed conflicting advice from his experts) and on August 14 announced the surrender of Japan and the end of World War II. While he was still sailing home from Plymouth, England aboard the cruiser, the U.S.S. Augusta, the White House released a statement he had labored over aboard ship, to tell the American public about the most harrowing decision of his life:

> "Sixteen hours ago an American airplane dropped one bomb on Hiroshima. . . . It is an atomic bomb. It is a harnessing of the basic power of the universe. . . . We are now prepared to obliterate more rapidly and completely every productive enterprise the Japanese have above ground in any city. . . .we shall completely destroy Japan's power to make war. . . . If they do not now accept our terms they may expect a rain of ruin from the air. . . ."

From war to anxious peace

Relief and excitement swept over the country at this news, which everyone took to be the sign that the war would soon be over. Yet news of the bomb also brought new anxiety, even terror, to Americans, and to people everywhere. Newspaper editorials had a grave tone: The Washington Post compared the bomb to "the worst imaginary horrors of science fiction", and the Kansas City Star called it "an invention that could overwhelm civilization." Truman had agonized over the decision to use the bomb, finally deciding it would save millions of American *and* Japanese lives. The public's mood was mixed, but very anxious.

Truman symbolized the mid-20th century average citizen awakening to the awesome possibilities of new technologies, especially nuclear technology. He was not only the first world leader to know about and use this incredible new force, but also the first person in history who had to make a decision about using the most terrifying manifestation of power ever developed by science. From the moment of that history-changing bomb drop, a new and frightening era opened for Americans and for mankind. No one was stirred more deeply than this simple man by the true terror and potential danger to the human race represented by the new weapon. Against those anxieties he had to weigh what he considered to be his prime responsibility as President—the securing of peace and freedom among nations. To act on that priority required a very painful and lonely kind of courage and will.

In the Oval Room of the White House, at 7 p.m. on August 14, 1945, Truman touched off a sensational display of American spirits when he announced the unconditional surrender of Japan. "Across America," wrote Eric Goldman in *The Crucial Decade*, "the traditional signs of victory flared and shrieked." In New York, as the V-J news flashed in Times Square, two million people milled about hugging and kissing each other, cheering and celebrating for more than 24 hours. In Los Angeles yelling paraders commandeered trolley cars, played leapfrog in the middle of Hollywood Boulevard and hung Hirohito from scores of lampposts. In Salt Lake City thousands of people snake-danced in pouring rain. In St. Louis a church service was held at two o'clock in the morning. In Washington crowds at the White House shouted: "We want Harry!" The president, reflecting the anxieties that all Americans would feel after the celebrating ended, more mindful than anyone of the uncertainties that the atom bomb had raised over the new era, welcomed "a great day" with the crowd but warned everyone that the nation was entering a new era still facing a crisis no less significant than Pearl Harbor.

Truman's snappy style, his long hours at the job and his trademark early-morning speed- walk, were soon admired even by many of those who had expressed doubts about him. Reporters called him "chipper", "jaunty" and "bouncy", wrote McCullough. Columnist Westbrook Pegler said Truman looked "like his old maw just dressed him up and slicked his hair for the strawberry social." One revealing note on the new president was sent to a friend by Acting Secretary of State Joseph C. Grew, who wrote: "I think he is going to measure up splendidly to the tremendous job... he seems to know the score all along the line and he generally has a perfectly clear conception of the right thing to do and how to do it. He is personally most affable and agreeable to deal with but he certainly won't stand for any pussy-footing..."

The honeymoon for Harry Truman—and for the nation's elevated spirits—lasted about one year. Despite his fast start as a world leader, the combination of Truman's initial vacillation over Soviet threats abroad and, at home, the longest, most costly period of labor troubles in U.S. history caused his popularity to dive. In early January 1946, 800,000 steelworkers staged the biggest strike ever, followed by workers in one industry after another determined to make up for the wage controls of the war years. By February Truman's popularity went down to 63%. He was attacked from every direction—by J. Edgar Hoover for tolerating "Reds" in government, by the Republicans for appeasing the Soviet Union and for trying to control meat prices and by some even for his devotion to his mother.

In April the President announced in a radio-television broadcast that he was seizing the steel mills (an act soon declared unconstitutional) and in the same month John L. Lewis called a nationwide coal strike. Conservative publications like *Life* began to question whether Truman was up to the job of handling all these problems. In May the president issued an executive order for the government to seize and operate the railroads, whose stoppage had brought the country to a virtual standstill. In a grim-voiced broadcast to the nation, he said the crisis had been caused "by a group of men within our own country who place their private interests above the welfare of the nation." He threatened to call out the Army if the strikers didn't return to work by four o'clock the next afternoon.

Just as he was speaking to Congress the following day, calling for emergency legislation, Truman was handed a note from Clark Clifford telling him that the union had accepted his terms for settling the railroad strike. "The whole Congress rose to cheer and applaud," wrote McCullough, "…like something in a movie." Whatever doubts the pundits had expressed about Truman, he had proved again to be very tough and decisive when the chips were down, and his popularity climbed again. Leaders of both parties recognized, as a *New York Times* columnist put it, that he was "a man who could rise to the occasion." Only a little more than six months later, the President scored once again by breaking John L. Lewis's strike in the coal mines, after taking Lewis to court. The President's popularity recovered after his put-down of Lewis and the important, visible performance of George Marshall as his Secretary of State, which helped greatly to reinforce confidence in the Administration.

Busy again with foreign troubles in March 1947, Truman rose to the challenge of picking up from a thoroughly exhausted Britain the responsibility for rescuing Greece and Turkey when Stalin was arming guerrillas in Greece and planning to grab naval bases in Turkey. Truman drove through Congress a request for $400 million in aid to those two countries, thwarting Stalin's thrust into the Eastern Mediterranean that had cast a cloud over the whole Middle East.

The Truman Doctrine and the Marshall Plan

"The Truman Doctrine," as this strategy became known, was a sweeping historic departure in U.S. foreign policy. Pronounced by Truman in a joint session of Congress on March 12, 1947 in a bold, forceful speech broadcast by radio, this new policy placed the U.S. squarely in the path of Soviet expansion, taking up responsibility for Greece and Turkey but also going far beyond that. With this doctrine the U.S. adopted the policy of supporting free people around the world who were resisting subjugation by outside powers or armed minorities.

This bold "containment" policy marked the beginning of the Cold War, the open conflict between U.S. dedication to freedom everywhere and Communist ambitions to dominate the world. It committed the U.S. to a new internationalism. Truman's popularity, which had sunk as low as 32% in the Gallup poll during the labor troubles, was up to 50%, on the strength of the display of leadership represented by the Truman Doctrine, despite the public's wariness about foreign entanglements. The press was overwhelmingly favorable. The *New York Times* compared the new policy to the Monroe Doctrine, and the popular magazine *Colliers* said the President had "hit the popularity jackpot."

The President's and the nation's spirits were clearly lifted in the spring of 1947. Truman's approval rating shot up to 60%. *Time* magazine and other media noted a new confidence in the president. Truman was after all an incurable optimist (though sometimes a naïve optimist, as when he thought he could have a trusting though competitive, relationship with Stalin.) Sometimes his optimism was catching (inspiring millions in his one great presidential campaign, besides inspiring himself to Olympian stamina in that remarkable drive.) His optimism, he said, was based on "a deep and abiding faith in the destiny of free men" and grounded in his belief that people in general were more good than evil, and that even the most complicated problems could be solved by getting people, and nations, to understand one another better.

One great legacy of Truman's humanitarian instincts was the Marshall Plan, dedicated to helping the millions of people facing starvation in the "rubble heap" of Europe, as Churchill called it. This colossal U.S. aid program was announced on June 5 at Harvard by Secretary of State George Marshall only three months after the decision to prop up Greece and Turkey. Based on ground-breaking work by George Kennan, Dean Acheson, "Chip" Bohlen, William Clayton, Clark Clifford and others, the $17 billion European Recovery Program was one of Truman's proudest achievements.

This extraordinary national gesture to aid European recovery reflected Truman's belief that morality should guide foreign policy and his beneficent concern for ordinary people throughout the world. Calling on the Europeans to work out their own recovery programs with America's money, it was the most magnanimous act ever undertaken by a victor on behalf of the victims of a war. "In all the history of the world," Truman proudly wrote, "we are the first great nation to feed and support the conquered."

Turning to the most tenacious problem on the home front, in a speech before 10,000 people on June 29, 1947 delivered from the steps of the Lincoln Memorial, Truman made the most forceful statement on civil rights since Lincoln's time. Addressing the National Association for the Advancement of Colored People, he called courageously for state and federal action to stop the lingering evils of lynching and poll taxes, for an end to the persistent caste system in education, employment and other areas that continued to deny opportunities to millions of people of color. Just two months before, the color line in major league baseball had been broken at Ebbets Field when Jackie Robinson ran out to his position at first base for the Brooklyn Dodgers, beginning the career (at second base) that would make him a role model for millions of young black men. For many black people, Robinson was the real pioneer in breaking the color line, eight years before Rosa Parks refused to give up her bus seat and the civil rights movement began in earnest.

Truman had set up a blue-ribbon civil rights commission in late 1946, and based on that commission's findings, still bucking resistance in Congress, he issued early in 1948 the first presidential special message on civil rights, once again asking for federal legislation to protect the right to vote, to abolish poll taxes and to establish a Fair Employment Practices Commission. Frustrated by the slowness of Congress in enacting civil rights legislation, Truman took matters into his own hands in the special session of Congress in July that year when he announced executive orders to end discrimination in the armed forces, a momentous step forward, and to guarantee fair employment in the civil service.

In that same summer of 1948 Truman showed his spunk again in his reaction to Stalin's blockade of Berlin. Stalinist Russia had been putting pressure on everywhere following the Red-army coup in Czechoslovakia. Stalin's crude threat to Berlin, however, was met by Truman's mulish resistance as the President, without consulting anybody, ordered a full-scale airlift of supplies to the beleagered city. That bold act raised morale throughout the Western nations and altered the course of the Cold War, as well as improving Truman's own chances of reelection, though at that time no one was the least bit optimistic about his public support. Truman's basic goal in foreign policy was simple and sound, as it was when Wilson first voiced it in 1917, and as it is today — the goal of making the world "safe for democracy."

On May 12, 1949 the President, and the American people, tasted sweet victory when Stalin backed down, the blockade ended and the lights came on again in Berlin.

War had been averted. And thanks to the heroic effort of nearly 300,000 airlift flights, delivering well over two million tons of food and supplies, America was seen again as a muscular champion of peace and freedom abroad.

Equally important in assuring Americans and their friends abroad of future peace was the signing in April 1949 of legislation creating the North Atlantic Treaty Organization (NATO), a defense pact of the U.S., ten Western European countries and Canada whereby each of the parties agreed that any attack on one would be taken as an attack on all. As the first American peacetime military alliance since the birth of the republic, it broke new ground. Truman was instrumental, having, in his first major act after his 1948 election, instructed his State Department to begin negotiating such an alliance.

The home economy

After peace, the other great pillar of public morale was the economic state of the nation. The war had given a big boost to the U.S. economy. Production of goods and services in Truman's first year as president was more than double what it had been in 1939. The average worker's income had doubled and unemployment was less than two percent.

Two years after Truman's election the World Series drew public attention to the new medium of television, as crowds at bars and department stores gaped through the windows to watch the games. Within three years about one U.S. family out of eight had their own "television machine" (Truman's term), prosperity was greater than ever, Cadillacs were sprouting tail fins, the transistor was developed and Chuck Yeager broke the sound barrier. By the end of Truman's first term there were four million TV sets in the homes of Americans.

The "Truman era" was the greatest period of prosperity that had ever been experienced by private enterprise, as Henry Steele Commager pointed out, with corporate income, farm income and dividends all reaching new highs, and unemployment virtually disappearing. Republican Congresses blocked most of Truman's efforts to expand "New Deal-type" social legislation, though many of his ideas eventually found their way into law. (More than a decade after he left office, a frail but still chipper Truman witnessed Lyndon B. Johnson sign the new Medicare bill into law at the Truman Library, providing the health care for the aged that Truman had proposed 20 years before.)

From the time of his very first major domestic message to Congress, Truman called for the revival and extension of New Deal policies. Only four days after V-J day he called a special session of Congress and gave it the longest message of any president since Teddy Roosevelt—a message calling for a full-employment law that would guarantee the right to work for everyone able and willing to work as well as a comprehensive unemployment compensation program, a Fair Employment Practices Committee to eliminate every sort of job bias, a broad aid program for small business and a housing program to build 1.5 million homes a year for ten years. He proposed a wide-ranging veterans program, and one month later he proposed a year of military training, as a civilian, for every young man in the country (he later said he was convinced that the Korean War and possibly the war in Vietnam would have been avoided if such universal military training had been in effect.)

Truman supported government efforts to restrain prices through FDR's Office of Price Administration (set up to stem wartime inflation), a control system that was relaxed and re-imposed, relaxed and re-imposed again during his administration. He supported a hike of the minimum wage and greater spending on social welfare programs. Business leaders lobbied fiercely for removal of the leftover wartime price controls, which were a blind spot for Truman that handicapped business recovery.

It is worth remembering that Republican President Nixon, responding to inflation and unemployment in the summer of 1971, also froze prices, wages, rents and dividends, then set up a price commission and pay board to administer these controls (which caused the country more harm than Watergate), and finally replaced mandatory with voluntary wage and price controls, just as Truman had done. The Nixon team also sought to fight inflation by restructuring the capital markets with tight money, causing a rise in interest rates, a falloff in industry's investment and expansion and a rise in unemployment.

The result of these various efforts to direct economic forces from Washington was an erosion of the position of the U.S. economy vis-a-vis Europe and Japan and a trade deficit (the first in nearly 80 years) with former enemies Germany and Japan, whose economies began to boom and whose products began to elbow American goods off even American shelves.

The supreme irony of the "control by Washington" policies of the

Truman and Nixon administrations was the spectacular contrast between their results and the stellar performance of America's former enemy, Germany, when it was still under Allied direction and even before it became the Federal Republic of Germany. The genius who pulled this off was the cigar-puffing Bavarian professor, Chancellor Ludwig Erhard, who resurrected the spirits of the German people by putting his faith in self-regulation of markets, dismantling wage and price controls and rationing, handing out brand new Deutsche marks to every German citizen and, within eight years, wiping out German unemployment. His free-market policies channeled effort and resources to their most productive uses and made Germany the lead-engine of European economies just as, years later, the equally bold free-market policies of Chile taught a similar lesson to the economically fumbling countries of Latin America.

While Truman was resorting to wage and price controls, while Britain's Labor Government was putting its faith in rationing, controls and redistribution and France was barricading itself with economic protectionism, the burly Bavarian fearlessly took an opposite path and became enshrined in history as the father of the "miracle" of postwar Germany.

A cool candidate

No period of Truman's presidency evidenced more cool self-assurance of this surprising man in the face of crisis than the three and a half months of his 1948 election campaign. As he relentlessly traveled to middle-size and small cities all over America in the old presidential Pullman car, the *Ferdinand Magellan,* something was going on under the surface of news and editorial opinions and the smug predictions of all the pundits that he would be trounced by Thomas E. Dewey.

That "something" was this: with extraordinary vigor and stamina, he was making direct contact in his whistle-stop campaign with a huge part of the electorate, especially in the smaller towns and cities, and he was convincing the growing crowds that lined the streets to greet him—40,000 in Ardmore, Oklahoma, 60,000 each in Cincinnati, Akron and Duluth, 25,000 in a rainstorm in Grand Rapids, more than 100,000 in Seattle, 90,000 in Dexter, Iowa and a quarter of a million in Miami, for example—that he was one of them, that he spoke their language and understood their problems.

While Dewey stood aloof and over-confident, Truman stirred the spirits of millions. He campaigned from dawn to midnight, traveled nearly 32,000 miles by train and gave an average of ten, off-the-cuff speeches a day, usually blasting the "do-nothing" Republicans ("the party of the privileged") that had blocked his domestic agenda. "Between twelve and fifteen million people had cheered or at least seen us", Truman's daughter Margaret estimated. "No president in history had ever gone so far in quest of support from the people," wrote McCullough. Truman himself called it "a crusade for the welfare of the everyday man." Looking the crowds in the eye, often from the campaign train's rear platform, he would tell them: "You are the government."

This phenomenal campaign was the reason why so many Americans turned out on election day to give Truman the biggest political upset in American history. The cry that had gone out from the people— "Give 'em hell, Harry"—had been answered. A *New York Times* reporter, surveying voters throughout Ohio, found that none of them had expected Truman to win, "but a majority of the 'little people' from the mines, mills and farms, having made their decision quietly and thoughtfully, went out and voted for him anyway." By January 1949, thanks to that upset election victory, Truman's popularity rating had shot back up to 69%.

On January 20, more than a million people lined up to see the President ride to the Capitol and take the oath of office a second time. It was the first inauguration broadcast on television, with some 10 million viewers in 14 cities, the largest audience ever to watch a single event by McCullough's estimate, and 100 million more listening on the radio. On orders from Truman, his daughter Margaret recorded, "for the first time in history black Americans were admitted to all official and unofficial functions."

At 10 o'clock Truman, his wife Bess and daughter Margaret went to a prayer service at St. John's Episcopal Church on Lafayette Square, just as FDR had done. Later, on the inaugural platform at the Capitol, Truman doffed his top hat and white scarf and overcoat and, with his left hand resting on his old Gideon Bible, he repeated the oath administered by Chief Justice Fred Vinson. Then he bent quickly to kiss the Bible, and in a strong voice delivered a speech that was devoted almost entirely to foreign affairs.

The speech was in an affirmative spirit, pledging support for the

U.N., the Marshall Plan and the North Atlantic alliance and making news with the announcement of a bold *new* program of U.S. involvement in the world. Known as "point four" of his address, it was a program to share the benefits of American science and industrial progress with underdeveloped countries, sharing America's store of technical knowledge in order to help other free people "realize their aspirations for a better life." It was to be a worldwide effort, with the U.S. and other nations working through the U.N. for the achievement of peace and plenty. "Only by helping the least fortunate of its members to help themselves," Truman said, "can the human family achieve the decent, satisfying life that is the right of all people."

At the conclusion of the speech about 700 planes, including transports like those that had ferried supplies to keep Berlin alive, flew over the Capitol in tribute to the ceremony. "The whole pageant," wrote McCullough, "struck countless viewers... as profoundly stirring. It was a day of dedication for the democratic spirit, with all the elements large and small momentarily in harmony." *The New York Times* captured the moment in these words:

> *"The clear sunlight, the President's evident high spirits, the patience and cheerfulness of the great crowds, such moving episodes as the presence of a guard of honor of Mr. Truman's comrades of the First World War...the slowly moving masses of men and vehicles coming down the Avenue from the seat of the national legislative power to the seat of its executive power, the booming of the Presidential salute, the planes overhead, the whole mood of the occasion—all these things seemed to speak of a confident and even exultant Americanism.... It was democracy looking homeward across a great continent, but also looking outward toward the world in which democracy will never again be impotent or ashamed or apologetic."*

Reversal of fortune

The President in his white tie and tails who watched joyfully the dancers and some 5,000 people at the inaugural ball could hardly have guessed that a combination of negative developments would once again alter the picture for him, and the public's enthusiasm for him, in the year that followed his surprise election. Scandal smoked in the White House when Truman crony Harry Vaughn and others ("five percenters" they were called) were investigated for receiving five percent commissions for securing contracts or influence from the government.

More important still was the bad news tumbling on the President from every quarter abroad. China went to the Communists; Russia developed its own atom bomb and built its military strength to exceed that of the U.S.; high-level traitors who had transferred vital U.S. military information to Russia were exposed in both the U.S. and Britain.

With such a pileup of worries, the American public was again in a state of high anxiety. Nothing contributed more to this alarm than the highly successful, demonical campaign of Senator Joseph McCarthy to spread fears that Communists and "Red spies" had infiltrated the U.S. government. By the end of March 1950, Truman's standing in the polls had plummeted to 37%, while half the American people spoke favorably of McCarthy and believed he was doing worthwhile work.

In the early part of Truman's second term, the public was shocked by revelations on the domestic front suggesting that American society was not only being eroded by Communists but also threatened by an underworld of organized crime. Americans watched months and months of televised hearings run by Democratic Senator Estes Kefauver, disclosing links between criminals and public officials. Compounding fears that the country's moral fabric was shredding were other disclosures about cheating on exams by West Point cadets, about corporations that had been bailed out of trouble with government loans and about members of Congress who had received favors from businesses in return for public loans. The scandals discouraged Truman and dampened public spirits. So widespread was the public concern that the national advertising agency Young & Rubicam took full-page ads in the newspapers lamenting that millions of Americans were asking: *"What's happened to our ideals of right and wrong? What's happened to our principles of honesty in government? What's happened to public and private standards of morality?"*

Corruption, communism and the continuing Korean problem all contributed to the defeat of the Democrats and the election of General Eisenhower in 1952. Many Americans felt that Truman left office in near-disgrace because of the scandals and also because of his misguided, defeated efforts to impose a virtual war economy of price and credit controls on the nation. But no one could deny his magnificent successes in foreign affairs.

Korea: victory from the jaws of defeat

Just as FDR had to meet challenges in the West and East simultaneously in his efforts to keep peace, Harry Truman, having taken his bold and sucessful steps to hold Russian expansion in check, had to face an equally dangerous situation in Asia. Once again, this episode began with public fear and trepidation, escalating in this case with initial military disasters and driving Truman's popularity to an all-time low.

A phone call from Secretary of State Dean Acheson on the evening of June 24, 1950 alerted the President back home in Independence that North Korean forces had crossed the line drawn after World War II separating them from the South Korean zone of occupation. Almost immediately Truman ordered U.S. air and naval forces to South Korea and three days later, having briefed Congressional leaders, he ordered U.S. ground forces into action to stem the invasion. Privately, he referred to Korea as "the Greece of the Far East."

For the first time in a long while, millions of Americans throughout the country, including many veterans of World War II, felt their spirits lifted when they heard Truman's declaration on the radio. Whatever their anxieties, they knew that this president was taking a stand, that he had learned the lessons of Munich and other capitulations to aggressors hostile to democracy and that he was upholding an American tradition in riding to the rescue of friends under siege. As happened with many other great men, his courage and rightness was recognized far more by succeeding generations than by the nervous and somewhat confused public that he led at the time.

A week after Truman ordered Americans into battle, the United Nations, prompted by Dean Acheson's fast action in the Security Council, placed forces of 15 other countries under U.S. command, and Truman appointed General Douglas MacArthur supreme commander of the combined military. For the first time, a world body had voted to meet armed force with armed force. The U.S. public bombarded the White House with phone calls, telegrams and letters expressing overwhelming approval.

After the U.N. forces had been pushed back in retreat to the southeast tip of Korea, the anxious American public was cheered when MacArthur launched a counter-offensive with a bold landing on the west coast. MacArthur's forces pushed north and took the Communist capital of Pyongyang and drove the Communist fighters almost to Red China's border. Then, to everyone's surprise and alarm, the Chinese Communists entered the war to rescue their Communist neighbors, counter-attacking and pushing south to recapture the South Korean capital of Seoul.

The American-led forces were forced back in the longest retreat ever made by an American army, and there was even some talk of evacuating the U.S. forces altogether in what would have been a virtual Dunkirk. Although he remained calm and steady throughout this ordeal, Truman worried deeply that a third world war was in the making, and agonized over what his own response should be to avert such a disaster. Keeping his cool throughout these dark days, Truman made headlines when he replaced MacArthur for insubordination after the general over-stepped his authority. Truman put General Matthew Ridgeway in command of the Eighth Army at its most excruciating moment.

That decision proved brilliant, because Ridgeway restored the U.N. forces' spirits and by March recaptured Seoul, driving on to the 38th parallel. The retreat of American forces, and the constant news of bloody losses, had by that time horrified Americans and driven the President's approval rating to an all-time low of 26% and, with corruption scandals involving the Internal Revenue Service making the news, falling to 23% by December.

Throughout his presidency, Truman showed a remarkably gutsy, independent mind, especially in asserting civilian control over the military and departing from the advice of "experts" —rebuffing his National Security Council when it opposed his decision to aid Greece, approving MacArthur's daring Inchon landing despite the doubts of the military chiefs, firing MacArthur for his habit of making political public statements conflicting with administration policy, rejecting advice from his Joint Chief's at the war's nadir when they advocated destroying Chinese cities with nuclear weapons and standing firm against political opponents like Robert Taft when they supported MacArthur even after Truman sacked the popular general.

Following the dismissal of MacArthur, calls for Truman's impeachment came from the Chicago Tribune, from Senator Taft and from countless others who besieged the Republicans in Congress with telegrams. On April 20 the president was booed when he threw out the season-opening ball at Griffith Stadium, and it was MacArthur, not Truman, who drew cheering crowds of millions when he returned to a triumphal welcome in Washington and a ticker-tape parade in New York that drew over seven million people, more than greeted Lindbergh in 1927 or Eisenhower in 1945.

But the editors of major newspapers endorsed Truman's decision to fire the Supreme Commander. The *New York Herald Tribune* praised the President's strength of character and said: "With one of those strokes of boldness and decision which are characteristic of Mr. Truman in emergencies, a very difficult and dangerous problem has been met in the only way it could have been met." This indeed has been the verdict of history, or at least of a growing consensus of historians who saw the wisdom of Truman's decisive actions and his insistence on "holding the line." Despite his questionable approval of the move north of the 38th parallel that provoked China, he was instrumental in turning the tide of the Cold War and, quite possibly, avoiding a third world war—the possibility of which he and the American people had so often dreaded during this very trying time.

The Korean War ended after Truman had left office, but his role in it earned him the esteem of all who understood the critical role that his determination and decisive action had played in once again turning the tide of world events very definitely in favor of America's ideals as well as its strategic interests. The action of the U.S. and its U.N. allies in Korea, as The *New York Times* put it, "represented something of a regaining of our national soul and conscience. We did a difficult and costly thing because we thought it was right."

Harry Truman was indeed a most unusual leader and a remarkable American, lifted from obscurity by history and inspiring a nation that gradually recognized his natural talents, not least of which his élan vital. Eight years after leaving the White House this still-frisky elder statesman, who in his time had faced off with Stalin, Molotov, MacArthur, John L. Lewis, Robert A. Taft and an obstinate Republican Congress, returned to what he once called "the white jail," where he had put in so many 18-hour days. On this particular occasion he entertained President John F. Kennedy and the assembly of distinguished black-tie guests by sitting down at the piano and playing for them a selection from Paderewski's *Minuet.*

Vietnam and the sixties

Americans had solid moral convictions, and unflagging optimism, about both of the "great wars" and also, with more mixed opinions, about the Truman-led Korean war against Communist expansion in Asia and the George Bush-led Gulf War to throw back Saddam Hussein's invasion of Kuwait. The exception in this century of wars was the longest, bloodiest and costliest war of all, the Vietnam War, a watershed in American history and the most brutal shock ever administered to the traditional, optimistic spirit of Americans. It was an aberration in American history.

U.S. public support for halting Communist North Vietnam's aggression was high initially—as evidenced by the unanimous war-policy vote in the House of Representatives in 1964 and the endorsement of military action by leaders such as Senator J. William Fulbright and was propped up by the increasingly deceptive assurances of Lyndon Johnson. But when casualties escalated as American military strength in South Vietnam reached half a million by end-1967 with still no victory in sight, the spirits of many Americans began to sink.

In 1965 and 1966 student activists had begun organizing war protests on college campuses. President Johnson's escalation of the war brought these protests to a boil and in 1968 more than 40,000 students were demonstrating at over a hundred colleges and universities. Student activists, like the public, were divided, however: in January '66 the College Republicans presented a petition with more than a half million student signatures in support of the Vietnam war.

Psychologically, the Communist "Tet offensive" in early 1968 had a devastating effect on the American people, increasing their doubts about this frustrating conflict and its sickening carnage. Since the Civil War, nothing had ever divided, disillusioned and embittered the public more than the repeated, day after day, agonizing TV coverage of American servicemen returning home in body-bags. This was a new and unique experience right in their living rooms. Amplified by the live television coverage of the war's horrors, the shattering experience of Vietnam marked the all-time low in the history of the nation's spirits.

The largest protest on college campuses followed the tragic shooting of students by state troopers at Kent State in 1970, prompting demonstrations by about a quarter of the total eight-million university students across the nation.

The counterculture spawned by this increasingly unpopular war galvanized a new generation that sang of "peace", "coming together" and "love, not war". The dark side of this new culture—the nascence of the drug epidemic that would ravage the nation, the defiance of law and order, the scorn of patriotism, the explosive growth of illegitimate, single-parent births, the promiscuity and vulgarity—have been well documented. The easy access to birth control pills and illegal drugs created a lifestyle that would have been unthinkable to the parents of these youngsters. But in time, most hippies realized it was impossible to reform society by "dropping out." And after many years, most of them realized that their emotional return to childishness, especially their glorification of the self and their view of life as "doing your own thing", which was nobody else's business, should not supersede traditional loyalties to family, community and old institutions like the church.

Still, the history of the American spirit would be incomplete—especially for those who were young and free in that era—without also acknowledging the perverse optimism of this subversive subculture and its lasting effects on American society. The sixties was a highly original variation on Americans' search for Eden—a colorful, chaotic period that left a deep imprint on American culture. The children of this Age of Acquarius were optimists, even though their "movement" began with student uprisings from Berkeley to Harvard seeking to overturn traditional culture and end the Vietnam war.

Their innocence, or naiveté, was personified by thousands of young people, many from the suburbs, who headed for places like Haight Asbury in San Francisco and the East Village and Greenwich Village in New York, frequently disconnecting from parents in suburbia who they felt were preoccupied with "making it" in business or other pursuits of wealth. As one guitar-playing, 16-year-old runaway explained her reason for leaving her prominent family and comfortable home in upstate New York: "The hippies are for love and beauty."

The initial optimism of the youngsters, who thought they could end war by holding hands and singing together with the fellowship of mankind, was in some ways a naïve re-emergence of the Edenic visions of Thoreau and other poets who sought escape from a harsh, mechanistic, materialist world. There was a very real sense of community—unconditionally welcoming rich and poor, black, white or brown, and searching together for answers to their spiritual hunger. The "flower children" were optimistic because they believed they could humanize society, challenging what they saw as the sterile, conformist stereotypes of the white-collar Eisenhower fifties—people who, they believed, took themselves too seriously and too selfishly. They rebelled not just against the war but against the culture of PTAs, country clubs, Little Leagues, department stores, family television and the other quiet, domestic pleasures, and the blandness, that their parents had been happy to settle into after two grueling decades of depression and war.

The new generation was crying out, especially in music and in its huge gatherings, against the cold impersonality and money-infatuated business society. More than half a million of them gathered on a 600-acre dairy farm near Woodstock, New York in August 1969 to make their statement (as simple as Joni Mitchell's anthem sung by Crosby, Stills, Nash and Young, "We are star dust, we are golden..."). They presented an unforgettable picture: kids with long hair and bushy beards strumming guitars, "bizarrely-dressed hippies with beatific smiles", as one reporter described them, and Volkswagen Beetles with daisy decals creating traffic jams in the mud. Such carnival-like gatherings produced high spirits because they represented an achievement of community among the counter-cultural crowd and what seemed at the time to be a healthy loosening of puritanical inhibitions about sex and drugs and a glorification of "self-actualization" and "natural" foods.

By comparison with their starchy elders, the flower children were whimsical, fun-loving, totally open, absurd and sometimes grotesque. Holding hands, in couples or in groups, became a happy norm for them. They recoiled from bourgeois values, narrow-minded authority and the traditional codes of American life. Probably the closest they ever came to gaining establishment recognition was when a *New York Times* editorial appeared in 1994 that praised their creativity and political activism and admitted that they "profoundly altered the way Americans think about their inner lives, their fellow citizens, the earth upon which we live and the process by which older citizens in Washington decide when and where young Americans die in combat." Perhaps more typical of the "straight" population's attitude were the words of Joan Didion in an essay on hippie culture: "We were seeing the desperate attempt of a handful of pathetically unequipped children to create a community in a social vacuum."

New music, often sung in groups, carried the themes of love, gentleness and social justice in the counter-culture. In the early sixties Bob Dylan became the most influential folk song writer. "The Times They are a Changin'", "Blowin' in the Wind" and his other songs captured the alienation of American youth and the concerns with social protest, poverty and politics he had inherited from Woody Guthrie. Pete Seegar ("Where Have All the Flowers Gone?", "If I Had a Hammer") got the crowds to sing along and influenced Joan Baez, who sang and marched for civil and student rights and peace. Sentimental love songs were sung and danced to, but these too were original, no longer putting women on pedestals but expressing the warm and close relationships of lovers, with titles like "You don't have to say you love me—just be close at hand" and "You light up my life", usually song by young women whose voices embraced crowds with electronic amplification.

Many of the young people shared a naïve belief that wonderful, magical changes were about to take place—as soon as people learned to express their feelings honestly and behave naturally. By 1963 four Liverpool-born singer-musicians who called themselves "the Beatles" had become objects of wild adoration in America, singing their lovely, original songs of love and peace (later, with allusive, drug-inspired lyrics), strumming bold rhythms on their electric guitars, less harsh and strident than Guthrie and Dylan, and introducing the cello, trumpet and sitar and new electronic techniques into their soft rock. They were followed everywhere by crowds of shrieking adolescent girls. The "Age of Acquarius" dawned in 1967 at New York's Public Theater with the opening of the hippie musical "Hair", which moved to Broadway and mainstream audiences the following year.

The psychedelic euphoria of the '60s made saints of pop music stars and the saint with the biggest, adoring legions of followers was the nine-fingered, bearded electric-guitarist and singer Jerry Garcia ("Captain Trips") and his nomadic San Francisco band, the Grateful Dead, which became the world's most popular touring rock band, touching deep emotions of three generations of Americans. As one devotee put it, "The world according to Jerry involved some basic precepts: Don't rip anyone off, don't discriminate, be nice, stay mellow, share stash." The concert-goers, who shared this philosophy and the idealism and communal bliss of Garcia's gatherings were like one huge, extended family living in a world all their own.

The Grateful Dead played their hybrid of rock, country, folk and blues to joyful audiences wearing "free spirit" clothes, tie-dyed T-shirts and Rasta hats, dancing in bare feet, eating vegan burritos and following the band's concerts from city to city—including the pop festival in Monterey in 1967, Woodstock in 1969 and Watkins Glen in 1973 and reaching as far as Egypt's Great Pyramid. They grossed as much as $50 million a year and gave tens of millions to charity. They set attendance records at one major arena after another. Their long, free-form concerts had a spontaneity that lifted the spirits of young people who saw themselves as pioneers seeking new ways to live in a complex world. Theirs was a virtual, secular religion of hope and celebration. The band's music radiated a new, original form of American optimism and adventure.

"Sunny, mischievous, cheerfully subversive, the band seemed to promise a better time always would come just up the road, around the bend," wrote Micah Morrison, an editorialist who believed the band evoked the same restless, nervous energy, the looseness and individualism, that Frederick Jackson Turner had identified as traits of frontier life. What inspired this comparison was Garcia's liberating, free-form ethos—letting music spring from his head and his heart in a spirit of risky exploration, in performances that never were the same. The band members played their hearts out, sometimes in cosmic five-hour marathons loaded with improvisations.

One newspaper, the *Seattle Post-Intelligencer*, called this band "the restorers of celebration in American life." The band's epic songs described America's mountains and cities, including the muddy rivers of Alabama and the Cumberland mines of Appalachia as well as their San Francisco homeland. Their songs were full of characters who often encountered disaster, but always laughed in its face. Jerry Garcia played with the flower-child optimism of one who really believed that sticking daisies into rifle barrels of National Guardsmen could help to stop the war.

This remarkable musical group mirrored the underside of the '60s as well as the bright, happy hopes of its enthusiastic worshippers. Garcia found inspiration in a massive, lifetime habit of hallucigens, ending in a heroin addiction that cut short his life. When the news came out that he had died at 53 at the Serenity Knolls drug treatment center in California, fans wept in the streets of San Francisco, Candlelight vigils were held in L.A. and Seattle and New York's Central Park and the Internet were flooded with eulogies and remembrances. One Internet mourner said "I can't believe it. I feel sick. But it's true, everyone. He's gone. It's over." Another fan wrote: "God is dead." A 29-year-old Starbucks coffee roaster in Seattle, who had followed Garcia for 11 years, spoke for many when he said he had been amazed by this "large group of like-minded people, people who were genuinely concerned about the thoughts and feelings of other people, about how we live in a community and how we live on the planet."

For all the attention it got and the influence it spread, the '60s psychedelic mania never went far beyond the youth cults in a few big cities and college campuses. Popular culture at the time included much more traditional fare—TV shows such as "Here's Lucy", "Marcus Welby, M.D." and "The Wonderful World of Disney" and Julie Andrews' hit movies of '64 and '65, "Mary Poppins" and "The Sound of Music." The movie box office champ of 1969, the year of Woodstock, was the road movie about the magic Volkswagen called "The Love Bug." But while the impact of the counterculture rebels didn't transform American society, its influence on the American consciousness continued for a long time to come.

Its humanizing influence and its smashing of stereotypes, for example, could not but have an effect on the younger workers on the business side of American life, which had been epitomized in Sloan Wilson's and William White's gray-suited "organization men". The influence of the '60s generation upon that business world has gone largely unremarked. There is no question but that this was the influence that led to a whole new breed of business people—the unstructured, jeans-clad crowd of entrepreneurs who founded high-tech companies that have grown at breakneck speed over the intervening years into some of our largest enterprises—as well as fostering greater openness of business in general towards employment of minority workers and encouragement of new ways to do things.

Many of the '60s flower children were still young when they started or helped build the high-tech companies of Silicon Valley and other hotbeds of computer technology and software. They pollinated those businesses with the humanizing influence of their generation, trying out on their own a proliferation of new ways to run an organization— "open offices" where supervisors and supervised were treated as equals, "think teams" where everyone was encouraged to share new ideas, elimination of hierarchies and meetings and other formalities, tolerance for big mistakes, huge rewards for innovators, company beer parties at the end of each workweek, and frequently stock options for every single employee, to make all of them feel like "family."

So the flower people did have a serious role in softening the hardness of a society that in the post-Depression and post-World War years had perhaps grown too stiff and standardized. They helped plant the seeds of the greatest business revolution in history, bringing with it a whole new culture of rapture, free expression and open collaboration.

As they grew up and entered the economic mainstream, they worked long and hard hours, energized by the greatest freedom ever enjoyed by workers in any society. The corporate apple-logo with a bite taken out of it was a whimsical reminder that a new, creative and exciting generation had taken charge and things would never be the same again.

The sixties were short-lived in the long arc of history, as were all the previous wishful efforts to create, on however small a scale, the Eden for which Americans were always reaching. But for many young people, leading sparse lives in their patch of Greenwich Village or Haight Asbury, the dream was lovely for the short time it lasted. And the hippies did raise a serious question that remains in the air: the question as to whether capitalist society can be humanized to the point that *all* citizens identify with the system, not just those with the capacities and contacts to richly aggrandize themselves.

Near the end of the sixties, feminists emerged more vociferously than ever as another force calling for change in American society that had to be reckoned with. They formed hundreds of organizations between 1969 and 1973—anti-discrimination bodies, campus collectives, centers for women's studies, political action committees and feminist publications. Their gathering power, as they demanded an end to unequal treatment, was indicated in 1972 when Congress approved the Equal Rights Amendment by overwhelming majorities, followed the next year by the controversial Supreme Court decision that women had a constitutional right to abortion. The ferment of the '60s was bringing American society closer than ever to fulfilling its promises of freedom and equal rights.

"Martin Luther" and the sixties

One of Vietnam's many tragedies was that the war clipped the wings of the civil rights movement by distracting presidential attention. The Viet Cong guerrillas and the North Korean Communists were already worrying U.S. officials in 1955–56, the time when the 26-year-old black Baptist minister Martin Luther King, Jr. was leading protests against Montgomery, Alabama's segregated bus system, marking the beginning of the civil rights movement. From then until King's assassination in Memphis in 1968 (the year of the Tet offensive) the White House was increasingly preoccupied with the agony of ending the highly unpopular war that Lyndon Johnson, even at the start of his administration in 1963, said he wrestled with "all the time, day and night."

Yet in little more than a decade Martin Luther King played the lead in bringing the nation nearer than ever to closing the gap between Jefferson's vision of equality and the reality of segregation, race hatred and unequal opportunity that for more than eight decades had polluted U.S. race relations. Against all sorts of obstacles, including the hesitancies of three American presidents, he managed to prevail by building upon the nation's religious and moral foundations, implicit in which he believed is the dignity of every individual.

King's amazing accomplishment was based on his strong moral convictions, his eloquence in reaching out to black *and* white people and his unwavering adherence to the principle of using nonviolent protest as a moral force, something he learned from his studies of Christianity, of Gandhi's devotion to nonviolence and Thoreau's ideas on civil disobedience and from his own tutor, the moderate black leader Bayard Rustin.

Being a minister who spoke in biblical cadences helped King arouse the spirit of the black people. And like King, the brave young "Nashville kids" who played such a big part in sparking the civil rights movement were devout Christians, two of their leaders having trained at Vanderbilt Divinity School, and their religious faith explained their resolution and their success in their struggle for equal rights, starting with the integration of lunch counters at Nashville's major department stores.

King holds a unique position in the tradition of great American optimistic moralists. When black churches were burning, black homes were being bombed, black citizens were being arrested for wanting to vote or share public facilities with whites, when young blacks were being beaten and killed and their murderers let loose from prison, King was preaching, "We are on the move now!" He carried the refrain, "We shall overcome" through a lifetime struggle that included his own repeated jailings, his stoning in Chicago, the bombing of his house in Montgomery and his stabbing in New York.

On receiving the Nobel Prize at Oslo University in 1964, his battle far from won, King called it "a great time to be alive" and declared he was "not yet discouraged about the future." In contrast to the bigots who hated him, King consistently spoke to the highest, spiritual senses of his audiences, seeking to inspire love and brotherhood and to discourage hate and violence. The moral and spiritual fervor he aroused among millions led to many transcendent events that became among the most memorable tableaux of American history.

Of the many scenes that epitomized the "overcoming" spirits of black Americans, a particularly poignant one was "The Children's Miracle" described by Taylor Branch in the first volume of his King biography. This was the scene at the Sixteenth Baptist Church in Birmingham, Alabama in May 1963 when police squads waiting outside to head off a youth march were suddenly overwhelmed when the church doors were flung open and long lines of teen-agers and even first-and second-graders, two abreast, marched out clapping their hands and singing "We Shall Overcome" at the pace of a ragtime march.

When the police halted the first line, another line marched out, then another and another until the brave children chanting freedom songs far outnumbered the capacity of the police paddy wagons waiting to haul them to jail, unstopped even by the sight of firemen with high-speed fire hoses. Nearly a thousand children, some as young as six years, were registered for jail during the three hours of this unprecedented spectacle, and 600 were taken into custody. It was one of the most moving displays of spirit and courage in all of American history.

Roused by King's sermons, and the inspiring music and singing that was so distinctive among Southern black churches, mass meetings kept up the spirits of black people across the country, courageously making their most strident outcries for delivery on the unkept promises of liberty and citizenship that had been made to Americans first in Jefferson's Declaration, then in Lincoln's Emancipation Proclamation.

King had learned about the power of mass demonstrations from evangelist Billy Graham, and from 1955 to 1965, under King's leadership, nonviolent protest achieved its greatest success—in the "freedom crusade" marches in Birmingham and Montgomery, the "sit-ins" at lunch counters and other segregated places, the "pray-ins" at churches and the "wade-ins" at beaches. After Montgomery, and the Supreme Court decision in 1956 ordering Montgomery to provide equal, integrated seating on buses and proving that nonviolent tactics could get results, King became a national figure and the "movement" begun by the Southern churches was on its way, accompanied almost always and everywhere by music of extraordinary spirit.

The first white mass meeting to which King took his message was in St. Paul's Episcopal Church in Cleveland, the first of his many mobbed stops in Cleveland. Shortly afterwards came word from Harry Belafonte that Los Angeles and Hollywood were mobilizing to give King a welcome that would top Cleveland's. King and "the heroes of Birmingham", now besieged with speaking invitations, were given a particularly memorable welcome in Chicago, where he rode in an open car with a limousine and police motorcycle escort to McCormick Place on Lake Michigan's shore. The cast for this mass meeting, with an overflow crowd that stayed until two o'clock in the morning, included no less than Chicago's Mayor Daley, gospel singer Mahalia Jackson, blues singer Dinah Washington and 21-year-old rising star Aretha Franklin, who sang the closing hymn.

Detroit was a similar story. King called his mass meeting at Cobo Hall in 1962 "the largest and greatest demonstration for freedom ever held in the United States." Something over 125,000 people listened intently to his 48-minute address, cheering almost every sentence he spoke. Branch pointed out that King delivered in Detroit a longer and richer version of the "dream" speech that he was to give two months later in Washington, with references in both speeches to Jefferson's democratic intuition and Biblical passages from Amos and Isaiah.

The apogee of King's nonviolent campaigns was the great Freedom March in Washington in the summer of 1963, a triumphant moment in American history. It was organized by King's friend and mentor, Bayard Rustin, inspired by joyous movement music and transfixed by King's "I have a dream" address, a speech that many believe to be the most important single piece of American oratory since Lincoln's Gettysburg Address and which became a glowing, permanent part of American legend. On that day, August 28, huge crowds of people poured into Washington—on 21 chartered trains and on chartered buses that arrived at a rate of one hundred an hour. Some people bicycled from as far as Ohio and South Dakota and one young black man, wearing a bright "Freedom" sash, roller-skated all the way from Chicago.

At the Washington Monument staging area, the spirits of the crowds were lifted by the freedom songs of Joan Baez and Odetta, the popular ballads of Peter, Paul and Mary and Bob Dylan, as well as the music of the Student Nonviolent Coordinating Committee's Freedom Singers from Albany. A huge sea of 300,000 or more people in all, black and white, waved their placards and gathered around the base of the Lincoln Memorial and on both sides of the reflecting pool between the Washington and Lincoln monuments. A. Philip Randolph, leader of the Brotherhood of Sleeping Car Porters, introduced King as "the moral leader of our nation."

With CBS, ABC and NBC television covering him, King faced a giant audience and a huge press corps and, in what Branch called "his clearest diction and stateliest barotone", gave the speech for which history would best remember him. Interrupted by ovations, and voices young and old calling out "Right on!" or just "Yes!", King went through his prepared text and then suddenly departed from it, speaking extemporaneously and, with characteristic optimism, urging the crowd to continue the work for freedom—urging them not to "wallow in the valley of despair."

When Mahalia Jackson shouted, "Tell 'em about the dream, Martin!", King, perhaps hearing her, decided to abandon his prepared speech altogether. He spoke from his heart of his "dream deeply rooted in the American dream…" With Mahalia chanting "My Lord! My Lord!" in the background, he said: "*And if America is to be a great nation, this must become true, so let freedom ring. And when this happens…we will be able to speed up that day when all God's children, black men and white men, Jews and Gentiles, Protestants and Catholics, will be able to join hands and sing in the words of the old Negro spiritual, 'Free at last! Free at last! Thank God Almighty, we are free at last!'*".

"I have a dream," King cried again and again in his speech, and each time the dream was a promise drawn from America's founding history. His speech rang with phrases from the Constitution, lines from the national anthem, guarantees promised by the Bill of Rights—all end-

226

ing with his vision that America's promises would all really come true.

The mass demonstrations drew enormous attention and support for the freedom movement and were influential, along with King's persistent prodding of presidents Eisenhower, Kennedy and Johnson, in leading eventually to passage by Congress of the Civil Rights Act of 1964 and the Voting Rights Act of 1965. What King and his followers did with his vision, based on devotion to a common American heritage rather than to any racial differentiation, was no less than to arouse America's moral conscience and move the country close to the ideal of civic equality, the founding ideal that "all men are created equal."

The black people King inspired may not yet have reached "the promised land" of equality he so confidently predicted for them; discrimination and segregation were not wiped out by the freedom movement and the legislation it inspired; prejudice lingers on throughout America, and de jure desegregation has not changed millions of prejudiced minds. But the gross bigotry and injustice and denial of basic rights that King lived through and preached against finally passed from American life, and blacks in America made great strides in joining whites at virtually all levels of personal and professional achievement, not least because of the great numbers of white Americans making an effort to enhance the status of blacks in the nation's life.

Had King lived a full life—had he not been cut down by an assassin a bare decade after stepping onto the national scene—he would have seen much of his dream come true; he would have seen black people emerge from the bleak life the South offered them in the '50s and '60s, and he would have seen the black American man and woman rise to remarkable positions of prominence. Though his assassination precipitated the worst rioting the country had ever seen in its big cities, betraying King's fundamental principles of non-violence, cooler heads in the years that followed proceeded on the peaceful path he had laid out.

The grass-roots drive for civil rights, and the heroic acts of civil rights activists, had acquired such moral power by 1964 that the Civil Rights Act was passed that year, the most important legislation in the history of American race relations. It banned racial discrimination in privately-run public facilities, authorized the Attorney General to eliminate de jure segregation in public schools and other public places, forbade discrimination in employment and created the Equal Employment

Opportunity Commission. The law had heart-warming effects on the black community, over time finally bringing down finally the barriers of Jim Crow—people could then begin to enjoy equal access to places formerly barred to them. Ten years earlier the stage had been set by another landmark action, the Supreme Court ruling on school deseg-regation, followed by other court actions to speed up implementation.

By the late 1960s, blacks in America could feel confident that most of the legal barriers to their full participation in American life had been removed. Twenty years of affirmative action at elite universities played a big part in integrating the professions, expanding the black middle class and preparing blacks for leadership. From scientists to musicians, writers to educators, from Gen. Colin Powell, who com-manded the world's most powerful military, to Tiger Woods, the daz-zling young golfer, role models have been encouraging young blacks that would have been almost unthinkable when King started out on his crusade. A magnetic black woman, Oprah Winfrey, became one of the nation's most influential people—owner of a major television pro-duction company and the undisputed leader of daytime television. In a *USA Today* survey of over 2,000 Americans on their outlook for the 21st century, about two-thirds of the people polled predicted that a black person will be elected president by the year 2025.

Over the past two generations the number of black professionals and managers and the number of black families with incomes over $50,000 have both quadrupled, the greatest step forward for any group in America in so short a period of time. Blacks are chief executives of some of the world's richest cities. (Peter Drucker wrote in 1996 that, "In the 50 years since World War II, the economic position of African-Americans in America has improved faster than that of any group in American social history—or in the social history of any country. Three fifths of America's blacks rose into middle-class incomes; before the Second World War the figure was one twentieth.")

Blacks today constitute more than 30% of the U.S. military and a majority of them are officers responsible for fighting forces that are primarily white. The U.S. Army set an example for the nation by com-bining disciplined training with color-blindness, with the result that the Army went from 3% black commissioned officers in 1973 to nearly 12% black officers in 1996. Today the Army, Air Force and Navy all have black four-star generals or admirals.

In the suburbs and across the land blacks moved up in the civilian social structure too. Between 1970 and 1995, seven million blacks moved to the suburbs, much more than the number who had left the South after 1940. Black buying power (personal income after taxes) rose approximately 73% between 1990 and 1999, compared with 57% for the total population. A third of American blacks live in suburbia today and five out of six blacks said in a recent survey by the National Opinion Research Center that they had white neighbors. And in the last Congressional election, 14 of the 37 blacks elected won in districts where less than half the voters were black.

Because of the progress blacks have made in achievements and recognition, a small but increasing number of black people are no longer supporting government policies that give their race favored treatment. They believe that such policies, if made permanent, as well as the activities of organizations promoting the separatism of black culture, only accentuate black feelings of inferiority and delay the achievement of the real, multiracial society—the real integration of races throughout American life—that King envisioned. They recognize too that the remaining black-white pay gap is explained chiefly not by prejudice but by the gap in education, skills and family structure.

This was the point of view of Ralph Ellison, author of the classic novel, *Invisible Man*, who repudiated the notion of a separate black culture, resisted the trendy black politics of segregation and insisted throughout his life that black identity is inseparable from American identity.

Thanks in great part to Martin Luther King, and thanks to the national spirits of both black and white people that he unleashed and led, America today is closer to being one, truly multiracial nation than any country in history. That certainly qualifies King as an epic American hero, and that is why he became the second American, after George Washington, whose birthday is a national holiday. Nearly every major city in the country has a street or school named after him, mostly in black neighborhoods, where just about everyone remembers King well as the man who more than anyone stirred the spirits and hopes of black people.

PART FOUR

THE REAGAN "REVOLUTION"

Forward to the Founders

Riding around his beloved *Rancho del Cielo* in the spring of 1975 on his big horse "Little Man", Ronald Wilson Reagan thought about the "lost vision of our founding fathers and the importance of recapturing it", he wrote in his autobiography. Getting into the saddle of a good horse helped free his mind to mull over problems. He and Nancy had bought their "ranch in the sky" on a huge green meadow above the granite peaks of the Santa Ynez mountains after he wound up eight successful years as governor of the nation's largest state. He was already 64 years old, but he would continue to spend a lot of time in the saddle in the coming years, mulling problems far beyond California.

In one sense this president-to-be was destined to complete a cycle of American history. Philosophically he was closer to the Founders than any president since Lincoln. Whether the simple, revolutionary 18th-century concepts of the country's early leaders could fit again the nation he knew—a polyglot, urban society without a physical frontier and without a common backbone of religious faith—history will judge. What is certain is that Ronald Reagan was passionately convinced that the country had made a terrible mistake in veering from its early principles.

He wrote in *An American Life* that the Founders "never envisioned vast agencies in Washington telling our farmers what to plant, our teachers what to teach, our industries what to build." The Constitution established sovereign states, not administrative districts of the federal government, he wrote, "and the Founders believed in keeping government as close as possible to the people; if parents didn't like the way their schools were being run, they could throw out the Board of Education But what could they do about the elite bureaucrats in the U.S. Department of Education who sent ultimatums into their children's classrooms regarding curriculum and textbooks?"

By the 1980s, many Americans vibrated to that iron string. An uneasy sense had come over them that New Deal big government had gone too far, that government was taking too much of their earnings and intruding too much into their lives and businesses with ever-expanding rules and regulations. Ronald Reagan was seen by many as the steward of America's first principles who could lead them out of what he called the "malaise" of the Carter years, which had ended with the nation's "misery index" (inflation rate plus the percent unemployed) far higher than when President Carter took office.

This was the theme that won Reagan the first of his two landslide presidential election victories. His optimistic verve energized the nation, drew middle-class, black, Hispanic, young and old citizens into the conservative fold—all but the poorest sectors of society. The tectonic political realignment he produced was as momentous as the liberal realignment produced by FDR nearly a half-century earlier. It was "the most decisive turning point in American national politics since the New Deal," in the judgment of historians William A. and Arthur S. Link. It sought to alter substantially the role of government in national life.

"His rejection of the moderate to liberal consensus that had come to dominate both Republican and Democratic administrations over the previous 40 years, his vision of a better America based on less government and more individual enterprise, and his efforts to translate this vision into a new agenda for the nation have been both distinctive and controversial," wrote John L. Palmer and Isabel V. Sawhill in *The Reagan Record.* "Not since 1932," they said, "has there been such a redirection of public purposes."

Ronald Reagan was not Superman. He was, and will remain in history, a complex human being with faults and weaknesses that made him prey especially to pundits and other intellectuals who still thought like New Dealers. But he was a force that turned America in a new direction. And most importantly, he was the embodiment of the optimistic spirit that is the American's most characteristic trait.

A bulldog on his favorite issues

During his eight presidential years Reagan concentrated with bulldog tenacity on two fundamental issues, stuck with them, held his ground against both domestic and foreign opponents and in the end made historic headway on both of his objectives. On the domestic side, his goal was to arrest the rate of government expansion, restore individual independence and free Americans from the octopus tentacles of government regulations and restraints that he saw strangling the nation. He put the brakes on after 48 years of federal government expansion that had been engineered by two great Democrats whom he admired, Wilson and FDR. He made it "intellectually respectable to question state intervention and the inexorable growth of presidential power," as historian Richard Norton Smith told a July 1998 conference at the John F. Kennedy Library. His pro-business posture raised the spirits of business entrepreneurs across the country.

In foreign policy, his goal was to restore the nation's military might to first place among nations, from a poor second place to Russia, so that America could negotiate from strength for world peace. Like Harry Truman, for whom he had once campaigned and voted, he became convinced that military strength was everything in talking to the Russians. In Reagan's vision of the future, U.S. military might would ultimately provide the leverage for ridding the world of nuclear weapons.

As a result of his perseverance on these two primary objectives everyone , whether they agreed with him or not, knew what he stood for and where he wanted to take the nation. He was scorned by much of the media and the intelligentsia, but he succeeded in lifting the country out of economic stagnation, leveling the rate of growth of government and halting Soviet expansionism, accelerating the process that lead to the downfall of Communism in almost every country it had ruled.

Nothing did more to rid generations of Americans of their anxiety and fears of Communism and nuclear war than the stubborn persistence of this President in forcing Moscow to back down on issues of disarmament, to trim Russian ambitions for world domination, to free millions of Russians to emigrate to America and—perhaps most important—to change Russian perceptions of America and American leaders and of democracy itself. Reagan's confidence in himself and his country paid off handsomely in restoring the spirits of the nation. By reducing public fears about the economic future *and* about the chances of nuclear war he restored Americans' self-confidence and at the same time gave them more confidence in their leadership.

Reagan and JFK: bringing optimism back in style

In the story of America's rising and falling spirits, a comparison of Ronald Reagan and John F. Kennedy is instructive. Each, in his own way, brought optimism back in style. Each of them aroused Americans by articulating the American dream of a perfectible society. Each of them attracted young, idealistic "revolutionaries" into government service— people who believed passionately that a new age really was dawning.

Reagan energized and politicized American youth. His youthful conservatives were just as fired up with optimism as the young liberals who had worshipped JFK. "The young people who came to Washington for the Reagan revolution came to make things better," wrote Peggy Noonan, a writer who served in the Reagan White House. "They had such spirit, such idealism…The thing the young conservatives were always talking about, the constant subtext, was freedom, freedom," meaning freedom from excessive taxation and interference by government, as well as freedom for people everywhere who were fighting Communist dictatorships.

Both JFK, at 43 the youngest president ever elected, and Reagan, who became at 78 the oldest person ever to complete a presidency, were superb communicators who could fire up freedom-lovers and inspire the kind of loyalty usually won only in wartime. Each of them was courageous—Kennedy at 21 captaining his wartime PT boat, and Reagan when he sprang back lightheartedly from an assassination attempt after only four months in office. Each of them believed in capitalism as the most powerful driver of prosperity. (The views of the Eureka College economics major have been more widely known than was JFK's advocacy of reducing the capital gains tax and his firm belief in the importance of providing incentives for individual risk-takers who create jobs through their private enterprises.*)

---

* JFK, like Reagan, believed the best way to raise government revenues in the long run is to cut taxes. In 1962 he made the point that "an economy hampered by restrictive tax rates will never produce enough revenues to balance the budget—just as it will never produce enough jobs or enough profits." The Kennedy tax rate cut was one of the greatest economic successes of the postwar era.

Of course one *difference* between JFK and Reagan was the relative power—military power—each of them wielded when he came to office. When JFK faced down Premier Khrushchev in the Cuban missile crisis of the early '60s, the U.S. had 10 times as many nuclear weapons as the Soviets; by the early '80s, Soviet nuclear arms outnumbered those of the U.S. and they were expanding their nuclear forces rapidly. So, a few weeks before Reagan made his big pitch for peace in a globally televised speech on November 18, 1981 (calling for elimination of all intermediate-range nuclear missiles in Europe) he had ordered a multi-billion-dollar modernization of U.S. strategic forces—bombers, missiles, nuclear submarines and space satellites. He knew the Russians would pay no attention to him if he led from weakness.

The big difference between Reagan and JFK was in *results*. Kennedy's ringing inaugural ("...the torch has been passed to a new generation of Americans...") stirred spirits and raised giddy hopes that this young Galahad, riding the shoulders of "the best and brightest", would lead the nation to an upland paradise. Kennedy's charisma, his personal charm, dazzled almost everyone who met him, especially women, and made him a mythic figure. Columnist Frank Rich fitted Kennedy to the morals of his time when he wrote: "In our Hollywood culture, star quality is everything. A handsome, charming, witty man who has a fling with Marilyn Monroe is as close to a god as we have."

But after Kennedy's sensational start, after the "new frontier" rhetoric of his acceptance speech, there was nothing like the *action* that his followers had expected. Historian Sydney Hyman said the phrase "new frontier" died on JFK's lips in his inaugural address, never mentioned by him again. Something was missing in JFK's leadership, James Reston wrote in The New York Times: "He plays touch government and tackles nothing." Time magazine, in November 1963, speculated that in the long view of history "his administration might be known less for the substance of its achievements than for its style." Historian and JFK biographer James MacGregor Burns said, after JFK's first two years in the White House, that the young president had simply not shown the commitment of heart, as well as of mind, that would produce the passion and power his followers expected of him.

And as for setting moral standards, JFK outdid Harding in his philandering White House trysts with a paramour who cavorted with Mafiosi. As regards respect for wives, or respect for the White House, there was quite a contrast between conservatives Teddy Roosevelt and Ronald Reagan and liberals Kennedy and Clinton, but this was not a subject likely to be touched by the mostly liberal press, at least not until the "Clinton scandals" erupted like a mushroom cloud near the end of the century.

In any case, JFK's 1,000 days in office was too little time to make a significant difference to the majority of Americans. His high points were his pledge of May 1961 to put a man on the moon, fulfilled in July 1969 by the Apollo project, placing the country first in space; his wise handling of the Cuban missile crisis, bringing relief to a nation suddenly alarmed at the real possibility of nuclear war; the conclusion of the treaty banning above-ground nuclear weapons testing; the Peace Corps; the use of federal troops to enforce school desegregation, and new presidential initiatives to foster literature and the arts.

By comparison, Reagan's broader influence on the national sense of well-being resulted from the transforming effects of his domestic and foreign policies. His domestic policies set the nation on a long-term course of economic growth, job creation and profit creation, while beginning the process of reforming the welfare and tax systems and slowing the rate of government regulation. In foreign affairs, the demise of the Soviet Union, the receding threat of nuclear war, the signing of the first treaty to reduce the superpowers' nuclear arsenals, the ascension of free enterprise in country after country as they shook off the shackles of their command economies, the North Atlantic Accord that Reagan proposed (later called the "free trade agreement"), the new strength of democracy in the Southern Hemisphere—all these things in which Reagan personally had a strong hand helped to revive national pride and vigor.

Reagan stood for American exceptionalism at a time when, the English journalist-author Godfrey Hodgson wrote, the liberals were "running America down". In Hodgson's opinion, "It was Reagan's conviction, his living faith, that the United States was a great society and must prevail. He believed that if the United States put forth its strength—military, material and moral—the Soviet Union could not live with it. And he was right."

For Reagan, as for Wilson and Truman especially, politics was above all a moral cause, not simply the pursuit of power. He believed just as Wilson had that America was a force for good and his ideas on foreign policy, such as his emphasis on aiding anti-Communist insurgents around the world, were conceived in moral terms. As William Kristol has written, "his confidence that God was looking out for America and for the right seems to have helped give him the courage to do all that he did."

More than anything, however, it was the economic recovery during the Reagan years that accounted for America's soaring spirits. Since the spring of 1983 the gross national product had expanded faster than it did in the previous decade. In September 1984 *Time* magazine published a cover story on "America's Upbeat Mood", cheering the "slam-bang economy." In euphoric prose, it said: "Old Glory is being waved like crazy. After years of confusion, America feels fat and sassy, loose and sure-footed… The new mood could lead to complacency or jingoism, but for now it is as refreshing as a summer romance."

All this did not mean that public anxieties about the future were swept away by the time the Reagan regime ended. Besides the big federal deficit, among the most important things left unresolved after the Reagan era was the central conflict between the public's desire to pay less taxes and the challenge of ballooning middle-class "entitlements", business and agricultural "welfare", tax breaks for home ownership and other subsidies, all of which remained as obstacles to realization of Reagan's dream of a smaller government. In the post-Reagan years "entitlements" grew to more than half of total federal outlays.

Surprisingly little was done in the Reagan years to replace public programs for social welfare with new initiatives in the private sector or new models of public-private partnership. The Presidential Task Force on Private Sector Initiatives created in his first year to "promote private sector leadership and responsibility for solving social needs, and to recommend ways of fostering greater public-private partnerships" had few tangible results. *Newsweek* took a dig at this effort by noting that one of its most "substantive accomplishments" was delivering 5,000 copies of singer Pat Boone's record, "Lend a Hand", to radio stations around the country.

The trend of government self-aggrandizement that Reagan warned about turned out to be even more unstoppable than he imagined; this was his major failure. By 1993, for the first time in U.S. history, the number of workers in the public sector surpassed the number in the entire manufacturing sector. The federal non-defense workforce has almost doubled since 1960. This worries those who believe, as S.E. Morison once put it, that "there must be a halt short of every American adult being on a government payroll, as happened in Newfoundland before it went bankrupt." Not even Reagan had ever contemplated the implications of having people in government, who distribute wealth, rising faster than those in the private sector, who create wealth.*

Government in fact lays a heavier hand on the American economy today than ever, cornering resources that could otherwise go to wealth-creating private enterprise. The U.S. federal government today spends close to a quarter of the wealth created annually, and the share of the national economic pie going to taxes continues to grow. The average American had to work for four-and-a-half months in 1998 to make enough money to pay his or her taxes. As the U.S. entered 1998 federal taxes hit a postwar high of nearly 22% of gross domestic product, the highest level in American history. Taxes including state and local took away just over 35% of America's entire national income, the biggest bite of the century. Taxes have increased at almost double the rate of increase in personal income. In terms understandable to ordinary Americans, the median family with two earners was paying nearly 40% of its income in federal, state and local taxes by the latter part of the century—more than they spent altogether on food, clothing, housing and medical care.

Reagan instinctively understood the fundamental role taxes play in peoples' lives, and he jousted against Big Government, but never reached his goals. He saw the role of government not as an instrument of social engineering or regulation but as an instrument to ensure law and order and a minimal safety net for citizens, and to provide *incentives* for the wealth-producing private sector The lion's share of the government spending he lamented is for "entitlements"—programs like Medicare and Social Security mandated by law. Reagan would have winced at such latter-day Clinton Administration proposals as the effort virtually to transform child care into another federal entitlement, one more "perverse incentive" that tends to encourage, rather than dis-

---

* By comparison, it is interesting to note Tocqueville's comment, describing the America of 1848: "Nothing is more striking to the European traveler in the United States than the absence of what we term the government, the administration."

courage, the decline of parenting time with children and the conception of children by unmarried women.

Part of the continuing growth of federal spending also is for regulation, the excesses of which are the bane of businesses across the nation and were one of Reagan's main targets. The total cost of federal regulations actually topped $700 billion a year by the end of the nineties, with heavy costs falling particularly on the smaller enterprises, and start-up enterprises that have produced the greatest job growth of recent times.

A personality for the age of TV

Ronald Reagan was a natural star in the history of the American spirit. What Americans consciously or unconsciously longed for in 1981—a leader with strong personal convictions and a convincing optimism about improving the world—was what they got, and the vast majority of them loved it. He rode in out of the West like the Marlboro Man, the embodiment of the old American movie hero—like Jimmy Stewart in *Mr. Smith Goes to Washington*, Gary Cooper in *High Noon* or Henry Fonda in *Young Mr. Lincoln*—and the champion of old-fashioned values that those screen idols represented.

Like Jimmy Stewart, Robert Mitchum and other film icons of his era, Reagan had been part of a Hollywood that "valued character over personality", as film critic Janet Maslin wrote in a Stewart obituary. She described the classic "good guys" of those days as "quintessentially American heroes who embodied a rock-solid moral code, deeply resonant ideas about good and evil."

Reagan spoke with warmth and disarming conviction, carried himself well and radiated, with Mickey Rooney enthusiasm, an attitude that "anything is possible in this great nation of ours." Howard K. Smith, one of the most respected liberal journalists of the postwar years, wrote in his memoirs that "Reagan was a different kind of campaigner. It made you feel good just to be within the range of that cheery smile and those really funny quips." After the double dramas of Vietnam and Watergate, and the pale years of Ford and Carter, the nation needed such a leader to restore its lost spirits and to stand up bravely to Soviet expansionists. Modern times favors leaders who can raise spirits with TV-charisma, and that's exactly what Reagan had.

The optimism he projected was enhanced by the most disarming sense of humor possessed by any president since Lincoln.

Reagan felt that during the late '70s the U.S. had begun to abdicate its historical role as the spiritual leader of the free world. Looking back on his first presidential campaign, after he left government, he wrote that "America had lost faith in itself… We had to recapture our dreams, our pride in ourselves and our country, and regain that unique sense of destiny and optimism that had always made America different from any other country in the world. If I could be elected president, I wanted to do what I could to bring about a spiritual revival in America. I believed… America's greatest years were ahead of it."

Reagan's first political hero had been FDR. He was 22 when FDR came to office in the depths of the Depression. "Reagan thrilled to the buoyant optimism he heard from Roosevelt," wrote biographer Lou Cannon, the most authoritative Reagan-watcher, a highly respected journalist who covered Reagan from his first run for governor of California to his last days in the White House. As a youth Reagan listened to FDR's fireside chats on radio, learned a style from them that was reflected in his own speeches years later, and even developed a good imitation of FDR, waving an imaginary cigarette holder in the air.

During Reagan's presidency, some liberals put labels on him that historians are only now beginning to remove. They regarded him as an aging Grade-B movie actor, a puppet who moved when others pulled the strings, a speaker who was lost without his four-by-five prompt cards and a lackey for big business. To a degree, Reagan's physical characteristics contributed to this impression. He suffered all his life from extreme near-sightedness (which kept him out of wartime battle duty); he was plagued with loss of hearing (the result of an accidental gun-firing in his ear during a filming) and, towards the end of his second term, the Alzheimer's that finally brought him down might have begun its lethal work, although his doctors found no signs of it then.

Reagan had strongly-held ideas of his own, and he often made major decisions in defiance of advice from his own advisers and senior people. There were no "handlers" involved when Governor Reagan cracked down on rampaging students at Berkeley or when President Reagan pressed hard on Congress for *both* "guns and butter"—tax cuts and a huge military buildup—or when he broke the crippling strike of air traffic controllers by firing 12,000 of them or when he blew his top and angrily stomped out of his first summit with Mikhail Gorbachev after the Soviet leader reneged on a dramatic arms reduction deal proposed by Reagan, attempting to scuttle U.S. development of the space defense system, which was one of Reagan's "untouchables" because he saw it, correctly, as a way to put stress on a regime that he believed, contrary to most people, was becoming economically strained.

One Russian general remarked later that the Soviets weren't accustomed to such an unyielding American President (especially after the way Stalin had duped the Western leaders in previous summit deals.) That was clearly all right with the American people, who by and large showed their enthusiasm for a leader with the guts to stand up to Communist bullies for a change. Reagan's steady popularity was displayed when he won the vote for his second term by the largest electoral-vote landslide in U.S. history, carrying 49 states.

Thanks to a surfeit of memoirs by people who were close to Reagan in his White House years, we know there was much truth in criticisms of him. He was considered intelligent by his aides, and acknowledged to be a quick study, with a photographic memory, but he was short on intellectual exploration of new ideas, or even curiosity about them, unless, like "Star Wars", they had some drama in them to stir his imagination. In part this was because he came to office with such absolute conviction about a few favorite issues and deliberately kept focused on them to make sure he would never get pushed off track.

In the Iran-Contra fiasco, he let his emotions override his reason. He became obsessed with the plight of the American hostages held by the Islamic Jihad in Beirut and with their grieving relatives at home. The indescribable frustration that causes leaders to do weird things when their countrymen or women are taken by savage captors abroad had been experienced by others before him, but it absolutely threw Reagan for a loss, nearly unraveled the great optimist and gave him enormous pain when, for the first time in his life, he confronted critics who didn't believe his word, especially about what he did and didn't know about the convoluted money and arms trails to Iran and to the Nicaraguan Contras.

Reagan often made decisions on matters as important as deployment of MX intercontinental nuclear missiles with seriously inadequate preparation. Cannon's most damaging criticism was that "the nation paid a high price for a president who skimped on preparation, avoided the complexities and news conferences and depended far too heavily on anecdotes, charts, graphics and cartoons." But the public saw little of this side of the great actor-president, and the remarkable thing was that his ability to rouse spirits and sustain public morale was for so long unaffected by these faults.

Reagan's hands-off management style fostered clashes among his top people, especially in his second term. His single-minded focus on two or three favorite policy areas—exemplified by his demonization of the Soviets and government-bashing at home—caused him to neglect other national problems that needed attention. And his contempt for government blinded him to the good things that government, and only government, can do in peacetime, such as punishing discrimination, rescuing people at the bottom of the heap and ensuring the basics of a healthy environment.

But despite his serious failings, everyone who worked with Reagan admired his way with people and with the general public, admitted that he had an almost magical talent for lifting audiences from despond to hope and more or less agreed that he performed magnificently what is probably the most important role of a president in lifting peoples' spirits—giving them a sense of optimism about the future and a confidence that things will come out right if only they stick to the fundamental moral and spiritual values of their ancestors. He was like FDR in recognizing that Americans respond to assertions of optimism even when solutions to their problems are anything but clear.

Peggy Noonan commented that a lot of people, after meeting Reagan, "wanted to dance down the stairs" of the White House. She felt that "through the force of his beliefs and with a deep natural dignity he restored a great and fallen office." Nobody disliked this president. James Baker, a key man in the trio of himself, Mike Deaver and Edwin Meese who were the powerful backfield players in the president's first term, called his boss "the kindest and most impersonal man I ever knew." Even Mikhail Gorbachev ended up liking Reagan as a friend, enjoying among other things their efforts to top each other's jokes.

Reagan wasn't ashamed of his Hollywood roots. He remembered how the Hollywood of the Depression had cheered up the nation. "He came of age in the middle of the most eager-to-please city in the most eager-to-please country in the history of the world... a country where people were laughing and dancing on the tops of skyscrapers, who were rich and spirited," wrote Noonan. "Even if it wasn't quite true that any place was this happy, it gave him an intimation of joy, of civic comity, that he ever after associated with film and childhood and America."

One Reagan presidential touch that symbolized his ardent, can-do enthusiasm was the routine he originated, during major televised speeches, to interject into his address a recognition of "heroes in the balcony." His critics thought this a corny stage device, but it went over well on TV and helped boost Reagan in the polls. Corny or not, the gesture was a way to highlight the heroism of ordinary American men and women. In his 1985 State of the Union address he pointed to a young Vietnamese girl in the balcony who had graduated from West Point 10 years after leaving her native land; he pointed to Mother Hale of Harlem and praised her good work. "Your lives tell us that the oldest American saying is new again," Reagan said. "Anything is possible in America if we have the faith, the will and the heart. History is asking us, once again, to be a force for good in the world."

When Reagan became President, Cannon wrote in the second volume of his biography, "public confidence in government was at its lowest ebb since the Depression. Double-digit inflation was eating up peoples' paychecks, the economy was sluggish." Interest rates were over 15%, discouraging investment, and unemployment was at 7.5%. Jimmy Carter, trying to cope with the loss of confidence, had made the mistake of blaming the American people for the nation's problems, saying in 1979 that Americans suffered from a "crisis of confidence" that "strikes at the very heart and soul and spirit of our national will."

Reagan didn't believe this, then or ever. One week after his debate with Carter, near the end of his first presidential campaign, Reagan's last campaign speech, taped in Peoria, was broadcast on television. He called it "a vision for America." He conjured up the Pilgrims landing in New England, the return of American prisoners of war from Vietnam, the American astronauts landing on the moon. There are some, he said, who say that "our energy is spent, our days of greatness at an end, that a great national malaise is upon us.... I find no national malaise, I find nothing wrong with the American people."

Reagan's own self-assurance, wrote Cannon, "was a tonic for a nation." In a New York Times-CBS poll soon after his election, nine out of ten people were confident that Reagan would see to it that the United States was again respected by other nations. "But his greatest service," said Cannon, "was in restoring the respect of Americans for themselves and their own government after the traumas of Vietnam and Watergate, the frustrations of the Iran hostage crisis and a succession of seemingly failed presidencies."

His personality played a big part. "Reagan's geniality, his stubborn individualism and anti-intellectualism, his self-deprecating wit and his passionate opposition to taxes set the tone for a decade that was at once a period of national renewal and national excess," Cannon wrote.

Gary Wills pointed out the irony that "we regained our youth by electing the oldest president in our history...He made us young again." Wills said "Reagan not only represents the past, but resurrects it as a promise of the future."

Stoking an awesome boom

Reagan believed that an overdose of government had stifled national spirits. He believed that the most effective way to cut government was to cut taxes. He had learned from fellow Californian-economist Arthur Laffer that tax policy was the main factor affecting investment, by lowering the cost of the capital needed by entrepreneurs. Understanding that private-sector people, not government, create wealth through profits, he was one of the few national leaders in the last half of the 20th century who recognized the vital importance of strong economic incentives to work harder, save more and invest in the future, provided by government's growth policies. Government's role, as he saw it, was to provide these incentives for private enterprise—not to regulate, control or interfere with free play of private markets. His wealth-producing policies led the nation out of the malaise that gripped it throughout the 1970s. He put the U.S. on an upward growth path that continued with little interruption for two decades, right through the '90s.

More than a year before his election, at the "Reagan for President" office, a policy memorandum worked out by Reagan and his advisers proclaimed that "the level of taxation in the United States has now become so high that it is stifling the incentive for individuals to earn, save and invest. We must have a program—of at least three years duration—of across-the-board tax cuts... Tax rates that are too high destroy incentives to earn, cripple productivity, lead to deficit financing and inflation and create unemployment."

When Reagan's inauguration took place in January 1981, tens of thousands of people stood on the Capitol grounds and streamed down the Mall. In his inaugural address the new President repeated his most familiar theme, saying that "In the present crisis, government is not the solution to our problems; government *is* the problem... It is time to reawaken this industrial giant, to get government back within its means, and to lighten our punitive tax burden... These will be our first priorities, and on these principles there will be no compromise..." The first blow to "free the people" from Washington bureaucracy—and Reagan's first official act as president—was struck that same day. Executive orders removed price controls on oil and gasoline.

Reagan addressed the nation's economic lethargy at a joint session of Congress only a week after he left the hospital following his injury in the assassination attempt of young John Hinckley. After a huge ovation that lasted several minutes, he told the Congress he was gratified by the support being shown by both parties for his "Economic Recovery Program". Then he went on television, asking the public to express their support to their representatives.

The day after his TV address phone calls and wire messages to the White House broke all records. There were 4,745 phone calls supporting his program, 1,103 against. There were 2,723 telegrams supporting his program, 373 against. Bowing to the obvious public support for the president, Congress passed Reagan's budget bill and a 25% cut in income taxes over three years, the largest tax cut ever. In Reagan's first year federal spending was reduced by $40 billion, the biggest cut ever in federal expenditures. The rate of growth in federal spending was cut in half. Anti-poverty programs were substantially cut for the first time since the New Deal and federal restrictions were reduced in the areas of environment and civil rights.

From 1982, the first year of the Reagan tax cut, to 1989, the top tax rate was cut from 70% to 28% (two post-Reagan tax hikes pushed it back up to 39.6%), yet federal tax revenues increased from $618 billion in 1982 to $991 billion in 1989, despite the recession of the early 1980s. The soaring revenues of the mid-1980s, when Reagan chopped tax rates, taught a lesson in economics worth remembering. Few politicians have ever understood as well as this President did the impact tax policy can have on national spirits and productivity.

In his life story, Reagan wrote that "the nation had begun the process of spiritual revival that was so badly needed." He was unfazed by the breathtaking dip in the U.S. economy before the turnaround began. Offsetting the inflationary aspects of his policies, Paul Volcker's Federal Reserve Board had put the brakes on monetary growth. Swallowing this bitter medicine as Reagan had expected they would, Americans endured a deep recession in the second and third years of the "revolution". Unemployment rose to 12% and, between 1980 and 1982 Americans suffered a 3.5% drop in real (inflation-adjusted) income. The federal budget deficit climbed from $56 billion to $200 billion a year by 1986. (Deficit spending helped to stimulate the economy, but the national debt was almost $2.7 trillion by the time Reagan left office and the share of gross domestic product absorbed by federal spending was still over 20% in Reagan's last year as president.)

In November 1982, one year after the first tax cut, the economic turnaround began and the U.S. entered a period of prolonged expansion, with only one mild eight-month dip in all of the 1990s. Reagan's policies unleashed the greatest wave of prosperity anywhere at any time in world history. Unemployment declined steadily; by 1989 it was only 5.3%. From the start of the Reagan era to the end of the century the U.S. added more than 35 million new jobs—more than the combined total for all the rest of the industrialized nations.

Reagan's political opponents and many media pundits called the 1980s a decade of "greed and excess", ignoring the gains in productivity, efficiency and welfare. Attacks on the "junk" (high-yield) bond market that thrived during the period ignored the fact that these bonds opened public capital markets to a great many small, risky but agile enterprises and helped to force many big corporations to restructure by shutting down inefficient operations or be taken over.

Among the policies initiated by Reagan none was more fundamental in fueling this prosperous era than the cuts in personal income taxes, which unleashed new capital that was invested in new technology, increasing productivity and creating jobs. Reagan understood that the way to create wealth is to encourage private interests to take risks, and that such investing is the only way to increase the nation's ability to produce goods and services in the future.

He had been persuaded by Laffer that tax reductions can be self-financing by producing incentives that actually increase government revenue, validating Friedrich Hayek's theory in *The Constitution of Liberty* that free people and free markets engender a wealth-producing discovery process. (Unfortunately, in the post-Reagan era, taxes were twice increased, bringing total Federal tax and fee receipts up to 20.5% of gross domestic product.)

An unplanned result of Reagan's policies was the explosion of the high-tech information age, which was central to the economic expansion of the '80s and '90s. Just three years into his presidency Apple Computer's Mac was born and the next decade exploded with information technology. This technology wave, unlike previous ones, was based on knowledge and information and among the tools for it were personal computers and micro-chips, micro-processors, cell phones, fiber optics, the Internet, DNA analysis, biotechnology and molecular engineering. Of enormous importance, the new technologies made American workers more productive than ever, which meant that the economy could grow without producing dangerous inflation and without putting growth-stifling pressures on the labor market.

This revolution was fueled by government policies that encouraged maximum entrepreneurial efforts and private risk-taking. The 1981 Kemp-Roth tax cuts restored entrepreneurial incentives as well as lower interest rates, lower inflation (which is a form of lower taxation), lower tariffs and stable currency. The greatest bull market in the country's history was underway. "President Reagan's vision tapped into a rich vein of optimism that lies deep within all of us," economist Lawrence A. Kudlow has written, describing "the emergence of a long wave of prosperity based on information-age, high-tech innovation and a populist democratic capitalism that has created more abundance than anyone dreamed possible."

During the "seven fat years" of the '80s, real after-tax income rose 16% for all Americans, 12.5% for the median of all Americans. There was striking upward mobility during this period, as 86% of the lowest fifth of Americans moved up, 60% moved out of the second lowest fifth and 47% moved above the middle fifth. The largest relative income gains were won by women.

The Information Age helped American corporations become world leaders and spurred the growth of new enterprises. There were an estimated 1.5 million business formations in the 1980s. The creation of new businesses rose dramatically in both decades of the 1980s and

1990s, reaching close to a million annually by the end of this period. Small businesses accounted for about two-thirds of the nearly 34 million jobs that were created between November 1982 and 1997, even while many of the large companies were downsizing. Many of those "small" businesses grew faster than anything ever seen before—becoming billion-dollar, then two-billion-dollar or three-billion-dollar companies within a few years and breeding young millionaires by the hundreds.

Among other factors behind the boom was deregulation, which had been started by Carter in the late 1970s (in airlines, trucking and banking) and was extended to the energy industry, the transportation industry and the banking and financial services industry under Reagan.

While Reagan pursued his growth policies the Federal Reserve's tightened monetary policy brought the inflation rate down from 13% in 1980 to a low of 2% in 1986. In the trade area, the Reagan cuts in tariffs on imports, the negotiation of new trade treaties and the pressure on Japan to open its markets helped to globalize industry, to the benefit of businesses and consumers everywhere. And finally, Reagan's progress towards ending the cold war yielded a "peace dividend" as the government was enabled to cut back defense spending and defense contractors shifted their sights to civilian markets.

Critics on the left and right howled warnings of doom throughout this rosy period. Labor unions warned that American jobs were being "exported" and many conservatives were horrified by the big budget deficits. Near the end of the Reagan era, Ravi Batra's scary book, "The Great Depression" became a best-seller. The pessimistic mood of the critics, reinforced by such repeated warnings of impending doom, proved to be amazingly resilient, and wrong, throughout these boom years.

But nothing sustains a nation's spirits like a good spell of prosperity. Defying the "declinists", the American economy from Reagan on put on a performance like nothing ever seen before in world history. More than 20 million new jobs were created in the 1980s, some 70 million during the two decades following Reagan's election. American industrialists began to learn to become more efficient by exploiting technology, training their workers in new technology and using global sourcing for their supplies. Reagan's tax cuts and deregulation moves stirred the productive energies of Americans. And through the Budget

Enforcement Act his administration also set the stage for deficit reduction by putting limits on discretionary spending and setting new "pay as you go" rules that helped to rein in entitlements and taxes.

The U.S. gross national product doubled during the 1980s. Between 1983 and 1990 alone, the economy grew by a third and per capita average disposable income grew by a fifth. The stock market went on an unprecedented roll. Foreigners took note of all this—the Reagan tax cuts started a tax-cutting trend worldwide, and foreign investors poured money into American investments on a scale dwarfing anything seen in the past.

Average real incomes rose in every income group from 1982 to 1989. "What happened in the 1980s," wrote the Hudson Institute's Alan Reynolds, was that "a much larger percentage of U.S. families moved up above income thresholds that used to define the 'rich'". Millions of families left the middle class.

Not the least of Reagan's economic legacies was his influence in the reform of welfare programs, both in California and in the nation. He believed that the Welfare State had devalued individual responsibility and character-building and eroded morality. He believed that in one way or another it had encouraged welfare dependency, illegitimate child-bearing, family breakups, teen pregnancy, alcohol and drug addiction and crime.

His initiative led to the Earned Income Tax Credit, which ended the pernicious policy of penalizing the poor for working. It liberated the poor from the perverse effects of a program that discouraged work. The new policy of allowing low-income people to take significant tax deductions for money earned by working represented almost as large a federal "investment" as the former principal welfare program of Aid to Families with Dependent Children, which was terminated. The earned-income credit proved to be so effective that liberals as well as conservatives came to support it. It liberated the poor from the perverse effects of a program that discouraged work.

Of course, as in every free-market boom, there were big gains for some people that seemed excessive to others. This was a decade in which wealth and conspicuous consumption returned to fashion. It was also the era of financial wheelers-dealers who made fortunes in their twenties and thirties. Some 100,000 Americans became millionaires every year, the "junk bond king" Michael Milken made $550 million in 1987 alone and the huge scandal of the savings and loan industry proved that bad things as well as good can happen when the government plays "hands off".

Nevertheless, the boom spread its rewards broadly among working Americans. The number of "affluent" black families, adjusted for inflation, doubled during the 1980s, according to the Population Reference Bureau. The black middle class grew by nearly a third from 1980 to 1988 and became the dominant black income group. The number of black professionals jumped 63% during the same period and black corporate managers and officers increased 30%. Unfortunately, the poverty rate among blacks resisted change, and in the inner cities black youth unemployment remained very high; the majority of black babies were born out of wedlock and twice as many poor blacks were dependent on public assistance in 1990 as had been a quarter-century before.

The general public voted its approval of the new direction in which Reagan had taken the country in the 1994 Congressional elections. The Republicans won control of the House of Representatives for the first time in 40 years, as well as control of the Senate, and they won eleven new governorships and control of both houses of 19 states. The shift from "New Dealism" to "Reaganism" was reflected too in the rejection by the Congress, and the public, of the Clinton administration's efforts later on to expand government influence through a centralized national health program.

The Reagan economic policies and the boom they produced justified, more than anything else, linking the words "Reagan" and "revolution." The 1980s taught a simple lesson: that lower tax rates can boost growth, and growth *increases* the tax base by boosting wage and business income. When more Americans are working, government revenues rise. The American public moved so far in the direction of Ronald Reagan's thinking that Democratic president Bill Clinton himself was forced to proclaim that "the era of big government is over." A *Reader's Digest* poll in 1994 had marked the trend by its finding that 67% of the people queried picked big government over big business or big labor as the threat to the nation's future that they took most seriously. In 1965, only 35% had felt that way about big government.

Although the Reagan steamroller was slowed later when Congress voted to raise taxes during the Bush administration, some of the Reagan magic re-appeared when the Rupublicans took the House of Representatives in late 1994. They pledged to cut taxes, reduce regulations, shrink government and balance the budget. The result was a wave of new optimism in the financial and business communities that washed across the markets, lifting stocks, bonds and the dollar up out of their slump.

When Reagan was nominated to be his party's candidate for another term at an ecstatic party convention in Dallas, his second presidential campaign proceded "like a coronation", as one White House staffer put it. There were few new ideas but still plenty of Reagan "magic"—and humor. In his second and last presidential debate with Walter Mondale, a reporter asked whether Reagan was too old, at 73, to handle the job. Reagan straight-facedly promised that he wouldn't make age an issue, then smiled and followed through with a characteristic one-liner: "I am not going to exploit, for political purposes, my opponent's youth and inexperience."

The strategy of this second presidential campaign was for Reagan to play it above partisan politics or even issues, on a broad theme of leadership and high hopes for the future. Reagan used the summer Olympic games as a metaphor for America's striving for excellence. The campaign's advertising team turned out feel-good ads with the unassailable theme: "It's morning again in America." On election day the super-popular president scored a massive electoral victory, the first back-to-back landslide since Eisenhower. Even Tip O'Neill, the Democratic House Speaker, admitted to Reagan that, in his 50 years of public life, "I've never seen a man more popular than you with the American people."

At what looks in retrospect like the apogee of Reagan's years in power, the 75-year-old president presided over the 100th birthday of the rebuilt Statue of Liberty on July 4, 1988. He spoke to a crowd of thousands in New York harbor and an audience of millions on television. On that spectacular evening some of the press representatives noted that he seemed to rise above politics, above his own remarkable political history, more like a symbol of American visionary optimism.

He "was treated by the press, by scholars, even by his opponents as a special, almost supernatural phenomenon," wrote two Washington scribes, Jane Mayer and Doyle McManus, in their book *Landslide*. *Time* magazine said the president had "found the American sweet spot", that he was "hitting home runs". *Time* described Reagan as "a sort of masterpiece of American magic—apparently one of the simplest, most uncomplicated creatures alive, and yet a character of rich meanings, of complexities that connect him with the myths and powers of his country in an unprecedented way." Even Reagan's political opponents agreed, at this high-water-mark for him, that Reagan, having restored the majesty of his office, had achieved an almost untouchable status with the American electorate.

What Reagan gave his country, in a word, was optimism, and the good feeling survived his presidency. As *FORTUNE* magazine was to write early in 1990: "That most American of character traits—optimism—is as strong in this era of fierce global competition as it was when the nation was triumphing over the worst economic depression in modern times."

A lifetime of lessons

Ronald Reagan's life was a build-up of experiences that molded the man and gave him passionately-held, nearly immovable opinions. His personal experiences on the road to the White House made him the kind of leader who could transfer his own self-confidence and optimism to a people jaded by wars and scandals. To understand where the 40th president "came from", what he stood for and how he came to have such impact on American spirits, one can do no better than examine literally where he *did* come from. His life, and the lessons he learned, reflect the traditional sources of American optimism over two centuries—where *it* came from, what sustained it, what threatens it and whether it is likely to survive into the 21st century.

The woman who bore him on February 6, 1911, had very little in life. Nelle Reagan lived in a flat above the local bank in Tampico, Illinois (population 820) with an alcoholic husband, a good man and a great storyteller, who lost his chance for business success in the Depression. Perhaps due partly to her Scots-English ancestry, she had, nevertheless, an inner optimism that ran "as deep as the cosmos," according to the son who would one day become the world's most powerful leader. Her optimism was based quite simply on her belief that everything in life was part of God's plan.

When Reagan was nine years old his family moved to Dixon, Illinois, a tight-knit little community surrounded by dairy farms, where he lived a Tom Sawyer-like life, swam and fished and hiked and, he later wrote, "learned standards and values that would guide me for the rest of my life." One of those values was racial tolerance. His older brother's best friend was black and Reagan's color-blind father refused to patronize hotels that discriminated against blacks. When Reagan was a college football player, he brought black teammates home with him when they were refused rooms in a hotel.

Reagan grew up in a simple world of small towns, neighborly values and unquestioned beliefs in religion, morality and patriotism. During his time in Dixon young Reagan liked to visit the town's only movie house, where his middle-class morals were personified by "good guys" like Tom Mix and William S. Hart who galloped over the prairies and dealt out justice and by idealized women like Pearl White and Mary Pickford.

Nelle showed a flair for public speaking, becoming the star performer in a group that staged readings, mostly in church. She seldom missed Sunday service at Dixon's Disciples of Christ church (the strict, Bible-based church of temperance leader Carry Nation) where her son Ronald decided on his own, at age 12, that he wanted to be baptized. She taught both of her sons the value of prayer, and Ronald was given to churchgoing and to prayer for the rest of his life, apparently never questioning his faith. His faith would be important in building the self-confidence and optimism that would later inspire the nation.

Contrary as it might seem to the movie-actor image of Reagan, one little-known aspect of this very private person was his lifelong religiosity. While quite young he got into the habit of praying for everything—for his family, his town, his country, and he prayed before football games, asking that his team do its best and that there would be no injuries. He tithed ten percent of his earnings to the church, until he decided, with his minister's approval, to divert his contributions to his needy brother during the Depression. The first time he entered the Oval Office as president, Reagan recounted much later, he said a prayer asking for God's help. When he returned from the hospital to the White House after would-be assassin John Hickley tried to kill him, he wrote in his diary: "Whatever happens now I owe my life to God and will try to serve him in every way I can." Four times in four pages of his autobiography he mentions praying for Hinckley as well as for himself. And when his agnostic father-in-law was seriously ill,

Reagan urged him to turn to God, speaking to him of the value of faith. Reagan sought advice and guidance from Pope John Paul II on numerous occasions during his presidency.

Also perhaps stemming from his spiritual convictions was Reagan's persuasive way with an audience and his spontaneous talent for connecting with ordinary people, as Harry Truman had done. His development as a public speaker started way back at those church readings, when he first performed before he was a teen-ager, discovering that he could arouse an audience's emotions, make people laugh and draw their applause.

No doubt the self-confidence building with these talents had its part in his becoming student body president and captain and coach of the swimming team in high school. Eureka, the college owned by his church which he attended on a "needy student" scholarship, supplemented by dish-washing in a girls dorm, was so small that it gave almost every student a chance to shine. Reagan became student body president. After college, he hitch-hiked to Chicago, trying and failing to land a job as radio sports announcer. Then he borrowed his family's old Oldsmobile to check out radio stations in small nearby towns. He got hired in Davenport, Iowa broadcasting Big Ten football games for $5 a game and bus fare.

As his sportscaster career progressed, he learned a lesson in communications that he carried to the White House. As he reported a game, he tried to imagine that he was speaking personally to his friends, especially the old small-town crowd back at the barber shop. And just like his hero, FDR (whose fireside chats he and his family had listened to intently in their impoverished days) he began to get mail from people all over the Midwest who told him he sounded as if he'd been talking directly and personally to them. His sports background and his speaking skills paid off when he became the best-known radio sports announcer in the Midwest.

But the art of public speaking was not the only thing Reagan learned in his early career, starting in the Depression. When his father was put in charge of the W.P.A. (Works Progress Administration) in Dixon, young Reagan formed his first impression of federal bureaucracy. His father found it difficult to get workers to take W.P.A. jobs, for which they got paid, because welfare didn't require them to work, and the welfare bureaucracy, as Reagan saw it, encouraged such dependency because it wanted to perpetuate itself. This was to be a sticking point for Reagan all through his political life. It accounted for his distaste for the rigidity of government and regulatory-agency bureaucracies (and incumbent legislators and their huge staffs) who always wanted more money, more staffs.

From the time he drove his Nash convertible through the gates of the Warner Brothers lot in Burbank in 1937, all through his 53-picture Hollywood career, Ronald Reagan learned many more lessons—about the deceitful, manipulative practices of Communists who were trying to take over the movie industry, about the high taxes paid by big stars and especially about government intrusion into the industry when the Justice Department forced the studios to give up their theater chains. Those chains had given some stability to the industry, enabling it to afford stables of good actors under contract. But most importantly, he learned about the federal-tax problems of movie stars and other highly paid people when he himself entered the 94% tax bracket and began giving the government most of what he earned.

His disillusionment with welfare-statism was deepened further when he observed bureaucratic inefficiencies in Washington during wartime work on government motion picture films for service people, which drew on film footage shot abroad. And his disillusionment was reinforced when he lived for a while in Labor Britain filming the movie "The Hasty Heart" and he noticed how the British welfare state "sapped the incentive to work."

In the late '50s, when he was television host of the new General Electric Theater, G.E.'s chairman, Ralph Cordiner, got him to travel as a company goodwill ambassador to G.E. plants around the country. In talking with workers and other local citizens, he heard more stories that made him question government's intrusion into economic life. Among other things he found out, as he told the story later, that the government "had six programs to help poultry growers increase egg production—it also had a seventh program costing almost as much as all the six others to buy up surplus eggs."

By 1960, these lessons drawn from experiences of ordinary Americans, including ordinary people like his California businessmen-cronies whose enterprises had made them rich, caused Reagan's conversion from Democrat to Republican. He had worshipped FDR and Harry Truman, partly because he inherited from his father a distrust of the business class as well as the notion that people in distress should look to government to solve their problems. He noted in later life that he had admired his old Democratic heroes for some rather ironic reasons: namely, that FDR had argued against permanent welfare dependency, and Truman had believed strongly in budget-balancing.

His experience in the private sector strengthened Reagan's belief that the country needed a government that could provide incentives to private enterprise, a government of people who understood the economics of a free society and who understood how incentives can motivate private enterprise to do things like worker training more efficiently than by creating new government bureaucracies. Instead, he saw a government more bent on regulation of the private sector, a government of career politicians many of whom had never even had exposure to private businesses and the market environment as he had during his G.E. days. He knew from experience that only people who make profits create new wealth, from which all social services are financed; the rest of the people distribute wealth, measure it, envy it or use it for worthwhile activities like education and public health.

Reagan had another chance to mix with the general citizenry during the last half of 1965 when he drove drove up and down California, testing the waters for a run for the governorship of the nation's largest state. His timing was perfect. California was ripe for new leadership. Its citizens paid the highest per capita taxes in the country and it had the highest crime rate and the most profligate state welfare program. The state that had been known as the land where the American dream comes true had become the prime example of fat government.

"A new wind was blowing across America," Reagan wrote later in his autobiography. He sensed correctly that people were tired of "wasteful government programs and welfare chiselers… and arrogant bureaucrats, and public officials who thought all of mankind's problems could be solved by throwing taxpayer dollars at them." States had become addicted to payouts from Washington just as welfare recipients had, and Reagan believed that the narcotic of give-away programs had "sapped the human spirit."

A generation of middle-class Americans "who had worked hard to make something of their lives was growing mistrustful of a government that took away an average 37 cents of every dollar they earned and still plunged deeper into debt every day," he wrote in his memoirs.

Government, he told Californians, was "becoming master of the people, not the other way around." The people were restive, he found, "and it was spreading across the land like a prairie fire."

As governor, Reagan learned how to tap the organizational genius of the private sector to make government more efficient and accountable. By visiting black and Mexican communities around the state he learned that minorities were not getting a fair shake in hiring for state jobs; he saw that the state's testing and job evaluation procedures were changed, and he brought blacks into executive, policy-making jobs.

He learned in California that one of the main causes of growing government and taxes was the influence of "permanent" bureaucrats with a personal interest in prolonging spending programs beyond the time they had been designed for. In education, he killed government rules that shut out parents from active participation and instead enlisted their help in the early education of their children. (The state education bureaucracy survived him, however, and almost half of California's public school workers today are in administrative, support and other non-teaching positions.)

But the most important political lesson of those years was the one that helped him fire up public support for *action* on state and, later, federal issues—the value of "taking my case to the people." He recalled frequently how FDR had gone over the heads of legislators to the people with his fireside chats. He went on TV and radio—the media he handled so well—and as leader of the state, and later of the nation, he explained social problems and explained how he planned to solve them in language anyone could understand. The Reagan magic in communicating with the people helped to produce a historic shift of public attitudes, restoring some of the fervor of the citizenry for greater freedom from authority akin to America's revolutionary days.

In summing up Reagan's impact on the nation, The Urban Institute of Washington gave this president generally good marks. "When candidate Reagan was campaigning in the fall of 1980," said the Institute's report, "the majority of Americans were pessimistic about their future financial prospects and those of their children. Four years later that pessimism has all but disappeared. Whatever else President Reagan may or may not have achieved, he has been able to rid the country of what his predecessor perceived as a national malaise."

In foreign affairs, Reagan learned a lot—and put his learning to use—especially from his long, personal dialogue in meetings and exchanges of private, hand-written notes with Soviet Premier Gorbachev. He learned quickly that the Soviets not only lacked any real understanding of Americans but were genuinely afraid of the United States. His perseverance in changing this dictator's views of himself and of America, convincing him in the end of America's sincere desire for peace, contributed importantly to reducing the fears of generations of Americans *and* Russians.

The final lesson that Ronald Reagan learned from his long experience in office was a sobering one. He learned that no matter how strong his convictions about what was right and what was wrong they could not justify end-running the processes prescribed in the U.S. Constitution. His riverboat gambles on huge deficits (based on his faith that unfettered private enterprise would create the wealth to pay for them) and his determined pumping-up of military spending, as well as his "cowboy" gambits in ordering attacks on Communists in Grenada and on Quaddafi's troublemakers in Libya had all been "wins" that added to this president's popularity. But when he failed to rein in aides who were improvising their own foreign policies on Iran and Nicaragua, violating the law that outlawed support for the Contra rebels and carrying these policies out in secret, he set the stage for the big setbacks of his administration.

For six years Ronald Reagan had enjoyed enormous popularity and success. But in the months after news broke that he had secretly sold weapons to Iran, despite his own previous exhortations about never rewarding terrorists, his popularity slid, he became more disengaged than ever and the White House became so chaotic that a top aide there advised the new chief of staff, Howard Baker, that consideration should be given to invoking the 25th Amendment, which provides for handing presidential powers to the vice president if the president is unable to do his job. The alarms behind the scenes in the White House were not heard by the public, which in 1984 had given Reagan a 70% approval rating along with his colossal re-election victory.

"Reagan's strength had been the public's perception that he was a man of his beliefs," wrote Mayer and McManus in their harsh assessment of the president. "He might compromise on the margins, but he would not sell out his principles wholesale. The shipments of weapons to Khomeni shook the foundations of this belief, squandering

Reagan's moral authority, which by 1986 was the main asset of an administration whose intellectual energy had long since run low…His was a rhetorical presidency, capable at best of uniting the country behind a common vision and moving the political center a long step to the right. But the Iran-Contra affair revealed his rhetoric to be disconnected from his actions, and his actions to be disconnected from his policies. Ronald Reagan's talents had hidden his flaws too well; inevitably, his unmasking was his unmaking."

With the Iran-Contra debacle the republic once again faced a Constitutional crisis. And once again, it corrected the abuses, and healed itself. The excesses of both Reagan and Nixon in misusing the immense power of the presidency met more than their match when the workings of the Constitution brought balance back to government, just as the Founders had intended it to do. In this sense, the real hero of American history in the last decades of the 20th century was not a president, not a single man or woman. It was really the U.S. Constitution.

Still, the remarkable popularity of Ronald Reagan survived even his final misadventures and Constitutional setbacks. The American public tired of the televised hearings of the joint congressional committee on Iran-Contra. It made martyrs in some quarters even of some convicted Reagan staffers, and it turned cool on the interminable investigation being carried out by the special prosecutor whom Reagan himself had ordered into being to sort out the mess. In the summer of 1987 public opinion seemed to have turned decisively against "investigators". The president himself was bloodied, but still popular.

So Ronald Reagan left the nation's highest office with a higher public approval rating than any other modern president had achieved. By the end of his second term, 71% gave him "thumbs up" on the job he had done. Everybody still liked him, many loved him and, when the day came for him and Nancy to board the U.S. Marine helicopter in their final departure from the White House, there were few dry eyes in the crowd in front of the Capitol that had come to see them off. Even a veteran hand as tough as Jim Baker wept openly at this last, moving moment of the Reagan presidency. It could have been the final scene of a sentimental 1930s movie, the kind they don't make anymore, when the audience sat stunned in silence, too choked up to talk, as the music comes up on a happy ending and the closing credits start to roll.

PART FIVE

FIN DE SIÈCLE, A SLIDE FROM TRADITIONAL VALUES

Morals and Optimism Both Fade

The history of the American ethos, especially the trait of self-confident optimism that has most distinguished Americans, throws useful light on the outlook for America's new century. The first conclusion to draw from this history is that the nation's Presidents have been by far the greatest single influence on public spirits, particularly in times of crisis such as those highlighted in this book. As America grew more pluralistic, and ever faster change took place, great leaders, with great communications skills, were instrumental in giving purposeful direction to national life. Carlyle's dictum played out in the 20th century as well as in his 19th century: history is written in the biographies of great men—and great women, he would have added today.

Following on the heels of this is another conclusion: that moral character has been enormously important in American national leadership and its ability to sustain public spirits, and optimism, in good times and bad. Americans benefited greatly from the leaders of high moral stature they were fortunate to have in critical periods of national life. One of the reasons why American historians consistently vote Washington and Lincoln as our greatest presidents is their unblemished reputation for high moral standards and their courage and tenacity in leading fellow citizens and their own lives by those standards (though the historians steer clear of such "judgmental" opinions on the touchy subject of morality.*)

---

*Daniel Boorstin noted in *The Image* how much our thinking about national leaders has changed: "Two centuries ago, when a great man appeared, people looked for God's purpose in him; today we look for his press agent."

As one of the most highly respected television news commentators, Eric Sevareid, once put it, the essence of any Presidency is "character, just character."

Our national history makes clear that of all the factors influencing public spirits and national optimism the most important, along with economic prosperity, has been the strength of the moral convictions that rise primarily from religious faith. This has been true of all of the greatest American leaders and the majority of American citizens. America's leading Founders set the tone: they were not unlike the Greek philosophers who taught virtue to the youth of Greece in its prime. In fact they read the classics of social and political philosophy specifically to study models of moral excellence and to discern what type of government best enhances virtuous life and protects citizens from tyranny. The nation's leaders who followed them, particularly up to Vietnam and the sixties, perpetuated for the most part the tradition of high moral standards in high office.

In early America the national compass was set to follow a code of morality based squarely on spiritual faith. Washington put the new republic on its course by declaring that morality, based on religious belief, is the indispensable prop for a democratic government's success as well as the source of human happiness. His parting words to the nation echoed the observation of the Enlightenment philosopher Montesquieu, who maintained that "the principle of democracy is virtue."

The Declaration of Independence, the cynosure of all American historical documents, asserted an ideal of government based on the theory that citizens are endowed by God with certain natural rights and the purpose of government is to secure those rights. Lincoln called the Declaration "the father of all moral principle." The Declaration's signatories, members of the Second Continental Congress meeting in Philadelphia, appealed in their closing paragraph to "the Supreme judge of the world" for the rectitude of their intentions, declaring their reliance on the protection of "divine Providence" in their epochal mission to form a unique new nation.

The Declaration placed Americans' freedoms and responsibilities firmly in a context of God-given natural rights. And the framers of the Constitution "considered religion to be a great public good, to be carefully protected," as Harvard law professor Mary Ann Glendon has written. On his arrival in the United States in 1831, Toqueville observed that "the religious aspect of the country was the first thing that struck my attention." The longer he stayed in America, he said, "the more I perceived the great political consequences resulting from this new state of things. In France I had almost always seen the spirit of religion and the spirit of freedom marching in opposite directions. But in America I found they were intimately united and that they reigned in common over the same country." He also wrote: "There is no country in the whole world in which the Christian religion retains a greater influence over the souls of men than in America, and there can be no greater proof of its utility... its influence is powerfully felt over the most enlightened and free nation on earth."

The United States Constitution "was made only for a moral and religious people," wrote America's second president, John Adams, who played a leading role in the adoption of the Declaration as a member of its drafting committee. "It is wholly inadequate for the government of any other". A century and a half later a liberal Supreme Court justice, William O. Douglas, declared in a high court opinion: "We are a religious people whose institutions presuppose a Supreme Being."

Theologians were the drivers of early American society—the best-educated, most articulate citizens, the ones who set society's tone. Reaching back to the Bible's Old Testament for guidance, just as Columbus did, the Puritan leaders compared their new land to ancient Israel at the time of the Exodus and set a theme that resonated up to present times—the theme that America has a moral mission, a unique destiny, a challenge to excel among nations and to open up new opportunities for higher forms of human achievement and fulfillment.

Religion was central to education as well as politics and public morale in America's early days. In the entire ante-World War II period of American history (which was three-quarters of American history to present time) U.S. educational institutions, elementary through secondary, considered the development of moral character to be a prime responsibility. As the public school system was emerging, Horace Mann wrote that the system "earnestly inculcates all Christian morals; it founds its morals on the basis of religion; it welcomes the religion of the Bible." Similar responsibilities for moral training were taken for granted by most parents. Books, and later the early motion pictures, reinforced these efforts with their own portrayals of heroic figures who acted on moral principles regardless of consequences.

Religion inspired the creation of America's first colleges and the first duty of the colleges was to educate ministers of the gospel. In early America the moral philosophers were the best minds of the time—Franklin, Jefferson, Jonathan Edwards and others, as ethics scholar and teacher, Albert R. Jonsen, has pointed out. At Harvard, Yale, Princeton and many smaller schools in the Republic's first decades, it was often the college president who taught the important senior course in moral philosophy, the capstone of higher education—often, as in the case of Brown's Francis Wayland and Williams's Mark Hopkins, putting their moral philosophy into lectures and textbooks (Wayland's book became a best-seller.) They openly professed their Christian beliefs—in fact, they urged Sabbath observance, daily prayer and discussion of moral matters in hopes that this would instill a high sense of moral probity in public life.

At the beginning of the 20th century America was fully a Christian nation. Jurors were required to believe in God, teachers to read from the Bible, and in some states citizens were required by law to observe "Lord's Day." Many of the immigrants who teemed into America sustained this moral tone of American culture, even though morality gradually became separated from any particular clerical associations and, in some cases, with any connection to religion at all. Irish Catholic immigrants brought with them a dedication and adherence to moral scruples unrelated to Puritan theology. The Irish Catholic and German immigrants who dominated immigration in the 19th century, the Italians and Eastern Europeans, including many Jews, in the latter half of that century all brought with them leaders who appealed on moral grounds for every policy or program they promoted, domestic or foreign, even though their appeals increasingly were to *individual* moral responsibility without reference to church or religion.

Americans have never been lacking in response to a moral cause when their leaders presented it as such. Ralph Waldo Emerson went so far as to say that to be an American is actually not a nationality but a "moral condition", and for most of American history that moral condition sprang from religion. In literature, America's influential writers—Hawthorne, Emerson, Melville, Stowe, Dickenson, William James, Mark Twain, T.S. Eliot, Frost, Faulkner among them—all concerned themselves in one way or another with God and religious issues. The dean of American criticism, Alfred Kazin, points this out in his book, *God and the American*

Writer. The scholar Malcolm Bradbury noted in reviewing Kazin's book that its theme is "the omnipresence of God in the core writers" and that Kazin's aim is to characterize American culture as "essentially a religious culture, born in the predestined certainties of Calvinism."

The deviation of America's moral bearings

In the last decade of the 20th century most Americans, consciously or not, had split personalities. On one hand, they were optimistic about the way things were going for them personally because unprecedented prosperity brought them the highest standard of living they had ever enjoyed. On the other hand, beneath the sense of their own well-being, they indicated time and again in the polls their sense that moral decay in the nation at large had made this a less-than-perfect picture and that this was the most important problem to address in the new century.

America's moral bearings had in fact been wavering for a long time, and in tandem with moral decline came a weakening of optimism. Despite their prosperity, this dispirited many Americans and contributed to the loss of some of their certainty about their nation and the world, their self-confidence and optimism. The gloominess of the new breed of "declinist" writers was as extreme as the early optimism of Whitman and Emerson.

The decline in America's morals is an important explanation for American malaise after World War II, excluding the Reagan years, because the two appear to be closely related.

Many people dismissed the scandals of the Clinton presidency with the comment: "It's always been this way" and they unearthed long-past dalliances of Jefferson, Hamilton, FDR and others. But the fact is that it has *not* always been that way and American history reveals that moral slippage post-World War II across American society has moved faster and farther than ever before in the past.

Religion-based morality began to lose its grip back in the mid-19th century, particularly in the face of new scientific and sociological thinking. In the 20th century one turning point was the famous Scopes trial of 1921 in Tennessee, when the cynical atheist, lawyer Clarence Darrow, took on William Jennings Bryan, a champion of Christian faith, in defending the teaching of evolution in high school. Although tradition prevailed over science that time, the case marked the beginning of religion's retreat from the academic world and, to a large extent, from the professional world as well.

Colleges born of religious faith ceased to recognize that fact or, frequently, even to include religious studies in their curricula (even though their faculties still wear monks' robes at their rituals.) Many higher-learning institutions either abandoned departments of religion or relegated such subjects to a minor elective course or two, a fringe status in the changing world of education. Reflecting back on his graduation from Yale in 1950, the devout Catholic, William F. Buckley, Jr. wrote that he had become convinced that Yale, and presumably other colleges like it, "were engaged in discouraging intellectual and spiritual ties to Christianity."

In elementary schools, children stopped saying the Lord's Prayer after the Supreme Court prohibited school prayer in 1964. The Warren Court had already, in 1948, forbade released time for religious studies in public schools. The Court subsequently forbade almost all uses of public money to aid children attending religious schools. Private secondary schools followed in step, virtually exorcising religion too. Over time, various justices, hostile or indifferent to religion and determined to remove it from first place among freedoms, often set government interests above the individual's rights to free exercise of religion. Lincoln's concept in his second inaugural, that God and country were one, no longer reflected the thinking of most jurists.

Throughout the professions even the mention of "morals" or "virtues" became thoroughly depassé. In disciplines such as medicine the notions of physician ethics receded and the subject of ethics was avoided in public discussion. Gradually, traditional ethics was superseded by the development of "regulatory ethics" and political/judicial judgments about such things as medical experimentation and controversial practices such as abortion.

Progress in medical technology, as in other fields of technology, spurred *earthly* hopes for the future, often replacing spiritual hopes. Just as they had been stirred by inventions such as telephones and automobiles, Americans drew confidence from news of progress in medicine—from new wonder drugs to heart-lung bypass machines to magnetic resonance imaging, artificial organs and transplants. To some extent technological optimism succeeded scriptural optimism in the evolution of American culture.

In government and politics, as in academe, "progress" lost whatever religious and spiritual connotation it had left. By the mid-19th century, links between state and church were broken. The First Amendment to the Constitution ("Congress shall make no law respecting the establishment of religion, or prohibiting the free exercise thereof...") left no doubt that from then on religion was personal and voluntary, no longer sanctioned by, or in any way involved with, political or institutional authority. In fact, Supreme Court decisions declared it unconstitutional to display the Ten Commandments in a schoolroom, to introduce graduation ceremonies with a prayer or even for an athletic coach to rally players with a pre-game prayer. In no other country, wrote Irving Kristol at the end of 1995, "has official secularism been so belligerent."

Over the years Americans' moral fervor, originally directed to salvation, shifted to social causes. The moral inheritance was showing, but gradually it was loosened from institutional creeds. "Progress", "social revolution", "renewal" and special-interest "rights" were the new metaphors replacing religion to stir human spirits. In recent times labor rights, women's rights, minority rights, environmental rights and other special causes all rode on moral or pseudo-moral exhortations.

All sorts of initiatives for social, political and economic reforms grew from these diverse roots. But whether they took the name of Progressivism or Liberalism or Reformism they all had one thing in common: something Dr. Jonsen characterized as a "melioristic" feature, a belief that things can be made better, which of course is fundamental to the American ethos and the traditional optimistic spirit of Americans. For some, this is one basis for carrying hope into the new century, rather than despair. But before exploring the chances for revival of America's traditional optimism, consider recent history, which has been marked by a dramatic turning away from the faith and certainties of the Founders.

America's lost innocence

If America lost its bearings on the voyage to the 21st century, history shows that what was lost chiefly was the nation's *moral* bearings. The traditional high spirits of the nation arose from its combination of high moral standards and devotion to freedom—with those standards carried through thick and thin on the shoulders of extraordinary leaders of great conviction and moral integrity. This history lesson is significant because in modern times American intellectual and political leadership and American culture have tended to *de-emphasize,* or ignore, morality, a trend accompanied by the breakdown of the American family, which once was in charge of teaching morals.

When we look back, for example, on the prayerful Puritans, the resilient pioneers, the swashbuckling Rough Riders, the doughboy crusaders of World War One and the idealistic, fully committed soldiers and sailors of the second great war—we realize the extent to which we lost our innocence. It was uprooted by the awful traumas of three murders between 1963 and 1968—the Kennedy brothers and Martin Luther King Jr.—as well as the cultural upheaval of the sixties and, at the end of that decade, by U.S. failure in Vietnam, a war that gained little if anything and cost 50,000 U.S. fatalities, as well as the disintegration of Lyndon Johnson's regime. All that was followed by the dragging-down of a president, Richard Nixon, in the Watergate scandal, an experience that finally soured much of the American public altogether on politics and government.

Lincoln once worried, in a letter to his best friend, that "American progress in degeneracy appears to be pretty rapid." One wonders what the great Protector would think of the state of the nation's morals today. What would he think of the fact that close to two million citizens are serving time in prisons and jails (not counting an even larger number on parole and probation), triple the number less than two decades ago, a higher percentage of the population than in any other nation?

Or of present predictions that one in four black Americans born today will serve time in prison? Or of the fact that new prisons are being built at the rate of one a week? What would he make of the fact that across the country criminal bombings have almost tripled in the last two decades to more than 3,000 a year? Or the fact that teachers list drugs, alcohol, pregnancy, suicide, rape and assault as the main problems in schools (as recently as 1940 the main problems were talking out of turn, chewing gum, making noise and running in the hall.)

He would surely be amazed that, through most of ther nineties, the U.S. was first among industrialized nations in the percentage of children who are poor, that some two million American teen-agers are homeless, that more students meet death by firearms in his country than in any developed nation, that as many as 6,000 students a year are expelled from schools for carrying guns and that students in many schools pass through metal detectors to screen out guns and knives, while illegal drugs are sold in and around their schools. Or that guns are kept in roughly one-third the nation's homes and more Americans feel unsafe without them than in frontier days.

One can imagine how surprised he would be to find that the main problems at colleges are alcoholism and binge drinking by students, whose alcohol consumption ran to an estimated $5 billion a year by the end of the nineties. What would he think on learning that half of American marriages today end in divorce, that illegitimate births have been rising for 30 years and that two-thirds of black newborns and three-fourths of teenagers' children are born out of wedlock, while some 70% of the offspring of never-married mothers live in poverty? Or that the United States is the largest consumer of illegal drugs in the world (nearly $60 billion a year, two-thirds of it cocaine), with drug addiction growing year by year to an estimated 810,000 heroin addicts, most recently among pre-teenagers, and with underground drug labs operating even in many suburban neighborhoods.

All this surely is a starker picture of national degeneracy and neurosis than Lincoln could have imagined. It is the dark side of a society that has at the same time, paradoxically, produced more wealth by far than any society in history. America's moral affirmations that began with the Puritans and were manifest in such leaders as Washington, Jefferson, Lincoln, Wilson and the two Roosevelts expanded into the nation's conduct of foreign affairs with the two "great wars", but then American society lost its bearings, beginning in the post-World War II era and accelerating in the sixties. The second world war was a turning point for American attitudes. The generation that had danced to Glenn Miller and his saxophones—and defined success as raising a family just like their parents, and sending their kids to good colleges— returned from war hardened and made more serious by their exposure to a complicated world.

The optimism and traditional high spirits of Americans derived in high degree from the high moral standards that marked the race from the beginning. There can be no doubt that the present age is short on optimism and common purpose, long on cynicism; short on spiritual faith and long on personal consumption and agglomeration. For perspective on these changes, one has only to review recent history.

Despondent voices

Now and then throughout the 20th century American writers raised rather lonely voices warning of the erosion of traditional American values. Daniel Bell dated the beginning of the moral decline in the 1920s, when mass production and the emphasis on consumption began to transform the life of America's middle class, replacing the Protestant ethic and the Puritan temper with "a materialistic hedonism" and "a psychological eudemonism."

In *The Cultural Contradictions of Capitalism* he noted that religion had been the mode of consciousness traditionally concerned with moral values and the basis of a "shared moral order". But with the decline of family, church and synagogue and of stable communities, social bonds snapped, and Americans lost their traditional ways of regarding their place in life. With the mid-19th century breakup of religious authority and its restraints, what Bell called "modernism" took over and society "began to accept the demonic, to explore it, to revel in it… moving the center of authority from the sacred to the profane."

"Is America falling apart?" asked Anthony Burgess after spending the year 1971 in the United States. Describing his impressions in *The New York Times Magazine*, he wrote that with the Vietnam war, and especially the Mylai horror and America's "massive crime figures", Americans were beginning to realize that despite their virtuous ancestry they were capable of "absolute evil." (This observation of a European-in-America was a reverse twist on the view of the best known American-in-Europe, the late 19th century American writer Henry James who, after living in Europe for 20 years, created the tale of a naïve American Christian gentleman from the New World, still possessing the "innocence of Eden", encountering the corrupt Old World nobles of Europe, in James' novel, *The American* and his commentaries in *The American Scene*.) Everything seemed to be going wrong in America, as Burgess saw it, "hence the neurosis, despair, the Kafka-feeling that the whole marvelous fabric of American life seems to be coming apart at the seams", while American politicians, having created a timocracy, seemed to him to be concerned mainly with protecting personal wealth and big fortunes.

Barbara Tuchman, another sagacious witness to American postwar life, contended in her commentaries of the eighties that World War II marked a major turning point in public morality for the nation and the world. "It does seem that the knowledge of a difference between right and wrong is absent from our society, as if it had floated away on a shadowy night after the last World War," she wrote in 1987. "So remote is the concept that even to speak of right and wrong marks one to the younger generation as old-fashioned, reactionary and out of touch."

So much evil was perpetuated in the Nazi years, she argued, "that harm done to fellow human beings began to appear normal, and there was a consequent failure to regard wrongdoing in general as out of bounds and punishable." A year later, taking her message to television, she declared that life in America had come to be characterized by "the loss of a moral sense as a guide to life." In modern life, she said, heroes were characterized by celebrity and notoriety, not by nobility of purpose as had been the case with the "giants" of early America.

In that same year the distinguished scholar, Robert Nisbet, in *The Present Age* (a Jeremiad not unlike those to come of Allan Bloom, Paul Kennedy and others) also made the case that the serious virtue of the founding fathers had been steadily eroded by commercialism and moral decay. Two of Nisbet's examples were the American sports hero's conversion into a commercial corporation and the devaluing of the honor of government service, which had become a way to the big book advance, the profitable lecture tour and lucrative lobbying consultancies. In place of the old collective standards of moral behavior, what Nisbet called the new "loose individual" made up his or her own mind about what was "right" and what was "wrong".

Other Cassandras had even grimmer takes on the changes in American life. One was Gertrude Himmelfarb in her 1994 book, *The De-Moralization of Society*. "Moral principles, still more moral judgments," she charged, "are thought to be at best an intellectual embarrassment, at worst evidence of an illiberal and repressive disposition." Among her arguments were the fact that the U.S. led the industrialized world in teen-age pregnancies; the six-fold rise in illegitimacy in just three decades; the rise in crime, violence and drugs; the acceptance of divorce and illegitimacy as 'alternative life styles'; the embrace of substance-abusers in government welfare programs and the dissolution of two-parent families.

Others have been sounding similar warnings more recently. "Today our entire culture flaunts and exploits sex and aggression—in movies, television, the Internet, rap music and, not least, the version of theater called politics," wrote Robert Coles, the respected author and child psychiatrist, in October 1996. "In recent decades we've taken every scrap of religious faith out of the public schools, and civic religion—the flag, for example—has become in many minds suspect. With God and country gone, what remains to guide or children and teachers ethically…?"

A Pepysian diarist of the century's dwindling days, Roger Rosenblatt, wrote in an essay summing up 1996 that "the only things missing in the year were nobility, honor, beauty, moral action and a sense of how to live in the world." The personality of the past quarter-century, he wrote, was the ex-football player and accused wife-slayer O.J. Simpson "along with his enlarging retinue of lawyers, prosecutors, agents, accusers, defenders, police, forensic experts, talk-show hosts and Faye Resnick" (one of the witnesses at the Simpson murder trial.)

Most of the media, charged Rosenblatt, behaved as if the Simpson case and all its sideshows was the most important subject for the public to know about, eclipsing other world and domestic events. "America's involvement with O.J.," he noted, "was nearing the length of its involvement with World War II, which was not covered as thoroughly." The fact that Broadway had chosen this particular time to revive the musical "Chicago" seemed entirely appropriate to this scribe, since it dealt with people who got away with murder.

Politics descending

In the last half of the 20th century, the baby boomers—the generation that grew up in the divisive '60s, a generation touched by the demoralizing culture of drugs and crime and destabilized family life—set new standards when they came to political power. Two of the principal new leaders setting the tone in the early '90s were the man in the White House and the Speaker of the House of Representatives.

Following the '96 election there was a gradual escalation of evidence that the Clinton administration, the last administration of the 20th century, was seriously flawed both in its standards of morality and its obeisance to law.

The lapse in moral standards was most shocking in the White House but it was not confined to the Democratic Party. The House of Representatives dealt an unprecedented reprimand and a $300,000 fine to

Republican Speaker Newt Gingrich for turning tax-exempt funds into political hush money, a breach of moral standards that discredited the House. The public viewed with dismay this extraordinary situation when leaders of both elected branches—their President and their House speaker, both representatives of the same new generation—were charged with serious ethical and legal transgressions. No wonder that Americans became even more profoundly cynical about their government.

About 75% of the people trusted the federal government when Lyndon Johnson took office in 1963, according to the polls; by early 1997 about the same percentage said they *didn't* trust the federal government. Public respect for government suffered particularly from the spectacle of the 1996 presidential election and its overdrive fundraising. Jimmy Carter, Ronald Reagan and George Bush had each run their election campaigns chiefly with funds provided by the federal government, but by the nineties both parties had found ways to circumvent the fund-raising limits of the post-Watergate reforms. In 1996 the two major presidential campaigns raised close to $300 million in "soft money" (donations from special interest groups, led by unions and corporations, supposedly to pay for things like "issue advertising".) Incumbents in Congress, the principal beneficiaries, ignored the public disgust and dragged their heels on any further reform of the system.

The nation's key moral barometer, and very often the key to national spirits, is the presidency. The last presidential election of the 20th century was not encouraging in this regard. More than half the people polled as they left the voting booths said they did not trust the man who won re-election, and fewer voters turned out to vote than in any election since 1924. In early 1997, polls indicated that 71% of the public put "scandals" first among the things they associated with the President, even though 60% expressed approval of his job performance, a paradox and a metaphor for cynicism all around.

The public's loss of confidence in political leadership, and the decline of moral standards during William Jefferson Clinton's two terms, did not substantially diminish the general good feelings of a large part of the public. Rather, the period illustrated how closely the citizen's mood was linked to his or her personal prosperity. Gloomsters like William Bennett and Gertrude Himmelfarb described this as a dark and tragic period of American history. They railed that there was no outburst of public outrage and claimed that this proved that the public in general had forsaken its morals. Realists knew that public sentiments during this period had less to do with morals than with the feeling on the part of the average American that he or she had never had it so good. For many people, this was "as good as it gets"— better, in terms of their well-being, than they had ever imagined for themselves. Nevertheless, beneath their enjoyment of the goods of life, Americans were far from happy about the obvious drift of national morals symbolized by the Clinton White House scandals.

The Clinton era: prosperity and unease

Despite the unprecedented prosperity that marked the Clinton years, reflected in the soaring stock market, many Americans were uncomfortable for a number of reasons. One of course was the White House scandals, but other concerns ran deeper. Harvard professor Michael J. Sandel, in his book *Democracy's Discontents* cited two concerns at the heart of public anxiety and discontent: "One is the fear that, individually and collectively, we are losing control of the forces that govern our lives. The other is the sense that, from family to neighborhood to nation, the moral fabric of community is unraveling around us."

In a cover story titled "20ᵗʰ Century Blues", *Time* magazine in mid-1995 documented the stress, anxiety and depression that ran through modern society and, among other things, noted that the "isolating technology" of television had contributed to the loss of community, and the loss of bonding, that characterized earlier American society. "When you're watching TV 28 hours a week—as the average American does—that's a lot of bonding you're not out doing," *Time* observed. In the quarterly, *The American Prospect*, Harvard professor Robert D. Putnam noted that television usually gave a negative picture of American life and declared that "heavy TV watching may well increase pessimism about human nature." Recent surveys have indicated that many people who spend time on the Internet also tend to be more pessimistic than those who are more engaged with people in live situations in their communities.

The 1996 presidential election convinced most Americans that the election process had become a money game of special interests, with little hope of reform coming from their entrenched, incumbent representatives in Congress. A *New York Times* editorial called it "a corrupt system that elevates the voice of the wealthy special interests over that of the average voter." The electorate's growing awareness that money was driving politics, and introducing a new type of inequality in American life, could not help but disillusion voters. Money bought television time, television time made celebrities of those who could pay for it and the average American felt increasingly impotent. The liberty and equality that Jefferson had placed high among American virtues seemed to be washing away in a Niagara of special interest and corporate and union money. The TV campaigns of special interests were taking control of most political outcomes, and the public knew it.

There was also unease, conscious or unconscious, over mounting evidence that the breakdown of marriage and family and the ballooning population of fatherless or single-parent young people were destabilizing American society. The number of married couples with children had fallen to one-quarter of all U.S. households in 1997, from 40% in 1970. Also, the realization that best-intentioned welfare programs had actually contributed to the breakdown of families and the virtual cult of dependency among the lower classes contributed to the malaise of many liberals who had once hoped for very different results. The cumulative weight of dashed Great-Society, Age-of-Entitlement expectations led to what *Newsweek* called the "free-floating gloom" that surrounded the 1996 election.

Still another destabilizing factor was the huge wipe-out of jobs in the century's last two decades, mostly by corporate restructurings. More than 43 million jobs were erased between 1979 and 1996. Because many *new* jobs were being created at the same time, there was actually a net *gain* of 27 million jobs, but the new jobs were often very different from the old jobs, particularly in requiring special information-age skills.

Defining immorality down.

As the 20th century drew to a close a dearth of moral leadership and a spread of transgressive behavior infected many parts of American life, taxing the nation's optimism and sapping its self-confidence. In a country where "everything from parricide to political scandal is instantly transformed into a multi-media freak show", as a *New York Times* pundit put it, the media in particular, especially television and motion pictures, stood out as insidious depressants of the traditional, optimistic American spirit. Author/Senator Patrick Moynihan's phrase, "defining deviancy down" captured the trend of shrinking morals.

Comedian Woody Allen did a show in Greenwich Village's Bitter End in 1996, the year President Clinton was re-elected, which portrayed pointedly a very unheroic figure—the wistful "little guy", the confused intellectual, contending with a world no longer comprehensible; for years that character served as a metaphor for a new breed of more cynical and seemingly values-shorn Americans.

Past images of "evil" were tame compared to new standards of behavior. Things once thought evil were actually *advertised* as "come-ons"—to sell motion pictures, fashion clothes or pop singers. "SEX, MURDER, BETRAYAL—EVERYTHING THAT MAKES LIFE WORTH LIVING" was just one of many such newspaper ads for movies running in late 1997. Describing the trend to *noir* in movies, books, fashion and music, one critic called it a sinister new lining to the American dream, a world of "light and shadow, where only crime is colorful and kisses kill." Motion pictures in the last decade of the century plumbed new depths to arouse audiences numbed out by mere violence. The old horror film genre like Frankenstein in the '30s was Pablum compared with the new slasher movies filled with body-shredding carnage, spectacular new-age special effects and gratuitous brutality.

Movies and TV shows made what formerly was considered wickedness downright heroic. The culture-commentator Michiko Kakutani railed against deconstruction's anti-humanist agenda, "our hip culture's obsession with the clever and the mocking and its suspicion of the serious and the sincere... applauding the bravura style of a maniac." Big-name movie stars like Robert Redford and Clint Eastwood made motion pictures glamorizing adultery, while top-paid film actress Demi Moore titillated a Congressman by stripping on his coffee table.

One movie-star life that mirrored the loss of innocence in America was that of Judy Garland. She was called the world's greatest entertainer but her life careened from joy to tragedy. Remembered as the wholesome girl next door in "Meet Me In St. Louis" (which lifted spirits of sailors and soldiers in World War II with its idyllic vision of life back home), and remembered too as the sweet innocent farm girl Dorothy having her unforgettable dream in "The Wizard of Oz", her real life was actually rocked by neuroses and excesses—five marriages, recurrent bouts with drugs and alcohol, a suicide attempt and finally premature death at 47. In his review of a TV special about Garland's life, the critic John J. O'Connor sighed: "As the century peters out rather ingloriously, we are all so damnably sophisticated."

On TV news shows, one CNN commentator complained, "almost every prime-time news magazine program uses techniques and subjects that would have been unthinkable a generation ago." Scenes of brutality including murders and police beatings of criminals became common and were featured day after day. The networks' standards toppled when they were forced to compete with explicit sex and crime pouring out of cable channels. "There's now so much air out there to be filled," commented CBS's chief Washington correspondent, "that I don't think there's any question standards are lower these days."

Commenting on the admixture of banality and evil in the movies, *Times'* critic Ben Brantley wrote that "being young, affectless and homicidal has become a staple of murder movies and TV shows...the evening news abounds with descriptions of such things as serial killers sitting down to eat sandwiches in the kitchens of their still-bleeding victims." Some syndicated TV talk shows were described as "cesspools overflowing into America's living rooms" by the executive producer of the news program "60 Minutes", which somehow carried on decade after decade broadcasting special reports more or less in the tradition of old-time journalists of character like Edward R. Murrow, Howard K. Smith and Eric Sevareid. On one daytime TV talk show, the Jerry Springer show, Nielson ratings were kicked up by lewd language and on-screen fisticuffs. As television claimed an increasing amount of Americans' time, commonplace life experiences that once raised the innocent spirits of Americans—such as romance, humor, wit and even good conversation—seemed to be disappearing.

Crime stories on TV tripled in the 1990s. Most troubling was their impact on children, even those in elementary schools who, by the time they got to high school, had watched an estimated 8,000 murders (26,000 by the time they were 18—some estimates put it at 40,000) and 100,000 acts of violence, according to a 1992 report of the American Psychological Association. Hundreds of studies demonstrated a linkage between children's exposure to such violence and their own behavior, hardly surprising in view of the fact that most inner-city children returned from school to parentless homes where they watched four or five hours of TV daily. In her book, *Mayhem—Violence as Public Entertainment*, Sissela Bok asked: "What happens to the souls of children nurtured, as in no past society, on images of rape, torture, bombings and massacre that are channeled into their homes from infancy?"

Nothing illustrated how far America's morals had down-shifted than the pop trends in an old medium—radio. The children and grandchildren of Americans who once gathered as a family in the evening to listen to "One Man's Family" or "Fibber MaGee and Molly" now tuned in their Lexis or Honda or Jeep car radios to the new "shock jock" world of Howard Stern or Tom Leykis. These shows reached millions of listeners and proved that talking about relationships, adultery, bisexuality and breast implants attracted far more young listeners than broadcasting music or drama.

As for hard-core pornography, which has been called "capitalism's most noxious industry", by the late '90s Americans were spending more than $8 billion a year on this form of entertainment, including things like video cassettes, adult cable programming and sex magazines— more than they spent on Hollywood movies and more than they spent on rock and country music recordings, according to *U.S. News & World Report*.

The Unabomber, the Net and murder

The print media's moral standards sagged too, particularly when giving recognition in headlines and sometimes near-respectability to wrongdoers and sensational crimes. After the "Unabomber" excited national attention by mailing bombs to randomly selected scientists and other academics, *People* magazine named this pervert one of the "most intriguing" people of the year. Essays flashed on the Internet hailed Kaczynski as a hero, even suggested a "Unabomber for President" write-in campaign. The national newspaper *USA Today* put an incredible headline on its front page quoting a university professor who described the monster as "a high-tech Robin Hood. He's going to save us from ourselves. There are plenty who feel the same way about technology." In one episode after another journalists in print and TV got caught in the act of reporting false stories, sometimes simply concocted out of their imaginations.

Women's magazines became so unjudgmental about adultery that "they practically recommend it to their readers as a fun and healthy activity, like buying a new shade of lipstick or vacationing in the Caribbean," observed writer Katie Roiphe. More recently a *Vogue* editor, quoting sex therapists and advisors, compared monogamous life with "having to eat the same meal every day" and implied that sex—not love, child-rearing or marital companionship—is the be-all of marriage and that married people who don't stray had "sexual dysfunction." *

In the slickest magazines and best stores, skinny models with stoned or angry junkie expressions promoted ghoulish "heroin chic". On the stage, the "best musical" of 1996- 1997 was about the whores and pimps who worked New York's 42nd Street before its cleanup. The smash hits "Angels in America" and "Rent" gave their audiences dispiriting views of AIDS, homelessness, gayness, poverty and helplessness, without suggesting much more in conclusion than the platitude, "We all must care." While such shows did their best to legitimize gay culture, an appalling promiscuity within that culture not only spread AIDS but also disgusted many straight people who otherwise would have had sympathy for gay causes. Unlike "Hair", the upbeat late '60s musical that celebrated hippie love, "Rent" animated audiences with death and H.I.V.

In literature, the popular horror novels of Stephan King and Anne Rice contributed to the sense of pervasive evil. The Library of America's executive editor called the *noir* trend "the dominant style of the American 20th century… It pulls together all the big themes of the power of money and corruption and sexual obsession—and a kind of craziness." In the field of teen-age literature, young adult novels became known in the trade as "bleak books" because they dealt with murder, drug addition, rape or incest.

A game called "Ultima Online", which became the fastest-selling role-playing game on the Internet after its introduction in September 1997, was described by *Wired* magazine as "an online world in which

---

* "I just do not understand why marriage breaks down in America," Anthony Burgess said in an interview. "It's quite exceptional in the whole world… It's as though they don't understand what marriage is about…it's not about sex at all. It's a matter of setting up the primal social unit, and this isn't just a matter of begetting children. It's a matter of building up a kind of miniature civilization in which there's a culture, in which there are immense subtleties of language, immense subtleties of communication. In some ways, this is what life is all about."

it's easy, tempting and lucrative to commit lethal crimes." Players entered a "Kingdom of Britannia" ruled by intimidation, power dynamics and conspicuous consumption, overrun by "maniacal, brutal, twitchy-fingered Quake killers who are ready to murder anyone on sight," the magazine reported. The game sold 100,000 copies in its first three months.

"America has become almost impossible to embarrass," wrote Christopher Hitchens in *Vanity Fair*, under the headline, "The Death of Shame." High-profile art in the nineties frequently focused on the human body and its previously unmentionable parts. A 1998 exhibition called "Bathroom" at a Chelsea gallery in New York featured Andy Warhol photographs of urinals. At a Beverly Hills art gallery in the mid-nineties, art collectors paid up to $20,000 for paintings by a condemned serial killer who had murdered 33 boys and young men. In Seattle, an art show featured obscene paintings of Jesus on the cross, a pope seemingly engaged in a lewd act and pages of the Bible defaced with satanic marks.

Rock music metamorphosed out of the gentle romanticism of the Beatles into crass, blatant songs about senseless violence. Gangs were romanticized in rapper songs like "Murder Ballads". Raunchy music videos and "beyond-bad" metal bands carried vulgarity into the mainstream. While music in earlier eras had sought to lift peoples' spirits, the nihilism and obscenity of Doggystyle rappers fed anger and hatred. Gorkian depths were sounded by the hard-rock group called Marilyn Manson, which screamed obscenities in concerts around the country, ripped up Bibles and used the American flag as bathroom tissue.

What scholar Mark Edmundson called "Fin-de-siècle American gothic" of the nineties purveyed a dark, pessimistic view, a fatalistic view that "all power is corrupt, all humanity debased, and that there is nothing we can do about it." He attributed such modern cynicism to the fact that in our time highly visible people who might otherwise have been role models—from transgressors like O.J. Simpson to the President of the United States—were associated with one foul deed after another, and also to the fact that faith in God had declined and spiritual content had slipped out of daily lives.

Mainstream moral melt

It became difficult in the nineties to find any corner of society untouched by moral relapse. In the business world, the tsunami that broke on the West Coast on the eve of the nineties decade and rolled over the whole country for years was the massive, pervasive fraud in savings and loan institutions. This became a national crisis, and cost the nation some several hundred billion dollars in bailouts and investigations.

The nation's largest insurance company was found to have cheated customers for more than a decade; the largest health care company was charged with a sweeping fraud scheme involving government health insurance; the largest landlord-developer of federally subsidized housing was accused of diverting federal funds into private pockets and the largest private union, the International Brotherhood of Teamsters, had $1.5 million embezzled from its treasury by its president's re-election campaign. Unions in the private sector misused political campaign funds and violated members' rights by forcing them to pay into political war chests, and unions in the public sector muscled non-union entrepreneurs out of opportunities to provide services to the public.

Frauds got bigger as the nineties' stock market surged. Stock promoters telemarketed scams. Eight New York Stock Exchange firms were charged with illegal trading. A top corporate executive was charged with a $9.5 million embezzlement from his firm and a banker was found to have committed a $10 million fraud against his bank. Some business executives reported phony profits to push up stock prices. Retail businesses reported losing $8–16 billion a year to shop-lifters plus another $10 billion in thefts by their own employees.

Acts of violence were reported increasingly in workplaces and on highways where "road rage", sometimes including shootings, rose markedly in the nineties. Stories spread about doctors who submitted fraudulent medical claims and hospital administrators who also committed frauds and used hospital funds to build luxury homes and finance overseas golf trips. Many schools practiced deception by padding attendance figures so they could collect more student aid, doled out on a per capita basis.

Stockbrokers were arrested for criminal fraud in the fixing of tests for licensing people in that industry; teachers cheated their way into public school jobs, and immigrants cheated their way to citizenship by buying answers to questions in tests arranged by the principal educational testing service. The president of the nation's largest black religious organization was convicted of racketeering, grand theft and immoral relations with an aide. A 1998 poll of 20,000 students showed an increase in lying and cheating, with 70% of high school students admitting to cheating on exams in one year and 47% admitting to stealing from stores.

The moral power of the law was vitiated daily as judges and prosecutors bargained with criminals. Sociologists and psychiatrists characterized criminal behavior as the result of external influences on criminals, and news publications sometimes gave as much space to criminals' opinions as to their accusers and victims. Trial lawyers became more skillful year after year in fleecing companies with frivolous class-action suits (more than half of the leading high-tech firms in Silicon Valley reported that this "legal killing field" had become a serious obstacle to their performance.) In a major feature on "incivility", *U.S. News* cited a 1996 poll indicating that to people outside the legal profession "lawyers have become symbols of everything crass and dishonorable in American life" while, among themselves, lawyers had become increasingly combative and uncivil.

In sports, coarseness and incivility became common. "Throughout the country", noted *The New York Times,* "in almost very sport in every region, officials are reporting increasing instances of verbal abuse, attempted intimidation and even physical assault."

Baseball icon Hank Aaron berated the $10-million-a-year baseball players of the late '90s and charged: "Their collective mission is greed...There's no discernible social conscience among them... People wonder where the heroes have gone. When there is no conscience, there are no heroes." Pro football players grabbed annual product-endorsement contracts for as much as $50 million (plus stock options in some cases) while erring-do in that sport included assaulting umpires, groin-kicking opponents, using cocaine and sexually assaulting women fans. More than a fifth of the National Football League players were charged with crimes in 1998. Gambling scandals rocked college football and basketball as players were indicted for fixing games.

Violent behavior by star basketball players was punished lamely if at all. In the case of a player who had choked, punched and threatened his coach, an arbitrator ruled that his team could not fire him and cited a state court ruling that simple battery doesn't involve "any appreciable degree of moral turpitude in American society today." Illegal sports gambling exploded on college campuses and college basketball players were charged with taking bribes to fix Big Ten games. Heavyweight boxing was called a "sewer of a sport" by sportswriter Pete Hamill because fights were fixed by racketeers.

Over the course of one generation there was an explosion of juvenile violence, a rise in juvenile crime to unprecedented levels, with some 4,000 murders a year, many of them random and gruesome. The experts predicted that the incidence of crimes would increase substantially if only because of increases in the youth population.

Across the board, behavior, art and language once considered "evil" actually became so mainstream by century's end that Columbia University professor Andrew Delbanco wrote a book, *The Death of Satan*, arguing that the very concept of sin had so faded from American life that evil, or what was once evil, was being packaged like any other consumer product, technologized, internationalized and often rhapsodized. In his "national spiritual biography" of Americans, Delbanco recalled that in the writings of Edwards, Emerson, Dewey, Niebuhr, Martin Luther King and others, evil was once an enemy, whereas now we lack even a symbolic language for describing it. "We certainly no longer have a conception of evil as a distributed entity with an ontological essence of its own," he wrote.

The President and the intern

Against this social background, the series of revelations of wrongdoing by the most important player on the national and international stages, the President of the United States, was not entirely surprising. William Jefferson Clinton was a product of his times, and a reflection of some of the deplorable characteristics of his generation. The historical significance of the Clinton scandals was that they forced the American public, or a large part of it, to acknowledge that the country's moral standards had slipped badly since World War II and, equally important, to realize that they really did *care* about their moral roots. This was a major climacteric, signaling—at least to some people—the need to turn back from the trend to amorality and immorality that had besmirched the half-century since World War II and that in large part had created the atmosphere in which scandals could occur without causing public outrage.

If public respect for the moral standards of the nation's chief executive fortified American spirits in difficult times such as those of

Wilson, the two Roosevelts, Truman and Reagan, so too the break-down of the moral standards of political leaders can temper peoples' spirits and cause them to lose some of their native optimism about their country and their country's future. That, unfortunately, was one of the lessons of the Clinton years. In the century's last decade the defining political and cultural influence in America was the Clinton White House scandals.

Bill Clinton strode onto the national stage in 1992 broadly supported by a host of enthusiastic, optimistic followers not unlike the youthful boosters of Jack Kennedy and Reagan. He combined the youthful charm of his beau ideal, the young Kennedy, with a fine intellect and an extraordinary, ingratiating poise in discussing public issues unmatched in Washington since Franklin Roosevelt. Despite the swirl of doubts and suspicions concerning Clinton's veracity and moral values that dogged him throughout his career, the Clinton loyalists by and large remained firm in their support right up to his crucial, and tragic, less-than-five-minute televised confession of his White House trysts with a 21-year-old White House intern that was broadcast on August 17, 1998 and seen by 70 million viewers. More than half of U.S. households tuned into this speech, more than the number who had watched Neil Armstrong's walk on the moon in 1969. Until that historic moment his image as a pro-active leader concerned with social issues, among Democrats at least, eclipsed his image as a pro-active philanderer.

Clinton's supporters gave him credit for helping the Republican Congress balance the budget after three decades of red ink, for preaching racial reconciliation and Social Security reform, for showing compassion for the underprivileged—especially young people lacking the means and skills demanded by the modern world—as well as for relating to working families concerned with issues like family leave, health insurance and the rising costs of their children's education. Appealing to conservatives, he promoted free trade, joined the Republicans in welfare reform and even intercepted the Republican theme that "the era of big government is over" as well as other Republican policies such as welfare reform, IRS reform and missle defense.

Much of the goodwill he had gained was squandered, however, when this bright, articulate man was trapped into admitting to gross, indecent behavior by the accretion of evidence presented against him to the independent counsel, Kenneth W. Starr. This included the testimony of the intern herself, the taped recordings of her phone conversations discussing her 18-month affair with the president and, most sordid of all, the DNA evidence on a dress worn by the young woman during their final White House encounter, forcing Clinton to confess when he became the first President ever called before a federal grand jury in a criminal investigation of his own conduct. After having forcefully denied to associates, to his family and, on national television to the general public, that any such affair had existed, the president was forced to admit he had misled the nation and attempted to put the scandals behind him.

But when he failed, during that brief, prime-time TV appearance, to admit to lying and to apologize for his libertine behavior and his betrayal of allies, his high-wire act became an inflection point in his political career. At that moment he lost the trust of virtually all of his betrayed supporters and his party, many of whom were dismayed by the president's brazen, cavalier attitude towards his misbehavior. He took the position that his affair in the White House was strictly private, "nobody's business but our own."

The President failed to understand that reckless, indecent behavior in the Oval Office—some of which was too obscene even to be described in most of the general press— was indeed a fit subject for attention by citizens who had any concern for moral standards. They were the ones who paid for his house, who had pointed to the President as a moral standard for their children. Clinton appeared insensitive to public concern over the moral character of the person holding the highest office in government and his standards of behavior, particularly in chambers of the White House where former presidents had made history of a very different kind. Clinton's conduct left a stain on the White House and the presidential office that George Washington had tried so diligently to raise above any reproach.

In a seeming paradox, former White House aide George Stephanopoulos, in a tell-all book after he quit his job, expressed his view that the President's shamelessness and capacity for denial were actually the basis for "the optimism that is his greatest political strength."

Notwithstanding their differences in age and status, the President and the intern seemed cut from similar cloth: both from broken families, both "loose individuals" influenced by postwar social changes, including the diminished role of the traditional family and the presence of a loving father and mother. Both needed much affection and attention to reinforce their sense of self-worth. Both of them astonished many Americans by their virtual Bonnie-and-Clyde lack of moral remorse for the damage thay had done to others and to the honor of the Presidency.

To some Americans, Clinton personified what Shelby Steele has called "a moral idea that blossomed rather notoriously in my baby-boom generation: that political and social virtue is more important than private morality in defining a person's character."

The bitter conflict between the President and independent counsel Starr was to some extent a clash of cultures— a battle royal between a prosecutor with the zeal of the early Puritans (the son of a Fundamentalist preacher in Texas) and a President who personified a generation of "loose individuals" (as Nisbet had called them) who identified themselves with this man and his mix of amorality and social compassion, which was not unlike that of the free-wheeling activists of the sixties.

Members of his cabinet, his staff and his party who had stood up for Clinton publicly were saddened and embittered by his betrayal of them. In one year he had committed perjury in legal proceedings, lied to Congress, lied to the American public, tampered with witnesses and obstructed justice. The minority of the American public who were paying attention, which had up till now suspended disbelief in the president, became more concerned.

Newspapers around the country condemned his angry, unrepentent attitude and his belligerence towards the independent counsel. In a lead editorial the *Times* referred to "a tidal feeling of betrayal and embarrassment running across the country today, from the grass roots to the White House." Shortly after the president's TV admission of misconduct, 17 newspaper editorial boards called for his resignation. Among many critical editorials, the *Seattle Post-Intelligencer* called it "a sordid tale, capped by a confession of startlingly reckless behavior." The *Houston Chronicle* wrote that "the man is immoral and not fit to hold office." *The Charleston Daily Mail* in West Virginia said it was "a hell of a comedown from a fireside chat with FDR."

Even worse, the foreign press published lead articles lampooning the "liar" in the White House, further dishonoring the American Presidency. In early 1997, the Sunday *London Times* magazine ran a cover story caricaturing Clinton as a liar and philanderer. The influential *Economist* of London lamented that Clinton should have resigned "if he were capable of shame or had any sense of honour." Europeans writing to American friends made similar comments, like the Englishman who wrote that Americans "appear to care little how their president's conduct diminishes the stature of his high office so long as he brings home the bacon." By early '99, following Clinton's surprise bombing of suspected weapons development sites in Iraq, even top Iraqui officials were scorning the president who had "lied to a grand jury."

Despite the fact that American society had become inured to "loose individuals" and lowered its expectations of public and private morality, it certainly seemed that this major presidential crisis had touched a deep chord, causing the old Puritan strain once again to re-assert itself in many Americans. Yet a week after the President's televised *mea culpa,* the *USA Today*/CNN/Gallup poll showed that the nation's strong economy and the prosperity it was creating continued to have a major, countervailing influence on public opinion. Some 63% of those polled said they were satisfied with the way things were going in the nation; 62% approved of the way the President was handling his job. But 67% said the President was not honest or trustworthy, and 29% thought he should be impeached and removed from office. In early February a Gallup poll indicated that 73% of the public believed Clinton had committed perjury, a felony, yet only 31% wanted him convicted.

The explanation for these odd opinion polls was relatively simple. The public was conflicted in spirit because of two opposing influences. One was their embarrassment over a President and a Congress who were being ridiculed in the domestic press and in the press worldwide, and indeed even denigrated by some foreign diplomats. But against this degrading of America's *public-sector* leaders, the U.S. *private sector* was functioning in top form, creating wealth on a scale and at a rate never imagined in history. The impact of this superb performance on the American public was to create a feeling of *individual* well-being among all but the poorest citizens.

The American citizen's positive feelings about his or her own economic success countered the sense that the nation politic was headed downhill, a view encouraged by the media's emphasis on negative news and scandal. As Americans made a clear distinction between their own individual situations and their view of the state of the country at large, in their answers to polls, social scientists began to refer to this as "the optimism gap." To complicate matters further, the besieged President, like a rooster claiming credit for the sunrise, took credit for "seven" years of unprecedented prosperity, whereas the nation was actually in the 17th year of an unprecedented wave of prosperity launched in mid-'82 with the supply-side, free enterprise revolution of Ronald Reagan.

Sex, power and money

One striking metaphor for the age of the "loose individual" that philosopher Nisbet lamented was the image of President Clinton, during a spring 1998 African tour, beating a bongo drum and hopping with delight in his hotel room in Dakar, Senegal, cigar in hand, after receiving news that a sexual harassment suit against him in Arkansas had been dismissed. Virtually no one doubted that he had committed an obscene act when he lured a government employee to his Arkansas hotel room, but he escaped censure because of the judge's fragile definition of "harassment."

The release on September 11 of the special counsel's initial report focusing on Clinton's White House trysts, with all the salacious details gathered from Grand Jury testimonies and other investigations, was probably the broadest, almost-instantaneous transmission of news in history and the first electronic communication between the U.S. government and its citizens on a massive scale. The 453-page report was flung into cyberspace through hundreds of Internet web sites. It deepened disillusionment with political leadership among the millions of Internet users who received it within hours of its release.

Growing public discomfort over the President's morals grew as the evidence of presidential misconduct piled up. The magnitude of the scandals around the Clinton Presidency had been masked partly by this president's political brilliance and issues-literacy; he seemed capable of communicating persuasively with the public without a trace of concern for the charges of personal sexual misbehavior that had followed him from the early seventies, his earliest days in politics.

A team of *New York Times* reporters, canvassing the country trying to explain why Clinton's support held up despite the lurid allegations against him, detected "deep-seated changes in the country's mores and political culture." Many Americans, they reported, no longer expected their President to provide moral leadership. When times are good, nothing else matters, seemed to be the public's attitude. A Roman Catholic priest in Chicago asked: "Have we as a nation become so corrupted that, as long as we get what we want, as long as times are good and the money rolls in, that we don't care what the hell goes on?"

Some people said that the public indifference to scandals simply reflected the shift of American attitudes towards sexuality. After all, a theme song of the baby boomers in the sixties had been that consensual sex should not be subject to moral scrutiny—so they could scarcely condemn the President for reflecting their generation's values. Evolutionary psychologists and biologists reinforced moral indifference by condoning acts that once were considered immoral as simply natural behavior governed by hormones, which in turn are controlled by genes. Indiscriminate male lust is a natural way to perpetuate the species, they argued, and power, magnified in the presidency, is the greatest aphrodisiac of all.

The revelations of Clinton's sexual escapades, and the reports of his extramarital affairs lasting as much as a decade or more, were rationalized by the public to some extent on grounds that these were just examples of general moral decline or that they were at least no worse than could be expected from a politician. While most people brushed off, or tried to ignore, the President's sexual peccadillos, they were increasingly troubled by evidence that he had lied under oath to a Grand Jury about his tawdry White House encounters with women.

With the liberal press joining conservatives in airing these allegations, public alarm reached a crescendo on January's "Super Bowl" weekend, and it took only a week for the public's positive feelings towards the president to plummet from 57% to 40%, troubling world markets as well as the American electorate, before the President's brilliantly-delivered State of the Union speech bounced his job ratings right back up again. Americans on the whole were prospering from the still-roaring economy and, rightly or wrongly, giving Clinton the credit. Hardly anyone wanted to turn against the handsome, energetic, loquacious president who was demonstrating his ability to seduce not only a White House intern but also the President and the TV viewers of China, on his visit to that country, and just about everyone else— especially when times were so good and so many people were making so much money.

The widespread abuses of power and alleged obstruction of justice by the executive branch of the government could not compete with the headlines about bawdy sex, but in historical significance were very likely to be seen as a flagrant violation of public trust by the most powerful branch of the American government. While Clinton's indiscretions with women in government positions subservient to him were abuses of power in terms of *personal* morality, his careless use of government for his own benefit was equally censurable. Charges repeated over and over again included obstruction of justice, manipulation of the IRS to harm political enemies and foreign espionage keyed to political contributions, as well as questionable uses of soft money.

Revelations seeped out over many months during Clinton's second term indicating that the fund-raising for his re-election campaign showed moral disregard and contempt for the intent of the laws and the interests of the public. The president's party used $450 million of soft money, theoretically raised for public education on issues, to finance TV spots savaging the opposition, paid for by the party's national committee but masterminded by, and run on behalf of, the President, deliberately circumventing post-Watergate reform legislation. What the televised hearings on campaign financing by both houses of Congress revealed was a President who seemed infinitely elastic in seeking funds wherever he could, prostituting his office and the privilege of access to it to people—including convicted criminals and a Chinese arms merchant—who could provide money needed to keep him in office.

The huge rivers of money sloshing through the '96 election greatly influenced voting, and "checkbook politics" added further to public distrust of government and politicians. From the public, and from those politicians who had *not* lost their sense of morals and ethics, came an outcry that the political campaign system had become truly corrupt, and that politicians had to spend too much time raising money instead of going about the public's business and governing the country. In the '98 Congressional elections, the combined fund-raising by both parties totaled $628 million, 41% more than the previous midterm elections, mostly due to a doubling of "soft money" contributions.

What damaged the office of the presidency most was the accumulation of evidence that funds from foreign sources were accepted illegally, with the President's knowledge and direction, flowing into the

Democratic National Committee, from which they were later returned. Most disturbing was the discovery that Chinese military people and arms merchants had secretly slipped funds into U.S. political coffers, apparently in exchange for access to top U.S. military-technology secrets. Also, unprecedented access to the President and the White House was given to campaign donors, including hundreds of overnight stays in historic White House rooms.

The New York Times, increasingly critical of these excesses, wailed that "everything was for sale." Various charges of wrongdoing distracted all three branches of government. They required appointment of an unprecedented seven independent counsels to investigate Clinton administration officials since he took office. At one time seven Senate panels and more than half the House committees werre carrying on 31 inquiries about wrongdoing charged against the President, his administration and the Democratic Party.

Anyone doubting that this administration's deviance from ethical norms was on a grand scale had only to reflect on the types of behavior that had caused scandal in earlier times—for example, when President Eisenhower's chief of staff was busted for accepting a vicuna coat, or when that straight-shooter President expressed mortification at having lied about the downing of a U-2 pilot over the Soviet Union during the Cold War and expressed his feelings of guilt that he had betrayed the public trust.

Because of the extraordinary number of witnesses who had either fled the country or been paid off to keep silent, or invoked the Fifth Amendment (60 in all), the independent counsel could not build strong cases on any of the abuse-of-power charges against the President. Starr was boxed into only one foolproof case against the President, the one concerning his flings with the young White House intern and his lies about it. Since the counsel was confined to these charges, his report dealt primarily with sex—which got him branded as a prude, a sanctimonious zealot and even a pornographer.

Because of the still-fresh scars of Watergate, the American public for a long while buried its head in denial over the mounting Clinton scandals. But voices on all sides that began to describe the Clinton record as one of the most pervasive, reckless flauntings of traditional ethics since Watergate could not be ignored forever. The first prominent call for impeachment of the President in a national newspaper was an op-ed piece entitled "Impeach" by Seattle writer Mark Helprin featured in *The Wall Street Journal* of October 10, 1997. It drew little comment.

The general public remained quiet, enjoying the generally good economic times and world peace that had been inherited by the Clinton administration. Clearly it would take more than conservative manifestoes to plunge the nation into another Watergate-sized crisis of confidence in its leadership. But the long state of siege between Clinton and Kenneth Starr, who persisted in investigating Clinton's behavior as relentlessly as Victor Hugo's famous Inspector Javert, was sure to join Watergate and the Vietnam War as yet another cause of Americans' cynicism toward their government institutions and the lies told by their leaders.

The absence of public outrage about Clinton's behavior did not reflect public approval of his lies and adulteries. The "everybody does it" argument of some Clinton supporters did not stand up against national studies showing most men and women to have been faithful to their spouses; a study at the end of 1998 indicated, for example, that roughly 86% of women and 75% of men had never strayed, and very little sex with co-workers took place. Those numbers would have shocked past generations—and they surely understated the prevalence of adultery among Hollywood stars and many entertainment and sports celebrities—but they meant nonetheless that Clinton was in a minority group of American men who betrayed their wives and took advantage of women who shared their disdain for the marriage bonds.

If a President's wife and family could not trust him to be loyal and tell them the truth, many citizens asked, how could the country trust him? If he was unfaithful to his marriage vows—not once or twice but many times—how could he be trusted to keep his oath of office? The heart of the matter was that the president had lied and persuaded others to lie and, finally, told lies to a federal Grand Jury, while obstructing justice by covering up his lies through the use of public employees and public funds to delay and derail investigations.

A bipartisan poll of voters shortly before the November 1998 Congressional elections showed that "moral and religious issues" had climbed up to the level of "drugs and crime" on voters' agendas. Many voters regarded the political system as "on the brink of moral bankruptcy," according to one of the pollsters. "It's important for us to be able to believe our elected officials," Congressman Jerry Moran told a town hall meeting with his constituents in rural Leoti, Kansas two days after Clinton's fateful TV confession of wrongdoing, in effect his confession that he had lied to the American people seven months before. "Truth and integrity matter...This is about what makes our country different from other nations. We have to preserve that sense that we are unique."

Like tripwires, the president's August 17 confession and the report of the independent counsel that followed tumbled the part of the nation that was paying attention into anxiety and, in a great many cases, sheer denial. Reacting to the independent counsel's report, the dean of Washington journalists, the *Washington Post*'s David Broder, had this to say: "This brings the whole subject of morals and values up before the nation. The November election will be about morality."

Many voters turn their backs

Broder's prediction was fulfilled on November 3 in the last Congressional election of the 20th century, but in some unexpected ways. Exit polls showed that "moral and ethical concerns" about candidates topped the list of issues that voters said had brought them out and influenced their votes. Many voters were troubled by the President's conduct, and 61% of them had an unfavorable opinion of him as a person.

Other interviews indicated that many among the astonishing two-thirds of eligible voters who failed to vote, including many young people, stayed away because the President's misbehavior, and the Republicans' release of torrential details about his sex life, had left them without respect for politicians of either party. These "no shows" continued a very worrisome 38-year downward trend of citizen participation in the political process, putting the U.S. at or near the bottom of all democracies in voter participation. In interviews before and after the election, many of these apathetic people said their non-vote was a protest against all politicians, whose standards of behavior seemed to many of them to be lower than those of ordinary Americans.

One sign of heightened concerns about morality in this election campaign was the finding in exit polls that the majority of voters felt President Clinton should be punished or severely reprimanded for his misconduct. They did not generally favor the extreme punishment of removal from office, presumably because that would add to the dishonoring of the office of the American presidency. But a good majority agreed that the offenses charged against the President were serious enough to warrant an inquiry as provided for in the U.S. Constitution or some form of censure or a presidential resignation.

In the race with the most significance for the forthcoming turn-of-century presidential election, Texas Governor George W. Bush's landslide re-election pulled in multi-party support, including a large Hispanic vote, partly because of the Governor's talk about moral decline and the need to raise character standards in government. By comparison, a prominent Democratic African-American woman in Illinois lost her Senate seat chiefly because of charges of unethical behavior in office. The morality issue surfaced also in the campaigns of other candidates who threw the slurs "liar" and "lies" back and forth at each other in nasty advertising and debates.

Yet while the shadow of the muddied president hung over the election, the conservatives' expectation that disclosures of presidential immorality would increase the Republican hold on Congress was turned on its head. Largely because of the Republicans' reliance on the scandals—instead of articulating their stands on issues more directly affecting voters—the Democrats seized the opportunity to paint their foes as psyched-out on sex scandals and impeachment, while Democrats focused on issues like education and Social Security.

The Republicans spent $10 million in the election's last week on a barrage of TV ads questioning Clinton's honesty, hoping this would shore up slipping turnout projections. Instead, the strategy misfired, because the public was already so tired of hearing about investigations and presidential sex. The conservatives came nowhere near achieving the gains in Congress they expected as a result of the Clinton scandals. For the first time since 1934 the party not holding the White House failed to gain any seats in the Senate and actually lost seats in the House of Representatives.

The Republican strategy of attacking opponents, instead of promoting their own ideas, was the wrong way to stir the spirits of voters who might otherwise have supported them. They failed utterly to articulate their important innovative ideas on issues—such as tax measures to stimulate long-term economic growth, private medical savings accounts, private choice on a portion of Social Security investments, privately-funded scholarships for poor students, school vouchers to give poor students an escape from the horrors of the worst public schools, more local control of education, reform of the Internal Revenue Service and a slim-down of government spending.

After the election, professor Everett Carll Ladd of the Roper Center for Public Opinion Research wrote that Americans "for the most part want their politicians to be sunny. Ronald Reagan exuded goodwill; he was unfailingly confident and optimistic. Republican politicians who followed Mr. Reagan's course—such as governors George Pataki of New York and John Rowland of Connecticut and the Bush brothers in Florida and Texas—had no trouble striking a responsive chord with voters."

Despite the spending of a record $200 million of "soft money" received from special interests by both parties in this election, as well as mammoth efforts by unions and black communities to get out the Democratic vote, the status quo more or less prevailed in Congress. And once again, basically, money talked. The candidates who could raise the most money, largely the incumbents, who commonly have beaten their opponents four to ten-times over in fund-raising, were the winners. Their challengers, who were a riskier bet for big givers seeking favors, were the losers. If nothing else, the election made a convincing case that the nation still badly needed campaign finance reform. The dominance of money in influencing the outcome of elections was one of the factors, along with the Clinton scandals, that turned off the 64% of eligible voters who no longer bothered to vote.

When the Republican-dominated House of Representatives made history by voting for the first time to impeach an elected President, charging perjury and obstruction of justice, Democrat charges that Republicans were driven by politics failed to stand up to reason. The Republicans knew that nothing could strengthen them more in the upcoming presidential campaign than to have a dishonored Democrat president as their easy target in the White House rather than a President Gore who would have had presidential experience. Some credit, therefore, had to be given to Republican Congressmen and Congresswomen for studying the Constitution and voting their consciences on principle, trying to find a just solution to a problem they detested just as much as the Democrats did.

A President on trial

Since the majority of Americans were better off financially than ever before, they were willing to give Clinton credit for their individual prosperity. Some 72% of total adults approved the way he was handling his job, according to a *Times*/CBS poll even *after* the President had been impeached by the House of Representatives. But people worried that the turmoil over Clinton might upset the nation's apple cart. And for some interest groups—notably women, blacks, unions and others who had come to depend on government support or intervention in their lives—the prospect of losing their intervenor and most ardent advocate was alarming.

While the House debate on impeachment was taking place in December, the media generally reflected the public's abhorrence of the President's behavior as well as its preference for censure over removal. In the minds of his critics, regardless of party, Clinton had disgraced the Presidency, which Franklin Roosevelt had once described as "preeminently a place of moral leadership." In one of its sharply critical editorials, the *Times* urged censure, not partisan impeachment, on the House, while at the same time castigating Clinton with this comment: "He is, in sum, a man you cannot trust whether you have his handshake, his signature or his word on a Bible."

Outside the Washington Beltway, the general public had a split mind about impeachment, which made the solons' job even harder. On one hand, most Americans wanted to feel that justice was being done; no matter how much they might disparage the members of Congress, they basically trusted the process created by the Founders for dealing with presidential misbehavior. At the same time, however, Americans had a gut instinct, going back to frontier days, to oppose any efforts by government—in this case the intrusive tactics of special prosecutor Starr— to interfere with their liberties by prying into their personal lives.

Whether is was because of public contentment with the thought that the Senate was handling this case according to Constitutional processes, or because there was general fatigue with this whole prolonged scandal, the public at large seemed somewhat benumbed. The major TV networks' coverage of the historic Saturday vote by the House to impeach the president drew far fewer viewers than the CBS coverage of the Buffalo Bills-New York Jets football game.

Astonishingly, Clinton's optimistic mien when he gave the State of the Union Address—at the very time when he was being tried by the Senate—jacked up his rating in the polls once again, this time to the highest level ever, at least insofar as his job performance was concerned. The speech was vintage Clinton—responding to each voter's "hot button" interests by promising something from the federal government to everyone, in tax breaks or spending increases. James MacGregor Burns referred to these as "policy bites"—little things that "simply do not add up to a systematic program." But they did help to add up to high "job performance" ratings, because Clinton typically found out from polls what people wanted and then assured them that's what he wanted too. This was one explanation for his high ratings even when Americans abhorred his behavior.

Clinton also proposed a short-term rescue of the Social Security System, which Harvard economist Martin Feldstein characterized as an "accounting sham", economist Milton Friedman characterized as a bogus sleight-of-hand to fool "a gullible public" and The Wall Street Journal characterized as a "shameless" act of "utter political cynicism."

The President, by implication, claimed credit for the nation's extraordinary prosperity. He omitted praise for the men and women managers and workers in American corporations whose innovations and hard work had produced the prosperity and wealth being enjoyed by most of the populace.

The widespread criticism of the President's program did not augur well for a second term that would be remembered for anything much beyond the scandals. Throughout the House impeachment and Senate trial proceedings the president gave no indication that he believed he had done anything wrong. In fact he was described as "exuberant" when he received "a rock star's reception" at a huge rally in Buffalo the day after his address to Congress. The President described it as "one of the great days of my presidency." To many observers he appeared cavalier in his lack of humility and the blithe disregard he had shown for the historic goings-on in Congress.

Even the Senate impeachment trial had failed to dent the Clinton armor. Clinton canceled a foreign trip in order to be present for the final vote. The Senate, obviously sensitive to public opposition to an ouster of the President, split 50–50 in its vote on the obstruction of justice charge and 55 to 45 on the perjury charge, with five Republicans breaking ranks on the obstruction of justice charge and 10 on the perjury charge, while the Democrats cast both votes as a partisan bloc. The prosecutors failed to obtain the two-thirds vote required by the

Constitution to remove the President from office. It remained to be seen what effect the President's acquittal would have on the rule of law in America—especially in future cases concerning perjury, obstruction of justice and sexual harassment in the workplace.

For most Americans, the year 1998 could not end too soon, as far as politics was concerned. In choosing Clinton and Starr as "Men of the Year", *Time* magazine characterized the two as "a faithless President and a fervent prosecutor, in a mortal embrace, lacking discretion, playing for keeps, both self-righteous, both condemned, Men of the Year."

This was certainly a period of American history without real heroes—except of course for the St. Louis Cardinals' Mark McGwire, who hit a record 70 home runs in one season, providing the most stunning moments in baseball history and giving a shot in the arm to America's most traditional sport. It was obvious that the scandals in the highest reach of government would depress Americans for some time to come; it was discomforting to say the least to have an American President under a criminal inquiry just when the outlook for the world economy and the taunts of rogue nations had produced new anxieties. But at the same time, more positively, the White House scandals were bringing about a reappraisal by many people of the moral side-tracking of the nation throughout the postwar period.

The last year of the century began with two phenomenal spectacles characteristic of the era's wild surprises, both of them statistical "highs". One was the leap of the Wall Street bull, reaching for the moon as the Dow Jones industrials soared past 9000, completing their first-ever four-year streak of double-digit gains and bringing unimagined riches, at least on paper, to millions of Americans. The other was the surreal spectacle of a State of the Union speech to Congress by a President who Americans had voted "most admired person" for the sixth year in a row in Gallup's annual survey, well ahead of runner-up Pope John Paul II, but who also had been impeached by the House of Representatives and was at that very time being tried in the Senate. This was something that had never happened, or even been imagined, in all of American history.

Trying to take all this in, the American citizen, and particularly the Clinton supporters, could look back wistfully to simpler, brighter times—for instance, when this President won re-election in 1996, portraying himself as a new "transformational leader" like Teddy

Roosevelt, in his case an activist "New Democrat" whose social achievements would leave him a legacy as brilliant as that of the two Roosevelts. Instead, Clinton's policy initiatives had been blunted by his immoral behavior and by opposition from a Republican Congress that regarded him as a "tax-and-spender" throwback from the pre-Reagan years. By his sixth year of office, Clinton's actual "success rate" of accomplishing legislation in the Congress was the lowest of any president in 46 years.

By his own doing, Clinton would be cast in history with Andrew Johnson and Richard Nixon, the only other targets of presidential impeachment inquiries in the nation's history. He would be remembered as the only elected American president to be impeached by the House and tried by the Senate. It remained to be seen whether the country could find a leader for 2000 who could begin the 21st century, despite its dangers and technological transformations, with the optimism and energy of Teddy Roosevelt when he charged like a bull into the 20th century.

PART SIX

THE AMERICAN SPIRIT AND
THE 21ST CENTURY

Optimism Surviving

In the face of the manifest demoralization of significant segments of American society in the last half of the 20th century, so ironically a time of great general prosperity, what are the chances of reviving the optimistic self-confidence and idealism that had been Americans' most prominent trait throughout their history, before the post-World War II traumas? As Americans move into the new century, what can be done to replace the fear, confusion and cynicism that are rife today with hope for the future?

Where do we go in the new millennium—when the nation has filled up from sea to sea, when the population has become polyglot, when opportunities for work are no longer in the agricultural pursuits that Jefferson found most conducive to the good society, or in traditional manufacturing, but in information sciences and technologies that require new knowledge and skills and interact instantaneously with others throughout the world? When a great part of the American population possesses more luxuries than their ancestors could ever have imagined?

One must admit to the permanent loss of some important sources of optimism, self-confidence and good spirits: the homogeneity of the Puritans' religious faith; the excitement of creating a new government and a new breed of citizens; the wide, physical frontier that opened such vast opportunities to those brave and hardy enough to go after them; the simplicity of the agrarian life that gave way to a complex urban and industrial society; the traditional positive influence of strong families and respect for parents, even the *presence* of parents, and the relative safety of citizens from dangers of bodily harm.

The breakdown of moral standards probably did more social damage than anything. As Daniel Bell declared two decades ago, the abandonment of Puritanism and the Protestant ethic and the advent of the "hedonistic age" left capitalism "with no moral or transcendental ethic." Religion had been the most civilizing influence in Western society, in effect the conscience of the society. It was the traditional mode of understanding oneself and one's country and the place of each in history. Religion, as Bell pointed out, had provided "a continuity with the past." It had imposed moral norms and restraints and a framework for public policy, and it laid the basis for traditional American optimism.

The idea of the Puritans, and of Jefferson and other early leaders, was that God's design would be unfolded on the virgin continent. But the cultural movement often called "modernism" shifted the center of authority "from the sacred to the profane," as Bell said, substituting individual self-interests and special-interest agendas for the social compact that had given unity of purpose to the republic.

One way in which Americans can approach the future, and at least begin the process of renewing the optimism about American life that characterized our first two centuries, is simply to recognize the moral dimensions of the nation's major problems and the price we have paid for losing our historical moral perspective. While there is absolutely no question that, across the board, Americans' moral *behavior* has sunk to a low ebb, there is also no question that the moral conscience planted in Americans by their forefathers and "foremothers" is still very much with them, and the friction between the two is troubling them.

The great issues that will determine our future are moral issues. The recognition that moral convictions have been the underpinning of American optimism and confidence in the past—and, in fact, are intrinsic to every important issue we face in the 21st century—is the only ground on which we can regain our traditional optimism about America's future. Through the osmosis of our history, and of such positive traditional influences as families, friends and churches, Americans still retain a core of moral reserves, notwithstanding the fact that they don't talk much about this and no recent leader has called up those reserves as Wilson tapped our moral impulses to fight the Kaiser, or FDR tapped them to fight the Great Depression and World War II.

To regenerate the Republic and meet 21st-century challenges, Americans must re-assert their moral responsibility to elevate the standards of government; their moral responsibility for the education of young people to help them prepare for a changed, high-charged world; their moral responsibility to care for the poor; their moral responsibility for public health; their moral responsibility to replace drugs and other forms of escape with re-emphasis on individual responsibility; their moral responsibility to nourish the free-market system as the fairest, most wealth-creating way to benefit all people, while at the same time correcting its excesses.

Public opinion surveys throughout the '90s have shown an underlying unease among Americans about the state of the nation's morals. A *Newsweek* poll in 1994 showed that 76% of adult Americans thought that their country was "in moral and spiritual decline," mostly attributed to the breakdown of the family. The following year a study of voters by the Wirthlin Group indicated that 60% of voting Americans felt that the nation's problems were "primarily moral and social in nature" as opposed to economic in nature, with three out of four believing the country was in a state of moral decay.

A Wall Street Journal/NBC News survey of several thousand Americans on the eve of 1997 reported: "All around them, Americans see a decline in morals and values. They deplore the diminished authority of the four great repositories of their values—religion, the law, schools and families." But this report added: "Yet despite their pessimism, Americans passionately believe in the importance of values, and they have given them a lot of thought."

Again, in March 1998, the largest number of respondents (25%) said "moral decline" was the greatest threat of all to the U.S. future—far ahead of racial tensions, recession, national debt or foreign economic competition.

This survey showed a quite remarkable persistence of qualities that were described as "quintessentially American: a moralism ranging from religiosity to equal rights; an abiding regard for integrity; and a commanding respect for hard work, patriotism, ambition, family and self-fulfillment." Although for the most part they were quiet about them, Americans even retained Puritan attitudes on matters of sex, adultery and divorce—with 90% opposing adultery.

The public's concern over the decline of morals seemed to prove that if the old moral standards were partly buried, they were still intact. A fundamental factor turning people back to traditional values is the middle-aging of the boomers who had families and became more preoccupied with investments and retirement plans than with social rebellion. The headline on *The Wall Street Journal*/NBC report on their huge mid-1999 survey was: "Americans Decry Moral Decline." The vast majority of Americans, this report said, "yearn for what they remembered as a more moral time with less pressure on kids and families." As for which group or institution could best improve the country's values, 70% named the family, only 4% picked government.

American character did in fact show some improvements during the Clinton years. The epidemic of out-of-wedlock births slowed down, after rising steadily through the 1980s; teen pregnancies, especially among black girls, was dropping; the abortion rate dropped in 1995, the latest year for which statistics are available (perhaps because unmarried mothers are more accepted today); the murder and violent crime rates have been declining; the high school dropout rate has declined since 1990. And, very importantly, the percentage of children living in single-parent families, which doubled from 1970 to 1990, has slowed its rise, in part because of a slight decline in the divorce rate. Guarded optimism was expressed by some social observers that the culture of violence, vulgarity and random sex in movies, TV, video games and music is finally spurring a backlash from parents. "As the culture becomes more noxious, people think more clearly," said Mary Pipher, a social critic and best-selling author.

Fallout of Clinton impeachment

A heightened sensitivity to moral issues across the political spectrum, and a reinvigoration of public concern over them, appear to be one positive consequence of the Clinton scandals. This of course was symbolized by the President's own repentance for his misdeeds. Despite the lying he had done to cover up his repeated past abuses of women, his religious counselors and his closest associates were convinced that this time he was sincerely contrite.

The fact that Americans in general wanted him to be not just contrite but also punished was itself a sign that Clinton had become emblematic of a perceived moral decline, and the public did not approve. The American people proved that they had values by indicating by a huge majority that they considered the President to be immoral, that they believed he lied and that he was a very poor role model for their children. A *Los Angeles Times* survey at the end of January 1999 indicated that 77% of the public felt that the President did not share their moral values. For their part, the Republicans indicated in one poll that the number one issue in the next presidential election would be "moral leadership". In order for either political party to regain the optimism of their inspirational leaders of the past they would have to find a way to identify with the clear base of public morality reflected in the polls.

Certainly the awareness of, and respect for, the U.S. Constitution on the part of many citizens was heightened by the playing-out of the Clinton impeachment and trial. After the House of Representatives voted in favor of a presidential impeachment inquiry, the public was reminded, once again, as it had been during Watergate, that the Constitution provided for an orderly handling of such crises and this protection at times was as important to the republic's welfare as the leadership or behavior of any one person or persons, including the President. The spectacle of a democracy actually putting its leader on trial before an elected jury impressed some foreign observers more than any other aspect of this highly publicized period of American history; it showed that the "American system" worked, even in such a disordered time. In a CNN poll, a majority of Americans also said they believed that the Constitution had worked.

It was the Founders' genius to provide a governing charter that anticipated crises such as this one. Just as it provided for a smooth transfer of power after elections, it provided for dealing with a President charged with abusing his high office. It gave the House the power to make such an accusation, and the Senate the power to try the president and remove him from office. With their typical acuity, the wise Founders had sought to restrain partisan passions by dividing the process between two legislative bodies with different constituent bases and different election cycles, and to impress all with the seriousness of this process by requiring a two-thirds vote of the Senate to convict, leaving it up to the courts to prosecute the president for crimes after leaving office. They added a final element of balance by making the Chief Justice the presiding officer of a presidential trial.

In the House impeachment debate, Representative Henry Hyde of Illinois, manager of the impeachment team, challenged House members to strengthen the Constitution by giving it "content and meaning" in this case. In the Senate trial that followed, Hyde referred to "the unique brilliance of America's constitutional system of government" as the guide for his impeachment team. In another eloquent speech before the Senate, former Democratic Governor Dale Bumpers declared his "reverence" for the Constitution, calling it "the most sacred document to me after the Holy Bible." In its comment on the verdict, the *Times* noted that "the Constitution has prevailed once again" and called the Constitution "the great anchor rock of the republic, enduring through partisan storms in the Congress, immune in the end to even so large and unpredicted a betrayal as a President's dereliction of duty."

The heightened sensitivity to moral issues produced by the impeachment ordeal was reflected in the statement made on December 18 by Henry Hyde in the House debate on articles of impeachment, the one statesmanlike speech during that raucous and rancorous squabble among House partisans. In remarks that the *Times* called "stirring" and "impassioned", Hyde said the matter before the House was quite simply "a question of lying under oath." He said "this is a public act, not a private act. This is called perjury." Hyde declared that the President had "corrupted the rule of law" by putting himself above the law, and violated his oath of office by lying under oath repeatedly as well as obstructing justice. As for the President, he finally apologized, in the Rose Garden after the Senate's acquittal, "for what I said and did to trigger these events and the great burden they have imposed on the Congress and on the American people."

In his commencement address to the last Harvard graduating class of the 20th century, Federal Reserve chairman Alan Greenspan admonished graduates that transcending all other goals in life is "being principled." Their success, and the success of the country, he said, "is going to depend on the integrity and other qualities of character that you and your contemporaries develop and demonstrate over the years ahead."

A group of leading trend-watchers reported in the January-February '99 issue of *The American Enterprise* that a moral turnaround was underway in America among diverse age groups, with Americans placing moral decline at the top of their list of things needing repair. Among many positive findings, they reported that a majority of teens, reflecting their own bitter experiences and badly burned by their parents' experiments with sexual liberation, now "disapprove of and avoid early sex."

After the Senate's decision on the President, civil rights leader Rev. Joseph E. Lowery also saw some positive results coming from the "hell" the country had been through when he made this statement: "I think there will even be a tightening of moral standards because he's been thoroughly rebuked…and people will be even more aware of the need for marital fidelity." Those sentiments were reflected in this statement by John Kasich, a young candidate-nominee to the office of President: "Over time… we'll look back and say that our actions helped to restore notions of right and wrong, and the belief that ordinary people shouldn't get shafted while big shots get away with everything."

Newspapers like *The Seattle Times* were flooded with letters to the editor commenting on moral standards, criticizing the indignities visited on the nation by the President. The real lesson of the Clinton impeachment, one Seattle man wrote, "is that we must again demand of our politicians—and ourselves—the devotion to principles which once made this country the greatest on earth." A liberal historian, Douglas Brinkley, said: "We've learned that character does matter. It is always going to be scrutinized in elections after this, because people are going to want to know answers."

There was nearly unanimous public condemnation of the President's behavior, with 84% of the public believing him guilty of the charges brought against him, according to one CBS poll. There was general anger at both Starr and Congress for releasing the salacious details about Clinton's sex acts in the White House (details that Starr had wanted to leave out of his report, before his lawyers persuaded him to change his mind), which gave the President's supporters an opportunity to turn the "moral issue" against the Republicans by labeling them as pornographers. There was a heightened self-consciousness among government leaders about their own moral behavior, such that columnist William Safire claimed that "no high official will be tempted to lie under oath or obstruct justice again soon."

Some "confessions" of past personal sins by politicians were carried to excess. The newly-appointed Republican House speaker resigned because of his past marital infidelities, uncovered by a sex magazine, and at least four Republican presidential contenders made statements assuring the public that they had been faithful to their wives.

America's past as anchor

The cumulation of moral traditions that are embedded, if not always acknowledged, in the American consciousness is the place to look for hope on entering a new century and a new era. The American past is a well-entrenched anchor. "We have the playbook of morality—everything from Moses' tablets to our inherited Puritan scruples and two centuries of American preachers and moralists—but we lost the habit of even talking about morals," says Dr. Jonsen.

"From the sixties on, such talk would have made us feel uneasy and out of touch with mainstream America," he said. "Traditional morality had been replaced by misguided nouveau-moralities: the loose 'morality' of the defiant sixties; the 'morality' of instant repentance and instant rebirth promoted by TV preachers; the perverse 'morality' of Larry Flynt; the naïve 'morality' of environmental extremists and the misguided 'morality' of the militias, the Unabomber and others who see evil in government and authority and technology." For many people, "worship" in modern times has meant not worship of God but worship of celebrities—sports figures, Academy Award winners, rock stars, even—on the fringes—worship of criminals who defy law and authority and get away with it, or who are justified on the grounds that they have been victimized by society.

Yet each of the serious challenges facing the nation today *has* important moral dimensions. *The recognition of this fact will be the key to bringing 21st-century problems into focus and reviving the old optimistic strivings for an Edenic America.* It is a simple way to get ourselves back on track, to provide the consistent national vision for the future that was lost along the way. The new century will call for courageous and optimistic leaders who understand the American heritage of freedom and moral values, who recognize the American past as their anchor, who find their hope in their history.

To illustrate the moral aspects of private and public life and policy, take just for example one new moral issue that arrived on the coattails of the Information Age. This is the problem, or challenge, of making certain that the revolutionary new technology of the Internet—a development comparable in importance to the industrial revolution—will adhere to moral standards and will be applied for the maximum benefit of society, not turned to anti-social uses. First, consider the positive side of this epochal change in modern life, especially its role in creating a new frontier for young Americans who are as optimistic for the future as any of their ancestors. This is where optimism is most easily found in modern America.

The Western frontier redux

The fabled American frontier and its risks and adventures—and even the gold rush to the West—haven't really disappeared in American life as Turner prophesied. They have been transmogrified into a newly flourishing pioneer society. Living up to their Klondike legacy, the new pioneers in and around the gold-rush city of Seattle, for example, are an energetic and hard-working lot, working and living at the edges of their human capacities to produce wonders from modern technology. In their hyper-competitive world, products become outdated virtually the day they are released.

Theirs is a frontier that's wider and more unlimited than the geographical frontier that beckoned the early pioneers. The new pioneers are high-spirited because their aim is nothing less than to change the world and that's exactly what they have been doing as they stormed out across the oceans, colonized the world with their manufacturing plants and sales organizations, revolutionized the way products are made and sold on every continent and added words like "Microsoft", "Intel" and "Oracle" to the vocabularies of people all around the globe.

Their frontier mentality has romanticized the idea of unlimited opportunities in technologies just as the trekkers romanticized the seemingly infinite natural resources on the North American continent a century and a half earlier. The new-frontier men and women are engaged in a heroic sort of enterprise. With typical cool, Bill Gates, the man most responsible for the information revolution, who at 39 became the richest man in the world, had this recent comment from his Seattle home base at Microsoft: "It's kind of a neat thing to have the Internet exploding and to have this gold-rush atmosphere."

The Internet empowers individuals in strikingly new ways—giving people everywhere new confidence in their ability to effect change. A single activist in Vermont, for example, working from her home, mobilized an international coalition of more than 250 organizations against the use of land mines; the result was the first international treaty to ban production of those devices, winning a Nobel Peace Prize for the young woman. A Chinese father of a three-year-old boy with a rare heart problem posted an urgent appeal on the Internet that was answered by strangers who helped bring the boy to the U.S. for life-saving surgery. Through the Interent, students take courses from far-distant teachers; patients learn about treatments from world experts and ordinary people swiftly use investment tools as advanced as those formerly used by big institutions on Wall Street. Young people around the country are inspirited today by being able to do things never before possibel—such as talking directly on the Internet with scientists exploring the North Pole.

South of San Francisco, the valley stretching from Palo Alto to San Jose that once sported bumper crops of plums, cherries and apricots, is today the famous Silicon Valley mecca of feisty, high-tech engineers and programmers referred to by one of its superstar financiers as "the cauldron of creation". In the new globally competitive world, Emerson's call to individualism, his challenge to be your own man or woman, has taken on new meaning. On the job, in places like Silicon Valley, individuals and teams of individuals have unprecedented autonomy today to come up with innovative new ideas and find better ways to run their enterprises. In cyber-space, they break free entirely from their surroundings and tap into boundless information and knowledge. These new workers are enfranchised with stock options and profit-sharing plans as part-owners of their enterprises, drawing out their maximum efforts.

It is these creative individuals, more than governments or political leaders, who are pointing the way to the future. In contrast, for example, to Jefferson's presidential leadership in opening the western frontier, individual entrepreneurs, scientists and engineers today are in the lead moving society beyond old boundaries. By dispersing power, technology is reducing the importance of politicians and raising the importance of individual human vision and effort. It will be a challenge in the new century to make the most of the Internet's power to make us interactive with government without enervating the constitutional system of our Founders. In corporations, human capital represented by "knowledge workers" is replacing hard assets like factory equipment as the key to progress.

Already, web communities of people everywhere with common interests—bankers and lawyers, universities, churches, sellers of products and services—are expanding relationships and freedom of communication. Silicon Valley and the Internet, where there are no rules or borders, have become hotbeds of libertarianism and the talk in cyber-space today sounds like born-again Jeffersonianism—arguing for a marketplace free from government interference and a govern-

316

ment limited in its powers to protecting public safety, safeguarding personal liberty and providing for national defense.

Individualism thrives in the Silicon Valley culture, and in the culture of all high-tech companies that provide incentives for individual creativity. A great deal of America's superb economic performance of recent years traces to innovative products and services created by the young, energetic people responding to these incentives, at the heart of the wealth-producing process. Their energy and daring—their zeal in leaping into technological change and profiting from it, rather than being dismayed by the breakneck pace of change—has resulted in the creation of unprecedented numbers of new enterprises just in the last two decades. Innovation is the key to their excitement—and the key to productivity.

Driven by the world-shaking takeoff of the Internet, Silicon Valley exploded, creating exciting new jobs faster than they could be filled, affecting commerce and industry more than any force in history, and in 1996 sailing past Detroit as the nation's leading export industry. Young entrepreneurs in the companies calved by the venture capitalists, who are pouring over $4 billion a year into Internet ventures alone, are becoming millionaires in less time than it takes to go to college, often becoming "angels" themselves, grub-staking some of their newly won capital into *other* nascent ventures and sometimes watching their million-dollar investments grow into stakes worth tens or hundreds of millions of dollars within a few years. One venture capitalist in the Valley recently described "the rush you can get from being involved with young people who have got great plans and ambitions and are prepared to break down walls by force of energy and ideas." They are living in the future, he said: "This is the modern world in the making. This is the true frontier."

The Internet and new devices for utilizing it are well on their way to becoming as much a part of American life as the automobile and the telephone became in the past. In homes across the country (60% of which will have personal computers by 2001, up from 40% today), men, women and children are finding excitement, pleasure and knowledge at the touch of their keyboards. In only seven years the Internet has invaded a quarter of American households, not to mention others throughout the world. It took the telephone 35 years to reach such penetration of society—26 years for television, 16 years for the personal computer.

The "networked economy" is arriving ten times faster than the industrial revolution did. Computer networks of corporations will do for knowledge what the steam engine did for manpower—leverage it and make it available efficiently to people everywhere. The number of people using the web is expected to be as high as 320 million by 2002, compared with about 100 million in 1999. Every aspect of economic, personal and political life is being changed by the microchip and the networks that allow it to communicate freely.

The acceleration of radical change is unprecedented, creating a society-wide ferment of entirely new activities and opportunities. The commercial Internet only dates from 1995, yet in the brief span since then E-mail has become the preferred communication medium for business and students; more than 100 million public web sites have been set up; retail sales over the Net exploded to some $43 billion in 1999; Amazon.com became the nation's third largest bookseller in three years and America Online, with some 18 million subscribers by the beginning os the 21ˢᵗ century, was expected to have $16 billion annual revenues early in the new century.

One field that excites these new pioneers is the field of education, where PCs and the Internet can increase the access of rich and poor students to vast stores of information and the best teachers from around the world. Bill Gates cites as an example the Christopher Columbus Middle School in New Jersey's Union City where, with help from the local phone company, a network of multimedia PCs was created linking students' and teachers' homes with each other and with the Internet. Within two years dropout rates and absenteeism dipped virtually to zero, and the students were scoring nearly three times higher than the average inner-city school on standardized tests.

The pursuit of these new technological horizons, and the proliferation of systems and products flowing from it, has created opportunities and wealth undreamed of for the millions of young people who have the education and skills to profit from it. Software engineers who not long ago were working in garages and living on credit cards and rice and beans have become instant tycoons. Not since Western frontier days have so many young people been able to work so enthusiastically in such freedom to transform their nation. The optimism of the young programmers, engineers and system managers today is no less than that of the pioneers who whooped it up in Missouri as their wagon-trains loaded up for the Western trek. They have an exciting new orientation towards space and time. Their neighborhoods are not the streets of their towns—*their* neighborhoods are up in space. They are online with people all over the world, communicating and interacting electronically. Today the associations among citizens that Tocqueville considered the central feature of democracy are global, and the single most important factor behind this transformation is the Internet.

The Internet is the most productivity-enhancing, life-changing technological development since the harnessing of steam and electricity. Widespread as its use is already, the Net's capabilities are taking a giant leap forward as revolutionary new technologies expand its bandwidth communications power. Among other things the Internet has speeded up research and the birth of new enterprises. The creation of virtual syndicates blending technical expertise, financed by "angels" with venture capital, is a very far cry from the enterprise Columbus launched when he was staked by Queen Isabella. In all, about 62 million Americans were using the Net by the end of 1998, nearly a third of the over-16 population.

The Net's dark side

Like all revolutionary technology, however, the Internet—glamorous as it is, and promising for human progress—has raised major moral issues. Amoral and independent of value issues itself, the new technology can be used, and has been used, for anti-social, even degenerate ends as well as good, life-enriching ends. Ironically, our children, who are the most computer-literate members of society and who accept the Internet as the main medium of their lives, are the ones most vulnerable to predators on the Net.

Among the first entrepreneurs rushing into this new medium were the purveyors of pornography, sensing their greatest opportunity ever to fly beyond moral bounds. A sea of digital muck spread with amazing speed across the cyberscene: "adult" web sites soon were taking in millions of dollars a month, *Penthouse* magazine was visited more than two million times in a month, pedophiles lured victims thousands of miles away, prisoners offered tips on kidnapping, dozens of web sites helped college students cheat by getting other people's term papers and anyone with a credit card could order X-rated pictures and products online. By the late '90s there were more than 40,000 porn sites on the world wide web, and still growing. New types of fraud multiplied on the Internet as sophisticated individuals and companies touted stocks and gambling scams, using false and misleading information.

"Right now the Internet is exactly like the frontier," said one of the nation's top "cybercops", in a Washington State county prosecutor's office. "There are lots and lots of bad guys out there and very few cops." Epitomizing the worst of this phenomenon of capitalism-gone-amuck is the 24-year-old Seattle entrepreneur who grossed some $20 million in his second year and $50 million in his third year running "an empire of sex—of virtual vulvas and clickable dildos and strippers on live video", as *Wired* magazine put it. Internet porn sites were the first web sites to turn profitable.

Most troubling is the easy access to pornography that children have when they graze the Internet. Increasingly the explorers in this new wild west are children—nearly ten million of them online in 1998, with their number expected to grow to 45 million by the year 2002. Most of them are only a mouse click away from porn sites. "We're seeing technology run ahead of ethics here," says a spokeswoman from the Washington Family Council in Bellevue, Washington.

Under the cloak of anonymity that cyberspace provides, space vandals learned quickly how to cripple whole networks and web sites and deface online businesses. Junk e-mailers bombarded unprotected computer-users and stalkers entered "chat rooms" to identify their targets, find out personal information about them and send them threatening messages. Sophisticated criminals printed counterfeit money, downloading images from the Internet. Disreputable stock promoters conned investors.

The Internet quickly became an engine of racist prejudices as more than 200 sites and chat rooms spewed out hatred of blacks, whites, gays, immigrants, jews and arabs. The Internet also became a thriving bazaar for drug information, where hundreds of thousands of mostly young Web "surfers" downloaded information from glitsy Net sites on everything from the chemical formula for methamphetamines (speed) to how to grow and use hallucinogens and how to trip out on LSD, with online testimonials from high school kids and others. Among crimes committed by Internet correspondents perhaps the worst was the murder of a 17-year-old boy who lived in Vermont with his mother. The teen-ager received a pipe bomb in the mail from his Internet correspondent, a 35-year-old truck driver in Indiana who was incensed over a trade of CB radios they had agreed to after the boy sent him a radio worth less than the one he had promised.

The explosion of new information technologies thus is both an obvious blessing and a potential curse, depending upon our moral judgments about using them. As the prescient historian Frederick L. Schuman warned many years ago (when it was nuclear technology that was stirring public fears and as we have been reminded by old terrorists like Hitler and new terrorists who bomb buildings in America for philosophical or political reasons) technology in the wrong hands can bring terror, depravity, fraud and crime just as, in the right hands, it can spread knowledge and creative and constructive ideas bountifully to people everywhere.

Almost from its birth, the Internet created a new moral challenge. Because it's the freest, unpoliced community ever created, it poses issues of freedom and responsibility never imagined by the Founders. Efforts thus far to clean filth from the Internet—or at least put it out of reach of children—have roused the ire of free-speech extremists. The contest now is between libertarians who put First Amendment rights first and foremost and traditionalists who believe that the moral standards that governed the formation of the nation take precedence over everything else. The most desirable solution to this controversy will be for technology itself to provide a compromise in the form of "do it yourself" censorship so that government intrusion can be avoided, providing we have the moral will to take the responsibility for our children.

Besides the moral challenge of electronic smut there is another challenge that confronts us as this revolution blasts its way through our society. The information revolution is widening the gulf between those who can profit by it and all the rest—producing, as it is already doing today, a culture almost as split as the Colonial culture was split between propertied men and slaves. The Internet phenomenon has created a "digital divide", a growing gulf in society between those with online computer access and those who lack the money, the skills, the literacy and education to become players in this speeding transformation of human life and work. The battle of the "haves" and the "have-nots" has already begun, witnessed for example in demonstrations by inner-city dwellers angry at being deprived of information-age opportunities.

Other moral issues

The new challenge of the Internet is just one among the innumerable public and private issues confronting us in the new century that raise important moral questions. In fact, all the big issues facing us, public and private, are moral issues. Retiring Senator Dan Coats remarked that "many of our worst social problems will yield only to moral solutions." The first requirement for nurturing virtue in our culture, he said, is "to defend the existence of virtue itself, celebrating it in our families and churches."

Consider, for example, the plight of the lowest-spirited, least optimistic group of Americans—the "underclass". The 21st century opens on a world where, more than ever before, an individual's place on the social scale will be determined by his or her cognitive ability. Those without access to science education and technology are disadvantaged indeed.

In contrast to the people profiting from the surge of new technology and enterprises, a large number of inner-city adults do not work at all in a typical week. Many of these people are not represented in unemployment data because they've given up trying to find work. Nearly a third of the unskilled men who haven't completed high school are out of the labor force altogether, almost double the rate a quarter-century ago. Work has disappeared from many poor areas even at a time when national employment generally soared and unemployment fell so low that economists began shaking their heads. Yet when jobs are not available for those left out of this pretty picture, crime rises, drugs fill the void and the traditional American social structure crumbles.

It has been estimated that the U.S. boasts an unprecedented 170 billionaires, 250,000 deca-millionaires and nearly five million millionaires. The average pay package of some 280 chief executives of large companies amounted to $8.7 million in 1997. But the system that creates such enormous rewards has left behind a large underclass that feels alienated from the system, and the gap between the rich and the rest of the population has been growing for at least a decade or more, according to the Congressional Budget Office, the Economic Policy Institute and the Center on Budget and Policy Priorities.

More than 21 million Americans had to seek help from emergency food programs in 1997 and in some cities there are ten times more people seeking shelter than public services can provide. The lines at soup kitchens and food pantries swelled after welfare-to-work programs cut off assistance to many of the poor. Beyond the inner cities, raw poverty still plagues Appalachia, the coal mining areas of West Virginia and other rural areas and Indian reservations. Yet the nation is far wealthier than it was when John Winthrop, first governor of the Massachusetts Bay Colony, reminded the Puritans arriving in the new world of their social covenant: "We must be willing to abridge ourselves of our superfluities for the supply of others' necessities." The percent of Americans living on "poverty" income remains in double digits (some 28–35 million people, depending on whether non-cash benefits are counted; also, Census Bureau statistics make no allowance for ownership by the poor of homes, cars, trucks, etc., which is higher than ever.) The average after-tax income of the poor, adjusted for inflation, has apparently fallen since 1977, while the top one percent of Americans (2.7 million people) increased their income to the point that in 1999 they had as many after-tax dollars to spend as the 100 million at the bottom.

American corporate leaders are becoming sensitive on this subject. Debunking the notion of a rising tide lifting all boats, the chief economist of Morgan Stanley recently told Hedrick Smith, "There are millions of workers who have never seen the harbor let alone even know what a boat looks like." And the chairman of Lucent Technologies, a superpower in the new Information Age, added: "There is no way a society can have this much of its accumulated wealth distributed to these few people."

Although political leaders almost never give them credit for their vital role in driving the economy and producing wealth, American corporations have taken important steps to help workers at the lowest level. Some 7,500 companies, for example, are participating in the Welfare to Work Partnership—recruiting, training and hiring welfare recipients for entry-level jobs. General Motors works in partnership with community colleges to see that students develop the skills needed for the future. Cisco Corporation has set up its own academies to develop badly needed skilled workers. Working together, private companies have set up a National Academy Foundation that sponsors special training "schools within schools." And individual business-person philanthropists have donated hundreds of millions of dollars to give needy children scholarships to private schools.

The ultimate moral test of government is how it treats the poorest members of society.* The persistence of poverty at the bottom of America's social scale while those at the top enjoy unprecedented wealth and prosperity weighs on the spirits of Americans with a social conscience. The percentage of people living in poverty in America was more than twice as high as in other industrial democracies in the late nineties.

Most Americans would admit that such disparity in enjoying the richness of American life is downright immoral. Most would agree that the world's most prosperous nation should feel shame over the fact that there are more than 600,000 Americans homeless every night, with less than 300,000 shelter beds to accommodate them.

As the most prosperous nation in history, America of all nations should see that *all* of its citizens can seek their fortunes in freedom and dignity. Over the years people as disparate as Winston Churchill and Kurt Vonnegut have spoken out for a guarantee of work for all citizens. Churchill looked forward to establishment of minimum standards for work and for healthcare, especially for children—"…and beyond that," he said, "free run!"

The top income group, by shifting focus even moderately from making more money to giving it away, could narrow significantly the nation's wealth-poverty gap.** Charitable giving, by some estimates, could quite easily be increased by $100 billion a year. So far, the young techno-millionaires lag behind average Americans in such giving—perhaps because they've made their money so fast, and perhaps also because they are not as closely involved with communities as were the philanthropists of earlier times. Change is in the air, however. The new Carnegies and Rockefellers may be the hugely wealthy young entrepreneurs of companies like Microsoft, Dell and America Online who are innovating "venture philanthropies", utilizing technology and management skills to establish learning centers, high-tech libraries and other resources that give poor people training and access to the fruits of technology and new medical breakthroughs.

---

* "A decent provision for the poor is the true test of civilization," the English literary lion Samuel Johnson once said. The condition of the lower orders especially, he called "the true mark of national discrimination."

** In general, the ultra-rich in America have devoted their nonprofit contributions less to social services for the poor than to organizations such as art museums, orchestras, opera houses and other institutions that serve the wealthier members of society.

Reforming dollar democracy

Among the many other moral issues to be faced in the new century is the problem of reforming a democracy that has become so money-corrupted that a citizen cannot become a serious candidate for the highest office unless he or she can raise tens of millions of dollars, or a candidate for Congress unless he or she can raise typically $12,000 a month mostly from special interests, a total of $3 million to more than $30 million to run a successful Senate campaign, depending on the state but chiefly coming from special interests outside the state. The present corrupt system not only distorts democracy, denying public office to many outstanding people (Lincoln wouldn't have a chance in this system) but also sours the public on government by threatening to turn the Congress into an auction house where public policy is sold to special interests such as labor unions, casino operators and arms manufacturers.

Incumbent office-holders, the chief beneficiaries of the rivers of money flowing into politics, have resisted reform. Only widespread *public* pressure for reform will ever get it done. A spirited reform movement at the state level has been catching on, producing legislation in the states to replace private with public financing of election campaigns and limiting expenditures. The process has been complicated by free speech and jurisdictional decisions coming from the Federal courts.

Another extremely important unresolved moral issue is the challenge of assuring basic healthcare for the poor. More than 43 million Americans lack health insurance, the highest percentage (over 16%) in a decade. A million or more Americans each year are losing their health insurance. A rich society should be able to insure the growing numbers of uninsured poor against catastrophic illness and mental disorders, on the principle that it is just as immoral to ration medical help for major illness on the basis of wealth as it is to accord political office only to those who can raise huge sums of money.

Another moral issue concerns the political football that politicians play with claims of budget "surpluses" or "deficits", without making clear to the public the underlying influence of past government borrowing of hundreds of billions of dollars from Social Security funds, plus windfall tax revenues that pour in when a strong economy pushes citizens into higher tax brackets.

A moral issue is raised also by the nation's convoluted tax system, which is tilted towards those who can afford professional help in avoiding taxes by exploiting the complexity of the infinitely contorted 12-million-word tax code. Still another moral challenge is that of reforming the American public education system, which at the high end is still too much a segregated caste system and at the high school level is producing graduates with the worst records among industrial nations in math and science—the most needed skills of the Information Age.

There are also the still-challenging moral problems of eradicating the remaining barriers to racial integration in American life so that Constitutional equality of opportunity is finally and fully realized; the moral challenge of rescuing the Medicare System and the Social Security System from bankruptcy for our future generations; the moral challenge of reining in "entitlement" spending for social benefits for high-income people, which could be done with affluence tests (the government already has some $17 trillion of unfunded liabilities for entitlement programs that were intended originally for citizens in need.)

New technologies have raised altogether new moral dilemmas outside the realm of traditional moral codes, such as dealing with scientific and technical developments like cloning animals and humans, which are seen by many people as intrusions into the prerogatives of God. In addition, there are moral issues raised by government over-regulation—typified, for example, by the jailings of citizens for failing to comprehend the complex paperwork of environmental rules or for simple errors like putting dirt in an ill-defined "wetland".

As for social issues like drug abuse and crime, our communities—including the courts, the policy-makers, the professionals and social workers—must recognize more than they have in most of the post-sixties era that these are moral problems, issues of right and wrong, not just medical or living-environment problems. There is also the moral issue of gambling, which has become a bigger economic activity than books, music and movies and, some say, is threatening the work ethic and the already frayed institution of family.

In the private business sector, there are unexamined moral issues such as the payment of CEOs at hundreds of times the rate of ordinary employees' compensation (a study of the 500 biggest firms in the country showed that their CEOs' pay, including bonuses and stock grants, was roughly 200 times the salary of the average American

326

worker in 1995, compared to about 40 times two decades earlier) ; the "stealth compensation" of corporate executives who receive mega-options (rights to buy stock at a specific future price and time) unrelated to their performance (about 2,000 companies granted options from 1992 to 1997 valued at $45.6 billion, a huge increase over past practice); and the questionable actions of corporate boards that award stupendous severance benefits and perks like chauffered cars worth as much as several hundred million dollars to corporate leaders who have failed to perform for their employees and investors. Without denying the importance of options as incentives for performance, some of these practices serve to deflate public morale and the public's sense of fairness.*

In order for workers generally to enjoy the full promise of American opportunity, one challenge is to empower more of them as stock and option holders and profit-sharers, as our most progressive enterprises do already. Without movement in this direction, the nation could become a modern version of 18th-century pre-revolutionary France, with people of immense wealth living lives of luxury at a far remove from those stuck on lower rungs of the social ladder.

There is a moral question too about the ganging-up of the growing elderly class in America—the largest and most powerful voting bloc— to protect and enlarge its government benefits and vote against such things as education levies, while segregating themselves in communities where they do not have to pay for schools. The fact is that the group accounting for the highest proportion of poverty in America is by no means the elderly: it is the population of under-18 young people.

The government's presently planned spending on federal entitlement benefits will exceed all federal revenues within 30 years after the start of the new century, leaving nothing for national defense or service on the huge national debt. The only ways to meet that upcoming crisis are either to cut federal spending or increase revenues through high-growth policies.

All of the above are examples of issues with important moral dimensions that must be dealt with in the 21st century. And, beyond these domestic issues, there are moral challenges to foreign policy—

---

* One CEO was paid $73.8 million for her "positively awful performance" in 1998, according to consultant Graef Crystal, who characterized such overcompensation as "complete and utter greed."

such as standing up to foreign tyrants who are developing weapons of mass destruction, avoiding U.S. financial and military aid to odious, undemocratic and corrupt regimes abroad and dealing with the continuing gross violations of human rights by foreign regimes with which our nation has become increasingly linked through global commerce.

It is somewhat ironic that in the end, as we come full circle in this brief account of some of the highlights in American history, that the perils most threatening to our way of life relate so directly to our departure from the morality symbolized by our first Puritan forbears. The enterprise system we have created has done wonders in lifting our citizens to the world's highest standard of living and making our nation the most powerful economic competitor among nations. But because of the freedom that the system provides, it is open to exploitations and excesses that have the potential to disgrace and undermine it.

The American way has produced the most bountiful society ever to exist on earth. But it has survived longer than any other system because, for most of its lifetime, our people have exercised their freedoms with a strong moral sense to guide them. That is the most important condition for progress in the new century. Even among the ancient Greeks, whose democracy our Founders held in such esteem, it was recognized that the handmaiden of liberty is morality and self-restraint.

Resurging religion: closing the circle

Traditional, activist religion provided the broad foundation of our moral impulses for much of the American past. We haven't really met the challenge Daniel Bell put to us two decades ago, when he advanced the "unfashionable" idea that a return to the concept of religion could answer the hunger in Western society for a greater reality, and a greater hope for the future, than that society had found in the dead ends of nihilism and hedonism. "I believe," he wrote, "that a culture which has become aware of the limits of exploring the mundane will turn, at some point, to the effort to recover the sacred." He was not the first to observe a vacancy in peoples' lives, nor the first to point out that religion had given the early generations of Americans a sense of meaning to their lives that seems missing in so much of modern life.

It is the churches and synagogues that have reasserted the existence and value of the human spirit. To a great extent, the success or failure of the free society depends on whether the public is virtuous, a point emphasized by our first President two centuries ago. Religious faith, and the moral convictions it engenders, is more often than not the basis for the optimism that characterized Americans for most of their history. Faith, optimism and liberty are interdependent—this is proven by history as well as logic. The periods when Americans were most optimistic have been periods when faith was strong: consider the optimism of the Puritans especially concerning the hereafter, or the turn-of-the-century optimism of Teddy Roosevelt's era especially concerning the vistas of perfectibility of American life promised by science and industry.

History confirms a close and natural connection between morality and optimism. Religion has turned out the idealists, and the idealists become the optimists—the people with faith in the future. Optimism, after all, is simply faith in the future, here on earth and beyond, and nothing has nurtured such faith more than religion.

One of the remarkable things about early American character noted by Tocqueville was its unique ability to combine the *spirit of religion* and the *spirit of liberty*—seeking at the same time and "with almost equal eagerness" both material wealth and moral satisfaction, making sacrifices for others while striving for well-being and liberty for oneself. Earlier, Adam Smith, the patron saint of free market capitalism, in his *Theory of Moral Sentiments*, argued the importance of tying the commercial spirit to the moral spirit.

With the loss of, or indifference to, faith in recent times, and the public's immersion in temporal images—images of celebrities, of wealth and material aggrandizement—many Americans lost the sense that their lives are significant, that they are in deep rhythm with the universe, as Emerson might have said. "We should try to reach outside our images," Daniel J. Boorstin has written. "We should seek new ways of letting messages reach us; from our own past, from God, from the world which we may hate or think we hate."

So many excesses and inequities arise within the capitalist system that capitalism is always in danger of self-destructing if things get out of hand. The drive to succeed in America—to "make it" materially— sometimes recognizes no limits. It thrives among thieves as well as CEOs. That's why we need institutions like church and family to brake the forces of excess, temper them with moral standards and provide the kinds of role models that help in development of character among young people.

Fundamentally, the "American spirit" of which this book is a modest biography is an expression of belief in something grander than the individual self, and nothing is grander than God for people of faith. In the last year of the twenties, Walter Lippmann commented that modern man is haunted by "the need to believe." In *A Preface to Morals*, he wrote that a vital religion can bring people into adjustment with the whole of their experience. "Our forefathers had such a religion," he wrote. "They quarreled a good deal about the details, but they had no doubt that there was an order in the universe which justified their lives because they were a part of it. The acids of modernity have dissolved that order for many of us..." Modern man, wrote Lippmann nearly 70 years ago, has lost "that ineffable certainty which once made God and his Plan seem as real as the lamppost." And by parting from their ancestral faith, he said, Americans became "deprived of their sense of certainty as to why they were born, why they must work, whom they must love, what they must honor, where they may turn in sorrow and defeat."

Hopeful signs of change

Yet despite the deviations from traditional belief, despite the scandals of the Clinton era, there are signs that things are changing. "My optimism for the future of our country rests on the growing dissatisfaction among our people with hedonism and materialism as a way of life," wrote Boston University president John Silber in his book *Straight Shooting*. As they move into the new millennium, Americans "grow hungry for spiritual refreshment, for truth and religious conviction", Washington journalist Philip Terzian commented recently. That hunger reminds us of the strong faith of the Puritans and the Founders: this is what was nearly lost, and this is what explains much of the searching and hand-wringing, the anxiety and the moral and ethical confusion of the modern world.

That hunger is manifest today in some signs of renewal in the conservative Protestant and Catholic churches (the latter gaining nearly one million new adherents in the last year, to a total of some 60 million); in the efforts of organizations like the Family Research Council to improve the moral atmosphere for child-rearing; in the relatively small but blooming New Age religious groups; in the increasing popularity of "spiritual" retreats (including those featuring Hindu practices like yoga or Chinese practices like Tai Chi); in the continued popularity of mind-levitating drugs and the highly emotional, near-apoplectic audience-rousing performances of TV and radio evangelists. The number of religious TV stations jumped from 191 in 1997 to 242 in 1998, and religious radio stations grew to 1,616 over the same period. There was also a surge of interest in spiritual and sacred music during the last years of the century—ranging from Gregorian chants to the new-found spiritualism of Madonna's "Ray of Light" album.

"America is experiencing a religious reawakening of sorts," said the *American Enterprise* report, noting that church attendance is "gently rebounding" from its lows in the '70s, especially among young people. The percentage of Americans who say God is an important presence in their lives is rising (and is far higher than in any other industrialized country.) Ministers and rabbis say increasing numbers of teens are going to houses of worship in search of spiritual experience and experimenting with everything from Middle Ages-labyrinths to cabalas and "rave masses." Interest in spirituality is at an all-time high, according to a MacArthur Foundation study in early 1999. And a Princeton research survey indicated that the number of women who believe politicians should be guided by religious values rose from 32% in 1992 to 46% in 1998.

Evangelism has been growing ever since Billy Graham began his crusades to unite people of all races and beliefs, introducing the use of new technology such as lapel microphones, television, radio and satellite links. Conservative evangelical Christianity is thriving today. The number of evangelicals—who adhere to traditional habits such as churchgoing and reliance on the Bible—is growing. The evangelical Christians find modern ways to reach out to masses of people—stadium events called "festivals" or "crusades", television, radio, books, CDs and web sites. Powerful pastors draw thousands to services in their megachurches. The evangelical Christians are also out in front in participating in politics, voting and volunteering in community programs. It has been estimated that membership of what some have called "the enthusiastic churches" has grown to more than ten million people, including fundamentalist, Protestant charismatic and Pentecostal denominations, in addition to some 31 million "born again" Protestants, Catholics and Mormons.

One example of a new desire among Americans to halt moral decay was the "Great Awakening" in October 1997, the largest major religious revival in American history, which brought more than half a million evangelical Christian men to the National Mall in Washington, a huge gathering as large as the civil rights marches and anti-Vietnam protests of the '60s. The First Great Awakening occurred when New England's famous Congregational preacher, Jonathan Edwards, roused the American colonies to fasting and prayer in the mid-18th century; this movement introduced revival meetings and, through its criticism of British corruption, played a part in the origins of the American revolution. The Second Great Awakening occurred with an explosion of religious zeal early in the 19th century—starting with students at Yale college, spreading to camp meetings in the South and Midwest and to several million soldiers in the Civil War, who formed prayer groups and carried Bibles to battle. A Third Great Awakening began in 1890, brought on by the problems of rapid urbanization and labor strife; these Modernists developed the theories of government intervention to redistribute income to the urban poor, which led to the welfare state and labor and feminist reforms.

The Fourth Great Awakening began about 1960 and the "enthusiastic religions" associated with it accounted for most of the growth of religion from then on, providing the roots of the broad movement called the Christian Coalition formed in 1988. In the highly publicized Great Awakening of 1997, the evangelical men's group called the "Promise Keepers", founded by a former University of Colorado football coach, drew several million men to dozens of athletic stadium rallies over several years—at which they were urged to be loyal to their wives, loving to their children and devoted to Jesus—leading up to a huge Washington Mall rally. Rich and poor, men came from all over the country to this mass demonstration of faith and optimistic hope—businessmen and doctors and other professionals, hand in hand with construction and factory workers.

They fasted, prayed, hugged, confessed their sins to one another and laid plans for 19 more such rallies across the country. At the Washington Mall they were spurred on by speakers on 18 giant video screens who repented their past misdeeds and proclaimed their belief that "getting back to God" is the answer to virtually all of the nation's social problems, including racism among both blacks and whites, crime, drugs and pornography. A motorcyclist attending the event expressed the general sentiment when he told *The New York Times*: "This country was supposedly founded on the Bible. It's kind of gotten away from it, I feel." A million Bibles were handed out to the men attending this rally.

Other prominent evangelicals, led by Bill Bright of the Campus Crusade for Christ and Pat Robertson of the Christian Broadcasting Network, summoned two million Christians to a 40-day fast from March 1 to April 9, 1998, seeking to build their own national spiritual revival. And nearly 13,000 women packed Seattle's KeyArena in August 1998 for a program called "Bring Back the Joy", the third annual series of conferences by "Women of Faith", a growing national Christian movement that complements the Promise Keepers' ministry to men. Half a million women were expected to attend these upbeat conferences in 29 cities, with joyful music and speakers telling how they got through difficult times through their faith.

Seeing broad implications in the Great Awakenings, Nobel Prize winner Robert W. Fogel of the University of Chicago Graduate School of Business, wrote that "The new religious revival is fueled by a revulsion over the corruption of contemporary society. It is a rebellion against preoccupation with material acquisition and sexual debauchery; against indulgence in alcohol, tobacco, gambling and drugs; against gluttony; against financial greed and against all other forms of self-indulgence that titillate the senses and destroy the soul."

"As the 20th century wanes," wrote religion columnist Gustav Niebuhr, "America's religious landscape is increasingly a place of mass movements." Everywhere across the country today there are signs of people reaching out in less spectacular ways to assuage their spiritual hunger, reaching out this way and that for some connection beyond the temporal, some system of belief that allows people to regain meaningful control of their lives.

"We have come through a long and bloody century, and something new is stirring everywhere," Michael Novak wrote recently. "It is none too soon." It seems clear from all this activity that the spirits of Americans today cannot really be fulfilled without the reinforcement of spiritual connections. The economic well-being of the '80s and '90s apparently has not been enough to satisfy other needs—the needs of the spirit. As the demographics of America change in the new century, a greater proportion of Americans will find themselves becoming elderly and it is in this late term of life especially that people tend to look for meanings beyond the material.

"Religious observances," wrote columnist George Melloan, "elevate morality as it is defined in different cultures and circumstances. It is a subject at once so simple (the Ten Commandments as the basis for Western law) and so complex, as seen in the fact that civilized nation states routinely send soldiers out to violate the 'Thou shalt not kill' commandment in protection of national interests from usurpers or tyrannies."

Perhaps the greatest social role of churches, synagogues and the newer religious organizations in the new century will be in fulfilling the church's traditional role in serving the poor and the homeless. Church-anchored programs have always played a role in attending the needs of the poor, devoting a very large part of their income from donations to troubled people outside their congregations. In the second half of the 19th century, the Catholic Church, through faith-based institutions like the Catholic Protectory in New York, helped many thousands of poor, abandoned Irish children develop the values that enabled them to enter the mainstream of American society.

Faith-based programs have worked in the inner cities in part because, unlike government aid programs, they have a pastor living in the neighborhood who can offer help every day, every hour it's needed. Unfortunately, this basic function of religion, above politics and beyond controversy, seems sometimes to have been forgotten by the extremist ideologues who are fixated on divisive issues such as abortion, homosexuality and sex.

Religious groups received about half of the record $144 billion philanthropic donations to charity in 1997, about $10 billion more than the previous year. Americans also donate an estimated 20 billion hours or more of their time to charity each year, much of this as part of the "outreach" and other programs of the churches. As welfare and social-spending programs get cut back across the country, communities are looking increasingly to the churches to fill the gaps with major expansions of their programs to provide shelter, training, mental health treatment and spiritual comfort to American society's growing numbers of "left outs."

The recent nationwide effort to move people from welfare to work has found strong allies among churches of many denominations, which have been effective not just in providing services but in raising the

334

spirits of those at the bottom of the social heap. The state of Michigan, through the Salvation Army and Good Samaritan Ministries, contracts with religious groups to provide trained mentors who help poor people build self-esteem and self-sufficiency. Religion, these mentors say, helps welfare people gain spiritually-based hope and confidence while also breaking free from poverty. Catholic schools in many inner cities not only offer a safe and caring environment, with strict discipline and parent involvement, but also send a higher share of their students to college than do the inner-city public schools.

In Texas a Christian ministry runs a prison pre-release program. In Chicago, a private nonprofit homeless shelter program of the Missionary Sisters of the Poor was named one of eight model programs by the National Alliance to End Homelessness; its nuns have provided refuge and "tough love" for thousands of homeless women and their children.

And in Des Plaines, Illinois, the Second Family Program of the Lutheran Social Services of that state, which provides AIDS services to H.I.V.-infected parents and develops family placement for their children, received the Peter E. Drucker Award for Nonprofit Innovation. And the lay ministers, women's auxiliary leaders and other volunteers of the Mormons (The Church of Jesus Christ of Latter-Day Saints) today have at their disposal 106 Church-owned storehouses of commodities for the poor, 87 canneries, more than 100 farms and 100 employment centers.

Unfortunately, during the years of de-emphasizing religion in American life, many social workers cut their ties with organized religion. Yet the churches have carried on, even in the most desolate streets of urban areas, and the public supports them with the largest part of its charitable contributions and over half the nation's volunteer workers. "It's time to notice these sacred places and to appreciate the service to the needy that goes on in them," says John J. Dilulio, a senior fellow of the Manhattan Institute and director of a research program on public/private ventures to connect religion to at-risk youth. Recent proposals by Republican congressmen have called for federal grants to religious-based organizations assisting welfare recipients and nonviolent criminal offenders as well as tax credits for contributing to charitable organizations such as churches.

Besides fulfilling their traditional role of helping the poor, the churches of America have played an increasing role in bringing black and white Americans together. "Sunday is still the most segregated day in America," black columnist Armstrong Williams wrote recently. He cites examples of how some churches have been reaching out across color lines, such as when the conservative Christian Coalition became the first organization to announce a $10,000 pledge to repair black churches when they were burned down in the South. New efforts are being made by religious traditionalists to practice "Biblical racial reconciliation"—to reach out to non-white churches and worshippers on the grounds that Scripture calls for racial harmony and that the church has a responsibility to bring the community together.

Churches are uniquely qualified to address the moral decay in the ghettos, and indeed throughout society to address the loss of the sense of right and wrong and personal responsibility that has been caused by such things as family breakdown, the "entitlement culture" and the morals-free media environment. Churches have the potential to play a particularly important role in answering the needs of the 40% or so American children who are living apart from their fathers—for, as recently pointed out by the president of the Institute for American Ethics, the God of the Jews and Christians has always been understood to be, as the Bible put it, "the helper of the fatherless." In fact, Catholic, Jewish and Christian churches in Baltimore are operating orphanages primarily for children deprived of parental care, either through poverty or other circumstances.

Church activities, when they have received support from society, have played an important role in giving drug users, and young people exposed to drugs, a reason to turn away from the drug life. Through prayer and music (like the addicts "rehab choir" of Harlem's Mount Moriah Baptist Church) churches have been influential in raising the spirits of many people and re-directing their thoughts and feelings beyond themselves. In one of the poorest Boston neighborhoods a parish house-recreation center works to rescue kids from drug and gang cultures; ministers, working closely with police, have given young people new values and new faith—and reduced juvenile crime dramatically.

In San Francisco, the Glide Memorial United Methodist Church and the Episcopal Grace Cathedral have helped to turn grief to faith among the city's huge AIDS population. A *Times* column recently described a seemingly tireless black woman at Glide sporting, not the red mourning ribbon that traditionally marked the AIDS victims and sympathizers, but instead a big button reading: "We Can Do Anything."

Reminders of America's traditional religious beliefs are all around us still, however inert and perfunctory. Every president still concludes his inaugural oath with "So help me God" and closes his State of the Union speech with "God bless America." Our coins and greenbacks carry the message, "In God we trust." Congress still has its chaplains, and judicial proceedings still frequently open with: "God bless this court."

The challenge of restoring religion to its traditional place in American life is of course compounded in a nation that has, ever since the Supreme Court's school prayer decision, spent three decades expunging nearly every vestige of religion from public life and discourse. Nearly four years ago Yale law professor Stephen Carter made the case, in *The Culture of Disbelief,* that American law, culture and politics all have discriminated actively *against* religion. This was the concern behind the call of U.S. Catholic bishops in December 1966 for Americans to put morality back at the center of decision-making, to shape all economic life and markets within a framework of morals.

One of the strongest voices lamenting recent trends and calling Americans back to religious faith has been Pope John Paul II, who stood before 75,000 people at Aqueduct Race Track in Brooklyn in October 1995, sounding like an optimist despite his 75 years, quoting the prophet Isaiah and expressing the Christian message of hope and salvation as the answer for all who "walk in darkness." Addressing the United Nations General Assembly on this same visit, John Paul spoke of the "moral logic which is built into human life," including "freedom, guaranteed by the exercise of self-determination."

He observed that "it is one of the great paradoxes of our time that man, who began the period we call 'modernity' with a self-confident assertion of his 'coming of age' and 'autonomy', approaches the end of the 20th century fearful of himself, fearful of what he might be capable of, fearful for the future." In this spiritual leader's view, the simple secret of solving the problems of political and social life is to understand properly the worthiness of individual human life in a universe with God at its center.

He concluded with a forceful invocation to people entering the new millennium, asking them to replace their fears with faith:

"We must not be afraid of the future. We must not be afraid of man. It is no accident that we are here. Each and every human person has been created in the 'image and likeness' of the One who is the origin of all

that is. We have within us the capabilities for wisdom and virtue. With these gifts, and with the help of God's grace, we can build in the next century and the next millennium a civilization worthy of the human person, a true culture of freedom. We can and must do so! And in doing so, we shall see that the tears of this century have prepared the ground for a new springtime of the human spirit."

PART SEVEN

OUR REGENERATIVE SOCIETY

Optimistic case for the new century

Looking back over the two centuries since the founding of the American Republic one realizes that, despite the troubled ending of the 20th century, one compelling reason for national optimism going forward is the very resilience of the system created by the Founders. Its self-correcting ability to absorb shocks and downslides and to recover, time after time, frequently from one presidential era to another, sets it above all other systems of government. The republic has heaved back and forth with the winds of change, righting itself after each storm no matter how badly optimism and confidence are shaken.

One explanation for Americans' adaptability has been their experience in settling what Daniel J. Boorstin has called "a whole continent of verges—of edges between the known and the unknown, of innumerable surprising encounters." Another was the genius of the Founders in creating a flexible government that would allow each generation to create in effect a new nation, what Boorstin called "the Sovereignty of the Present". As Jefferson once expressed his confidence in a free people: "The earth belongs always to the living generation; they manage it, then, and what proceeds from it, as they please... They are masters, too, of their own persons, and consequently may govern as they please..." Each generation, Jefferson believed, had "a right, by the will of its majority, to bind themselves, but none to bind the succeeding generation..."

Given the Constitutional right to elect their head of state directly, Americans hold the reins of power in their hands to a greater extent than citizens of any other major nation, a privilege they tend not to appreciate nearly as much as they should.

Dreamers and idealists in this drama of freedom seldom fully realize their dreams, but they do accomplish many worthwhile things. And new dreamers come along to start the process all over again, as if *they* were the first. In that sense America is a long succession of dreamers and their dreams, of births and rebirths.

For most of the 20th century the optimism for which Americans are known pulsated up and down. It rose, for example, when Teddy Roosevelt led the nation gallantly into that new century. The nation's spirits then transmuted into anxiety when the Kaiser disrupted European peace. Spirits rose again with Wilson's "New Nationalism" and "the war to end all wars". They ebbed in disillusionment over that president's broken dreams of world unity and peace. They soared again, at least for the relatively well-to-do, in the boom that was capped by the twenties. They plummeted with the Great Depression. They recovered under the steady hand of FDR, and soared in the heroic times of World War Two. They chilled in the anxieties of the Cold War and the dangerous confrontations between superpowers threatening each other with atom bombs.

The nation relaxed in the relatively calm interludes of the Eisenhower fifties, the brief Kennedy Camelot period and the foreshortened "Great Society" of Lyndon Johnson. But it was rocked by the horrendous blows of Vietnam and Watergate. After that concatenation of miseries, the consummate optimist Ronald Reagan produced a rebirth of national pride and self-confidence in the tradition of the first Roosevelt, reinforced by the fall of Communism and, in the early Bush administration, by the lightning victory of modern American military forces in throwing Saddam Hussein out of Kuwait and demonstrating superb skill and high technology, surgically striking that tyrant's military backbone.

But then disillusionment returned again with the scandals and investigations involving President Bill Clinton, the first President to emerge from the loose culture of the sixties. For the third time in the 20th century power had passed to a new generation, this time one whose formative years were influenced by the Vietnam defeat, by assassinations, foreign dangers including the threat of human annihilation and new domestic conflicts. All that makes it more understandable that the sixties' generation would have less confidence in the future, and less respect for the past, than the Roosevelt and Reagan generations.

But our history should leave Americans confident in their native ability to cope with crisis and move on. After all, the sturdy republic survived a Civil War, a World War, a Great Depression, a second World War, a challenge by a more powerful superpower that beat us into space, and innumerable other challenges—only to come cruising into the 21st century far and away the most powerful and prosperous nation ever to exist on earth. The rest of the world still turns to us for leadership when a rogue dictator threatens his neighbors or when mismanaged economies in developing nations threaten to disrupt world markets. For all our political and social discord we remain the longest enduring society of free people governing themselves without dictators or kings.

We saved the free world with Wilson, we saved it again with FDR and again with Truman. Challenged by Russia in the Cold War, we won that too, in the sense that our economic and military power and persuasive ideology caused politically opposite systems to collapse. Americans carry in their memories, consciously or unconsciously, the ideals of the nation's Founders and of millions more who came to America's shores in search of liberty of thought, liberty of religion, liberty of action, creating in the process the longest-enduring society of free people.

The achievement of Americans in their first two centuries was spectacular. As Commager wrote, they "formed a more perfect union, established justice, insured domestic tranquility, provided for the common defense, promoted the general welfare, and secured the blessings of liberty for themselves and for their posterity. They had lifted burdens from the shoulders of men and women, given immigrants from the Old World a second chance, cherished the principles and promoted the practices of freedom, advanced social equality, promoted material well-being, furnished a climate favorable for the nourishment of talent, championed the cause of peace, undertaken and largely fulfilled their responsibilities in the community of nations."

Within a century and a half of the founding of the republic "America had taken an indisputable lead in science, medicine, law, education, and the social sciences and made contributions of lasting merit to art, architecture, literature and philosophy..." Over the last century, innovations, driven by competition, became commercial products and helped to produce a tenfold rise in American families' living standards. And the vast majority of Americans continued to acknowledge, with Jefferson, "an overruling Providence, which by all its dispensations proves that it delights in the happiness of man here and his greater happiness hereafter."

All this is cause for national pride, but not for complacency. As the nation made its way into the 21st century, it had to face the reality of its failures and frustrations as well as its accomplishments. It had failed to provide education for all its children that would equip them to compete in the new age. It had failed to provide medical care for all citizens who needed it regardless of income. It had failed to find a place for the lowest-income Americans who had been by-passed by the Information Age. A national poll by *USA Today* declared that Americans were approaching the new century worried about the decline in respect for values, and seemed "more concerned about values than the standard of living over the next 30 years."

The nation had failed to realize fully the promise of freedom and equality of opportunity for all the races and colors of its people. It had failed to keep political rights meaningful because it had, to a large extent, allowed government's high positions to be auctioned off to the ever more powerful special interests who could make the highest bids. It had allowed money to become the dominant factor in election outcomes, while fewer and fewer citizens cast votes. It had allowed free-wheeling profit-seekers to lay waste to many of its natural resources. And by failing to enact sufficient economic incentives, it had seen the nation's economic growth rate slow in the '90s to not much more than half that of the '60s.

But the natural historic mood of Americans is one of optimism, and it is justified today by the immense opportunities the 21st century holds for America, including extraordinary opportunities for constantly unfolding new applications of technology. The advances in technology, trade and education are almost certain to boost the fortunes of most Americans. Considering how much society has been altered in the mere 25 years since invention of the microprocessor, the future promises even more dazzling changes ahead. Three out of four Americans in the *Wall Street Journal*/NBC News poll just three months before the end of the century said they optimistically believed the next century would be better than the last. Most of them believed the can-do optimistic spirit will flourish for another 100 years, sustaining America's world leadership. This upbeat outlook was most pronounced among blacks, Hispanics and young Americans.

The U.S. economy created unprecedented wealth because it drove up productivity by its mix of new technologies, skilled workers, agile managements and a system that rewards risk-takers handsomely. The digital world and e-commerce became the new drivers of economic growth, holding down inflation by enhancing productivity.

America ended the 20th century with the longest peacetime economic expansion in history still continuing and with the lowest unemployment in three decades. Almost half of all American households owned stocks directly or indirectly as the century drew to a close, compared to less than one in ten in the 1960s.

The increasing diversity of our multi-racial, polyglot society qualifies us uniquely for an interdependent world. We have shown that we can adapt to change faster than any society in history; our government system and our social system have self-correcting properties unequaled anywhere; we reward risk-taking pioneers more than any other nation; we are more open to immigration and its stimulus of fresh brains and enthusiasms than any other nation and we are the leaders in the technologies of the future.

The nation's principles of limited government set by the Founders, and our reliance on the liberties, individualism and private initiative of our citizens, have fostered a spirit of optimism and individual self-confidence, not unlike the optimism that was generated by the philosophers of the European Renaissance succeeding the pessimism and fatalism of the Middle Ages. Our freewheeling culture promotes change and technological innovation at a pace never experienced before.

America has made large strides also towards greater social justice for its people who suffered discrimination in the past, including women, and workforce diversity will be more of a strength than ever in the future. All three major minority groups—Hispanics, African-Americans and Asian Americans—made great progress economically during the long wave of prosperity in the latter half of the century. The number of minority citizens in colleges doubled over the past two decades.

America's women enjoy today "the best and most rewarding job market in the world," according to a 1997 survey by the Independent Women's Forum and the American Enterprise Institute. The men-women wage gap has narrowed gradually, to the point where women's pay on average is slightly more than three-quarters that for men (88% where skills and experience are equal.)

For some time women have been earning more college bachelor's and master's degrees than men and taking more than 40% of the degrees in law and 35% of the degrees in medicine and dentistry. Their leadership pool is growing. They have invaded executive suites, they make up nearly half the managerial and professional ranks and they own a third of the nation's domestic businesses. Women are starting new businesses at twice the rate of men and they are managing billions of dollars of investments for institutions and individuals. Young women are completing high school and graduating from college at higher rates than their male peers. There are still glass ceilings to break, such as directorships on the boards of Fortune 500 companies, but there too some progress is being made. A big breakthrough came in July 1999 when Carly Fiorina became president and CEO of Hewlett-Packard, the first woman to head one of the 14 biggest industrial corporations. Granted a record $66 million worth of stock plus options and salary, she became one of the highest paid executives in history.

A crowning achievement for women in that same month was the victory of the American women's soccer team over China before 90,000 Rose Bowl fans (and 40 million watching on TV) in the final of the Women's World Cup Soccer match. it was the most important event in women's sports history and it swept the nation off its feet, making instant celebrities of the high-spirited, ponytailed U.S. team members. Only two weeks later, Air Force Colonel Eileen Collins broke into the top ranks of the male-dominated aerospace world by becoming the first woman to command a space mission. Capping the steady climb of women astronauts in space flights, she commanded the 135-ton shuttle Columbia, which put into orbit a telescope observatory to scan the heavens from 87,000 miles above the earth.

Women are voting in larger numbers than men (in 1900 they could not vote or own property.) As a voting bloc, they were responsible for President Clinton's re-election in 1996. In Washington State more than 40% of the legislators are women. In a recent USA Today poll 81% of the women said they expect a woman to be elected president within a quarter-century.

Americans in general are healthier than ever, their average life expectancy having risen from 47 years in 1900 to about 76 years today (85 years for the baby boomers, one in 26 of whom will live to 100), although health care for the poor remains a major unsolved problem. In one astonishing survey made on the web by Peat Marwick, 64% of college students believe they will retire before the age of 50. Winding up the century on an unprecedented buying binge, Americans had more of everything than ever before. The percentage of American households owning their own homes rose to a record 67% by the end of 1998. The main thing Americans wanted but couldn't buy was more leisure time outside the busy daily grind. Despite their affluence, they seemed to be more time-pressed than ever.

The 21st century is opening up new perspectives even to the growing population of elderly Americans. The 80 million Americans entering their senior years as the new century begins are starting "a second lifetime", in the words of historian and super-optimist Theodore Roszak. Writing of the "longevity revolution", Roszak points out that what he dubs "the New People", born between 1946 and 1964, will survive and remain active longer than any senior generation before them. Seniors over 60 will make up 25% of the population by 2020. Because of their health and the progress of medical science these elders, the first generation of senior dominance, are pioneering a new frontier. They have "hungry minds, physical vitality, keen perception, lively tastes, political know-how, even ambition." Already they are bringing their experience and wisdom to bear in many ways; for example, they are communicating via 100 Internet web sites of the SeniorNet Learning Centers in every state.

What some have called "The American Century" drew to a close with the U.S. standing as the lone remaining superpower, with by far the world's most vigorous economy and with U.S. corporations responding with incredible speed to dynamic changes, taking clear leadership in markets worldwide, especially in key fields such as technology, science, finance and management.

The American economy today accounts for more than a quarter of the world's gross national product, finances the most effective global military force, nourishes a well-ingrained rule of law, honors property rights, gives respect to a solidly democratic political system and remains the world's greatest "melting pot", assimilating freedom-seeking people from around the world, as columnist George Melloan has pointed out.

One of the most striking superiorities of the American system has been its fantastic record of jobs creation—some 70 million or more new jobs since 1980—resulting particularly from the unprecedented amounts of investment capital that has flowed into industry from private sources such as pension funds and other institutions and investors.

Ours has been the most dynamic jobs-producing economy the world has ever known.*

No less impressive than the record of jobs creation has been the record of enterprise-creation. Some $60 billion went into new businesses in 1998 alone, and more than $100 billion was available for venture financing (71% of the world's venture capital for start-ups.). No other country has a comparable new-issue market for young enterprises, where a Netscape or a Yahoo! can so easily find public partners. The new companies are pushing out the boundaries of technology today with new ideas, new products and new entrepreneurial energy and skills.

In the ferment of adapting to 20th-century dynamics as many as 385,000 U.S. manufacturing workers lost their jobs in a single year, but several million new jobs were created in the same period. The job boom and tight labor market drew many formerly alienated, unskilled young black men and single mothers into the business mainstream.

Increasingly, Americans favor the private over the government answer to social and cultural needs, except for the union-dominated public school system. With their old welfare system discredited, new private initiatives are addressing the handicaps of the less fortunate. In the arts, America attains world cultural leadership largely through private funding. In medicine and healthcare, America remains a world leader largely through its huge network of privately-funded hospitals and private drug and biotech companies. Thanks partly to the advances of private medical science, Americans today lead healthier lives than any people have ever led throughout history.

In reinforcing the national prosperity, a leading part has been played by Congressional efforts to reduce federal spending and the U.S. budget deficit, and continuing efforts on this front will be crucial in the new century in holding down interest rates by cutting the government's need to borrow, freeing up private capital that can be invested for still greater productivity of industry rather than buried in bureaucracies that so often stifle productivity. Lower cost of capital, and higher U.S.

---

* One reason for this "jobs miracle" is that the U.S. resisted the generous European-style unemployment support systems that made unemployment virtually respectable and, for many people, removed the incentive to work, as well as the restrictions on layoffs that curbed European modernization. The result: Americans were starting new enterprises at a record rate in the latter part of the century, creating new jobs at an unprecedented rate.

348

capital and labor productivity have produced higher returns on savings, more jobs and greater national prosperity.

The political institutions created by our Founders and the relative freedom of the economy from government control have enabled private enterprises to adapt to dramatic changes without the turmoil experienced by many other nations in the roiling global markets. This fact was brought home in the last part of the 20th century when economic and structural problems caused radical dislocations in Japan and in the other East Asian countries handicapped by their largely planned economies and their cozy, inflexible business-government connections.

Of course America's strength is not in capitalism alone, but in individual human freedom and the moral, self-disciplined exercise of individual rights in a culture of freedom, without which capitalism must fail. Fundamentally, Americans have inherited the strength of character, the ideals and the history of those who built our nation on such strengths.

"Now we have come upon a very different age from any that preceded us. We have come upon an age when we do not do business in the way in which we used to do business... This is nothing short of a new social age, a new era of human relationships, a new stage-setting for the drama of life".

Those were actually the words spoken by Woodrow Wilson early in the 20th century, and they bear repeating a century later. In his speeches then Wilson reminded the American people that the liberty that immigrants had sought and found in America was "a fundamental demand of the human spirit, a fundamental necessity for the life of the soul". With a message as inspiring to Americans in the 21st-century and their diverse, multi-cultural citizenry as it was to the Americans of Wilson's time, he proclaimed:

*"The day is at hand when we shall realize on this consecrated soil a new freedom, a liberty widened and deepened to match the broadened life of man in modern America, restoring to him in very truth the control of his government, throwing wide all gates of lawful enterprise, unfettering his energies and warming the generous impulses of his heart—a process of release, emancipation and inspiration, full of a breath of life as sweet and wholesome as the airs that filled the sails of the caravels of Columbus and gave the promise and boast of magnificent Opportunity in which America **dare not fail**."*

BIBLIOGRAPHY

PROLOGUE

Bloom, Allan, *The Closing of the American Mind.* New York: Simon & Schuster Touchstone, 1987.

Lerner, Max, *America as a Civilization.* New York: Simon & Schuster, 1957.

De Tocqueville, Alexis, *Democracy in America* (Volume I). New York: Vintage Books, Random House & Knopf, 1945.

PART ONE: FROM NEW EDEN TO NEW NATION— THE FIRST THREE CENTURIES

Ambrose, Stephen E., *Undaunted Courage—Merriwether Lewis, Thomas Jefferson And the Opening of the American West.* New York: Simon & Schuster Touchstone, 1996.

Blum, John Morton, *Woodrow Wilson and the Politics of Morality.* Boston: Little, Brown, 1956.

Boorstin, Daniel J., *The Lost World of Thomas Jefferson.* Chicago: The University of Chicago Press, 1948, 1981, 1993.

_____ *The Americans: The Colonial Experience.* New York: Vintage Books Division of Random House, 1958.

_____ *The Americans: The National Experience.* New York: Vintage Books, 1965.

_____ *The Exploring Spirit—America and the World Experience* (The Reith Lectures, 1975.) London: British Broadcasting Corporation, Billing & Sons, 1976.

Burns, James MacGregor, *The Vineyard of Liberty.* New York: Knopf, 1982.

Clark, Ronald W., *Benjamin Franklin.* New York: Random House, 1983.

Commager, Henry Steele, *The Empire of Reason.* New York: Anchor Press/ Doubleday, 1978.

Cunningham, Noble E., *In Pursuit of Reason—The Life of Thomas Jefferson.* New York: Ballantine, 1987.

Cunliffe, Marcus, *George Washington—Man and Monument.* Boston: Little, Brown, 1958.

Daniels, Bruce C., *Puritans at Play*. New York: St. Martin's, 1995.

Debo, Angie, *A History of the Indians of the United States*. Norman, Oklahoma: University of Oklahoma Press, 1985.

DeVoto, Bernard, *The Year of Decision, 1846*. Boston: Houghton Mifflin, 1943.

Donovan, Frank, *The Benjamin Franklin Papers*. New York: Dodd Mead, 1962.

Ellis, Joseph J., *American Sphinx—The Character of Thomas Jefferson*. New York: Knopf, 1998.

Emerson, Ralph Waldo, *Essays & Lectures*. New York: The Library of America, 1983.

Flexner, James Thomas, *George Washington* (four volumes: *The Forge of Experience, In the American Revolution, And the New Nation, Anguish and Farewell.*) Boston: Little, Brown, 1965-1972.

Geiger, Vincent, *Trail to California* (edited by David Potter.) New Haven: Yale University Press, 1945.

Hafen, LeRoy and Ann, *Handcarts to Zion*. Glendale, CA: A.H. Clark, 1960.

Haigh, Jane and Murphy, Claire, *Gold Rush Women*. Seattle: Alaska Northwest Books, 1997.

Hall, Michael G., *The Last American Puritan, The Life of Increase Mather*. Middletown, CT.: Wesleyan University, 1988.

Howe, Irving, *World of Our Fathers*. New York: Book-of-the-Month Club, 1993.

_____ *The American Newness: Culture and Politics in the Age of Emerson*. Cambridge: Harvard University Press, 1986.

Hubbell, Jay B., *American Life in Literature*. New York: Harper & Brothers, 1936.

Johnson, Paul, *A History of the American People*. New York: Harper Collins, 1998.

Lavender, David S., *Westward Vision: The Story of the Oregon Trail*. New York: McGraw-Hill, 1963.

_____ *The American Heritage History of the Great West*. New York: American Heritage (distribution, Simon & Schuster), 1965.

_____ *Nothing Seemed Impossible*. Palo Alto, CA: America West, 1975.

_____ *Land of Giants: The Drive to the Pacific*. Lincoln, Nebraska: University of Nebraska "Bison" book, 1979.

_____ *The Overland Migrations*. Washington, D.C.: U.S. Department of the Interior, 1980.

Link, Arthur Stanley, *Woodrow Wilson, A Profile*. New York: Hill & Wang, 1968.

Malone, Dumas, *Jefferson the President: First Term*. Boston: Little, Brown, 1970.

_____ *Jefferson and His Time* (five volumes, including *Jefferson and the Rights of Man, Jefferson the President* and *The Sage of Monticello*.) Boston: Little, Brown, 1948, 1977, 1981.

Middlekauff, Robert, *The Mathers*. New York: Oxford University Press, 1971.

Miller, Perry, and Johnson, Thomas H., *The Puritans* (volumes one and two). New York: Harper & Row, 1938.

Morgan, Dale L., *The Humboldt: Highroad of the West*. Lincoln, Nebraska: University of Nebraska, 1985.

_____ *The Great Salt Lake, Overland in 1846*. Lincoln, Nebraska: University of Nebraska, 1986.

Morgan, Edmund S., *The Puritan Dilemma—The Story of John Winthrop*. Boston: Little, Brown, 1958.

Morison, Admiral Samuel Eliot, *Christopher Columbus, Mariner*. New York: New American Library, 1983.

_____ *Admiral of the Ocean Sea*. Boston: Little, Brown, 1942.

_____ *Builders of the Bay Colony*. Cambridge: Riverside Press, 1930.

_____ *The Oxford History of the American People*. New York: New American Library, 1972.

Myers, Gerald E., *William James, His Life and Thought*. New Haven: Yale University Press, 1986.

_____ *The Spirit of American Philosophy*. New York: Putnam, 1970.

Parkman, Francis, *The Oregon Trail*. New York: New American Library, Signet Classic, 1950.

Parrington, Vernon Louis, *The Colonial Mind, 1620-1800*. New York: Harcourt Brace, 1927.

Peterson, Merrill, *Thomas Jefferson and the New Nation*. New York: Oxford University Press, 1970.

Parrington, Vernon Louis, *The Colonial Mind*. New York: Harcourt Brace, 1927.

Phillips, William D. Jr. and Phillips, Carla Rahn, *The Worlds of Christopher Columbus*. New York: Cambridge University Press, 1992.

Pritchard, William Fowler, *Journal*, and *Overland Diaries*. Fairfield, WA: Ye Galleon Press, 1995.

Randall, Willard Sterne, *Thomas Jefferson*. New York: Henry Holt, 1993.

_____ *George Washington*. New York: Henry Holt, 1997.

Reynolds, David S., *Walt Whitman's America*. New York: Alfred A. Knopf, 1995.

Richardson, Robert D., Jr., *Emerson—The Mind on Fire*. Berkeley, CA: University of California, 1995.

Rhodehamel, John H., editor, *George Washington: Writings*. New York: Library of America, 1997.

Royce, Sarah Bayliss, *A Frontier Lady: Recollections of the Gold Rush and Early California*. New Haven: Yale University Press, 1932.

Sanford, Charles B., *The Quest for Paradise*. Urbana, Illinois: University of Illinois Press, 1961. (Lectures at Middlebury College, VT, 1950-51.)

_____ *The Religious Life of Thomas Jefferson*. Charlottesville, VA: University Press of Virginia, 1984.

Smith, Bernard (editor), *The Democratic Spirit—A Collection of American Writings from the Earliest Times to the Present Day*. New York: Knopf, 1941.

Smith, William Bradford, *Bradford of Plymouth*. Philadelphia: Lippincott, 1951.

Spalding, Matthew and Garrity, Patrick J., *A Sacred Union of Citizens—George Washington's Farewell Address and the American Character*. Lanham, Maryland: Rowman & Littlefield, 1996.

Stegner, Wallace, *The Gathering of Zion—The Story of the Mormon Trail*. New York: McGraw-Hill, 1964.

Turner, Frederick Jackson, *The Frontier in American History*. New York: Henry Holt, 1920, 1947.

Van Doren, Carl, *Benjamin Franklin*. New York: Viking, 1938, 1966.

Weisberger, Bernard A., *Many People, One Nation*. Boston: Houghton Mifflin, 1987.

Whitman, Walt, *Complete Poetry & Collected Prose*. New York: The Library of America, 1982.

Wilford, John Noble, *The Mysterious History of Columbus*. New York: Knopf, 1991.

Zvi Dor-Ner, *Columbus and the Age of Discovery*. Hammersmith, London: HarperCollins, 1992.

PART TWO: COMING OF AGE—THREE PRESIDENTS, IN THREE GREAT WARS.

Allen, Frederick Lewis, *The Big Change—America Transforms Itself, 1900-1950*. New York: Harper & Brothers, 1952.

_____ *Only Yesterday—An Informal History of the 1920s.* New York: Wiley, 1997.

Baldwin, Neil, Edison: *Inventing the Century.* New York: Hyperion, 1995.

Blum, John Norton, *The Republican Roosevelt.* Cambridge, MA.: Harvard University Press, 1954, 1977.

Boorstin, Daniel J., *The Americans: The Democratic Experience.* New York: Random House Vintage, 1974.

Buhite, Russell D. and Levy, David W., editors, *FDR's Fireside Chats.* New York: Penguin Books USA, 1993, University of Oklahoma Press, 1992.

Burns, James MacGregor, *Roosevelt: The Lion and the Fox.* New York: Harcourt, Brace, 1956.

_____ *Roosevelt: The Soldier of Freedom.* New York: Harcourt Brace Jovanovich, 1970.

Commager, Henry Steele, *The American Mind—An Interpretation of American Thought and Character Since the 1880s.* New Haven: Yale University Press, 1950.

Donald, David Herbert, *Lincoln.* New York: Simon & Schuster Touchstone, 1995.

Douglas, William O., *Go East Young Man: the early years; the autobiography of William O. Douglas.* New York: Random House, 1974.

Everett, Dick, *Sod-House Frontier, 1854-1890.* Lincoln, Nebraska: University of Nebraska Press, 1989.

Fromkin, David, *In the Time of the Americans. FDR, Truman, Eisenhower, Marshall, MacArthur—the Generation That Changed America's Role in the World.* New York: Vintage Books, Random House, 1995.

Harper Perennial, 1992.

Johnson, Paul, *Modern Times: The World from the Twenties to the Nineties.* New York:

Morris, Edmund, *The Rise of Theodore Roosevelt.* New York: Ballantine, 1979.

Leuchtenburg, William E., *Franklin D. Roosevelt and the New Deal, 1932-40.* New York: Harper & Row, 1963.

Link, Arthur S., *Woodrow Wilson and The Progressive Era.* New York: Harper & Row, 1954.

Link, Arthur S. and Catton, William B., *American Epoch—A History of the United States Since 1900.* New York: Knopf, 1955.

_____ *American Epoch,* Volume II, *Affluence and Anxiety, 1940-1992.* New York: McGraw-Hill, 1987, 1993.

Lord, Walter, *The Good Years*. New York: Harper & Brothers, 1960.

Ludwig, Emil, *Lincoln*. Boston: Little, Brown, 1930.

Manchester, William, *The Glory and the Dream, A Narrative History of America* (two volumes). Boston: Little, Brown, 1973.

Neely, Mark E., Jr., *The Last Best Hope of Earth—Abraham Lincoln and the Promise of America*. Cambridge: Harvard University Press, 1993.

Parrington, Vernon Louis, *The Romantic Revolution in America, 1800-1860*. New York: Harcourt Brace, 1927.

Parrington, Vernon Louis, *The Beginnings of Critical Realism in America, 1860-1900*. New York: Harcourt Brace, 1930.

Peterson, Merrill D., *Lincoln in American Memory*. New York: Oxford University Press, 1993.

Roosevelt, Franklin D., *Fireside Chats* (eight selected from 31). New York: Penguin Books USA, 1995.

Sandburg, Carl, *Abraham Lincoln—The Prairie Years* and *The War Years* (three volumes.) New York: Harcourt, Brace, 1926.

Schlesinger, Arthur M., Jr., *The Age of Roosevelt—The Crisis of the Old Order, 1919-1933*. Boston: Houghton Mifflin, 1957.

_____ *The Coming of the New Deal*. Cambridge: Houghton Mifflin, Riverside Press, 1959.

_____ *The Bitter Heritage: Vietnam and American Democracy*. Boston: Houghton Mifflin, 1967.

Sherr, Lynn, *Failure is Impossible, Susan B. Anthony in Her Own Words*. New York: Times Books, Random House, 1995.

Wills, Gary, *Inventing America: Jefferson's Declaration of Independence*. New York: Doubleday, 1978.

_____ *Lincoln at Gettysburgh: The Words that Remade America*. New York: Simon & Schuster, 1992.

Wilson, Robert A., *Character Above All*. New York: Simon & Schuster, 1995.

PART THREE: AGE OF ANXIETIES—BEARING THE SUPERPOWER MANTLE.

Anderson, Terry H., *The Movement and the Sixties*. New York: Oxford University, 1995.

Branch, Taylor, *Parting the Waters, America in the King Years, 1954-63*. New York: Simon & Schuster Touchstone, 1988.

_____ *Pillar of Fire, America in the King Years, 1963-65*. New York: Simon & Schuster, 1998.

Goldman, Eric F., *The Crucial Decade—And After, America, 1945-1960*. New York: Vintage, Random House, 1956, 1960.

Daniels, Jonathan, *The Man of Independence*. New York: J.P. Lippincott, 1950.

Halberstam, David, *The Fifties*. New York: Villard Books, 1993.

Lewis, John and D'Orso, Michael, *Walking in the Wind, A Memoir of the Movment*. New York: Simon & Schuster, 1998.

Miller, Merle, *Plain Speaking, An Oral Biography of Harry S. Truman*. New York: Berkley, 1974.

Murray, Charles, *Losing Ground—Americn Social Policy, 1950-1980*. New York: Basic Books, 1981.

Nisbet, Robert, *The Present Age—Progress and Anarchy in Modern America*. New York: Harper & Row, 1988.

Patterson, James T., *Grand Expectations, The United States, 1945-1974*. New York: Oxford University Press, 1996.

Pauken, Thomas W., *The Thirty Years War*. Ottawa, Illinois: Jameson Books, 1995.

Schlesinger, Arthur M., Jr., *The Cycles of American History*. Boston: Houghton Mifflin, 1986.

Schuman, Frederick L., *International Politics*. New York: McGraw-Hill, 1958.

Truman, Margaret, *Harry S. Truman*. New York: William Morrow, 1973.

McCullough, David, *Truman*. New York: Simon & Schuster, 1992.

PART FOUR: THE REAGAN "REVOLUTION"— FORWARD TO THE FOUNDERS.

Bartley, Robert L., *The Seven Fat Years and How To Do It Again*. New York: The Free Press, 1992.

Burns, James MacGregor, *John Kennedy, A Political Profile*. New York: Harcourt, Brace, 1960.

Cannon, Lou, *President Reagan—The Role of a Lifetime*. New York: Simon & Schuster, 1991.

Friedman, Milton and Rose, *Free to Choose*. New York: Harcourt Brace, 1980.

Kudlow, Lawrence, *American Abundance—The New Economic and Moral Prosperity*. New York: Forbes/American Heritage, 1997

Mayer, Jane and McManus, Doyle, *Landslide*. Boston: Houghton Mifflin, 1988.

Noonan, Peggy, *What I Saw at the Revolution*. New York: Random House, 1990.

Palmer, John L. and Sawhill, Isabel V., *The Reagan Record*. Washington, D.C.: The Urban Institute, 1984.

Reagan, Ronald, *An American Life*. New York: Simon & Schuster, 1990.

Schlesinger, Arthur M., Jr., *A Thousand Days, John F. Kennedy in the White House*. Cambridge: Houghton Mifflin, 1965.

PART FIVE: *FIN DE SIÈCLE*, A SLIDE FROM TRADITIONAL VALUES—MORALS AND OPTIMISM BOTH FADE

Bennett, William J., *The Death of Outrage*. New York: Free Press, 1998.

Bok, Sissela, *Mayhem—Violence as Public Entertainment*. Reading, MA: Addison-Wesley, a Merloyd Lawrence Book.

Bork, Robert, *Slouching Towards Gomorrah: Modern Liberalism and American Decline*. New York: Regan Books, 1996.

Carter, Stephen, *The Culture of Disbelief: how American law and politics trivialize religious devotion.*. New York: Basic Books, 1993.

_____ *Integrity*. New York: Basic Books, 1996.

Delbanco, Andrew, *The Death of Satan, How Americans Have Lost the Sense of Evil*. New York: Farrar, Straus and Giroux, 1995.

Edmundson, Mark, *Nightmare on Main Street—Angels, Sadomasochism and the Culture of Gothic*. Cambridge: Harvard University Press, 1997

Gelernter, David, *Drawing Life—Surviving the Unibomber*. New York: The Free Press, 1997.

Himmelfarb, Gertrude, *The De-Moralization of Society: From Victorian Virtues to Modern Values*. New York: Knopf, 1995.

_____ *On Looking into the Abyss: Untimely Thoughts on Culture and Society*. New York: Knopf, 1994.

Hughes, Robert, *The Culture of Complaint*. New York: Oxford University Press, 1993.

Johnson, Haynes & Broder, David, The System: *The American Way of Politics at the Breaking Point*. Boston: Little, Brown, 1996.

Kurtz, Howard, *Spin Cycle—Inside the Clinton Propaganda Machine*. New York: The Free Press, Simon & Schuster, 1998.

Lippmann, Walter, *A Preface to Morals*. New York: Macmillan, 1929.

Medved, Michael, *Hollywood Vs. America: Popular Culture and the War on Traditional Values*. New York: HarperCollins, 1992.

Sandel, Michael, *Democracy's Discontents: America in Search of a Public Philosophy.* Cambridge: Harvard University Press, 1996.

Shogan, Robert, *The Double-Edged Sword.* Boulder, CO: Westview Press, Perseus Books Group, 1999.

Soros, George, *Soros on Soros: Staying Ahead of the Curve.* New York: Wiley, 1995.

Steel, Ronald, *Walter Lippmann and the American Century.* Boston: Little, Brown, 1980.

Woodward, Bob, *The Agenda—Inside the Clinton White House.* New York: Simon & Schuster, 1994.

PART SIX: THE AMERICAN SPIRIT AND THE 21st CENTURY— OPTIMISM SURVIVING

Bell, Daniel, *The Cultural Contradictions of Capitalism.* New York: Basic Books, 1976.

Bok, Derek, *The State of the Nation.* Cambridge, MA: Harvard University Press, 1997.

Borstin, Daniel J., *The Image: What Happened to the American Dream.* New York: Vintage Division of Random House, 1992. Weidenfeld & Nicolson, 1961.

Gates, Bill, *The Road Ahead.* New York: Viking Penguin, 1995.

Jonsen, Albert R., *The Birth of Bioethics.* New York: Oxford University Press, 1998.

Lippmann, Walter A., *A Preface to Morals.* New York: Macmillan, 1929.

Moynihan, Michael, *The Coming American Renaissance.* New York: Simon & Schuster, 1997.

Novak, Michael, *The Spirit of Democratic Capitalism.* New York: American Enterprise Institute/Simon & Schuster, 1982.

Rosenberg, Claude N., *Wealthy and Wise: how you and America can get the most out of your giving.* Boston: Little, Brown, 1994.

Samuelson, Robert J., *The Good Life and Its Discontents: The American Dream in the Age of Entitlement.* New York: Times Books, 1995

Silber, John, *Straight Shooting—What's Wrong with America and How to Fix It.* New York: Harper & Row, 1989.

Wattenberg, Ben J., *Values Matter Most.* New York: Free Press, 1995.

Wilson, James Q., *The Moral Sense.* New York: Free Press, 1993.

Wilson, Robert A., *Character Above All.* New York: Simon & Schuster, 1995.

PART SEVEN: OUR REGENERATIVE SOCIETY— OPTIMISTIC CASE FOR THE NEW CENTURY

Commager, Henry Steele, *The American Mind—An Interpretation of American Thought and Character Since the 1880s.* New Haven: Yale University Press, 1950.

Roszak, Theodore, *America the Wise.* New York: Houghton Mifflin, 1998.

Wilson, Woodrow, *The New Freedom.* New York: Doubleday Page, 1919.

A.E. Jeffcoat turned to fulltime writing in the Northwest after a career as a foreign correspondent, corporate executive and communications counselor. He became a foreign correspondent for *The Wall Street Journal* while in his twenties, based in London and then as bureau chief in Paris. He later held executive positions at Ford Motor Company and IBM, and was president of his own firm, Jeffcoat Schoen & Morrell, counseling major corporations and non-profit organizations including the New York City bar association, the Carnegie Corporation, the Council on Foreign Relations and the Japan Society. He is honorary founder chairman of a nonprofit performing arts organization, The Manhattan Theatre Club, internationally recognized as a leading center for development of new American work for theater. He graduated from Williams College with a degree in American History and Literature and received his graduate degree from the University of Michigan.

A BOOK FROM THE NEW WEST

Spirited Americans is a prime example of the growing book publishing and electronic communications activities in the western United States.

The author, A.E. Jeffcoat (bio on p. 361), lives on Bainbridge Island, Washington, home to a growing number of writers who are gaining high national and international reputations. The designer, Steve Herold, has been designing and publishing books for 40 years in Seattle, while juggling at the same time his Books AtoZ Internet site and the Wit's End Bookstore and Teashop in Seattle, which is a center where Western authors meet and read their work. Herold was one of the first book publishers to adopt digital production and to later establish a Web site designed for producing and selling books over the Net.

The Spirited Americans diskette traveled quickly from the author's laptop to Herold's computer system and from there to other computers at CCS Digital in Redmond, Washington. There, an initial, low-cost small print run (bypassing the making of plates and other costly traditional printing methods) was printed for distribution to national and international reviewers. From CCS the revised electronic text was sent to Publishers Press in Salt Lake City, Utah where the first hardcover edition was printed for national distribution by Midpoint Trade Books in Kansas City, Kansas.

THE COVER ARTISTS

Front cover: John F. Clymer (1907–1989) was preeminent among American artists in depicting the pioneer men and women who endured the rigors of the frontier with courage and tenacity, as well as the Native Americans and wild animals they encountered. He created a vivid pictorial history of the Old West—incidents in the Lewis and Clark Expedition, experiences of frontiersmen, fur traders, gold seekers, cattlemen and Plains Indians. He and his wife Doris would spend many months researching his paintings, studying Western localities to be certain that every detail was historically correct. His tiny ink drawings emerged as magnificent extra-large paintings now displayed in the Whitney Gallery of Western Art in Cody, Wyoming and in private collections. Among them are *Alouette* (trappers dancing at their winter camp, on this book's cover), *The Cattle Drive*, *The Gold Train* and *The Homesteaders*. His early work as an illustrator included 80 covers for *The Saturday Evening Post* as well as illustrations for the *National Home Monthly*, the *Blue Book Magazine*, *Field and Stream* and the *Marine Corps Gazette*.

Back cover: Thomas Hart Benton (1889-1975) was the best known muralist of the 1930s and early '40s, noted for his graphic, colorful, rhythmic paintings expressing the vitality of American life. He was the grandnephew and namesake of the Missouri senator who was a power during the administration of Andrew Jackson and Martin Van Buren. *Changing West* (on the back cover) is a detail of one of a suite of murals entitled *America Today*. Contrasting with John Clymer's painting of the early frontier, this mural portrays the transformations and social flux brought on by America's industrialization. It evokes the boom rush of the burgeoning oil industry and its effects—pumps and rigs, storage tanks, billowing black smoke and, in the distance, a gas cracking plant served by rail tank cars. Workers weld pipes and lay new lines while surveyors search for new reserves by land and air. The windmill is a reminder of older, less modern sources of energy. The pioneers, cowboys and herdsmen nave been eclipsed by the onslaught of the modern age.